Modern Tsars and Princes

V

Modern Tsars and Princes

The Struggle for Hegemony in Russia

JEREMY LESTER

VERSO

London • New York

First published by Verso 1995
© Verso 1995
All rights reserved

The right of Jeremy Lester to be identified as the author of this work
has been asserted by him in accordance with the
Copyright, Designs and Patents Act 1988

Verso
UK: 6 Meard Street, London W1V 3HR
USA: 180 Varick Street, New York NY 10014–4606

Verso is the imprint of New Left Books

ISBN 1–85984–914–8
ISBN 1–85984–039–6 (pbk)

British Library Cataloguing in Publication Data
A catalogue record for this book is available from the British Library

Library of Congress Cataloging-in-Publication Data
Lester, Jeremy.
    Modern tsars and princes: the struggle for hegemony in Russia /
Jeremy Lester
    p.   cm.
    Includes bibliographical references (p.   ) and index.
    ISBN 1–85984–914–8 (hard). — ISBN 1–85984–039–6 (pbk).
    1. Russia (Federation)—Politics and government—1991   2.
Power (Social sciences)—Russia (Federation)   3.
Authoritarianism—Russia (Federation)   I. Title.
JN6692.L47   1995   95–23359
320.947'09'049—dc20   CIP

Typeset by M Rules
Printed in Great Britain by Biddles Ltd, Guildford and King's Lynn

Contents

The modern prince, the myth prince, cannot be a real person, a concrete individual. It can only be an organism, a complex element of society in which a collective will, which has already been recognised and has to some extent exerted itself in action, begins to take concrete form. History has already provided this organism, and it is the political party – the first cell in which there come together germs of a collective will tending to become universal and total. . . .

The modern Prince must be and cannot but be the proclaimer and organiser of an intellectual and moral reform, which also means creating the terrain for a subsequent development of the national popular collective will towards the realisation of a superior, total form of modern civilisation.

Quintin Hoare and Geoffrey Nowell-Smith, *Selections from the Prison Notebooks of Antonio Gramsci*

Preface

This book was first conceived in the early summer of 1991. At that time the Soviet Union had just completed its sixth year of reform under the auspices of Mikhail Gorbachev's campaign for *perestroika*. What had initially started out as a mild-mannered approach to improving the productive potential of the economy and tightening up labour discipline through such measures as the anti-alcohol campaign had eventually become a system-threatening process of revolutionary proportions. Territorially, the country was well down the road of disintegration, unable as it was to fend off the nationalist resurgence in many of its key republics. Economically, it was in virtual free fall as one programme of reforms after another either failed to make any significant impact or got stalled in the debating chambers of power. Socially, it was divided in ways it had not experienced for many generations as new social strata sought to carve out ever larger niches for themselves and old ones looked on bemused and disorientated by the ever-quickening pace of change. And politically, the old certainties of one-party monopolization had given way to a bitter factional struggle for control of the Communist Party, combined with the emergence of brand-new political organizations more and more capable of challenging the traditional supremacy of the communists.

The anti-Gorbachev August *coup d'état* was still only on the horizon at this time, but when it came the ill-fated actions of the conspirators, of course, only served to quicken the pace of change.

For the observer of Soviet affairs, it goes without saying that these were intellectually stimulating times. A country and a system of power which virtually everyone had previously assumed to be impregnable, one that had survived all manner of upheavals and challenges in the past, was quickly and inexorably coming apart at the seams. What had started out as a process of reconstruction had ended up as a near-definitive piece of *destruction*. In the shattered ruins of the old order, new nations and new societies were about to emerge, with new political and economic agendas and new social interests underpinning those agendas. The void that existed clearly had to be filled. Not *re*construction of something old, but a brand-new type of *con*struction was now the order of the day. The question of questions was: what exactly would emerge to fill this void, and what kinds of challenges and hurdles would it face? It is an attempt to give some kind of response to this question from the perspective of developments in Russia since the end of 1991 that lies at the core of the present study.

The intellectual stimulus of these times was matched by an intellectual challenge of exacting proportions. How could one best provide a framework in which to analyse and understand the historical changes that were taking place? What, if any, were the threads connecting the processes of upheaval in the different domains of national, cultural, social, political and economic life?

It was this desire to provide a broad framework for analysis, rather than simply a blow-by-blow account of events, that led me to adopt a Gramscian understanding of hegemony and hegemonic struggle. One thing that runs through all of Gramsci's writings is a constant desire to seek some kind of unity within all manner of constituent elements; to construct a more total and integral conception of the phenomena he is observing. This, then, was precisely the task I wanted to try to achieve in relation to developments taking place in Russia. The year 1991 also marked the centenary of Antonio Gramsci's birth, so there was no shortage of debates and material to stimulate a long-standing interest in this remarkable thinker. What was even more interesting was to observe the way in which a fresh approach was also being applied to Gramsci in Russia itself. From reform-minded communists to opposition figures of many different persuasions, Gramsci's influence would often be cited, either in directly political or in broader intellectual terms. In particular, the twin usage of the notion of hegemony both as political *strategy* and as political *analysis* was extremely fascinating.

The format of the book, therefore, is as follows. In the Introduction, the broad contours of Gramsci's notion of hegemony are outlined in order to set the scene for the empirical investigation that follows. Attention is focused on the way in which the concept was considerably expanded beyond its original roots in the late-nineteenth-century circles of Russian Social Democracy. The main 'battleground' of hegemonic struggle is identified; there is also a justification of its conceptual application to a society such as Russia, which is experiencing such a fundamental process of transition.

In Part I, the primary notion of a hegemonic struggle in contemporary Russia is analysed from the perspective of the difficult contextual conditions that currently exist. In Chapter 1 an in-depth analysis is made of Russia's emerging, yet still very fragile, realm of civil society and the associated problems of widescale economic dislocation and an immature party political system which is weakly correlated with identifiable social classes, conscious of their long-term aspirations. This is followed in Chapter 2 by a focus on the palpable threat of 'Caesarist', authoritarian solutions (as witnessed in the destruction of the first post-communist parliament in October 1993) achieving a status of permanence in the 'new' Russia. Similarly, attention is paid to the dangers posed by an increasingly politicized military and an unstable asymmetrical federal structure which, as graphically shown in the case of Chechnya, is subject to permanent strains and disintegrative tendencies.

In Part II, attention switches to the struggle that is taking place among the different social and political forces that have emerged in Russia, desirous of filling the void that has been left by the collapse of the old one-party-dominated order. Chapters 3, 4 and 5 deal with the three main contemporary combatants: Westerners, Russophiles and Centrists. In each case the 'collective will' of the respective combatants is clearly identified, together with their capacity thus far to weld together a complex array of social and political forces into a new type of 'historical bloc', cohesive enough to resist internal and external pressures. Each chapter is then concluded with an analysis of their respective short- and long-term potential of achieving a hegemonic condition in Russian society. Chapter 6, meanwhile, focuses on the state of the Left in today's post-communist Russia. While one should recognize that such forces should not be given equal status in the contemporary struggle for hegemony, it is clearly important to make some kind of assessment of the possibilities of a new socialist movement emerging in the country which might have the potential to activate an otherwise demoralized and highly contradictory working class. And once again, let me stress here that my aim in all these chapters is to try to focus on the *integral connections* between ideas, culture, economics and politics. If I have dealt in each case with the realm of ideas first, this is primarily due to reasons of methodological clarity. It is *not* an attempt to impose some kind of a priori determinacy to this realm — a determinacy in which it is somehow autonomously existing ideas that have given rise to social and political actors.

Finally, the study is concluded with an overall assessment of the hegemonic struggle in Russia, based on the situation that exists at the time of the manuscript going to press in early 1995. As with most books seeking to give an account of ongoing developments in a country subject to seemingly constant flux and change, such conclusions will intrinsically carry the risk of provisionality. At the very least, however, it is nevertheless hoped that the book will assist readers in gaining an understanding of recent events in Russia, and that it will map out a useful empirical framework for future analysis.

The Appendices, meanwhile, are used to provide detailed information pertaining to the December 1993 parliamentary elections, both from the perspective of a constituency-based as well as a regional/federal-based survey of the results. Parliamentary factions in the State Duma are listed and there is also an attempt to show the main axes of conflict and disposition of major political forces as of January 1995.

Acknowledgements

In writing this book I have had the invaluable intellectual input of many people whose time and generosity in speaking to me about the situation in Russia, either formally in on-the-record interviews or informally in conversations, warrants my deepest gratitude. Special thanks are due to Aleksandr Buzgalin, Ludmilla Bulavka and Andrei Kolganov for the frequent insights they gave me, and not least for the warm hospitality that they and their family provided during many visits to Moscow. Similar thanks and appreciation are due to Boris Kagarlitsky, Renfrey Clarke (and family), Boris Slavin, Sergei Novikov, Ludmilla Vartazarova, Mikhail Malyutin and Boris Kurashvili, as well as to those who graciously gave up their time to take part in a round-table discussion in Moscow in summer 1994: Vladimir Khazanov, Galina Rakitskaya, Aleksei Prigarin, Vladimir Kizima and Igor' Gotlib. On a number of visits to Moscow I was the guest of the Gorbachev Foundation, and for this privilege I would like to express my warm thanks to Grigorii Vodolazov, Aleksandr Galkin, Evgenii Malkin and Petr Fedosov. Similarly, Valentin Tolstykh proved likewise to be an invaluable contact and source of information at the Philosophy Academy in Moscow. Needless to say, any faults in the interpretation that follows are purely my own.

For the opportunity to undertake such research trips and much else besides, considerable thanks are due to the University of Reading Research Endowment Trust for their generous financial assistance. Pat Hicks, Ann Cade and Pam Allen from the Department of Politics at Reading University all gave me the benefit of their secretarial time and expertise throughout the course of the book's progress, and special thanks must also go to Ken Gladdish for his scholarly support and advice, and for his helpful comments on a previous draft.

For his editorial advice and assistance, Robin Blackburn at Verso deserves much of the credit for a final manuscript of manageable proportions.

Last, but most certainly not least, I would like to acknowledge the moral and intellectual support of my wife, Gemma. For her patience and tolerance, this book is dedicated to her.

Introduction
The Theoretical Framework

I have often been asked to affirm that my father was Lenin's pupil and my answer has always been: 'Pardon me, he was Croce's pupil!'

Giuliano Gramsci[1]

Despite – or possibly even *because* of – the times we live in, the interest in and enthusiasm for the writings of Antonio Gramsci continue to increase incessantly. In Western Europe this interest largely dates from the late 1960s, stimulated as it was by the events that were taking place at this time, and not least by the fact that his writings were increasingly beginning to reach beyond his native Italian confines. In Eastern Europe, meanwhile, and especially in the former Soviet Union, it was the Gorbachev era that did most not so much to renew as fundamentally to change the character of the traditional, often highly distorted interpretation of the intellectual and popular debate about the nature of Gramsci's legacy. In short, what was often an officially controlled monologue on Gramsci now became a genuine, multifaceted dialogue, and in post-Soviet Russia this dialogue has been keenly taken up by a new inquiring intellectual class desirous of applying new methodologies and criteria to the changing environment around them.

What is it, then, about Gramsci that makes him so sought-after at a time when most other theoreticians and ideological strategists from the days of the Comintern are being so disparaged? To what does he owe his continuing popularity and influence?

An answer to these questions depends to some extent on the direction from which you approach Gramsci. For the politically engaged, Gramsci's keynote political strategy of hegemonic trench warfare within the realm of a highly developed civil society is still one of the most plausible and optimistically inspiring routes to a radical overhaul of an entrenched order. Gramsci's own communist convictions are also not necessarily a barrier to other political forces making full use of his insights. As one participant in a Moscow round table on Gramsci in January 1991 cogently put it:

1

Of course, Gramsci's main interest is in the destiny of the working class, the peasants ('the subordinate classes') and their corresponding political party. Nevertheless, based on his analysis of common forms of questions concerning the overall correlation of forces, hegemony, power, the state and civil society etc., he also appeals to, and is certainly taken notice of by, other classes and different social groups and is therefore an acknowledged purveyor of accepted historical laws of development.[2]

For the theoretically minded, Gramsci's Marxism still offers one of the most cogent espousals of base–superstructure interaction, and also a theory of praxis which justifies and legitimizes the role and significance of intellectual pursuit and understanding. And for the political scientist, Gramsci's expanded theory of politics in general, and power in particular, again revolving around the notion of hegemony, likewise offers one of the most convincing frameworks for empirical analysis – not only as regards the functioning of developed stable capitalist systems, but also as regards transitional societies undergoing revolutionary upheaval from one type of system to another. Since the latter clearly best defines the contemporary situation after the collapse of the Soviet Union, what follows is an attempt to apply Gramsci's theory of hegemony and hegemonic struggle broadly to the new Russian arena.

The purpose of the study is basically twofold. First, it should go some way towards outlining the very complex nature of political struggle taking place in Russia in the aftermath of the disintegration of one-party domination and the attempt to establish some kind of overall framework in which a pluralistic democracy can emerge. Secondly, it should also relocate the important theoretical concept of hegemony back to its original birthplace in Russia, from where Gramsci himself first borrowed – some would say 'rescued' – it following the October Revolution in 1917.

The Conceptual Development of Hegemony

In his painstaking reconstruction of some of the 'shifting constellations' of the concept of hegemony, Perry Anderson was one of the first English-language writers successfully to indicate the true origins of the concept.[3] Taking issue with writers like Norberto Bobbio in Italy and Maria-Antonietta Macciocchi in France, Anderson belied the novelty of Gramsci's general conceptual and linguistic use of hegemony and successfully traced its origins to Russian Social Democracy at the turn of the nineteenth century; specifically to the writings of Georgii Plekhanov.

Plekhanov, a former Populist who had 'converted' to orthodox Marxism while in exile abroad, first started to employ the concept [*gegemoniya*] in the early-to-mid 1880s as a means of suggesting that the working class itself would have to *instigate* the bourgeois-democratic revolution in Russia, owing to the weakness and inconsistencies of the emerging Russian bourgeoisie. Under the influence of Plekhanov the concept was taken up by several other prominent Russian Social Democrats, and by the turn of the century Lenin himself was openly making use of this now 'famous' political term.[4]

For Lenin, the earlier evolution and development of the concept of hegemony proved, more than anything, to be of great strategic significance. Having taken on board the notion from Plekhanov, and extended in particular by Pavel Axelrod, that the proletariat itself must play a primary role in the bourgeois revolution against Tsarism, Lenin, from his 1902 pamphlet 'What is to be Done?' onwards, began to see the key task of the Social Democrats as being to organize and lead 'special auxiliary detachments' of all the working and exploited people of Russia in this new enlarged phase of the revolutionary struggle. 'The proletariat is revolutionary', he argued, 'only in so far as it consists of and gives effect to this idea of the hegemony of the proletariat.'[5]

At this stage, of course, the task was still limited to carrying out the bourgeois phase of the revolution, with only Trotsky arguing in any consistent fashion for a proletarian hegemony that would immediately go on to introduce the *socialist* phase, and hence an outright *dictatorship* of the proletariat. As the Leninist distinction between the two phases also became more blurred, however, so likewise outright proletarian dictatorship began to supersede the old strategic notion of hegemony; or at the very least, the two terms 'hegemony' and 'dictatorship' began to lose any real differentiation.

In the actual aftermath of the October Revolution, as Anderson goes on to outline, the notion of hegemony suddenly ceases to have much internal actuality in the new Soviet state, having effectively outlived its strategic usefulness. It is true that Lenin continued to refer to the concept, and the likes of Bukharin, Bogdanov, Brutkus and, later, Bakhtin also developed ideas on the subject that some commentators have seen as being, if not exactly close, then at least relevant, to the Gramscian version. These thinkers aside, however, especially after Lenin's death, the term was all too frequently interpreted as nothing more than a dogmatic parody of an already increasingly authoritarian form of domination over hostile 'anti-proletarian' forces. The one area where the term was still being debated was at the congresses of the Comintern, and it was during these debates in the early 1920s that Gramsci himself first came into contact with the concept.

In assessing the Gramscian interpretation and understanding of the concept of hegemony, it is important not to downplay the fact that throughout the Prison Notebooks there are consistent and explicit references to Lenin's considerable achievement in formulating and realizing his own powerful notion of hegemony. Such praise is undoubtedly genuine. For all that Gramsci was one of the first post-1917 theoreticians to elaborate a more developed analysis of the critical differences between political develop- ments in Russia and the rest of Europe, which thereby ultimately necessitated a totally different strategy of socialist revolutionary activity in the more advanced civilizations of the West, he was always adamant that the Jacobin-like acquisition of power by the Bolsheviks was the right course in the circumstances prevailing in Russia at that time. This explicit praise for Lenin and his specific strategic employment of the concept of hegemony during the preparatory stages of a revolutionary onslaught against the Russian state, however, has to be contrasted with Gramsci's own elaboration of a concept of hegemony, which began to differ markedly from its Leninist-inspired origins.

Three crucial differences in particular deserve to be highlighted. First, whereas for Lenin hegemony was a mere strategy or prescription of action evolving out of capitalism's inherent backwardness in Russia, for Gramsci, not only is the strategic nature of hegemony altered to fit the more advanced political societies of Western Europe, but he also fundamentally alters the concept from a mere strategy in itself to a whole new interpret- ative category: a general systemic theory of political struggle that is by no means transfixed in one specific geographical or time warp. Secondly, whereas for Lenin hegemony was definable solely in *class* terms, for Gramsci the terrain of hegemonic struggle is considerably broader. Without doubt, class is still the *underlying* aspect of hegemonic struggle, but he is well aware that there are innumerable aspects of political conflict that simply cannot be reduced to a fundamental class character. And thirdly, whereas for Lenin hegemony was about the *assimilation* and even the *manipulation* of like-minded interests in the preparatory phase of rev- olution, for Gramsci (echoing a criticism that had earlier been made of Lenin by Aleksandr Potresov) hegemony was a long-term trench warfare that was all about the ability to *articulate* different kinds of interests within a recognized pluralist, *consensual* framework.

If we now go on to elaborate in some greater detail the Gramscian understanding of hegemony, these crucial differences with the Leninist mode of analysis will be made that much clearer.

The more refined conceptualization of hegemony is noticeable right at the very beginning of Gramsci's reflections while in prison. In the first of his Notebooks, commenting on the French Revolution of 1789, Gramsci writes:

> . . . not only did [the Jacobins] organise a bourgeois government, i.e. make the bourgeoisie the dominant class – they did more. They created the bourgeois

state, made the bourgeoisie into the leading, hegemonic class of the nation, in other words gave the new state a permanent basis and created the compact modern French nation.[6]

Already, then, Gramsci has somewhat superseded Leninist strategic reductionism in favour of a more general, broader approach to the concept. Going on to clarify what he means by Jacobin hegemony, he begins to argue for the first time about the importance of being able to widen specific class interests – not so much to assimilate subsidiary interests, but to find some common ground, some consensus with them that will nevertheless leave the dominant group (in this case, the Jacobins) in a commanding leading role.

It is in the Fourth Notebook, however (compiled and written in 1933), that the really significant extension of Leninist analysis begins to emerge. As Chantal Mouffe has shown, Gramsci's fundamental task now is not so much to demonstrate the significance of a simple political alliance as to show how 'a complete fusion of economic, political, intellectual and moral objectives' can be brought about 'by one fundamental group and groups allied to it *through the intermediary of ideology*'. Here, then, we not only have a sense of a dominant class renouncing a strictly corporatist conception of itself by concerning itself with the specific *interests* of other social groups: 'it also presupposes a certain equilibrium [whereby] the hegemonic groups will make some *sacrifices* of a corporate nature'.[7] It is this that is, in essence, the beginning of a real discordance with Leninist conceptions. Lenin's concept of hegemony had always been limited to a notion of *political* leadership as an essential strategy of the proletariat; a political leadership, as already mentioned, that would over a course of time assimilate these subsidiary social interests to the needs of the proletariat. Gramsci now is not talking only of political leadership but, more importantly, of *intellectual* and *moral* leadership. Furthermore, he is not talking about the eventual assimilation of other social groups into the dominant class power, but beginning to recognize the importance of *articulating* different interests, whereby each group maintains a substantial degree of its own individuality.

When it comes to describing the actual mechanisms of articulating different interests, Gramsci is astute enough to distinguish between two different processes, only one of which he himself would favour. On the one hand, he argues, the interests of different groups might perhaps be articulated so as to neutralize them and hence prevent the development of their own specific demands (a process that will be referred to in more detail below). This would be a very *passive* type of articulation, which Gramsci himself saw prevalent in the actions of the Moderate Party during the *Risorgimento* in his native Italy. A more *active* type of articulation, however, would be a promotion of each group's specific demands to their fullest possible extent which would then intrinsically lead to a final resolution of the contradictions that each expresses.

The actual medium of articulation is ideology ('a battlefield of continuous struggle', as he calls it), and this in turn will act as the main 'cement' binding all the disparate forces together. For Gramsci, the hegemonic process is about the creation of a 'higher synthesis'. In terms of ideals, this synthesis will amount to a coming together of individual component beliefs into what he terms a 'collective will'. This will then form the basis of a physical synthesis in the shape of a 'historical bloc' of forces which will go on to be the key political protagonist in any given period of history during which its hegemony is maintained. The essence of such a historical bloc is its capacity to unite an ensemble of economic and political relations.

A key element for the actual foundation of a hegemony of the kind so far outlined is the process of intellectual and moral reform. By laying such stress on the intellectual and moral process, Gramsci is not stating that intellectuals are the *determining* forces of a collective will in society, but he is giving them a strategic place of great importance in the hegemonic struggle. As Ernesto Laclau and Chantal Mouffe have indicated: 'For Gramsci, political subjects are not – strictly speaking – classes, but complex "collective wills"; similarly, the ideological elements articulated by a hegemonic class do not have a necessary class belonging.'[8] If a sense of class solidarity, then, is not the force that keeps the groups united together in this collective will, it clearly implies that there is another factor of integration that is at least of equal significance.

On this issue it has to be said that Gramsci himself is not all that clear or consistent, though the preponderance of opinion is to argue that *cultural* unity is the strongest bonding mechanism, at least in the ethical-political realm:

> Culture, at its various levels, unifies in a series of strata, to the extent that they come into contact with each other, a greater or lesser number of individuals who understand each other's mode of expression in differing degrees, etc. . . . An historical act can only be performed by 'collective man', and this presupposes the attainment of a 'cultural-social' unity through which a multiplicity of dispersed wills, with heterogeneous aims, are welded together with a single aim on the basis of an equal and common conception of the world.[9]

Let me emphasize here that Gramsci is certainly not implying by this that class is insignificant in the development of a hegemonic force; far from it, and Laclau and Mouffe, in their post-Marxist critical study of Gramsci's concept of hegemony, totally undervalue the pivotal significance of class formations. Classes are what Gramsci terms 'the efficient cause' without which there would be no preparatory stage for a hegemonic struggle in society. Nevertheless, he does clearly argue that social classes which exist at the economic level are not necessarily duplicated at the political level, for part and parcel of the process of articulating a collective will able to effect a political hegemony in society is the ability to create 'inter-class' political subjects. While class, then, is for Gramsci the decisive *nucleus* of economic activity which determines the ethical-political realm of hegemonic struggle, culture becomes the key factor within the parameters of that realm and intellectuals, by implication, thus become key decisive players; they are the ones in charge of elaborating and spreading the 'organic ideologies' whence hegemony will be achieved.

As for the actual manner of spreading this ideology, Gramsci here turns his attention to the 'Modern Prince' – i.e. the political party.

> The political party . . . is responsible for welding together the organic intellec-
> tuals of a given group. . . . The party carries out this function in strict
> dependence on its basic function, which is that of elaborating its own com-
> ponent parts – those elements of a social group which has been born and
> developed as an 'economic' group – and of turning them into qualified political
> intellectuals, leaders and organisers of all the activities and functions inherent
> in the organic development of an integral society, both civil and political.[10]

How, then, does an actual struggle for hegemony arise, and on what basis is a new hegemony attained? For Gramsci, the truly political phase of a hegemonic struggle is undertaken when 'previously germinated ideol-ogies . . . come into confrontation and conflict, until only one of them, or at least a single combination of them, tends to prevail'. This, he goes on to add, brings about 'not only a unison of economic and political aims, but also intellectual and moral unity, posing all the questions around which the struggle rages not on a corporate but on a "universal" plane, and thus cre-ating the hegemony of a fundamental social group over a series of subordinate groups'.[11] More specifically, he writes:

> What matters is the criticism to which such an ideological complex is subjected
> by the first representatives of the new historical phase. This criticism makes pos-
> sible a process of differentiation and change in the relative weight that the
> elements of the old ideologies used to possess. What was previously secondary
> and subordinate, or even incidental, is now taken to be primary – becomes the
> nucleus of a new ideological and theoretical complex. The old collective will dis-
> solves into its contradictory elements since the subordinate ones develop
> socially.[12]

Gramsci makes it plain here that he is not talking about a *sudden* or even *total* destruction of a once hegemonic collective will. Rather, the process is much more gradual. First of all, the unity of the collective will is slowly dissolved or disaggregated. Then, the basic elements of the old collective will can be 'sifted through' with a view to seeing what, if anything, can be *re*articulated within the structures of a brand-new collective will.

As for the actual decisive moment of victory in a hegemonic struggle, Gramsci declares, using a somewhat erroneous phrase, that a collective will will successfully prevail once it manages to become a 'popular religion'. By this, he basically means when it becomes imbued in the national consciousness of a given society.

The Battleground of Hegemonic Struggle

Having dealt with some of the main component elements of Gramsci's theory of hegemony and hegemonic struggle, it is important that we now examine the actual terrain on which a struggle for hegemony takes place. For Gramsci, there is no doubt in his mind that that terrain of struggle is located firmly and squarely 'in civil society, through the private organisms of which the most important are the political parties and the unions, but which also reveal a multitude of ideologico-cultural forms', such as newspapers, literature, churches, schools and similar associations, not to mention things like architecture and even the names of streets. The actual solidity of any given state (apparatus of government), Gramsci goes on to add, thus depends on the consistency of the civil society which serves as its basis.

For the Marxist theoreticians of Gramsci's philosophy, the concept of civil society is, in fact, one of the most contentious issues of debate. Arguments about its setting within the superstructure of society rather than the economic base, as well as a whole range of other issues, have been the subject of much controversy over the years. Since this is an area of argument that has been well documented, there is no need to examine it in any great detail here.[13] It is important, however, at least to indicate the kind of relationship that exists in Gramsci's analysis of civil society and the state, for this will clearly have a significant bearing on the later empirical investigation.

One of the fundamental problems encountered by readers of Gramsci's Prison Notebooks relates to the different ways in which the 'state' is actually denoted. In some instances it is narrowly defined as simply 'the apparatus of government' and nothing else. In other instances, however, the state is defined in a much more *integral* way (a term borrowed from Hegel) as being the actual institutions of government (what Gramsci here calls 'political society') *plus* the whole range of activities undertaken by civil society. This different usage of the term is clearly very important, since in the narrow sense it implies a clear *demarcation* between political institutions and political activities defined in a much broader sense; while in the second definition it implies a clear assimilation of *all* political activities.

The perplexed reader is helped somewhat by referring to Gramsci's more historical texts. In these, it appears that the 'integral state' is a historical evolutionary advancement of the narrow institutional state that has so far been achieved only in the more advanced 'bourgeois' civilizations. Only in those societies which for one reason or another have not developed a civil society, therefore, should the narrow definition be applied.

A vital clarification of this basic distinction is provided by Gramsci when he refers to the actual means by which the institutional state ('political society') and the integral state ('political society plus civil society') actually carry out their functions. Political society, he argues, is characterized primarily (though not exclusively) by the use of domination. Civil society, on the other hand, is characterized primarily (though again not exclusively) by the use of *consent*. A fuller definition of the integral state, then, would go as follows: '[It] is the whole complex of practical and theoretical activities through which [a] ruling class not only justifies and maintains its domination, but succeeds in obtaining the active consent of those over whom it rules.'[14]

With this definition in mind, it is now possible to locate the concept of hegemony in the realm of the integral state complex. The struggle for hegemony occurs on the terrain of civil society; a struggle primarily for intellectual/cultural control, the outcome of which will result in a popular consent for the victorious historical bloc. If this victorious historical bloc also has control over the institutions of the state, then it will have access to explicit forces of domination as well. Domination, however, at least in an advanced political civilization, will be a supplement to consent only for as long as hegemony within civil society is adequately maintained.

Having established the basic linkage between hegemonic rule and consent, it is perhaps necessary to explain in a little more detail what precisely Gramsci implies by this. As Joseph Femia has written: 'When Gramsci speaks of consent, he refers to a *psychological* state involving some kind of acceptance of the socio-political order or of certain vital aspects of that order.'[15] Like most other general theories of consent, Gramsci's 'psychological' approach can be essentially characterized in an active and a passive manner; what is most interesting about this distinction, however, is the very thin objective line of demarcation between the two. A more active form of consent implies for Gramsci that a hegemonic force is able to rely on a level of agreement and consensus in civil society which is strong enough to overcome any possible division or disruptive force that might arise from conflicting interests of one kind or another. More crucially, it is also one in which there is an essential harmony between objective interests and needs at any given stage, and the critical ability to develop a course of action that suitably corresponds to these needs.

If this represents an optimal condition of active consent, Gramsci is fully aware of the difficulties in attaining such a condition. Further on, he indicates that wherever conflicts do take place, the aggrieved force, in isolation, rarely possesses the clear theoretical consciousness which would enable it effectively to comprehend and act on its discontent. This kind of phenomenon is labelled 'contradictory consciousness' by Gramsci, who then goes on to study the role of language in particular as a tool of hegemony capable of preserving a given status quo by effectively narrowing an alternative image of society.

Similarly, one should also note here Gramsci's important notion of 'common sense', or what he also calls 'the folklore of philosophy'. In essence, what Gramsci means by common sense is the whole gamut of human sentiments, human myths and human superstitions. It is his way of trying to understand some of the *uncritical* and *unconscious* ways in which all human beings try to make sense not only of their own lives, but of the world around them. In particular, it is an attempt to understand the manner in which people absorb long-established historical ideas and aim to fit them into a contemporary setting to provide some element or some desire for stability. In this sense, then, Gramsci makes it plain that common sense is by no means equivalent with, or reducible to, a ruling-class ideology. It is instead 'an infinity of traces without . . . an inventory. . . . It contains Stone Age elements and principles of a more advanced science, prejudices from all phases of history at the local level and intuitions of a future philosophy which will be that of a human race united the world over.'[16] Nevertheless, as a means of perpetuating fragmentary and superstitious attitudes, Gramsci equally makes it plain that a ruling class will inevitably be tempted to harness such sentiments for its own ends. And certainly, language (understood as 'a totality of determined notions and concepts and not just of words grammatically devoid of content'),[17] is one of the tools for reinforcing certain 'desirable' commonsensical values.

For Gramsci, then, if one is to free oneself from the restrictions of common sense, and if one is to look at the world from the perspective of a *senso buono* (good sense) – i.e. one that is able to define the *real* needs and interests of the masses of ordinary people – it is almost certainly incumbent to learn a *new* language so as to attack all the old encrustations embedded deeply in the existing language form.

Before leaving the 'battleground' of hegemonic struggle, it is necessary to continue the military analogy (so prevalent in Gramsci's own political analysis) for just a little longer to include a brief account of the main kinds of strategy a *potential* hegemonic force will use to try to gain victory over an existing dominant class, and the kind of counter-strategy available to the latter.

Having established an integral connection between the ethical-political terrain of civil society and the institutional arm of the state, and postulated that civil society operates very much as the outer trench of hegemonic power, Gramsci is now able to come to the conclusion that the only feasible strategy available to a potential *new* hegemonic force is one of trench warfare *within* civil society. This conclusion serves as the basis for the development of Gramsci's well-known strategic concept of a 'war of position'. In the most advanced states, Gramsci argues, 'civil society has become a very complex structure and one which is resistant to the catastrophic "incursions" of the immediate economic element (crises, depressions etc.)'.[18] Because of the very complexity of this structure, it follows for Gramsci that a direct assault on the state by a potential hegemonic force (a 'war of manoeuvre') will invariably end in defeat, precisely because of the way in which an existing dominant force has institutionalized itself in so many different spheres.

Instead, the requisite strategy for a bid for supremacy must be gradual and must involve 'a steady penetration and subversion of the complex and multiple mechanisms' of hegemonic diffusion. It must, in other words, engage in an ideological-cultural struggle for the control of the key agencies of civil society – the schools, the universities, the publishing houses and the mass media, and so on. This, then, is what Gramsci effectively means by a 'war of position'. As Chantal Mouffe has noted:

> In effect, the war of position is the process of ideological struggle by means of which the two fundamental classes try to appropriate the non-class ideological elements in order to integrate them within the ideological system which articulates itself around their respective hegemonic principles. This is therefore only a stage in the struggle, the one in which the new hegemonic bloc cements itself, but it is a decisive moment. . . .[19]

Indeed, in Gramsci's own words: 'in politics, once the war of position has been won, it has been won definitively', and he makes it perfectly plain that without a successful penetrative war of position in civil society, any kind of offensive aimed at overthrowing the state's institutional apparatus will come to grief precisely on the 'trenches and fortifications' of civil society.

As for the options open to a ruling hegemonic force in resisting an alternative force's incursions on its control, Gramsci examines a number of alternatives. First, the ruling forces will be ever vigilant in looking for ways to keep a potential hegemonic force weak and fragmented, and will always seek ways to 'pick off' elements of the opposition, either by itself articulating certain specific interests within its own sphere of hegemony, or by incorporating the leaders of potentially antagonistic groups into the elitist network of the hegemonic domain. Indeed, Gramsci is adamant that this process of readjustment and renegotiation is absolutely critical to the survival of a ruling hegemonic force, and should be periodically undertaken, irrespective of whether there is a specific crisis of hegemony or not.

If the hegemonic crisis is of a degree or depth which makes it difficult for the ruling force to continue to secure the conformity of other groups and classes, then another option that is frequently invoked, Gramsci suggests, is to make ever greater use of the incumbent bureaucracy such that the bureaucracy emerges, temporarily at least, as the only organization capable of discharging the tasks of the ruling force. One very important consequence of finding refuge in the bureaucracy, he argues, is the way in which the process of representation and the creation of consent is replaced by technical competence; and this, in turn, is bound to lead to a considerable decline in the importance of ideology.[20]

Should neither of these tactics produce the desired consequences for the ruling forces then, according to Gramsci, a third option will more and more come into play: the ever greater reliance on the institutional powers of the state and the outright mechanisms of domination, coercion and force.

> If the ruling class has lost its consensus, i.e. is no longer 'leading' but only 'dominant', exercising coercive force alone, this means precisely that the great masses have become detached from their traditional ideologies and no longer believe what they used to believe previously etc. The crisis consists precisely in the fact that the old is dying and the new cannot be born; in this interregnum a great variety of morbid symptoms appears.[21]

Gramsci, however, is adamant that the more coercion and domination are exercised in such a situation, the more the ruling class will reveal its vulnerability as a force able to exercise any kind of integrative capacity of hegemony. As a short-term strategy of survival, therefore, it might just prove effective. As a long-term strategy, however, extensive reliance on domination alone might well prove self-defeating.

A final response to a crisis of hegemony is the solution Gramsci calls *Caesarism* – a solution which brings to the fore charismatic 'men of destiny' (an issue that will be dealt with in greater detail in Chapter 2).

Gramsci's East–West Dichotomy

From the account that has been given so far, it is clear (whatever the arguments of someone like Togliatti on the Left and other figures on the Right) that Gramsci has moved an enormous distance from the conception of hegemony originally formulated within the ranks of the Russian Social

Democrats, and particularly by Lenin. From a strategic point of view, Gramsci was very clearly of the opinion that a replication of the Bolshevik type of war of manoeuvre (a direct assault) against the state in more advanced political conditions (i.e. in the West at this time) would be totally futile. And from a broader, analytical point of view, he has clearly evolved a conceptual form of hegemony far richer than anything Lenin was able to achieve.

In an interesting passage in the Prison Notebooks, Gramsci – ever determined, none the less, to defend Lenin's strategic use of hegemony in the Russian national context in 1917 – is adamant that:

> Ilitch understood that a change was necessary from the war of manoeuvre applied victoriously in the East in 1917, to a war of position which was the only form possible in the West. . . . This is what the formula of the 'United Front' seems to me to mean. . . . Ilitch, however, did not have time to expand his formula – though it should be borne in mind that he could only have expanded it theoretically. . . .[22]

The use of the word *theoretically* is significant, for it gives Gramsci the basis to develop a theme that is predominant throughout the Notebooks: the fundamental difference between political developments in the East and the West. It is worthwhile, therefore, devoting some space to Gramsci's analysis here, for it will provide us with a framework for a brief examination of the broad pattern of development in Soviet Russia after 1917, and in particular under Stalin.

The underlying aspect of Gramsci's distinction between East and West centres upon the relationship between state and civil society in the two geopolitical arenas. In a celebrated passage in the second of the Prison Notebooks, Gramsci states:

> In the East, the state was everything, civil society was primordial and gelatinous; in the West, there was a proper relationship between state and civil society, and when the state trembled a sturdy structure of civil society was at once revealed. The state was only an outer ditch, behind which there was a powerful system of fortresses and earthworks: more or less numerous from one state to the next, it goes without saying – but this precisely necessitated an accurate reconnaissance of each individual country.[23]

The importance of a 'proper relationship between state and civil society' in the West has already been dealt with. But what precisely did Gramsci mean by his reference to a primordial and gelatinous civil society in the East, and what significances stemmed from this?

Certainly one thing he meant by it was the way in which state power in the East was more explicit, more visible than in the West and far less reliant on the kind of *voluntary* – albeit largely passive – forms of consent that exist in the West. Precisely because state power was not camouflaged behind the plethora of rights ensconced in civil society – rights such as universal suffrage or 'freedom' of the press, etc. – a full-scale assault on the state was the only real alternative open to an oppositional force which desired to be in power. For all its explicit show of strength and domination, therefore, the Russian state was far more susceptible to a rival force than a Western state because of its *lack* of popular consent. This, then, is Gramsci's basic reason for continuing to justify the Bolshevik war of manoeuvre strategy in 1917, without wanting it to be considered as the most viable strategy of opposition in the different conditions in the West.

If we take Gramsci's East–West analysis a little further, however, we can begin to see the outlines of another significant factor relating to the lack of a fully functioning civil society in the East. Gramsci now begins implicitly to look at the kinds of *problems* associated with a capture of power by means of a direct assault on the state in conditions where a civil society is negligible or non-existent. One of the intrinsic problems of such a scenario is the way in which a degenerate form of statization, or what Gramsci terms *statolatry*, may well become endemically entrenched. That is to say, having been unable to rely on a mass popular initiative for the capture of power, the subsequent process of transition may also come to rely primarily on the state as the key protagonist of change rather than on a more expansive base of support. Should this occur, argues Gramsci, you are faced with essentially another form of a passive type of revolution, based on a totally passive form of consent in which politics becomes identified purely with the statist and instrumental domain of domination, characterized by such things as bureaucratic centralism, authoritarian paternalism, state fanaticism and totalitarianism. The inevitable result of all this is what Gramsci calls a *dictatorship without hegemony*, a phenomenon well summarized by Christine Buci-Glucksmann:

> In the event that the state becomes a partisan-state (or even a party-state), hegemony is restricted not only in its mass basis, but also within the class itself: 'The hegemony will be exercised by a *part* of the social group over the entire group, and not by the latter over other forces in order to give power to the movement.' . . . Thereupon, the hegemonic apparatuses . . . become ideological state apparatuses.[24]

The contextual location of Gramsci's discussion of the phenomenon of dictatorship without hegemony is explicitly set in Italy, forming part of the broader analysis of why the *Risorgimento* led to a 'bastard' kind of state, an illegitimate offspring that was unhealthy and corrupt – if economically progressive – and reliant on the twin themes of passivity, supplemented by the ever-present threat of violent repression. It does not stretch the imagination too much, however, to see that Gramsci was equally motivated here by an obvious concern that a genuine capacity for hegemony (as he understood it and not as Lenin understood it) might also fail to materialize in post-revolutionary Russia.

From his analysis of the *Risorgimento*, however, Gramsci does at least implicitly offer one piece of advice to his Russian comrades from his prison cell. If an expansive class, he argues, is to avoid being replaced by a narrow dictatorial state, it must gain hegemony both before *and* after the seizure of power. Now we know that Gramsci fully understood that the Bolsheviks had no chance to create a hegemonic base *prior* to the seizure of power in October 1917 because of the primordial and gelatinous nature of Russia's civil society and its all-encompassing state. But Gramsci's stress here on the need to gain hegemony *after* the seizure of power is very instructive. What he seems to be exhorting Stalin and the rest of the Soviet leadership to do at this time is to construct themselves a fully functioning civil society with a full range of non-institutional apparatuses which would in turn encourage a dynamic and positive sense of adhesion to the new socialist project through the 'socialization of politics'.

Gramsci fully recognizes that: 'For some social groups, which before their ascent to autonomous state life have not had a long independent period of cultural and moral development on their own . . . a period of statolatry is necessary and indeed opportune.' However, he goes on, 'this kind of statolatry must not be abandoned to itself, must not, especially, become theoretical fanaticism or be conceived of as perpetual'.[25] Instead, the capturing of state power must represent a 'movement to create a new civilisation, a new type of man and of citizen, *[it] must serve to determine the will to construct within the husk of political society a complex and well-articulated civil society*, in which the individual can govern himself without his self-government thereby entering into conflict with political society – but rather becoming its normal continuation, its organic complement'.[26]

As things turned out, of course, Stalin did not take up Gramsci's advice, and instead implemented a revolution from above, whose only links with the base of society were the social 'transmission belts' firmly under the control of the dictatorial state apparatus; in other words, instead of the new state giving birth to civil society, it smothered it. For all his references to the Communist Party's 'leading role' in society, then, the Stalinist process of development clearly resulted in a triumph of 'domination' over 'leadership' from a Gramscian perspective. Bureaucratic centralism, authoritarian paternalism and totalitarianism were indeed the results of this 'fanatical state domination', this dictatorship without hegemony. And there can be little doubt that even from the confines of his prison cell, Gramsci was well informed of the visible signs of degeneration permeating Stalin's Russia. His warnings about the dangers of the Party relying on *bureaucratic* rather than democratic forms of centralism, for example, is an obvious case in point. Bureaucratic centralism, he argues, might well be the appropriate organizational mechanism for a church, but a political party aspiring to create the nucleus of a new expansive type of hegemony must be able to go beyond the use of such regressive methods. The consequences for the Party if it cannot achieve this are clear. It will stagnate and ossify under illusions of unity and immutability.

Similarly, Gramsci's writings on totalitarianism, though first and foremost applicable to Mussolini, were also undeniably set in a Soviet context as well. Discussing the problems that arise when political pluralism is subjugated to the demands of a single totalitarian governing party, Gramsci is convinced that 'the functions of such a party are no longer directly political, but merely technical ones of propaganda and public order, and moral and cultural influence . . .. [In] such parties cultural functions predominate, which means that political language becomes jargon. In other words, political questions are disguised as cultural ones and as such become insoluble.'[27] For Gramsci, the most important consequence of this kind of totalitarianism is again its effect on the relationship between rulers and ruled, leaders and led, elite and masses. In all instances, the latter serves 'no other political function than a generic loyalty, of a military kind, to a visible or invisible political centre'. The mass exists for no other purpose than 'for manoeuvre, and is kept happy by means of moralising sermons, emotional stimuli, and messianic myths of an awaited golden age, in which all present contradictions and miseries will be automatically resolved and made well. . . .'[28]

At times, Gramsci's criticism of Stalin even penetrated the barriers of implicitness; as witnessed, for example, by his stinging critique of the Soviet regime's artistic policy of Socialist Realism. For Gramsci, 'art is art and not "willed" political propaganda', and any simplistic or mechanical attempt to harness the intrinsic aesthetic qualities of art to political control will make it fictitious and dull.[29]

In short, then, Gramsci remained a 'Leninist' in so far as he fully supported and justified the revolutionary onslaught against the Russian state in October 1917 as a historically necessary and progressive act. He was not a 'Leninist', however, if this implied, as it frequently did, a reduction of hegemony to a form of class dictatorship exercised primarily within and through the institutional realm of state (*qua* government) power. And he was certainly no advocate of the 'Stalinist' process of state-dominated developments after 1929, criticizing it, as we have seen, for its closed, dogmatic, rigid, uncritical and elitist methods.

The ultimate conclusion of Gramsci's analysis of the dichotomy between East and West, then, is this: capturing state power is one thing; being in a position, however, actually to *construct* a viable alternative to the old order which is genuinely hegemonic in an active, consensual, democratic, participatory way is another thing entirely.

Conceptual Application

Before going on to examine the struggle for hegemony in present-day Russia, let me briefly summarize the main aspects of the Gramscian framework.

A struggle for hegemony, following traditional Marxist thinking, has its origins in the mode of economic production in society. These material forces of production essentially follow their own inner logic of development and act as the primary determinant of the kind of class relations which will then ensue. These relations will not be of a harmonious kind but will reflect the contradictory interests of the different economic classes; contradictory interests which will also be reflected in the non-economic, superstructural realm of society. This leads Gramsci to draw the conclusion that although the economic realm is primary, it is not in itself *decisive*. One of its attributes is to create the necessary conditions and boundaries within which certain resolutions and solutions concerning the evolution of a society will be advanced. To put it another way, Gramsci argues that while material conditions of production have an objective existence, this objectivity in itself 'is not yet sufficient'. It is necessary, he says, to 'know' these conditions of production; to know how to use them; and, most important of all, 'to *want* to use them'.[30] It follows, therefore, that while human freedom is ultimately circumscribed by an existing form of economic reality, this economic reality is in no sense a passive phenomenon; man's creative spirit and man's ability and desire to utilize this reality are most decisive.

In any historical period, one class will achieve dominance over another. The primary attribute of dominance in any society is state power. This creates the basis for the dominant class to establish legal prerequisites for the continued functioning of a given type of economic system (by the establishment of a specific set of property rights, for example), as well as giving it various other levers of compulsion and control to maintain the required apparatus of production and create the required type of *Homo economicus* to operate this apparatus. State power of this kind has been used throughout the ages to buttress the power of a dominant class. What is of most interest to Gramsci, however, is the way in which in *modern* states an extra dimension of power has been created by its diffusion outwards; and it is this outward diffusion of power that is the real essence of Gramsci's concept of hegemony. By means of a complex and vast network of 'organically conceived' political and social alliances, together with the creation of an ethical-cultural set of values, a dominant class has achieved the basis for establishing a form of rule over society as a whole on a consensual basis.

By 'alliances', Gramsci means here the way in which an economic class is able to transcend its strict corporate character by engaging in a process of articulating different forms of social interests. A requisite process of articulation should produce a degree of equilibrium which is characterized by the prevalence of the interests of the dominant class, but not at the total, sacrificial expense of secondary social groups. The result of this articulation, meanwhile, is a plethora of organizations linked together in a historical bloc, cemented by a collective will which is capable of structuring and embodying the perceived national values and traditions of society.

In a modern state, then, the solidity of the social structure depends very much on the way in which power has been effectively diffused outwards within the realm of civil society, and the degree of consensual mechanisms underlying this diffusion. The more active and direct this basis of consent, the stronger the hegemonic nature of the social structure will be. The more passive and indirect, the more explicit and regular will be the recourse to the coercive levers of state power, producing in turn more instability and an increasing loss of legitimacy and hegemony. As for a potential alternative dominant force, it goes without saying that it too must take up the struggle for hegemony within the realm of civil society. It must strive to build an effective, cohesive historical bloc of forces which gives maximum credence to an alternative conception of the world, and it must seek to isolate the dominant class politically and ideologically, forcing the component parts of its historical bloc to disintegrate. Both sets of antagonists must constantly search for ways and means (active or passive) of preserving their own unity, while destroying the unity of the opposing force.

In seeking to *apply* this Gramscian framework of hegemony to the contemporary situation in Russia, a number of additional points must be stressed.

First, not all Gramscian scholars would necessarily approve of the idea of 'applying' Gramsci's notion of hegemony, especially in a non-Italian domain, justifying their objections with the conviction that Gramsci's writings clearly do not constitute a 'manual' in any sense whatsoever. This objection, however, can be overcome in two different ways.

There can be little doubt that Gramsci himself foresaw the potential and the desirability of his ideas on hegemony being subsequently used as a general overall framework of empirical analysis. Indeed, in many passages of the Notebooks, clear-cut methodological guidance is provided. For example, after demonstrating that various social groupings, each representing a function and occupying a specific position within the productive process, will arise in all economic systems, he notes:

By studying these fundamental data [material forces of production] it is possible to discover whether in a particular society there exist the necessary and sufficient conditions for its transformation – in other words, to check the degree of realism and practicability of the various ideologies which have been born on its own terrain, on the terrain of the contradictions which it has engendered during the course of its development.[31]

Consider, too, the following piece of crucial methodological advice:

A study of how . . . innovatory forces developed, from subaltern groups to hegemonic and dominant groups, must . . . seek out and identify the phases through which they acquired: 1. autonomy vis-à-vis the enemies they had to defeat, and 2. support from the groups which actively or passively assisted them; for this entire process was historically necessary before they could unite in the form of a state. It is precisely by these two yardsticks that the level of historical and political consciousness which the innovatory forces progressively attained in the various phases can be measured – and not simply by the yardstick of their separation from the formerly dominant forces.[32]

On top of this, a lot of the doubts that might be raised about the notion of applying Gramsci also depend to a large extent on the actual connotation of 'apply'. And here I am very much inclined to follow Stuart Hall, who, perhaps more than anyone, has sought to make full use of a Gramscian perspective in relation to our own contemporary political conjuncture. It is thus on the basis of Hall's reasoning that I would want to justify my own use of a Gramscian approach to contemporary Russian politics. In Hall's words: 'We mustn't *use* Gramsci (as we have for so long abused Marx) like an Old Testament prophet who, at the correct moment, will offer us the consoling and appropriate quotation.' Nevertheless, Hall continues, it certainly is possible to 'think' through problems and situations in a Gramscian way: 'Gramsci gives us, not the tools with which to solve the puzzle, but the means with which to ask the right kinds of questions. . . .' Above all, Gramsci

knew that difference and specificity mattered . . . [and] we should attend to this riveting of Gramsci to the notion of difference, to the specificity of a historical conjuncture: how different forces come together, conjuncturally, to create the new terrain on which a different politics must form up. That is the intuition that Gramsci offers us about the nature of political life, from which we can take a lead.[33]

Another question that might be raised about the suitability of a Gramscian hegemonic framework relates to its application to a country like Russia, which has traditionally been associated much more with pre-modern rather than modern political traits. Following Eric Hobsbawm in this matter, however, it is important to stress that Gramsci's concept of hegemony is not relevant only to a study of politics in established conditions of modernity, it is also equally relevant to those societies specifically embarking upon a fundamental systemic transition.[34] To give one illustration of this, for instance: one of the practical problems that becomes uppermost in such conditions is the manner in which new types of social forces set about trying to obtain the *consent* of the newly politicized elements. This, along with other major issues of a similar nature, again lies precisely at the heart of Gramsci's whole body of writings on hegemony. In general terms, then, we can say that the remit of Gramsci's hegemony is applicable *before*, *during* and *after* a process of power transition and, as such, is *uniquely* relevant to the Russian situation.[35]

What is more, the American scholar Walter Adamson has raised the extremely interesting question of whether Gramsci should in fact continue to be treated first and foremost as a political and revolutionary theorist firmly located in the modern, developed capitalist West, or whether his underlying influence could be *better* represented in those societies embarking on the *transition* to 'modernity'. According to Adamson, Gramsci is accurate in his historical analysis of how the French and the English bourgeoisie arrived at their hegemony in the early phases of capitalism by expropriating for their own purposes a weak and ill-defined civil society. Having given life to this seemingly autonomous sphere beyond the strict realm of state power, the bourgeoisie were clearly adamant that they would not give the same kind of freedom of manoeuvre to any potential class opponent. This, according to Adamson, thus left Gramsci's theory of Western superstructures in a rather 'paradoxical state':

> On the one hand, he recognized that in advanced western societies the key to political power lay in the hegemonic control of civil society; the image of a proletarian seizure of power in a 1917-style coup had become mere fantasy. Yet on the other hand, the ability of those controlling western political societies to block the formation of an alternative hegemony was unprecedently high.[36]

Adamson concludes, therefore, that Gramsci's discovery of the political importance of civil society was in many ways negated by the obstacles to institutional innovation within it – something that historical experience would certainly seem to bear out (as witnessed, of course, by Gramsci's own failure with the Turin Workers Councils in 1920). On the other hand, however, Gramsci's study of civil society does seem to take on even greater significance precisely in those non-Western societies where its existence is extremely weak and fragile. As Gramsci has clearly demonstrated, the actual opportunity to capture an *embryonic* civil society would open up all sorts of possibilities. And again, let us not forget that Gramsci did seem to recognize this in the case of the Bolshevik victory in Russia in 1917. The

Bolsheviks' failure to establish a workable and functioning realm of civil society seriously debilitated their chances of securing anything greater than domination and dictatorship. Now that a new opportunity to create and shape the contours of a civil society has thus emerged in Russia, it does seem that Gramsci's writings are remarkably pertinent.

The final point that must be made follows on from the 'transitional' status of contemporary Russia, and highlights the fact that the notion of a *struggle* for hegemony, as used in the title of this study, should be understood in two primary, contiguous ways. First, it is a largely self-explanatory reference to the struggle that is taking place among different social and political forces that have emerged following the collapse of Communist Party domination and the extent to which these forces can be considered to be the bearers of some kind of hegemonic project in Russian society. In other words – and this is very important – there is no automatic assumption that the nature of the struggle is necessarily of a hegemonic type. Secondly – and just as importantly – it is also a reference to the struggle that is taking place *to create the very conditions* in which hegemonic-type practices, in the manner first delineated by Gramsci, can actually operate. It is this latter, crucial, contextual issue that will thus be taken up first.

PART I
The Context for a Hegemonic Struggle in Contemporary Russia

The Frailty of Russia's
New Civil Society

[A]fter the emotional revolution comes traditional everyday reality [in which] the hero of the faith, and above all the faith itself, disappears or (which brings even more visible effects) becomes the object of the conventional rhetoric of political philistines and technicians.

Max Weber, *Politik als Beruf*

The Emergence of a Civil Society in Russia

Applying a Gramscian-based conception of hegemonic struggle to the current situation in Russia would clearly be impossible if the actual space for that struggle – i.e. a civil society – did not exist. The first task of the empirical study that follows, then, must be to explain not only the nature of the civil society in existence today, but also the actual manner in which an embryonic civil society began to form back in the days of Gorbachev, *perestroika*, and the Soviet Union.

In his account of Gramsci's theory of hegemony Joseph Femia has formulated an interesting distinction between three different levels or types of hegemony. In the first type, labelled 'integral hegemony', he argues, Gramsci had in mind a paradigm scenario in which 'society would exhibit a substantial degree of moral and intellectual unity, issuing in an organic relationship (to use the Gramscian idiom) between rulers and ruled; a relationship without contradictions and antagonisms on either a social or an ethical level'.[1] Although no reference is made to it by either Gramsci or Femia, such an integral type of hegemony seems to capture the *vision* of society Lenin had in mind in his 'State and Revolution'. More importantly, though, it also corresponds well to the kind of *myth* that was invariably promoted by the Communist Party of the Soviet Union (CPSU) concerning the relationship it would have liked to think it had with Soviet society.

A second type of hegemony, labelled 'minimal hegemony', is characterized by 'the ideological unity of the economic, political and intellectual
elites along with aversion to any intervention of the popular masses in state
life'.[2] This type of hegemony brings to mind the kind of corporatist structure that Brezhnev was able to develop during the zenith of his leadership
of the Soviet Union in the 1970s.

Femia describes the third type of Gramscian hegemony, meanwhile, in
the following terms: society is no longer

> capable of representing or furthering everyone's interest. Neither is it capable of
> commanding unequivocal allegiance from the non-elite . . . as soon as the
> dominant group has exhausted its function, the ideological bloc tends to decay.
> Thus, the potential for social disintegration is ever-present: conflict lurks just
> beneath the surface. In spite of the numerous achievements of the system, the
> needs, inclinations and mentality of the masses are not truly in harmony with
> the dominant ideas. Though widespread, cultural and political integration is
> fragile; such a situation might be called *decadent hegemony*.[3]

According to Femia's classification, 'minimal hegemony' is a much lower
form than 'decadent hegemony'. Be that as it may, the really interesting
thing to observe is the way in which this description of a decadent form of
hegemony parallels very closely the kind of analysis Gorbachev was himself enumerating about the problems affecting Soviet society from about
January 1987 onwards (i.e. from the time of the Party plenum representing
a fundamental switch to wholescale political reform and democratization).
This can clearly be seen in his first major literary exegesis on the reform
process, his book *Perestroika: New Thinking for Our Country and the
World*, which came out later that year. In one passage in particular, he
writes of the 'braking mechanism' which had hitherto prevented any kind
of ideological or even intellectual renewal and creativity. Instead, the
propaganda of success, 'real or imagined', had gained the upper hand.
Eulogizing and servility were prevalent everywhere, while no one paid any
attention to the needs and opinions of ordinary working people.
Superfluous and voluntarist assessments were constantly declared indisputable truths; and in the cultural domain, one could only ever find
mediocrity and formalism. Worst of all, however, was the fact that the
old-style presentation of a 'problem-free reality' had effectively backfired.
There was no recognizable correlation between words and deeds, only
utter disbelief in all the slogans that had previously been proclaimed. In
short, there was a serious 'credibility gap' between those on the rostrum
and those below. Public morals were decaying; alcoholism, drug addiction
and crime were rife, and all the old feelings of solidarity, so desperately
forged during the Revolution and the 'Great Patriotic War', were weakening almost by the day.[4]

Coming from the pen of the General Secretary himself, such words as these, and many others at this time, represented a huge indictment of the mistakes and failures of the Party, and of the decadent socialism the Party had fostered over the years. In one fell swoop Gorbachev had exposed the notion of society's 'single collective will' for the myth that it had always been. 'Communist Man' was now laid bare for all to see, and as the creator of this fiction, the Party had to take full responsibility. Getting the Party to take full responsibility, however, was always going to be the real problem and the real dilemma for Gorbachev. He himself was convinced that the Party had the capacity to rectify many of the mistakes it had made, and could continue to be the main force shaping the direction of future social change. But to do this it would have to undergo certain fundamental changes from within, and if it was to survive these changes it would have to remain a united and cohesive force at the same time.

From his experience of the January 1987 plenum and the reaction to his more radical proposals both beforehand and afterwards, Gorbachev must have been left in no doubt that change and unity were incompatible phenomena. Sticking to a rigid unity of the Party would always play into the hands of the 'braking mechanism' that he discusses so eloquently in his book, and this in turn would only add to a social and cultural disintegration all the more potentially explosive for not being recognized. But if retaining a fundamental unity of the Party was no longer possible, how was Gorbachev to set about disaggregating the Party while retaining some kind of control over the process of disaggregation – the key dilemma of any communist reformer since 1917?

His attempt at finding a solution to this problem was perhaps best represented by his espousal of a concept which, surprisingly, was either very much underrated at the time of its emergence, or variously miscomprehended in most Western analyses: *socialist pluralism*. In some analyses the discussion of what socialist pluralism entailed was virtually indistinguishable from the concept of 'institutional pluralism', a popular concept amongst 'revisionist' academics of the Soviet Union after the late 1960s who were primarily concerned to counter the scholastic hegemony of the totalitarian school of thought. Such an analogy, however, intrinsically weakened the more inclusive, engaging role of socialist pluralism.[5] In other analyses it was a term that was barely indistinguishable from an expansive interpretation of *glasnost'*, which therefore had the weakness of somewhat limiting it to a realm of combative intellectual discussion.[6] While in other analyses it was seen as an attempt by the 'Gorbachevite wing' of the Party 'to stage an ostensible withdrawal from society without giving up any real power'.[7] Certainly, the latter part of this equation was indisputable, but the former part was a total inversion of everything that the concept stood for, since the Gorbachevite wing was now precisely concerned to be more engaged *within* society in order to buttress the struggle going on inside the Party, while at the same time giving it a greater element of consent as regards its actual use of power.[8]

In essence, then, Gorbachev's espousal of socialist pluralism amounted to two fundamental points. First, a recognition that the Party, as a collective entity, was at one and the same time the main force shaping the direction of social change in the new climate and the main braking mechanism of that change. Consequently, if the process of social change was to continue in any fundamental and meaningful sense, the Party had to undergo a process of disaggregation; and this process of disaggregation would have to include an open debate about the different socialist ideological strands within the Party, as well as attitudes to structural change within the sphere of politics and economics. And secondly, it was a recognition, primarily by the reformist wing of the Party (but one which eventually affected the 'conservative' wing as well), that during this process of disaggregation elements of society would necessarily have to be *engaged* from below to buttress the primary struggle going on from 'on high'.[9] Hence the now open emergence and toleration of the so-called informal [*neformaly*] associations, especially in those towns and cities where party reformers were in the ascendant;[10] and hence also the plethora of sociological studies that now began to appear legitimizing the idea that society was indeed fractured and had always been fractured into distinctive groups (though not 'classes') with distinctive goals and aspirations, not to mention different levels of capacity for fulfilling those aspirations, all of which were now potential *subjects* of articulation by the different strands competing for hegemony *within the Party.*[11]

The important thing to bear in mind, then, is the manner in which Soviet society was now encouraged to be a potential subject of the political process in this new 'pluralist' phase of the reforms. Its emergence into the equation of political activities came as a *magnanimous gesture* from forces wishing to promote their control of the levers of state power against other elements of state power. In other words, society's emergence was granted from on high rather than won from below. Different sections of society might now have the chance to help influence the struggle taking place behind closed party doors to determine who the real wielders of state power might be, but they were still as far removed as ever from the objective control levers of that power.

Nowhere was this better demonstrated than in a round-table discussion on the significance of socialist pluralism held under the auspices of the *Novosti* Press Agency and the editorial board of *Sotsialogicheskie issledovaniya* in early 1988.[12] One concept that emerges throughout the pages of the discussion is the very amorphous one of 'mono-pluralism'. What this basically amounted to was a recognition that consciousness was indeed varied and pluralistic, but *power* is nevertheless always unitary or monistic. Allowing a 'multitudinous diversity of pluralistic forms' was one thing, but some kind of unity had to emerge out of this diversity – a unity 'in what is most important, basic, essential and fundamental'. And nothing, of course, represented what was more fundamental than the ability to have control and to have power – *political power.*

In fact, only one participant in the discussion, Boris Kurashvili, raised a spectre of dissent from this point of view with any consistency. 'Pluralism of opinions, comrades,' he argued,

> is simply the usual timid label for an unpleasant reality. The unpleasant reality to which we must accommodate ourselves and with which we must carry on a dialogue is political pluralism. Not pluralism of opinions, but political pluralism. If something does not reach the stage of political expression, does not reach the point where definite political demands are formulated, this means that something is not ripe in our society. And just such an unripe something is the idea of a pluralism of opinions that allegedly can substitute for political pluralism. Nothing can substitute for political pluralism – this must be recognised and studied.[13]

According to Mikhail Malyutin, a philosopher who set up an independent centre for research on the concept of civil society in the late 1980s, the formula of socialist pluralism that was promoted by Gorbachev throughout 1987 and much of 1988 was nothing short of a (self!) deception, precisely because it avoided nearly all references to the significance of *power* relationships in the state's interaction with society.[14] In a sense, of course, as has already been indicated, this was a perfectly legitimate criticism. At the same time, however, despite all these limitations, one should at least give credit where credit is due, and recognize that the mere mention of the term pluralism carried enormous significance in itself. Indeed, Malyutin's own position at this time as head of an independent research institute looking at civil society was itself a clear sign that, as with other areas of the whole reform process, an unstoppable momentum was generated over which few political leaders, if any, had any degree of control.

Quite clearly, Gorbachev's concept of socialist pluralism had no pretensions to be a fully functioning form of civil society, but it was perhaps inevitable that the logical next step of the reform process, linguistically and analytically at least, was to include the concept within the ambit of public discussions.

One of the first real serious analyses to be made appeared in the monthly *Voprosy filosofii* in August 1987, written by a senior researcher at the Academy of Sciences' Institute of the World Economy and International Relations, Andranik Migranyan.[15] In a wide-ranging overview of the concept's history and background, Migranyan lamented the fact that, on the basis of there being no previous clearly defined demarcation between the state and civil society under Russia's old regime, the new post-revolutionary state succumbed to the temptation of 'swallowing up' society and all individuals within it in the 'sincere' but false belief that it could best solve the country's problems by applying essentially bureaucratic solutions. Under this misconception, he argues, a full sense of democracy was inevitably forfeited, for instead of the state being under the control of society, 'as the founders of Marxism envisaged', society came under the total control of the state. Although this was a probable outcome, bearing in mind the country's economic and cultural backwardness, Migranyan (clearly echoing Gramsci here) is nevertheless convinced that the Bolsheviks had another option open to them. The task of the new state, he argues, 'along with its economic, administrative and culture-building functions', should have been 'the creation of a *new civil society*, the gradual limitation of state interference in economic and socio-cultural life and the nurturing of a civic consciousness and of voluntary associations, unions and organizations for the realization of the creative energy and initiative of the people'.[16] Lenin did at least recognize the validity of this during the phase of the New Economic Policy, Migranyan goes on, but unfortunately the forms and methods of Stalin's industrialization and collectivization 'resulted in a total regimentation of all spheres of the life activity of society and reduced to almost nil any possibility of spontaneous, unsanctioned self-realization on the part of individuals and groups'.[17]

Going on to look at the ways in which fully operating civil societies have benefited capitalist systems, Migranyan draws directly on the Gramscian analysis in his reference to the fact that where the state and society are quite perceptibly separated from one another, then there is a high probability that the political regime will maintain its stability, 'since the state and its institutions are sustained by society and its associations, political culture, customs and traditions. They are in fact the guarantee that the political system will survive in crisis situations.'[18] Sensing, therefore, that this was precisely the thing that Gorbachev most needed, Migranyan again took up the theme that the principal task of *perestroika* in the political sphere had to be 'the attainment of a newly created civil society, with the help of all the means now at the state's disposal and the means which it acquires as it is progressively strengthened and institutionalized'. Only by this process of the 'institutionalization of civil society', Migranyan concludes, would there be 'a swift destruction of the mechanism holding back development. . . .'[19]

In its fundamental analytical treatment of philosophers who have in one sense or another addressed themselves to the issue of civil society and its relationship with the state, Migranyan's article appeared grossly oversimplistic and highly reductionist in content. On the more practical level of offering Gorbachev and the reformist leadership of the Party a strategy to pursue in order to achieve a greater measure of – if not stability, then at least *protection* for the state, the article was extremely instructive, and clearly represented a landmark in the willingness of the reformist wing of the Party to *create* its own civil society.

Indeed, the fact that Migranyan himself was more willing to pursue the *strategic* implications of creating a civil society rather than the more esoteric benefits associated with any generation of self-government from below was very well indicated by two other contributions to the Soviet press in 1989. In June, in an article in *Sovetskaya Kultura* entitled 'Populism' (a reference to the so-called 'Yeltsin Phenomenon'), Migranyan implicitly stated that the construction of a civil society was fast becoming Gorbachev's main – if not only – hope of survival, and he argued categorically that, if necessary, Gorbachev should use 'authoritarian powers' to create the kind of civil society that would be of most use to him.[20] And in August, in a wide-ranging interview with *Literaturnaya gazeta* (along with Igor' Klyamkin), Migranyan was even more forthright in his determination to convince Gorbachev to construct a civil society as soon as possible, and by whatever means were available to him; even to the extent of creating a Committee of National Salvation to push through the desired reforms and to overcome the resistance of the party fundamentalists.[21]

In other words, then, what Migranyan seemed to be telling Gorbachev – and the references were nearly always to Gorbachev personally – was that a reform of a totalitarian system can be carried out only by authoritarian means; and a key part of the task of an authoritarian reformer was to find or develop a constituency of support in society at large strong enough to build a focus of criticism against opponents of reform which would help weaken their resistance. This process of weakening resistance, however, was not necessarily designed to 'open up' society. More importantly, it was designed to strengthen the power and authority of the authoritarian reformer himself for the future tasks of transformation. In short – and these are Klyamkin's words – there was now 'an urgent necessity to transfer *responsibility*, or at least some of it, to society, to a new structure, while at the same time retaining power'.[22]

That Gorbachev himself was taking heed of this (dirigiste) advice was indicated in his long article on 'The Socialist Idea and Revolutionary Perestroika', published in *Pravda* at the end of November 1989. For the very first time Gorbachev himself now openly endorsed the idea that creating the mechanisms of a civil society was the key political task of *perestroika*. As to how this was going to be done, Gorbachev made no attempt to hide the fact that the Party was going to have a special role here:

> *Perestroika* has set the Party a twofold task: on the one hand, it must determine
> its place in the conditions of a fundamental democratization of the political sys-
> tem, it must build a civil society and it must help in the transition to financial
> autonomy and economic management methods in the national economy[;] and
> on the other hand, it must implement *perestroika* within the party itself.[23]

In other words, then, a civil society could be built 'by the Party, out of the
Party', for the more it implemented reforms within its own organization,
the more tendencies of one kind or another would emerge, having to look
to society for support. It is also very noticeable that it was precisely at this
time that Gorbachev committed himself to the creation of an all-powerful
executive state presidency, whose basis of support was meant to lie totally
outside the realm of the Party. As the latter slowly disintegrated to form
the basis of a more widespread civil society, the unity of power, and the
role of arbitration that power entailed, could be preserved now in the
highest echelons of the newly emerging state institutions.

Once again, then, it is hard to escape the notion that this first embryo of
a civil society in the former Soviet Union was a deliberate creation by
forces from on high determined to manipulate it in a power struggle game;
giving it to all intents and purposes an appearance of autonomy, while
firmly denying it any real leverage over those higher sources of power. In
this sense it differed quite fundamentally from the kinds of civil society
that had begun to emerge at about the same time in many of the Eastern
European states. In countries such as Poland, Czechoslovakia and
Hungary, for example, the disintegration of Communist Party control was
accompanied by a much stronger, more developed, more autonomous and
more spontaneous 'parallel society' from below, primed and ready to take
advantage of the social vacuum that had appeared. As Janina Frentzel-
Zagorska has argued in relation to Poland, for example, as soon as the
Polish Communist Party had begun to relinquish its grip on power,
Solidarity was ready to perform an important cognitive function of the
civil society:

> Solidarity became a source of information, definitions of concepts and images
> of reality generated by society – a source which served Solidarity itself, society
> at large and the ruling elite. The process of elaborating new language began.
> This language could provide tools for the description of reality in terms differ-
> ing from those imposed by the conceptual network of official language. It could
> also promote a crystallisation of opinions and a rebuilding of the image of
> reality.[24]

All of this was a far cry from the kind of tasks civil society in the Soviet
Union was either capable of doing or *expected* to do at this stage. As a

means of engaging and providing legitimacy to a growing variety of distinctive interests and tendencies, civil society was fine. But as a means of intrinsically generating a whole new elaboration of images in terms of its relationship with the state on the basis of new conceptions of power, this was totally out of the question.[25]

Indeed, nowhere was this determination to retain full control over the affairs of this new-style civil society better encapsulated than in the legal provisions formally sanctifying civil society's existence, inclusive of the right to set up brand-new political parties. In Article 3 of the USSR Law on Public Associations, which came into force in October 1990, the state was given extensive powers to restrict those groups or parties which 'espouse the use of violence with the intent to overthrow or change the constitutional system or territorial integrity of the USSR; . . . who promote war, violence or cruelty; . . . who incite social, racial, national, religious and also class enmity; . . . and who carry out activities detrimental to the health and morality of society'.[26] Some of these restrictions were undoubtedly valid ones, but it is hard to envisage a proper civil society functioning in which the state has the *exclusive* right to determine what is moral or not, or what is conducive to class hatred or not.

What the provisions of the Law seemed to typify most was the way in which civil society had now formally established itself in the lexicon of Soviet politics – not on the basis of an organic growth from below, but on the basis of creation from above: 'a by-product of the liberation of the dominant class through the re-distribution of elites'.[27] And in this sense it was a classic illustration of a Gramscian *passive revolution* – a recognition by the state that if it wanted to preserve its most essential features of power, then *it* would have to be the force instigating change in society, rather than vice versa. Thus, while the process of developing this civil society undoubtedly engendered fundamental social, political and ideological changes, the real levers of power and control remained largely untouched. Different faces or different bodies certainly emerged to operate those levers, but the levers themselves remained unmoved by the social changes.

This is not to say by any means that the constant use of the term civil society throughout all sectors of the Soviet media at this time was a deliberate act of deception, a means by which the very use of words and rhetoric by the holders of power masked the actual manifestation of power. This would be too much bordering on the totalitarian. For all the limitations of this civil society that was being created, it was no longer an amorphous mass, and it was no longer atomized. Malleable it may well have been, but nothing like what it had been in the past. Certainly, when the Law on Public Associations first came into force, one had a feeling that there was still only an *illusion* of politics taking place, but even that illusion was better than a nothingness, a total void. As Malyutin has pointed out, none of the organizations that emerged on the scene with the label of 'party' attached to their name was structurally or psychologically geared for any kind of social struggle within the realm of society, but not all of them were prepared to be pawns in a game over which they had no control whatsoever. And not all of them were prepared to be defined simply by 'the badges they wore on their lapels', rather than by a more fundamental set of interests.[28] What basically existed, therefore, were the *rudiments* of a civil society, but a civil society that still nestled too exclusively within the interstices of the state.[29]

In the aftermath of the abortive *coup d'état* in August 1991 – itself an indication that a 'war of position' type of struggle in the much-trumpeted civil society that was emerging at this time was of less significance than the belief that a quick decisive victory in a 'war of manoeuvre' was still attainable; and in the aftermath of the definitive disaggregation and disintegration of the CPSU, it is certainly the case that a more genuine realm of civil society has begun to emerge. Nevertheless, it is important that one should be aware of the continuing problems and deficiencies still being experienced in this process of construction.

Writing in the summer of 1991, prior to the coup, one analyst identified a number of long-term obstacles to the emergence of a civil society in any post-communist Russia, and these indices can therefore be a useful framework to assess subsequent developments.[30]

The first of the obstacles refers to the central tenet of what has been discussed heretofore – namely, the basic antipathy in both the Soviet and, of course, the centuries-old Russian state tradition to the principle of legitimate and effective independent intermediation of diverse societal interests. Various examples can be cited here of how the new post-communist state authorities have continued this tradition of antipathy, though one of the first, and perhaps one of the most significant, examples concerns the manner – and, more importantly, the *justification* – of President Yeltsin's decree banning the existence of the Russian Communist Party in November 1991.

In the deliberations of the Constitutional Court, which was requested to assess the legality of the decree, a whole range of complex issues emerged which clearly called into question the nature of the new state's perception of its own rights and powers *vis-à-vis* organizations situated in civil society. Central to the proceedings of the case was the claim that at the time of the decree's enactment the only jurisdictional authority that appeared to be in force which could be used to prohibit a political party was the aforementioned USSR Law on Public Associations. According to the provisions of this Law, however – which allowed for the prohibition of a political party or other such organization where its activities were found to be 'purposely directed towards the violent overthrow of . . . the constitutional order' – such an enforcement could be given only by the Prosecutor's office and by the courts; that is to say, it could not be given by the Presidency. More damaging still to the Russian authorities' case – or so it seemed at first – was the recognition that, at the time of the decree, the USSR Law on Public Associations had not been adopted by the Russian parliament, nor had its general provisions been incorporated into the Russian Constitution.

What was most instructive in the case, then, was the nature of the state's defence. Since the USSR Law on Public Associations had no authority within the Russian Federation, and since Russia had already declared its legal sovereignty over USSR laws, it was thus claimed that the only valid piece of legislation at that time in existence in Russia which would legitimize the action taken by the President was nothing other than Stalin's own infamous Law on Voluntary Associations, dating back to 1932; a statute which did indeed permit the prohibition of any association by executive decree, without reference to any judicial hearing.[31] What this amounted to was that the very piece of legislation which had sanctified the abolition of free association and with it, of course, the right of a genuine, autonomous realm of civil society, was now being used by a President and a set of state authorities that had supposedly made the acceleration of the development of a civil society one of its primary legitimating aspects.[32]

As events turned out, of course, one year after the initial ban was introduced, the Russian Constitutional Court did go on to declare the presidential decree unlawful, and though it upheld the ban on the ruling bodies of the former Communist Party, on the grounds that they had usurped state power, the decision nevertheless removed all the restrictions on the re-emergence of a Russian Communist Party with much of its assets intact. More significantly, perhaps, the decision also lent a new sense of optimism to the prospects of a stronger civil society at last emerging in Russia, a civil society protected for the first time by a more clearly defined rule of law, and by a judicial system that would not automatically uphold the interests and authority of the state *vis-à-vis* the interests of individuals and non-state associations.

This optimism, however, must still be tempered somewhat by other actions of the Russian state authorities in this same period. Though it has since gone on to incorporate most of the general provisions of the USSR Law on Public Associations into its constitutional framework, there are quite clearly enormous discrepancies as to what degree of state interference and control can be exercised on the activities of groups within civil society, as well as discrepancies over who exactly can exercise state authority in this area. For example, the presidential decree 'On measures to defend the constitutional system of the Russian Federation', issued at the end of October 1992, banning the National Salvation Front, was also successfully challenged in the Constitutional Court on a similar pretext to the ban on the Russian Communist Party – in other words, the President has no personal authority to liquidate a public association, since this is a prerogative of the courts.[33]

Moreover, as was mentioned above, while the provisions of the former USSR Law on Public Associations were a step in the right direction in sanctifying a greater degree of automony for the realm of civil society, there were nevertheless severe limitations on this autonomy, all of which have been continued in the post-communist era. Thus, for example, a number of left-wing political organizations and workers' movements have found it difficult, if not impossible, to secure legal recognition for themselves under the provisions of the Constitution, since they have been adjudged to be organizations promoting or propagandizing class enmity. On the other hand, neo-liberal organizations and associations closely linked to the existing state structure and closely identified with the aim of promoting private entrepreneurial initiative and profit-orientated activities in a free-market environment, face no such accusations.[34] One effect of this is clearly the promotion of a two- or multi-tiered civil society, whereby some associations are fully recognized (and therefore protected) by the law, while others are not.

Recognizing, however, that the state itself might negate some of its own capacity to deal with associations in civil society which were formally outside the legal structure, yet another presidential decree was issued in January 1993: 'On measures for stepping up monitoring of the creation and activity of public associations'.[35] According to this new set of provisions, executive authorities were ordered to strengthen their existing control and supervisory mechanisms over the activities of all associations currently in existence, as well as those seeking to come into existence. Furthermore, they were also given additional powers to bring about the disbandment of those associations, whether registered or not, which were deemed to have breached constitutional provisions on public associations; which aimed at impeding the activities of recognized state structures; whose actions were deemed to go beyond the bounds of the aims and tasks contained in their rules; and which sought to discredit state structures through the dissemination of false information.

A second obstacle to the growth of civil society, cited in mid 1991, concerned 'the enduring political controls on, and backwardness of, communications and information in Russia'.[36] As regards the first element here, the picture has been very mixed in the period after August 1991. Initially it appeared as if the new independent Russian authorities were even more intent on controlling the affairs of the media than their immediate Soviet predecessors; this was particularly characterized by their active attempts to force the closure of many former pro-communist newspapers and journals throughout the autumn of 1991. In February 1992, however, considerable progress seemed to be made with the enactment of a radical new Law on the Media. Among other things, the new Law considerably extended the process of de-monopolizing the controlling ownership of the media; considerably liberalized some of the last remaining vestiges of direct forms of censorship; and also extended the rights of media organizations to obtain access to information on the activities of state bodies.[37]

While the provisions of the Law remain a radical testament *on paper* to the state's commitment to setting up a free and pluralistic channel of information and communication in society, *in practice* the extent of state control and leverage in this sphere has continued to be extremely widespread. In the period since the Law was passed, many newspapers (of all different political persuasions) have had to fight constant battles with different elements of the state apparatus to preserve their hard-won editorial independence. Some newspapers, such as *Izvestiya*, have indeed been strong enough to defeat parliamentary attempts to impose direct authority. Others, however, such as *Rossiiskie vesti* and *Rossiiskaya gazeta*, have since become nothing more than pliant tools of the presidential and government apparatuses.

Similarly, the state has not been averse to openly interfering in the editorial policies of television and radio companies. In November 1992, for example, the popular and well-respected Chairman of the Ostankino Television and Radio Company, Yegor Yakovlev, was summarily dismissed by presidential decree for transmitting an allegedly biased documentary analysing the ethnic conflict that had erupted in the North Caucasus regions of North Osetia and Ingushetia. In the aftermath of Yakovlev's dismissal, Ostankino was taken over by a new Board of Guardians with no less a figure than President Yeltsin himself assuming the responsibilities of Chairman of the Board.[38] Likewise, at the height of another North Caucasian conflict in late 1994, this time in Chechnya following the military's attempt to reimpose federal authority in this breakaway Republic, periodic threats were issued to the head of the All-Russian State Television and Radio Company chairman, Oleg Poptsov, that a similar fate of summary dismissal would befall him unless he too toed the state authorities' line.

Perhaps most worrying of all, however, for those who fear the reimposition of more explicit and more permanent forms of state-controlled censorship has been the creation of new types of agencies, exclusively accountable to state authorities, specifically designed to exercise a controlling influence over all types of media output.

One of the first such agencies was the Federal Information Centre. Created at the end of December 1992, it was designed to act as a supervisory agency with strong interventionist powers over all the country's national and regional television companies, as well as the two main national press agencies, ITAR-Tass and RIA-Novosti.[39] More recent examples of openly explicit forms of state control, meanwhile, have included the Federal Broadcasting Service, the Directorate on Informational Guarantees for the Presidential Administration, and the so-called Temporary Information Centre, which was specifically created to promote the government's interpretation of its actions in the conflict with Chechnya. Last, but not least, it is important to point out that the state still largely controls the purse strings of the vast majority of newspapers through its regulation of such things as newsprint; something that it has again used with some degree of effectiveness to limit the effect of any kind of criticism that newspapers might seek to vent.[40]

It is not just excessive state interference, however, that diminishes the effectiveness of civil society in this vital realm of information and communication. There are also long-standing problems of technological backwardness that clearly continue to undermine the communicational capacities of large sectors of the new civil society, and will do so for some considerable time to come. Access to basic things such as desk-top computers and photocopiers remains very difficult; and though the supply side of such vital equipment is gradually easing, the demand side is still (for obvious financial reasons) very restrictive. And even if these factors can be overcome, there is still a very debilitating large-scale monopoly on the actual distribution of newspapers and journals (in the form of *Rospechat'*), something that has largely been unaffected by any of the information-related reforms in the post-communist era, and makes it extremely difficult for the vast majority of citizens to obtain many independent publications.

Consequently, although there are a number of positive factors that one can point to – the undoubted political diversity of today's press, the manner in which many media outlets bravely defied attempts to subject them to state censorship (not least during the height of the Russian–Chechen conflict), as well as the fact that non-state publishing houses continue to represent a growth area in Russia's domestic economy – one should not downplay the fact that serious problems still remain. Taking up one of the points referred to in the mid-1991 analysis, one would still have to say that:

> Leaders of the new organisations are acutely aware of how problems of communication and information impede their capacity for articulating demands, attracting new members, holding conferences, influencing public opinion and establishing contacts abroad.[41]

A third long-term impediment on civil society, it was contended, was the structure of the Russian economy back in summer 1991. Two things in particular were implied here. First there was the general point that so long as there continued to be such a depth of fusion between the state and economy in Russia, then this would clearly reduce the ability of the vast majority of associations within civil society 'to obtain needed inputs without reliance on political authorities', and would also seriously impede every effort thereby to establish 'autonomous resource bases'. In addition, it was also much more specifically stated that what was needed to overcome this was the accelerated emergence of a new, capitalist business class, 'which in many societies has acted as a powerful counterweight to state power'.[42]

Clearly, what we have here is a general, normative statement on the one hand and a very specific, prescriptive statement on the other. The second statement certainly follows from the first, but there is no inevitability that if one accepts the logic of the first premiss, it *must* then produce the prescription contained in the second. In other words, it is crucial to recognize that de-statization (of capital assets, etc.) and marketization (de-monopolization, etc.) – the two necessary requirements here of setting up a more autonomous resource base for associations in civil society – can, in fact, take a *variety* of concrete forms, of which the emergence of a new private, capitalist business class represents just one possible outcome.[43] It is also crucial to recognize that depending on which option of de-statization and marketization is chosen, this will then very firmly shape the nature of the battlefield of any hegemonic struggle within the realm of civil society. That is to say, the specific interpretation and subsequent implementation of one type of de-statization and marketization will inevitably give *priority* to some social groups rather than others in their search for greater financial and resource autonomy from the state.

This issue is so important to the whole remit of the present study that it is logical that greater depth can be given to it in succeeding chapters when analysing the respective hegemonic combatants in Russian society today. Suffice it to say here that such was the continued level of state control of the economy at the end of 1991 that any programme of de-statization and marketization would necessarily be quite prolonged, which in turn would prolong any extensive activation of an effective realm of civil society. Similarly, any such programme of uncoupling the economy from the state was almost inevitably going to increase, for an undetermined period, the existing rate of economic deterioration and dislocation in society, with one of the main offshoots being the emergence of very high levels of inflation. Of course, quite whether there was anything inevitable about the fact that at the end of 1992 Russia stood on the precipice of *hyper*-inflation following a year's experiment with one radical form of neo-liberal-inspired de-statization and marketization is, needless to say, a very contentious question. Again, however, one would simply have to note here that the reality of prolonged periods of near-hyper-inflation has likewise had serious *negative* effects on the desired creation of a strong, vibrant civil society.

A fourth perceived impediment to the ultimate emergence of a civil society was somewhat less tangible or less structural than the preceding three arguments, but no less important for that. This concerned the probable debilitating factor of social attitudinal problems with the very notion of popular engagement in any emerging civil society; as well as questioning whether the Russian political culture was entirely amenable or apposite to this kind of development, in either the short term or the long term.[44]

To debate this particular factor in any sufficient depth would clearly require an extensive study of its own. For some analysts and commentators the notion that Russian society has somehow been historically shaped or conditioned perennially to desire servility in the face of state authority was firmly disproved, once and for all, at the time of the August 1991 *coup d'état*. For others, the nature of what was, after all, a very limited public response to the coup, in conjunction with developments that have taken place since, simply proves, on the contrary, the accuracy of the traditional view of Russian society's quiescence. Likewise, there is the vitally important issue here of the deeply embedded *patriarchal* nature of Russian (political) culture, and the effect this might have on the evolutionary patterns of a new realm of civil society.[45]

What I think can be briefly said on this general issue for now is that there has certainly been a great deal of *passiveness* among virtually all sections of the Russian population in the aftermath of the post-communist transformation, a passiveness which is certainly understandable and explainable in the light of the need of most citizens to expend their energies on struggling to maintain a basic everyday subsistence and survival in the face of low wages, continued shortages and the aforementioned imminence of hyper-inflation.

Similarly, there has been a perceptible growth in public *cynicism*, especially towards the whole process of political activity. Indeed, one could say that one of the primary characteristics of the initial period of post-communism in Russia has been the degree to which a notion of *anti-politics* has reigned supreme. This is certainly not a reference to the kind of anti-politics that was conceived of back in the 1980s among the intellectual forces of the Central and East European dissidents, an anti-politics that conjured up the vision of a new humanist morality pervading a post-communist state. Instead anti-politics, contemporary Russian-style, conjures up visions of yesterday's terminally ill political-administrative structures and today's political-administrative vacuum; it conjures up visions of overwhelming popular apathy and outright hostility to all things labelled politics; and it also conjures up a vision, graphically described by Neal Ascherson, of a phenomenon that passes itself off as politics, but is more truthfully analogous to mere charade-like symbolism.[46] A form of politics-as-symbolism which, despite its self-acclaimed impressive appearance, has no effect whatsoever on the things that should be under its control; and certainly has no effect on the daily plight of the ordinary masses. How quickly (and how ironically) the situation in Russia has been transformed from *non*-politics to *anti*-politics has thus been quite staggering to behold. Quite whether these traits of passiveness and political cynicism are temporary or more lasting aspects of Russian political culture is too hard to say.[47] That they have a negative effect on the establishment of a vibrant civil society, however, is indisputable.

Speaking at the 7th Congress of People's Deputies in December 1992, the prominent political activist Nikolai Travkin boldly proclaimed that a normal civil society had come into existence in Russia, the demonstrable proof of this being that Russian citizens 'are already in a position to act as [their] consciences and the laws dictate, and not just to hang on to the words of [their] leaders – whether they are presidents or general secretaries – and to salute them'.[48] That there was some obvious political manoeuvring and posturing in his claim was particularly noticeable when he later went on to suggest that the very day on which he was speaking should henceforth be regarded as the day on which Russia could celebrate 'the birth of a civil society'.

When Travkin's words were reported, the emphasis on the notion of civil society was partially lost in the stenographer's account. Not unlike Ernest Gellner's recent eulogy to the concept,[49] however, one can conceive of Travkin paying homage to his new 'pet' slogan by making use of a capital 'C' and a capital 'S' every time he makes reference to it, and in the process (also like Gellner) treating its existence almost as an end in itself, rather than demonstrating at least equal concern with what is *really* taking place within its confines. It is surely more prudent, therefore, to leave Travkin's kind of rhetoric and sloganeering aside and follow the recommendation of a scholar such as Professor Aleksandr Galkin, who has indicated that, at best, only a *quasi*-civil society currently exists in Russia;[50] a recommendation also attested to by another noted scholar, Vladimir Bibler, who has drawn considerable attention to the fact that the evolution of a more comprehensive civil society can be nothing other than an extremely long-drawn-out process.[51]

The Depth of Economic Dislocation

It has already been argued that if a vibrant civil society is genuinely to take root in Russia, then the country must avoid total economic breakdown and chaos. How close has it come to that?

Before attempting to give an answer to this question, let us be clear about one thing. No one can doubt that when Gorbachev came to power in the spring of 1985 the Soviet economic structure was in serious, almost certainly terminal, decline. The necessity and desire for change, if not unanimously recognized at first, *were* unanimously recognized by the end of 1986 following the outright failure of all attempts simplistically to 'accelerate' the existing mechanisms of production. In other words, going back to the old ways was no longer a viable option. Such unanimous desire for change, however, has produced only one unanimous outcome: the almost absolute incompatibility between rhetoric and reality. What will thus concern us here is not the rhetoric for change (whichever side it may emanate from) but the actual reality of change in economic and social terms.

Looking at the results of economic development since the mid to late 1980s, one would have to say that the Russian economy has been perched precariously right on the very precipice of total economic collapse. Take, for example, the figures for gross domestic product (or what the Soviets used to call net material product) since 1985.[52]

Table 1.1   Gross Domestic Product (GDP) and Net Material Product (NMP) since 1985

Year	GDP (R bn) (%)	Real growth over last 12 months	NMP (R bn) (%)	Real growth over last 12 months
1985			353	2
1986			359	2
1987			365	1
1988			385	5
1989	573		413	2
1990	644		445	−4
1991	1,300	−12	1,051	−14
1992	18,093	−19	14,652	−22
1993	162,344	−12	119,844	−13
1994				
Q1	96,900	−17		
Q2	148,100	−17		

Source: Russian Economic Trends, vol. 3, no. 2, 1994, p. 110

As Table 1.1 shows, notwithstanding the well-known (exaggerated) inaccuracy of Soviet-era figures, there can be no doubt that Russia's GDP (or NMP) has been in constant free-fall since 1990. Admittedly, the figures for 1993 were nowhere near as catastrophic as those for the preceding year.

More worryingly, however, the downward trend was not maintained in 1994, with the official end-of-year figures showing a further 15 per cent decline alongside an industrial slump rate that had gone from 16 per cent in 1993 to 21 per cent in 1994.[53]

As for the nature of the slump, the devastating effects have been felt across virtually all areas. Within the industrial sphere, for example, some of the biggest reductions have been in the engineering sector (down by a further 41 per cent in 1994 over the previous year); chemicals and petro-chemicals (down by a further 31 per cent in 1994); and light industry (down by no less than 48 per cent on the 1993 figure). In agriculture, meanwhile, the annual rate of overall decline has gone from 3.6 per cent in 1990 to 4.7 per cent in 1991, rising to 8.0 per cent in 1992. In January 1993 it was reported that meat production was down by 11 per cent on the pre-vious year; milk by 8.2 per cent and eggs by 10 per cent. Projections in agriculture for 1994 were, if anything, considerably worse, and underpin-ning all of this was the calculation that by 1996 perhaps as much as a quarter of all available land in the country would effectively be taken out of production.[54]

Turning to the realm of inflation, Table 1.2 gives the figures for con-sumer and industrial price indices since the beginning of 1991.

In the early 1980s Soviet official statistics on inflation, if they were ever mentioned, repeatedly referred to a figure of between 1 and 2 per cent. By 1990, according to Western estimates, the annual rate was approximately 10 per cent. By the end of 1991, as Table 1.2 shows, this had now increased to approximately 160 per cent.

Table 1.2 Consumer and Industrial Price Indices since January 1991

Year	CPI	CPI (food)	CPI (non-food)	IPI
Dec. 90	100	100	100	100
June 91	202	222	222	240
June 92	2,606	2,283	3,182	9,403
June 93	21,700	18,439	22,612	99,943
June 94	111,224	90,055	96,485	580,895
July 94	117,897	n/a	n/a	n/a

Source: Russian Economic Trends, vol. 3, no. 2, 1994, pp. 123–5

With the official liberalization of prices in January 1992 the picture altered dramatically. In that one month alone the rate reached 245 per cent and then averaged out at something approaching 20–25 per cent per month throughout the rest of the year, although occasionally it hovered dangerously close to the 40 per cent per month mark. In 1993 the monthly rate stabilized somewhat from a January high of 26 per cent to a December low of 13 per cent. And to be fair, the monthly rate continued to improve throughout 1994, eventually reaching a new low point of a 6 per cent increase in July.

As Table 1.2 shows only too graphically, however, given a starting index of 100 in December 1990, consumer prices had reached a staggering index of 117,897 by the summer of 1994. Moreover, as Prime Minister Viktor Chernomyrdin informed the Russian parliament (in a no-confidence debate in late October 1994), most of the predictions for 1995 indicated that the monthly inflation rate might well be set to increase (a prediction certainly supported by most Western economic analysts).[55] Meanwhile, one indicator not shown in Table 1.2 is the fact that since 1990 industrial prices have been rising far more rapidly than agricultural procurement prices, often by a rate of 3:1. This has subsequently led to the re-emergence of the classic Russian 'scissors effect', with many farmers refusing to sell grain to the state, while at the same time cutting back on their yields.

One of the main factors stimulating the fear of increasing levels of inflation in 1995 was the continued depreciation of the rouble. In April 1991 the official exchange rate with the dollar was 30 roubles. By December of that year the 100 mark was broken, and by May 1993 the rouble had crashed through the 1,000 barrier. While it stabilized at this rate for quite a time, increasing levels of depreciation once again set in by the end of the year, the rouble eventually going on to reach 2,000 dollars in early July 1994. As if this was not bad enough, in a five-week period between September and early October 1994, the rouble fell a further 29 per cent, and in one day's trading in mid October ('Black Tuesday') it lost a staggering 22 per cent of its value.[56] Granted that in Soviet times the rouble was always excessively overvalued, no one can doubt that it has since become enormously undervalued, and thereby cannot help but undermine all attempts at economic stabilization.

With inflation galloping ahead at such phenomenal rates for more than three years, one of the main concerns for ordinary citizens has been the extent to which wages have kept pace. Looking at the comparative statistics in this area, it is clear to everyone just how handicapped wages have been in the race to keep up with prices.

While nominal wages have indeed increased, it has been calculated that between 1985 and mid 1992 *real* wages declined by 27 per cent. In the period leading up to the first quarter of 1993 the decline in average wage levels reached 49 per cent, while in the same period the fall in the minimum real wage was a staggering 75 per cent. Looking at the period between 1992 and the beginning of 1994, Otto Latsis has calculated that while the rise in prices reached 245 per cent, average wages staggered a long way behind, at

109 per cent.[57] If one takes the figures for wages and then includes factors such as welfare payments and other possible means of obtaining income, it can be ascertained that between 1990 and 1994 the population's real income levels as a whole dropped by 30 per cent.

The actual decline in wages, of course, is by no means the only issue here. For one thing, the statistics assume that wages were actually being paid on time, which has been far from the case for a considerable period. In the summer of 1994 a conservative estimate indicated that workers in 35,000 enterprises were not being paid any wages at all (effectively amounting to one billion pounds in arrears); and if they were receiving anything, it was most likely to be some form of payment in kind.[58] Average delays in the actual receipt of wages, meanwhile, was three months, which often meant an additional value depreciation of up to 50 per cent in real terms. This delay was attributed mainly to the ever-increasing levels of state indebtedness to enterprises, as well as the extent of inter-enterprise debts. As an example of the first, by the middle of 1994 the state owed nearly 8,500 billion roubles to enterprises under its control. Inter-enterprise debts, meanwhile, had reached some 130,000 billion by the same period and, not surprisingly, many of these firms were clamouring for the state to bail them out if it wanted to prevent the economy grinding to a complete halt.

Given the overall condition of public finances, however, the possibilities for direct intervention were minimal (even assuming that the willingness was there). Since 1988 the budget deficit has grown constantly, and although in recent years the extent of the deficit has been reduced, the room for manoeuvre is nevertheless very small. It has been calculated that in 1991 Russia's deficit (while still part of the USSR) was some 350 billion roubles, or 31 per cent of GDP. In 1992 official government figures seemed to indicate that this was drastically reduced to 4.7 per cent of GDP (655 billion roubles), though this figure was seriously challenged by all Western experts. In the view of the IMF, for example, a more accurate figure was 22 per cent of GDP.[59] By the end of 1994 the deficit was down to less than 9 per cent, with a further reduction of 1 per cent planned for 1995.

Notwithstanding such reductions, a number of factors continue to add to the country's financial difficulties. Since 1988 gold reserves have been seriously depleted following attempts in that year by the Gorbachev regime to keep the economy from sinking into the abyss. Earnings from oil and gas revenues have likewise declined – dramatically in the case of oil (following a 50 per cent cut in exports in 1990) and somewhat less dramatically in the case of gas, where output remained stable throughout 1991, suffering a shortfall in 1992 of 0.4 per cent and a fall of 2 per cent in the first half of 1993. Exports as a whole fell by 12 per cent in 1992 and recovered only marginally in 1993. Imports also fell by approximately 40 per cent in the same period, and although this gave the country a significant trade surplus, one would nevertheless be hard pressed to see these figures in anything other than negative terms. And not the least of the government's financial concerns was that at the beginning of 1994 non-commercial debts to the major world capitalist powers exceeded 80 billion dollars. Debt service charges alone came to 20 billion dollars in 1993, and the periodic suspension of these charges by international creditors, while welcome, was nevertheless nothing more than a short-term financial reprieve.

Last, but not least, what underpins all these problems, especially in terms of future recovery potential, are the extremely negative figures for domestic investment, which are detailed in Table 1.3. Even more worrying is the lack of incoming investment from the West. According to one calculation, Western investors are 26 times more likely to invest in China at the moment than in Russia, and when outside investment is forthcoming in Russia it is on a very specialized, selective basis in areas such as telecommunications.[60]

Table 1.3   Gross Investment Figures since 1989

Year	R bn	As % of previous year (constant prices)	As % of GDP
1989	134	104	23
1990	133	100	21
1991	236	85	18
1992	2,670	60	15
1993	25,235	84	16
1994			
Q1	12,300	72	13
Q2	22,100	72	15

Source: *Russian Economic Trends*, vol. 3, no. 2, 1994, p. 120

As we shall see in Chapter 3, not all the economic statistics in this period need necessarily be given an exclusively *negative* gloss. As *The Economist* in particular is always keen to stress, while the official figures for GDP up to the summer of 1994 would seem to indicate a *per capita* income that would place Russia on nothing more than a par with Namibia, there are other ways of interpreting the statistics that could lead one to conclude that the average Russian citizen lives 'better than this figure suggests'.[61] Additionally, it argued, official GDP figures too often reflect what is happening simply in the state-controlled economy, thereby ignoring the very positive developments in the newly emerging private sector. Likewise, few can doubt that inflation in the past was always detrimentally hidden; or even that some of the industrial production slump is of goods no longer required, and is therefore to be saluted.

Even allowing for this more positive gloss, the full extent of the economic depression is hard to deny; and in social terms even harder to ignore. According to the State Committee on Statistics, in July 1994 the official unemployment rate was 4.6 million (or 6 per cent of the workforce). By the end of the year this was expected to rise to between 6 and 7 million (8–9 per cent). If figures for 'concealed unemployment' (i.e. those on short time and forced unpaid leave) were also taken into consideration, this would mean that at least 11 million (or 15 per cent) of the workforce were effectively out of work. Given the regional variation in the employment sector, this often means that in some locations anything up to one half of the workforce are unemployed. While such figures are by no means as catastrophic as many would have expected, it still has to be recognized that these are often conservative estimates in comparison with many Western studies, and virtually all the prognoses are of an unemployment crisis still very much in its infancy. Moreover, according to a number of observers, even if the present figures are accurate, the state currently has funds only to cope with an unemployment level of 3–4 per cent.[62]

Unemployment, however, is by no means the only social phenomenon that needs to be taken into account. By late 1992 it was calculated that at least 80 per cent of the population had suffered a decline in living standards. More recently, in October 1994 the Ministry of Labour indicated that 26 per cent of Russian citizens (38.5 million) have to survive on incomes that are no more than 40 per cent of the average wage, while a further 26.1 million citizens receive less than 28 per cent of the average wage, which is the official designated poverty line. This also was widely considered a conservative estimate, and even the State Committee on Statistics has indicated that upwards of one-third of Russian citizens were trying to survive on incomes below the barest minimum standard of living;[63] a figure that gives credence to the fact that life expectancy in 1994 was calculated at 64 years, down from 69.3 in 1986 (and for men was a mere 59 years).

Not surprisingly, in the light of these statistics, income differentiation has grown enormously. In early 1994 it was estimated that the wealthiest 10 per cent of the population received almost 30 per cent of all income, while the poorest 10 per cent received only 2 per cent. By the summer of 1994 it was expected that this gap would increase fourteenfold. The same report also indicated that changes in consumer production would also seriously aggravate the existing disparity in conditions of living. While most retailers were increasingly stocking products aimed at the higher end of the market, cheaper products, products for children and the most basic items of consumption were invariably being withdrawn from production altogether.[64] It was thus very noticeable that when an opinion poll was conducted in autumn 1994 on citizens' attitudes to living standards in the foreseeable future, the most popular *concrete* answer to the question of when they thought an improvement would take place was 'never'.[65]

It is undeniably clear, then, that in such conditions of economic depression and chaos, the emergence of a healthy civil society is not easy to sustain. As even Adam Smith himself was wont to point out: 'No society can surely be flourishing and happy, of which the far greater part of the members are poor and miserable.'[66]

Of the dangers that exist because of the depth of depression and chaos, two phenomena are more prominent than most. The first of these can perhaps best be labelled the 'Weimar scenario', and is self-evident in scope and nature. The perpetual economic depression with which Russia has had to cope in recent years is clearly grist to the authoritarian mill. It may well be, as some of the more optimistic commentators are keen to point out, that Russia has by now been on the edge of a cliff for so long that no one is quite sure any longer what will push it over.[67] Indeed, given the fact that the fall in the country's industrial output since 1989 has already far outweighed the experience of Weimar Germany in the late 1920s and early 1930s, perhaps nothing at all will push it over the edge. Be that as it may, familiarity with life on the edge cannot possibly breed contentment. It does, however, make the 'Weimar scenario' a constant threat, and few can doubt that there are plenty of willing Hitlers waiting in the wings.

As for the second danger to the development of a civilized and healthy civil society stemming from the proximity to economic chaos, this is something that all Russian citizens are now having to face in their day-to-day experience: the criminalization of the economic realm and the increasing scope of *mafiya* control and influence.

In his time at the head of the European Bank for Reconstruction and Development, Jacques Attali had indicated that Russia was embarking upon a race in early 1992 in which there were two main competitors: institutions which would abide by civilized rules aiming to create a functioning market economy and institutions which would abide by the rules of the jungle, whose victory would result in an economy largely controlled by the mafia.[68] Two years on, the race continues, and the latter competitor is undoubtedly getting stronger and stronger.

In a series of related speeches in the early part of 1993, President Yeltsin was forced to admit that Russia had become 'a mafia power on a world scale'. Organized crime, he implied, was destroying the economy, interfering with politics and undermining public morale. Robbery, embezzlement and corruption were all becoming the norms of social relations, and beginning to penetrate every aspect of citizens' lives.[69]

Exactly how penetrative such phenomena have been, virtually no one is able to say. Nevertheless, in arguably one of the most detailed surveys carried out so far, Stephen Handelman has painted a frightening picture of gangsters, swindlers, drug traffickers and corrupt officials in virtual absolute control of the new economic domain. In a book aptly subtitled 'The Theft of the Second Russian Revolution', he leaves his readers in no doubt that these are not peripheral attributes of the transition process. They are practices at the very heart of that process. The protection rackets and the gang wars, he writes, are everyday occurrences which have often made the streets of many Russian cities complete no-go areas.[70]

Certainly the few statistics that are available seem to back this view up. Up to 40 per cent of Russia's wealth is now believed to be controlled by criminal cartels. Eighty per cent of private enterprises and commercial banks are said regularly to pay up to 20 per cent of their earnings in taxes to racketeers. More than 50 per cent of Russia's criminal groups have close ties with government ministers and agencies. And as if all this was not enough, there are still virtually no laws effectively dealing with mafia organizations.[71]

Of the wealth that such groups possess, a vast proportion is illegally spirited abroad. Estimates vary, but according to some analysts somewhere between 6 billion and 15 billion dollars have been illegally exported each year since the collapse of the old order. This is also backed up by a Central Bank official who argued that by the summer of 1994 the monthly flight of such capital had reached at least 1 billion dollars.[72] As for the money which remains in Russia, this is most effectively laundered through the new stock markets and the buying and selling of property.[73] Indeed, it is not so much a question of gangsters opening bank accounts so much as opening banks themselves. And again, if some versions are to be believed, as many as half of the new commercial banks in Russia are effectively under direct mafia control.

Reading the accounts of the new Russian mafias, one is hardly inclined to come away with an image of a civilized competitive realm of civil society in the making. The predominant image, rather, is of a 'swindler's playground' that also often resembles a military front line. In 1992, one in every four crimes in Russia was committed by criminal gangs; and in 1993 such crimes rose by 28 per cent. As for the weaponry that is available, it is not unheard of for anti-tank grenade launchers to be used on the streets of Moscow.

Quite clearly, then, the more such criminal organizations take root in present-day Russian society, the more causes they will 'serve'. The mafia, for example, is already the predominant life force of the new breed of populist politician, and has become everyone's favourite 'bogey'. On the one hand, it is the mafia which is blamed for the failure of the new economic set-up; on the other, it is the same mafia that is used to justify the need for a new 'iron hand' to exercise authoritarian control over the developing situation. The ultimate political correlation that can be drawn from this was cogently summed up by one local newspaper editor whose city, Ekaterinburg, has become a mafia stronghold:

> If people begin to equate freedom and democracy with crime and anarchy, they will support political forces who say they can eliminate the disorder [*bespredel*] by strong arm measures. And there is really only one political force in this country strong enough to do that right now, together with the army . . . the fascists.[74]

Political Parties

Apart from perpetual chaos in the economy, one of the other major factors behind the perceived fragility of Russia's civil society at the moment is the existence of a weak, amorphous party structure in the Russian political set-up. This is not by any means caused by a dearth of political parties. In fact, if anything, the opposite is true. One of the primary causes of the weakness and ineffectiveness of the party system is the existence of *far too many* organizations calling themselves political 'parties' – more than fifty at the latest count, taken in the autumn of 1994.[75]

Political parties have been allowed a *de jure* existence in Russia since the enactment of the aforementioned Law on Public Associations in October 1990. Looking collectively at them, one can hardly say that any of them has really distinguished itself with honour or glory, let alone massive popular support and sympathy. Very few of them claimed at the outset to represent specifically organized interests in society or, for that matter, interests yet to be organized. This, in turn, frequently resulted in a very vague form of party programme being adopted by many of them; and in some cases no real programme at all, with both phenomena being largely justified by the misconception that all they had to do was sit back and wait for the Communist Party to collapse in order to gain more support. Even after the disintegration of the CPSU the need to evolve a positive, constructive programme of aims and policies was only slowly acknowledged; a phenomenon largely attributable to the inexperienced nature of the new leaderships or, worse still, leaderships based around certain headline-catching individuals more desirous of promoting themselves as charismatic figures than of promoting the cause of the party as a whole.[76]

Charisma-seekers aside, another common problem of the existing parties so far has been the image of elitism that has been projected. Formal organizational structures inside the parties are at best unclear, and at worst non-existent. Party debates, meanwhile, are monopolized by a few prominent figures at the top, and are prone to lapse into personalized disagreements and feuds. Lack of tolerance for dissenting opinions is all too frequent; as too are formal splits inside a new party, particularly over the most trivial of issues.

To be fair, of course, that most of the parties have remained small and elitist in appearance is not entirely their own fault, since until very recently it still took a fair amount of courage to be openly identified with many of the alternative forces. (Loss of job or position on a housing waiting list, for example, continued to be forms of possible retribution by unreconstructed communist-controlled localities even after the demise of the CPSU.) Moreover, one should also not underestimate the depth of negative connotations many Russian citizens still have with the very notion of 'party'. Nevertheless, for as long as they retain the appearance of being elitist, they will always find it difficult to enlarge their membership base and develop a proper functioning organizational structure. Last, but not least, on top of all these problems, the other obvious problem common to them all is lack of finances. Indeed, political parties that do seemingly have sufficient funds are inevitably treated with great suspicion.[77]

It is not only logistical problems, however, that continue to plague the emerging multiparty scenario throughout the country. For some time now – ever since the concept of pluralism found official favour – there has been continual open speculation as to whether some parties are in fact as legitimate as they appear; perhaps in reality, and despite their high-sounding names, they are front organizations for hardline sections of the old KGB or the new mafia organizations. Nor can one doubt that the current saturation of political forces, be it in some cases a tactical ploy or not, is resulting only in outright popular confusion and increasing signs of apathy. One must seriously doubt, for example, whether their own respective memberships can truly differentiate between the aims of the Party of Constitutional Democrats and those of the Constitutional Democratic Party. And was it a deliberate ploy to sow confusion in the public's mind or a genuine need to focus on a specific difference in outlook that necessitated the establishment of the Democratic Party and the Russian Democratic Party shortly after the foundation of the Democratic Party of Russia? If, as some commentators continually maintain, this was a deliberate ploy by the old CPSU to keep the opposition perpetually splintered, then one would have to recognize it as a very astute, if not necessarily original, tactic. Whatever the reasoning behind it, however, one cannot help thinking that in combination with all the other debilitating factors cited above, Viktor Kuvaldin probably got it right when he declared: 'we are setting sail on the high seas of the multiparty system in a poorly rigged ship with an uncouth crew'.[78]

Without doubt, if the main task of political parties is generally recognized to be the aggregation and mobilization of interests, the provision of a basis for articulation and representation, and also a mechanism for access to and control of the state's power structure as a whole, then it is clear that Russian political parties are only at the very initial stages of the learning process. Nor can one say that the holding of the first post-communist parliamentary elections in December 1993 did anything fundamentally to improve the situation, or even assist the process of party formation in any real sense. The nature of the electoral system that was eventually chosen gave far greater credence to a few prominent, usually Moscow-based, individuals than it did to the party or electoral bloc as a whole. Electors throughout the country were encouraged to vote not according to serious party manifestos that had been carefully drafted in the run-up to the elections, but for a handful of star names that topped the party's list. The Democratic Party of Russia, for example, had always been exclusively identified with its founding father Nikolai Travkin (to the extent that everyone referred to it as 'Travkin's Party'). The bloc led by Grigorii Yavlinskii made no attempt whatsoever even to think of a party label for itself; it simply adopted the most prominent three names on its list as its formal appellation. And Russia's Choice was never really anything but an amalgamation of prominent individual government ministers or presidential aides. As a consequence, few members felt any real attachment to an organization that could transcend individual loyalties; and such individual loyalties were always going to be excessively emotive, irrational and unstable. As Aleksandr Buzgalin adequately summarized the situation at the time of the elections: '[Russian political] parties represent nothing more at the moment than a kind of service for the interests of the political elite. Their function is to help smooth the way for their foremost representatives to play an enhanced role within the elite, and that is all.'[79] As for the situation in the first-past-the-post constituencies, this, if anything, was even worse.[80] The vast majority of candidates in these constituencies could not even be bothered to associate themselves with formal party organizations, often considering such associations to be totally detrimental to their personal, localized or regionalized ambitions. (See Appendix 2.)

Another significant attribute of the general environment in which political parties in Russia are currently operating is the existence of high levels of political linguistic contradictoriness. It is perfectly true, of course, that the notions of 'left' and 'right' have often been used in Russian political culture in a very different way than in the West. As Andrzej Walicki has rightly pointed out, the connotation of 'the Left' has nearly always been a powerful attraction for the Russian intelligentsia, and very few of them have ever openly sought to classify themselves as being on the ideological 'Right' precisely because of the negative aura that this creates in society.[81] Boris Kagarlitsky has also argued in a similar vein:

> In different cultures the terms 'left' and 'right' have a quite different emotional impact. In France rightists are not ashamed to call themselves rightists. In

Russia, by contrast, the term 'left' is seen as particularly attractive. Leftists speak out against the authorities, they establish an opposition, and in a country which has not known political freedoms, this in and of itself is widely considered a great benefit.[82]

Under present circumstances, however, this clinging to one's cultural heritage is often stretching credulity much too far; to the point at which, argues Boris Kurashvili, 'terminological confusion' is now paramount.[83] Certainly, when it reaches the point at which those who openly espouse a radical imposition of recapitalization of the country, according to Thatcherite and Reaganite criteria, still cling assiduously to the 'left' assignation, then one can see what Kurashvili means.

For Kagarlitsky, such a confusion of concepts is perhaps understandable after decades of cultural isolationism and totalitarian propaganda, as well as being indicative of the fact that no real, definitive delineation of class forces has yet emerged in post-communist society. It is only when the latter is in place, he argues, that one can really appreciate and understand the true significance of what Left and Right respectively stand for.[84] In the meantime, both the newly politicized Russian citizens themselves, and observers of the Russian political scene, are left to cope as best they can with the confusion that prevails. For others, meanwhile, it is perhaps more astute to avoid left and right terminology altogether. This, however, only seems to complicate matters even further. Although no one has yet suggested following Mayakovsky's sarcastic advice of simply distinguishing between the 'bastards' and the 'tripe', the ever more frequent use by some Russian political activists and commentators of a bemusing colour scheme of reds, browns, whites, greys, greens and various shades in-between appears only to be adding to the general muddle.

By far the most important issue concerning party political development in Russia since the collapse of the CPSU's monopoly, however, is the frequent charge (especially in the Russian press itself) that very few parties, if any, have sought genuinely to represent distinct social interests in Russian society.[85] For some commentators in the West, the mere appearance of such an accusation is conclusive proof that a lot of indigenous Russian commentary on developments taking place in society is still deeply mired in some kind of ideological morass. The fixation, they argue, which regularly appears in some of the Russian media between what is termed a *genuine* multiparty system underpinned by social and class distinctions [*partiinost'*] and an *artificial* kind of political pluralism underpinned by more populist-type appeals to the masses [*portsialnost'*] is a far cry from the kind of concerns and issues that preoccupy the vast majority of Western academic thinking on the nature of parties.[86]

Quite whether this really is an accurate assessment of Western academic thinking on the subject will not concern us here. What is much more significant is the type of debates this basic criticism of the emerging party structure has touched off in other areas. One aspect of this further debate revolves around the question of whether this perceived shortcoming is first and foremost attributable to the parties themselves, or might rather be due to the fact that *as yet* there are, as it turns out, very few real distinct, or at least *consistent,* sociomaterial interests in Russian society to represent in the first place. Moreover, this question, in turn, has also given new life to that long-standing debate in Soviet studies concerning the existence or otherwise of fundamental *class* interests in the old Soviet system, and the extent to which these class interests have been inherited and/or transformed in post-communist Russia.

For Boris Kagarlitsky – who, as one of the leaders of the Party of Labour, has tried and done more than most to pin his political organization to a firm social interest in society – such a general criticism of Russian political parties is certainly valid. Nevertheless, it is clear from some of his writings that subjective factors alone are not to blame for the social rootlessness of most of the new parties; certain objective factors have also conditioned such an outcome. Analysing some of the key aspects surrounding the collapse of the old Soviet system, Kagarlitsky has drawn particular attention to the following significant point:

> The incongruence of the Western and Eastern models of society [at the point of collapse] was obvious. It was simply impossible to understand the processes unfolding in the East by means of analogies with the West. Society to a significant degree remained declassed; people were not conscious of their interests, and the normal social bonds were missing. There were no classes. The mass movement was [thus] inevitably transformed into the actions of a mob.[87]

The crucial point here for Kagarlitsky is the emphasis on a *declassed* society; the sense in which all elements in society were essentially stripped of their class identity. This was not a recent phenomenon, he argues, but a long-standing condition of both Soviet and pre-revolutionary Russian life. It started with the destruction of existing class identities at the time of the Stolypin reforms during the first years of the twentieth century and the fragility, if not total failure, of new class allegiances to emerge definitively out of these reforms. It then continued because of the absolute volatility of social conditions that have prevailed in Russia ever since: the destruction of social bonds during the First World War, the Revolution and Civil War; the social destabilization of the Stalin years, with the massive programme of industrialization accompanied by terror, purges and the Second World War; and in the inability and impermissibility of stable social bonds being allowed to develop in any significant way in the postwar years.[88]

As for whether the bureaucracy became a ruling *class* in its own right, Kagarlitsky is adamant that it did not. 'Classes only exist', he emphasizes, 'where there are social structures distinct from the structure of the state.'[89] This clearly was not the case in the old Soviet system. The bureaucracy, therefore, must be equated with a statocracy, and despite all the privileges open to it, in all other respects it was just as declassed as the other social strata of Soviet society. Consequently, unlike traditional ruling classes in a Western capitalist society, who have been able perpetually to survive political crises of all different kinds, in the Soviet case this clearly meant that the very existence of the ruling bureaucracy was closely tied to the continued dominance of the state structure.

The major significance of this, argues Kagarlitsky, was that when it came to a real, fundamental crisis point in the political system, the *nomenklatura* found that it could no longer rule in the old fashion, but it also knew that no one could take its place at the helm of the state administration:

> Political slogans could be changed, and new ideological labels could be passed on to the state, but the fact remained: looming up ahead was a crisis and no alternatives. *There was no new class able to seize power from the old oligarchy and to give shape to a new model of society.* Only the oligarchy itself, or some part of it, could do this.[90]

This particular issue of the relationship (or lack of it) between political parties and a real social base in present-day Russian conditions has also been taken up by a close colleague of Kagarlitsky, Andrei Kolganov. He, too, has forcefully argued that there has been little real opportunity to create a genuine correlation between political parties and a distinct social base, precisely because the latter has not really had time to emerge properly and the former have been created largely as a result of the activities of a narrow stratum of the *old* bureaucracy and political elite.[91]

The activities of the state and those who comprise this sphere are therefore still independent of processes and developments taking place in the broader realm of society. And because political forces are not fully dependent on initiatives originating in society by one or another social stratum, it inevitably follows that the real force of political parties at the moment is determined more by their degree of access to state power mechanisms than by their membership figures or electoral popularity. Small wonder, then, that parliamentary deputies still feel little sense of *obligation* to a particular party or parliamentary fraction. What often makes it worse, however, is that in such a situation, social interests that are beginning to develop in society are often seen as an *obstacle* to the successful realization of state interests. 'The government', writes Kolganov, 'uses weaknesses or the absence of the political self-organization of different social strata in order to play the role of the supreme arbiter in the inevitable social conflicts. [Indeed] the government is [often] concerned with fanning such conflicts in order to demonstrate its own strength and its necessity.'[92]

Of course, this adherence to the idea that post-communist Russia has inherited a declassed society, with all the consequences that follow from this, is not the same as saying that no distinct social interests exist in that society. Clearly they do exist, and the pioneering studies of Russian sociologists (like Tatyana Zaslavskaya and Boris Kagarlitsky himself) since the early 1980s have contributed an enormous amount to our understanding of these interests. More than anything else, however, a conception of a declassed society emphasizes the extent to which perceived social interests are constantly subject to change and flux, and as such, therefore, lack any real *consistency*. It also emphasizes the fundamental lack of *consciousness* attached to these interests. To borrow the old Marxist notion, they are interests that exist *in themselves* (i.e. structurally), without necessarily existing *for themselves* (i.e. formationally).

In some crucial instances, however, it is debatable whether one can even say that specific interests exist structurally at this moment in time of post-communist transition. For all the references in some political quarters, for example, to the need to buttress the current transition with the backing of a very strong and powerful *middle class,* one would surely have to agree with Claus Offe (and before him, Max Weber) when he points out that such a category of social agents has never previously existed in Russian society. To this end, such a new class of entrepreneurs and private owners has first of all to be installed from above 'in a political way and through politically visible actors'.[93] Once again, therefore, we are left with a scenario in which certain political forces within the realm of the state are given the responsibility of creating mechanisms for the emergence of new social interests, rather than being reliant and dependent upon an already existing social class with a fairly well-defined set of interests, needs and ideological propositions.[94]

As for a *working class* in Russia, meanwhile, the problem here is altogether different. While it clearly it does not have to be created from scratch, it does nevertheless have to be *re*-created out of the previously declassed, atomized ranks of the working masses. And this task of re-creation is hugely complicated by the enormous depths of *contradictory consciousness* currently prevalent within those ranks. As Aleksandr Buzgalin has commented, for example:

> The old social structure [inherited from the Soviet system], in effect represented a mixture of different socioeconomic systems, so that in any real, concrete relation different aspects of social interests could be seen. For example, if I was employed in an enterprise as an engineer I would encounter different types of social relations in the workplace. Firstly, I would encounter a state capitalist structure in which the Director of the enterprise is a state representative and I am an employee, and therefore the relations are the same *vis-à-vis* the buying and selling of labour. But there were also elements of socialism here because

there was no unemployment, there were numerous social welfare guarantees and even some degree of self-management within the enterprise. On top of this there were elements of semi-feudal relations, especially as regards the maintenance of the system of *propiska* – the system of registration according to one's place of residence. Finally, there were also elements of a pseudo-capitalist type of relation to the extent that the black market was rife within the enterprise. So what we had, then, was a very confusing social picture where it was impossible for a clearly defined and distinctive social interest to emerge. In each individual person elements of different types of social systems and social relations would coexist with each other. To some extent we were all a bit of a bureaucrat, an employee of a bureaucrat, a bit of a private businessman buying and selling what we could on the black market, as well as being a socialist. In such circumstances, then, the crisis of this system [was bound to lead] to the appearance of a whole plethora of different [kinds of responses].[95]

Moreover, two other significant factors need to be borne in mind if we are fully to comprehend the depths of contradictory consciousness among the Russian working masses at this particular juncture. First, it must be remembered that under the old Soviet system there was always a great deal of *collusion* between workforce and management within the enterprise structure. As the post-communist transition progresses it is *assumed* that the structural basis of that collusion will eventually alter, but even if this assumption is correct it will inevitably take time for this structural change to impact on the old-style consciousness of the workforce *vis-à-vis* their former relationship with management. And secondly, there can be little doubt that what is perceived to be the growing *lumpenization* of society is also clearly going to have similar enormous contradictory effects on the Russian social realm.[96]

Quite clearly, attempts to overcome the former declassed nature of Russian society, whereby distinct social interests are provided with a sense of consistency and an underlying sense of consciousness, is not going to be an easy or a quick process. It is, however, an essential process if a strong multiparty, pluralist system, rather than some kind of socially rootless, floating party system, is going to be established in Russia. The sheer enormity of the task ahead in this sphere was nowhere made more abundantly clear than in an opinion poll of more than 1,500 residents of twelve Russian cities in the winter of 1992–3, carried out by the Moscow Institute of Applied Politics. Reporting on the findings of the poll, the director of the Institute, Olga Kryshtanovskaya, indicated that 'the people of Russia have only a vague idea as to what sociopolitical system now functions in Russia'.[97] Of all respondents, 51.6 per cent had difficulty answering this question; 9.2 per cent could only respond that it was a mixture of chaos, anarchy and rampant lawlessness; 10.5 per cent thought that they were already living under capitalism; 4.5 per cent still maintained that they were living in a socialist system; 4.3 per cent did not think that there was any system at all; while the remainder thought that the country was in a period of transition towards capitalism.

On the specific issue of political parties, meanwhile, Kryshtanovskaya was able to report the following: 52.3 per cent of the respondents were of the firm belief that 'all new parties have been founded by people who are thrusting towards power'; 39.7 per cent maintained that 'party activities have no bearing upon the life of common people'; 19.9 per cent were convinced that 'the new parties do not play any substantial role in politics'; and 11.8 per cent were of the opinion that 'present-day party activists are simply "dead ducks" who have really nothing better and more useful to do'. Finally, in answer to the question whether or not there were now any parties in Russia that the respondents thought expressed their interests, 77.9 per cent said 'no'.

How Many States;
How Many Caesars?

Unhappy the land that has no heroes.
No, unhappy the land that needs heroes.

Bertolt Brecht, *Leben des Galilei*

The Fragility of Russian Statehood

In the survey conducted by the Institute of Applied Politics, twelve cities in all were focused upon by the researchers in four separate regions of the Russian Federation, all of which could be said to be from the traditional national heartland of Russia. When the researchers asked respondents to name the party they most associated with, it was thus very noticeable that some of the most popular ones were those closely associated with protecting what were perceived to be pure ethnic Russian interests and ambitions. In the situation currently prevailing in the Russian Federation, one can certainly surmise that had a different set of twelve cities been chosen for the survey – cities more representative of the ethnic heterogeneity of the Federation – a similar set of findings would have been recorded. That is to say, political allegiance would still have been prioritized according to ethnic rather than social criteria. According to the analyst Andrei Kortunov: 'The road from communism to democracy is much longer than the road from communism to nationalism.'[1] In the context of the present survey one might also say that the road from a system based on absolute and coercive domination to one based on consensual hegemony might similarly be interrupted by an excessive number of nationalist, ethnic and regionalist roadworks.

That these kinds of cleavages have been more in evidence thus far, than the socioeconomic cleavage is in many ways, of course, a direct hangover from the last weeks and months of the Soviet Union. After all, it was the use of this cleavage by the 'democratic' opposition that eventually brought down the Gorbachev regime. Having thus prioritized this issue, and having demonstrated its ultimate power and significance at first hand, it is hardly surprising that the lesson was widely learned. As one journalist wryly put it: 'Nothing secedes like secession'.[2]

For some commentators, the upsurge of this kind of allegiance grounded in national and ethnic considerations is a healthy sign of a vibrant civil society in the making.[3] For many others, however, the present author included, in the contemporary context of Russian conditions it represents an enormous danger that may well prove uncontainable. As Paul Piccone astutely remarked, newly politicized subjects emerging on the stage of an embryonic civil society and acting according to exclusive nationalist and ethnic considerations tend on the whole not 'to behave like aloof Habermasian scholars gathered around a seminar table [engaging themselves] in undistorted communication . . . in the calm search for a democratic consensus'.[4] Going on to comment specifically on the situation in the Soviet Union at the height of Gorbachev's reforms, he noted: 'instead of galvanising a solid bloc of support to deploy against an entrenched apparatus, the lifting of the repressive cloak . . . only uncovered an embattled society – not in the sense of an orderly polity of citizens and competing interest groups . . . , but a Hobbesian *bellum omnium contra omnes* impossible to mobilise in any but the most irrational projects of nationalistic, ethnic, religious or corporatist vindications'.[5] What one needs to recognize, therefore, is that this kind of politics is nearly always a zero-sum game.

Quite clearly, then, just as the 'imagined community' that went by the name of the Union of Soviet Socialist Republics failed in the end to find a societal realm resistant enough to cope with this kind of predicament, so the same fate might well befall the 'imagined community' that is trying to emerge in the guise of the Russian Federation.

What, after all, is the Russian Federation? The question might seem a spurious one at first glance, but it does not take that much probing to realize just how relevant it really is. The recognized borders of the Federation, for example, have no historical analogy with any previously existing state structure of Russia. To make matters worse, in its former Soviet guise, unlike the other fourteen constituent Union Republics, it had very few attributes of national statehood that it could draw on once the old Soviet system disintegrated; and one need look no further than the extremely protracted crisis that has taken place between the executive, legislative and judicial branches of central authority in the aftermath of the August 1991 coup attempt to appreciate just how difficult it has been to establish a coherent state structure in such porous conditions. Nor is this situation helped by the regular appearance of opinion polls indicating that a considerable proportion of the population have a strong degree of nostalgia for a state that no longer exists.[6]

Addressing the Congress of People's Deputies in December 1992, just before the first anniversary of the formal demise of the USSR, the Congress Chairman, Ruslan Khasbulatov, told the parliamentary representatives in no uncertain terms:

> . . . you should not think that we in the Russian Federation today are dealing with an absolutely independent, classic state. It is very important for us to understand this. The evolution of one of the republics of the union into an independent state, with serious institutions possessing not only a strong legislative foundation but also a strong sense of tradition, is a matter of many long years, and we are therefore kidding ourselves if we think we currently possess the resources to run a classic independent state. This is the origin of many of our contemporary problems. We have to realize that we are only feeling our way towards an independent state, with all the attributes, with all the institutions and, of course, with legislation.[7]

In terms of its administrative set-up, the Federation consists of 89 constituent republics and regions of one kind or another (including Moscow and St Petersburg), divided into a complex ethnic as well as territorially based asymmetrical structure. According to the calculations of Ramazan Abdulatipov, no more than 15-20 per cent of these administrative units were previously subordinated to Russian structures in the old Soviet system; the rest were subordinated to all-union structures, which has likewise severely complicated the creation of a new coherent administrative system of power.[8] In the middle of March 1992 a Federal Treaty was signed by all but two of the constituent republics (Chechnya and Tatarstan) to try to bring some order and clarity to the administrative chaos, though most commentators quickly recognized that in practice the provisions of the Treaty rarely made any impact.

When one bears in mind as well that there are more than a hundred different indigenous ethnic groups within the Federation, speaking a similar number of recognized different languages, across eleven different time zones, then one begins to appreciate the real enormity of the hegemonic task in the country, even under the most optimal of conditions. The fact that those optimal conditions clearly do not exist only makes even more apparent the danger that the search for hegemony currently risks being submerged in the language of irredentism.

In Map 2.1, an attempt has been made to try and encapsulate some of the current fragmentary, dislocative trends.

At the time of writing, the major problem facing the integral unity of the Russian federal state is without doubt the separatist aspirations of the Republic of Chechnya.

Located on the northern side of the Caucasus mountains and a major strategic centre for Russia's oil routes, this Muslim Republic of just over

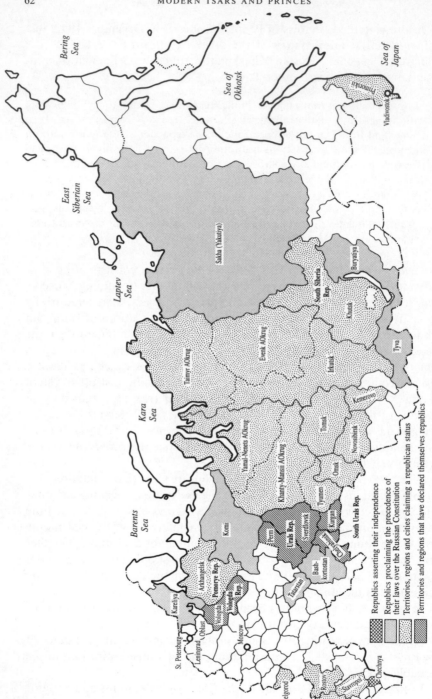

Map 2.1 The Process of the 'Sovereignization' of the Russian Federation *Source: Moscow News*, no. 40, 1993, p. 6

one million people has a long history of opposition to Russian control. Consequently, when, under the leadership of its new President, Dzhokhar Dudaev, the Republic announced its unilateral declaration of independence in November 1991, few observers expected that there would be anything other than acute and painful reverberations.

One of the first consequences of the Republic's decision to embark on its independent route was a separate claim for federal recognition by the region of Ingushetia, which had formerly been united with Chechnya in a combined Autonomous Republic within the old Soviet structure. In breaking away from Chechnya, Ingushetia laid claim to territories (in the Prigorodny region) which, since 1943, had belonged to neighbouring North Osetia. As a result of this claim, a fierce military struggle ensued which has been tempered only by the periodic imposition of Moscow-controlled states of emergency. The separation of Chechnya and Ingushetia, meanwhile, also encouraged other amalgamated entities likewise to achieve some kind of divorce settlement: something that has frequently been attempted, for example, in nearby Karachai-Cherkessia and Balkar-Kabardino.

Internally, Chechnya's declaration of independence also encouraged a protracted power struggle within the Republic. Since Dudaev had initially seized power by illegitimate means, his authority was never universally accepted by the myriad clans that have traditionally existed in the region. Consequently, after a short period of unity behind Dudaev's leadership in the face of a brief flurry of military activity by Russian forces towards the end of 1991, the Republic slowly but inexorably lapsed into a condition of civil war. When even this failed to alter the political state of play, the central authorities finally made the fateful decision to embark on a full-scale military (re)conquest of the territory, launching a much more determined offensive in early December 1994.

Just why the federal authorities resorted to the military option when they did has been a matter of much speculation. Whether it was to placate a restless military organization which perhaps naively equated Chechnya with some kind of American-style Haiti operation which would restore law and order to a crime- and drugs-ridden territory; whether it was a more sinister attempt in time-honoured fashion to divert public attention away from an embattled, scandal-ridden Defence Minister (Pavel Grachev, accused of widescale corruption) or an equally embattled President, whose popularity stakes were touching an all-time low; or whether it was more to do with protecting Russia's economic interests in the whole Caucasus region, few can doubt that the protracted war that then ensued (and continues as this is being written) has proved enormously costly. By mid February 1995, more than 24,000 civilians alone had been killed in the conflict, and more than 400,000 citizens had become displaced refugees. To add to the country's already depleted financial resources, it was estimated that the cost of restoring the Chechen capital, Grozny, alone would amount to more than 5,000 billion roubles. And, of course, the Russian authorities had to suffer the indignity of massive public as well as international reprobation.

As if all this was not bad enough in itself, far from enhancing the unity of the Federation, the conflict only made matters considerably worse. Many other ethnic republics in the Federation openly and vehemently opposed the brutal and excessive use of force, as too did many ethnically Russian regions.[9] Worst of all, the conflict also seriously inflamed a whole range of other ethnic and religious-based tensions throughout the Caucasus region, leaving many commentators fearful of a much wider Transcaucasian conflagration. In some of the neighbouring states – Dagestan, Ingushetia and Kabarda for example – the very nature of the Russian military action in Chechnya has led to increasing internal pressure on the incumbent leaders of the republics openly to espouse their own separatist aspirations. In republics such as Dagestan, meanwhile, long-standing ethnic and territorial disputes between groups such as the Kumyks and the Laks have been exacerbated by the Chechen war. As for political organizations such as the Confederation of the Peoples of the Caucasus – a movement set up at the end of 1991 amalgamating sixteen different ethnic groups in the region in a common struggle against 'Russian imperial ambitions' (as well as the imperial ambitions of Georgia and Azerbaijan) – they too have openly used the conflict to fuel their hopes of a breakaway North Caucasian confederation, and have likewise not been averse to playing the 'Islamic card' in their opposition to Russia.[10]

It is not only in the troubled Caucasus region, however, that the central Russian authorities have had to cope with ethnic and territorial disputes. In total, it has been calculated that there are more than seventy points of inter-ethnic and territorial conflict currently being waged within the borders of the Russian Federation.[11] While the vast majority have some kind of historical continuity, some of them are attempts to forge brand-new forms of territorial recognition. Such is the case, for example, in the attempt to create an entirely new Yenisei Republic out of existing Russian-populated regions near Krasnoyarsk, along with the districts of Taimyr and Evenki. Moreover, in a number of regions, territorial issues are currently being struggled over, and the outcome might well have serious implications in regions and territories outside the Russian Federation. This is the case, for instance, in the attempt to reunify the North Osetian Republic with the South Osetian region in Georgia. Similarly, there are also attempts to forge a Lesgin Republic out of territories in Dagestan and Azerbaijan.

If Chechnya is the republic that has gone furthest in its attempt to secure *de facto* independence from Russia, a number of other republics have likewise pressed their claims for strong degrees of autonomy on the federal authorities. In the case of Tatarstan, for example, an oil-rich republic in the heart of the Federation which has been developing ever closer ties with Turkey, this has been done by proclaiming an 'associate membership' of the Russian Federation; and while President Mintimer Shaimiyev rightly insists that this is a long way short of a full *de jure* attempt to secede from Russia, it is nevertheless clear that the extent of the Republic's autonomy is very considerable indeed,[12] just as it is equally clear that a good many political groups in Tatarstan will ultimately settle for nothing less than outright independence.

Both Chechnya and Tatarstan, it goes without saying, were among the first ethnic republics to adopt their own state constitutions. All the other ethnic republics followed suit, and six of them are adamant that their local laws will take precedence over all-Russian laws: Tyva, Karelia, Komi, Sakha (Yakutia), Buryatia and Bashkortostan.[13] In the case of the last-named, the Republic reserves the right to secede freely from the Russian Federation; something which is also claimed by Tyva and Sakha (Yakutia).[14] Bashkortostan has also moved closer to the position adopted by its neighbour, Tatarstan, in maintaining that its relations with Russia will be governed only on the basis of bilateral agreements; indeed, during the course of 1994 many such agreements were in fact signed with the federal authorities. Such moves, however – including the claim that the Republic has only one national entity, the Bashkirs – has only succeeded in stirring up further inter-ethnic tension inside the Republic. After all, the Bashkirs are only a minority within their own Republic, accounting for 21.9 per cent of the population in comparison with Tatars (28.4 per cent) and Russians, the largest ethnic group, comprising 39.3 per cent of the population. The same kind of situation *vis-à-vis* the minority status of the titular, indigenous nationality also applies to the other republics claiming legal sovereignty (the one exception being Tyva).

Perhaps most worrying of all in terms of the maintenance of the state integrity of the Russian Federation is the fact that the 'parade of sovereignty declarations and separation claims' is not solely or exclusively occurring along national and ethnic lines. Even long-established traditional parts of the Russian heartland are beginning to pursue very strong regionalist tendencies. This stems for the most part from a desire to acquire equal status with the national-ethnic republics within the federal framework, as well as a wish to acquire greater degrees of economic autonomy for themselves – especially as many of them are net contributors to the federal budget, in contrast to the ethnic republics, which tend to be net recipients of financial handouts.[15] None the less, one cannot *totally* rule out the possibility that in the future this might just conceivably lead to their breaking away from the current Russian federal set-up.

In essence, the process is occurring on two, not always complementary, fronts. First, it involves the attempts by a number of territories and regions to be recognized as fully fledged republics. In summer 1993, for example, the region of Sverdlovsk formally proclaimed itself to be the newly constituted Urals Republic, and this was accompanied by a similar proclamation of republican status in Vologda and in Chelyabinsk (which now took on the name South Urals Republic).[16] Similar claims have also been unilaterally made by Vladivostok (which would like to be known as the Republic of Primoria), St Petersburg (the Neva Republic) and a whole host of other regions and territories. Secondly, it involves a concerted effort in many regions and territories to amalgamate themselves into brand-new forms of supra-regional entities. By the summer of 1994 eight such entities were in existence, encompassing the likes of the Great Volga Association, the Great Urals Association and the Far Eastern Association.

By far the best-known of them all, however, is the so-called Siberian Accord, which was originally set up in October 1990 and is an amalgamation of nineteen different Siberian regions. Although it is primarily an economic-based association, co-ordinating such matters as intra-regional exchange and integrated investment schemes, the Accord nevertheless maintains a standing parliament and a number of co-ordinating councils (equivalent to ministries), as well as various other integrated political and administrative organizations. Taken in conjunction with such co-ordinated economic institutions as a common regional banking sector, it is not all that difficult to see here the *possible* makings of a future fully fledged independent state structure.[17] Indeed, during the crisis in Moscow in September and October 1993 which culminated in the forcible destruction of the national parliament, the leaders of Siberian Accord played a very prominent and explicit political role. At the very height of the crisis it was announced that unless the dispute in Moscow was resolved amicably and within existing constitutional norms, measures would be taken that might ultimately lead to the formal creation of a united Siberian Republic, which would certainly seek to loosen its affiliation with Moscow and might ultimately lead to a unilateral declaration of independence.[18]

As events turned out, the threats went unheeded and the resolution of the crisis in President Yeltsin's favour was followed by a series of resignations among the leaders of the Accord.[19] Nevertheless, a number of political organizations and prominent political figures continue to propagate the demand for outright secession, and while the separatist winds may be nothing more than a slight breeze at the moment, few can believe that they have blown away for good. If nothing else, the separatist trends in areas like Siberia will undoubtedly be sustained by the desires that outside powers have in investing in such areas directly, rather than through Moscow channels, which could easily encourage a potential divergence of interests with the rest of the Russian Federation. Likewise, and as indicated above, they will also be sustained by the resentment that exists to a tax regime which allows them very few autonomous powers, yet leaves them as considerable net contributors to the federal coffers in Moscow. Indeed, the fact that some areas (like Sakha) have already managed to negotiate terms with Moscow which allow them to keep all the taxes raised in their republic is a clear incentive for the rest to try and do the same. And if this does not work through negotiation, they can always resist paying their taxes to Moscow; something that Magadan did in 1993 and other regions have consistently done over the past few years.[20] What this also does in turn, however, is to continue an asymmetrical structure which not only pits region against centre but also increases intra-regional tensions, as one area feels aggrieved at the apparent advantages of another.

Quite clearly, then, in such circumstances it is hardly surprising that one encounters, virtually on a daily basis, constant references in the central Russian press to the possible disintegration of the Federation and its replacement by a whole range of, what are often termed 'feudal-type domains', vassals and suzerains. And although in most cases this is clearly over-the-top hyperbole, certainly as regards the situation prevailing in the Caucasus it is not far off the mark, particularly in light of the existence there of innumerable irregular armed detachments owing their allegiance to nothing more than 'clans' of one persuasion or another. It is also worth pointing out that throughout the Federation as a whole, there are approximately 150 exclusively national or ethnic-based political organizations; again, many of these also possess their own armed-combat detachments.[21] In contrast, virtually none of the recognized major political parties is truly 'national' in scope, and given the nature of the dominant cleavages at the moment, there are very few prospects of unified, national party organizations emerging.

If a struggle for hegemony is genuinely to take place in the existing boundaries of the Russian Federation, and not in a domain more equivalent to the old Grand Duchy of Muscovy, it is clearly imperative for any potential hegemonic force to be able to give credence to genuine regional and ethnic interests, yet also to be able to find points of reference which can *transcend* such parochial forms of allegiance. If this fails to happen, then the country will face a stark choice. One possibility will be ever deeper submergence into that much-feared chaos and anarchy forever associated in historical terms with the 'Time of Troubles'. And what will emerge from this will be an irrational, symbolic form of political activity that will feed off nothing more than the perpetual creation of enemy images and the arousal of strong, passionate and highly emotional prejudices. This, in the words of one commentator, will be a 'circular' form of political activity that will be extremely hard to deconstruct:

It is circular because it harms and exposes new surfaces to attack in every direction; it is circular because it concentrates only on itself; it is circular in the most vicious meaning of the term as it reproduces itself without the slightest chance of going beyond itself; and, most importantly, it is circular because it entraps thinking in a closed system rather than extending it into an open society. Such irrational-symbolic political discourse is always a monologue. Its fatal enemy is the logical and meaningful dialogue, for this could easily destroy its prejudices.[22]

The other non-hegemonic possibility is the (temporary?) abandonment of the whole transformational project of political modernity in Russia and the reimposition of dictatorial control, most probably in the guise of what Gramsci called the 'Caesarist' option; and it is this and other related issues that will now be focused on in the remaining part of this chapter.

Caesarist Tendencies

That there are very strong Caesarist tendencies in the post-communist transformation taking place in Russia is almost too self-evident to require any clarification. It is also apparent these tendencies have been underpinned by a whole plethora of legitimatory arguments confirming their logical *necessity* in the specific conditions of Russia's experience of transformation. Ever since the appearance of the aforementioned interview in *Literaturnaya gazeta* with Klyamkin and Migranyan back in August 1989, when they advocated the strengthening of the personal power of the state leader in acute periods of fundamental transformation so as to overcome the inevitable strains that would be placed on society by 'the absence of more organic forms of social solidarity',[23] the pages of newspapers, journals, think-tank reports and suchlike have been replete with similar kinds of assessments.[24]

Given the inevitable instability that has marked Russia's post-communist transformation, one can find no shortage of pretenders to the Caesarist throne. A much more interesting question, and certainly one with more direct and immediate concrete implications, concerns the extent to which the existing ultimate embodiment of personalized power in Russia, President Boris Yeltsin, is himself imbued with such Caesarist tendencies and inclinations. Any answer to this question, I think, would almost certainly have to be much more affirmative than repudiatory. Having said that, however, Tatyana Tolstaya is also surely right when she argues that Yeltsin's belief in his own Caesarist image is not necessarily matched by the reality of his capabilities.[25]

In assessing the Caesarist credentials of President Yeltsin, it is crucial to highlight three important aspects of the Gramscian understanding of this phenomenon.

First, Gramsci is very clear on the type of condition which perennially gives rise to a Caesarist type of solution. It is a solution, he writes, which appears when two or more forces in society and in the political realm are so balanced in their conflict that this cannot but produce a catastrophic outcome; and by catastrophic he is here referring to a condition in which the long-term continuation of such a conflict will ultimately lead to each side's reciprocal destruction, with all the resulting social consequences. Secondly, the solution which Gramsci sees arising from this situation is itself one in which an individual personality (i.e. a charismatic 'man of destiny') is thereupon required to play an *arbitratory* role, so as to resolve the crisis in a particular direction. Thirdly, Gramsci makes it plain that for all the outward appearance of supposed neutrality, the Caesarist figure will always objectively seek a resolution to the crisis to the benefit of one class interest over another. In other words, no matter what the national or populist credentials of the Caesarist figure, there is always a class-oriented structure underpinning it. The particular nature of the class orientation may not be clearly or explicitly defined; after all, the very essence of any Caesarist appeal must always be orientated towards such nebulous entities as 'the people'. Nevertheless, Gramsci affirmed, the apparent classlessness of the Caesarist solution is firmly rooted in the ultimate perpetuation of the interests of one social class as against another.[26]

It is this last point, of course, which is perhaps the most crucial in the Gramscian analysis, and clearly has enormous salience in the specific context of the analysis of President Yeltsin's position. As will be made clear in the next chapter, there is little doubt that President Yeltsin is a key participant in the current hegemonic struggle taking place in Russia. For the pro-Western combatants in that struggle, the President's explicit support of their cause (at least in the first crucial phase of the country's transformation) carried enormous legitimatory weight and significance. While the Westerners rightly seek to portray Yeltsin as a committed advocate of their cause, however, there is always a sufficient degree of ambiguity and contradictoriness surrounding the role and stature of the presidential office. For that reason, Yeltsin is often able to play the role of 'the man above the combative fray' whenever it suits him, or whenever circumstances dictate this. Indeed, it is precisely the *ambiguity* of President Yeltsin's position that gives him such strength and influence. He can be someone above the political fray without necessarily being outside it.

In what precise ways, then, is it possible to observe the Caesarist tendency at work; and how debilitating have such tendencies been in prohibiting the context for a genuine hegemonic struggle?

In some ways, it can be argued that the whole of Yeltsin's post-CPSU political career has been established on Caesarist foundations. In the aftermath of the defeat of the August 1991 coup, the old protracted crisis which had pitted 'liberal' communists against 'hardline conservative' communists, and had so stultified any kind of socioeconomic or political development over the previous eighteen months or more, finally came to an end. Portraying himself as the populist hero of the Russian people, Yeltsin emerged out of the coup attempt in a politically unassailable position – a position he was to use to quite considerable political effect over the course of the next several months, as he ruled almost exclusively by decree alone.

It was a period when once again newspapers were frequently shut down for not agreeing with the presidential line; when local leaders were removed on the totally spurious basis of disloyalty; when freely elected local parliaments were deprived of power and their authority was transferred to appointed representatives of the President (considered nothing more than his 'eyes and ears' in the regions); when national legislative institutions were deprived of many of the basic rights to check and balance the powers of the executive branches; when local and regional elections were suspended; and last, but not least, it was a period that represented an almost uncontrolled 'orgy of appropriation' of former CPSU-controlled property by the authorities loyal to the President and their respective 'hangers-on'.[27]

Even the well-known liberal philosopher Dmitrii Furman was forced to admit that in the immediate aftermath of the failure of the August 1991 coup, the Russian parliament was suddenly transformed into an institution where an 'age-old spirit of applause, rising into an ovation' now reigned triumphant. The democrats, he argued,

> are turning into 'so-called democrats' at precisely the moment when no one is prepared any longer to describe them in this way. The victory of democracy is turning into a serious threat to democracy, and the prospect is already emerging of an authoritarian populist regime led by a 'people's president', based on a 'democratic movement' devoted to this individual, and possessing an ideology and symbolism dominated by anti-communism.[28]

This period of almost unadulterated control by the President and the largely unaccountable structures he had created for himself lasted until spring 1992, when the legislative institutions slowly started to claw back some of their legitimate constitutional rights and powers. In the process, a far greater balance of power now ensued between the executive (governmental) structures and the legislative institutions. As the latter, however, increasingly became the main forum of opposition to the reforms that were being implemented, it was inevitable that sooner or later a new crisis point in the domain of power relationships would ensue.

The first serious indication that Yeltsin was not prepared to tolerate the stalemate that had been brewing up since spring 1992 occurred in December of that year. At the beginning of the month the seventh Congress of People's Deputies had tried all it could to revoke the special powers that it had awarded the President and the government in the aftermath of the August 1991 coup attempt. Many of the decisions taken at the congress were later 'frozen' to allow a cooling-off period between the different branches of power, though one decision remained firmly in place: Yeltsin was now forced to nominate a Prime Minister much more of the legislative's choosing, and in the process the radical free-marketeer Yegor Gaidar was replaced by the more cautious figure of Viktor Chernomyrdin.

Following a protracted crisis over personnel appointments in the new government later that month, Yeltsin took the diplomatically embarrassing step of cutting short an official visit to China. On his arrival back in Moscow, he made it plain that now that 'the master had returned home to sort things out', radical measures to solve the growing impasse in the power structures were well under preparation. For most observers this was a clear indication that he was again preparing to take full personal responsibility for the situation and impose another period of rule by decree; only this time he would not oblige in the courtesy of seeking parliament's approval for such a step.

In the event, lack of firm support and commitment to impose such a condition of presidential rule from the security agencies resulted in the threat not going any further. By early March 1993, however, the political 'gridlock' between the government and the legislature was, if anything, even more deeply entrenched. In a report 'On the State of Constitutional Legality in the Russian Federation', published by the Constitutional Court, the depth of the growing crisis was encapsulated in the opening paragraph:

Russia is experiencing one of the most complex periods in its history. The economy is in decline. Citizens' economic and social rights are not safeguarded. Inter-ethnic conflicts are continuing unabated. Crime is on the increase. Radical movements pursuing anti-constitutional aims are gathering strength. The state apparatus is affected by corruption. Legal nihilism is widespread even among top officials of the Russian Federation and its subjects. People's discontent at the inaction of the [executive and legislative] authorities and the confrontation between them is threatening to spill over into a social explosion. The constitutional system of the Russian state is under threat.[29]

When even this report failed to produce a workable solution to the executive-legislative impasse, Yeltsin once again attempted to take full personal control of the situation. In a television address on 20 March 1993, he announced that a period of 'special rule' would be imposed, pending a constitutional referendum in April. Once again, however, lack of support from the security apparatus and from a majority of the regional power structures meant that a climbdown was inevitable. While the constitutional referendum was endorsed, all notion of a period of special rule, which would have involved the dissolution or suspension of the legislative structures, was quickly dropped.

With two attempts at imposing a forceful resolution on the power crisis already having been thwarted, it was perhaps inevitable that any third attempt would either make or break the political influence of Yeltsin and his Presidency. When the third attempt finally came, therefore, it was likewise inevitable that the means used, and the tactics employed, would be far different.

On 21 September 1993, Yeltsin finally took the step of issuing a formal decree dissolving the existing national legislative structures, the Supreme Soviet and the Congress of People's Deputies. Direct presidential rule was imposed for a period of three months until such time as a new constitution and elections to a new type of parliament, the Federal Assembly, could be introduced. Glossing over the obvious illegality of his decree and the claim that such a step represented nothing less than a presidential-inspired *coup d'état*, Yeltsin sought to defend his actions in a nationwide television address by stating: 'The security of Russia and its peoples is more precious than formal compliance with the contradictory norms established by a legislative power that has definitely discredited itself.'[30] In what he later referred to as a form of 'political gangrene' that had manifested itself in the parliamentary domain and was threatening to infect the whole of the state and society, he also categorically insisted that he was merely responding to a whole series of demands for decisive action that had flooded in from all corners of the country.

Given the refusal of most parliamentarians to accept the presidential assumption of all the powers of the state, a forceful denouement to this latest stage of the power crisis was always likely. Consequently, when the leaders of the parliamentary forces, Ruslan Khasbulatov and Aleksandr Rutskoi (who had since been sworn in as Acting President), encouraged their supporters to launch an offensive on the Moscow Mayor's office and on the headquarters of the Ostankino television centre, this gave Yeltsin the pretext to issue an ultimatum to the previously hesitant security and defence forces: either put down the rebellion and the parliamentary opposition by force, or risk the consequences of a full-scale civil war.

With the army behind him, Yeltsin was once again in full control of the situation. Following the violent destruction of the parliament building on 4 October 1993, the earlier decree on presidential rule was now accompanied by a temporary (two-week) imposition of a State of Emergency in Moscow. In the time available to him, Yeltsin thus had the opportunity to re-create the political rules of the game in Russia very much in his own and his supporters' favour. Not unlike the situation that had accompanied the defeat of the August 1991 coup attempt, a whole series of decrees were passed, which were designed rapidly to force the pace of the country's ongoing transformation.

Opposition parties and newspapers were once again banned. Censorship was explicitly reintroduced for a temporary period during the State of Emergency, and implicitly maintained thereafter on a voluntary, self-regulation basis, with television and radio broadcasts, in particular, reverting to almost exclusive state-orientated coverage. Many important posts, such as the Prosecutor General's office, previously autonomous from direct presidential control, were now subordinated to Yeltsin personally; while any remaining vestiges of institutional control on the arbitrary use of power, such as those embodied in the Constitutional Court, were temporariliy prohibited from convening. Previously established civil rights and liberties for many groups, not least the ethnic minorities in Moscow, were curtailed, with some estimates claiming that upwards of 10,000 ethnic refugees from the Caucasus and Central Asia were arrested, beaten up and forcibly deported during the State of Emergency period. Dissident opponents of presidential rule were once again publicly denounced and often humiliated. Thousands of democratically elected councils throughout the Russian Federation were forcibly dissolved by decree and their powers passed to direct appointees of the President. And last, but not least, earlier concessions given to the republics as regards the nature of their status (and their accompanying autonomous decision-making powers) within the federal set-up were now simply withdrawn.[31]

As for the proposed elections to the two representative chambers of the brand-new Federal Assembly, the previous non-existence of any legal or logistical mechanisms for the actual holding of the elections now meant that the President himself could predominantly define the basic rules of the electoral contest, largely epitomized by his ability to appoint the members of the newly created Central Electoral Commission that was set up to oversee all aspects of the ballot. And as for the plans to introduce a brand-new Constitution, which would be able to underpin legally the basis of any new power structure, the President's ability now to change the rules concerning the calling of a referendum and the level of support needed for a referendum victory invested Yeltsin with very significant powers indeed. In effect, the new Constitution could now be passed by as little as 25 per cent of the eligible voting population.

Commenting on the nature of the all-encompassing powers invested in President Yeltsin after his September dissolution of parliament (and also lambasting the vast majority of the intelligentsia, who to all intents and purposes failed to defend many of the previous fruits of democracy that had been gained at such great cost), Andrei Sinyavskii highlighted an inevitable correlation between October 1993 and October 1917:

> I remember only too well how Russia lost the freedom that was declared in 1917, how newspapers which did not please the authorities were closed down, how censorship was introduced and opposition parties were suppressed, while the Russian intelligentsia, my beloved intelligentsia, gave its blessing to it all.
>
> Today the most terrible thing is happening. My old enemies have begun, occasionally, to speak the truth and my fellow Russian intellectuals have, instead of opposing Yeltsin and trying to correct the mistakes he and his team have made, welcomed the appointment of a strong leader and again call for strong measures to be taken. We have seen all this before. That was how Soviet rule began.[32]

Of the two events which were intended to signify the *formal* end to the period of absolute and arbitrary presidential control of the levers of state power – the elections to the new Federal Assembly and the desired ratification of the new Constitution, both of which took place on 12 December 1993 – it was certainly the latter that was always deemed far more important to the President and the apparatus around him – for reasons that are self-evident.

First, the new Constitution legitimized a huge imbalance of power between the Presidency (as head of the executive branch) and the new legislative branches. Under the terms of the new Basic Law, the President has the power to appoint the Prime Minister, the Chairman of the Central Bank, the Commanders in Chief of the armed forces and the top judges, including those belonging to the new-style Constitutional Court, the Supreme Court, the Highest Arbitration Court and the Prosecutor General. As for the appointment of the rest of the government, this is left to the Prime Minister, though the President's approval must be obtained. In the realm of policy, meanwhile, he is personally responsible for setting all the major guidelines of the domestic and foreign policy agenda. He can also issue decrees, edicts and directives at will; veto any legislation he does not agree with; and call referenda on his own authority. In contrast, the two chambers of the Federal Assembly – the Council of the Federation (the upper chamber) and the State Duma (the lower chamber) – are effectively reduced to 'rubber-stamping' institutions.[33]

It is not just in the domain of appointments and policy-making, however, that the President has an inbuilt advantage. Perhaps of more ultimate significance is the fact that the new Constitution provides the President with a series of rights that can allow him to dissolve the other branches of the power structure, if he so desires, with virtual impunity – something that even Yeltsin himself acknowledged 'might conceivably frighten some people'.[34] Included within this particular series of rights, for example, is the power automatically to dissolve the lower house if it rejects three presidential nominees for Prime Minister in succession. Alternatively, he can dissolve the Duma if it refuses a demand that it vote confidence in the government; or, if it initiates a vote of no confidence on its own, it can likewise be subject to dissolution at the President's own whim. A presidential sacking of the Prime Minister, meanwhile, can occur without any kind of consent whatsoever from the parliament.[35]

Above and beyond these measures, the President has a virtual prerogative in instituting a State of Emergency in any part of the Russian Federation; and he is almost totally beyond the realm of impeachment (other than for acts of treason, which would have to be determined by the Supreme Court, whose members are appointed by the President).

Given the nature of the new Constitution, therefore (which was ultimately adopted on the basis of a 58.4 per cent yes vote in a 54.8 per cent turnout), it is perhaps easy to appreciate why Vyacheslav Kostikov, President Yeltsin's press secretary, was so adamant that 'when all is said and done, the passing of the constitution is of primary importance. In comparison with this it is merely a secondary matter as to who gets elected into the Federal Assembly and who does not.'[36] Prophetic words indeed, especially bearing in mind the serious doubts that have since been raised as to whether the official figures were in fact accurate.[37]

Sentiments such as these also perhaps explain Yeltsin's own pre-election rebuff of all the political parties campaigning for the new parliament (even those most closely associated with his own stance). In a remarkable broadcast three days before the ballot, Yeltsin was not only keen once again to stress his credentials as the individual who shouldered the main responsibility for the country and should ultimately be seen as the main guarantor of its unity and well-being; he was also keen to 'rubbish in advance the verdict of the voters' in the parliamentary elections, drawing attention to the defects of all the candidates, their lack of experience and the way they were all hampered by their mutual recriminations and lust for ambition – an unusual case of 'electioneering in cynical reverse', as one newspaper editorial aptly described it.[38]

For the critics of President Yeltsin, of course, all of this was totally indicative of his long-standing authoritarian aspirations. In the view of Oleg Rumyantsev, the former Yeltsin-appointed Secretary of the Constitutional Commission, the sole purpose of the new Constitution is to 'legalise the authoritarian regime that has come to power and to preserve the vision of the state and society held by the radical liberals'. 'Boris Yeltsin', he went on, 'has lost his self-control. His personal ambition has been exposed.'[39] As for Valerii Zorkin, former Chief Justice of the Constitutional Court (who was sacked in the aftermath of the October 1993 uprising), the extent of powers granted to the President reminded him of the old Article 6 of the Soviet Constitution which granted a 'leading role' to the Communist Party: 'Then, at least, there was a whole party. Now there is just one man. . . . What should be a long-lasting document is simply being used to give the cover of legitimacy to the President's seizure of power by force.'[40]

Without doubt, then, the powers granted to the President in the new Constitution, *at the very least,* make the possibility of a Caesarist-type solution to the problems besetting the post-communist transformation process a permanent fixture on the political horizon. If a President, be it the present one or a future one, decides that it is somehow in the country's interests for him to adopt the Caesarist mantle, he now has an almost guaranteed prerogative to make that decision effective in practice. The very success of the new power arrangements, in other words, depends almost entirely on such nebulous factors as the President's own personal benevolence and personality.

Ultimately, of course, it is important to acknowledge, as Gramsci himself did in his writings, that no easy subjective or even moral judgement should be made concerning the imposition of a Caesarist solution. Not all examples of Caesarism possess the same kind of historical significance. That is to say, it is perfectly possible for there to be not only reactionary but also *progressive* forms of Caesarism. The former applies where the outcome is a series of changes that are merely quantitative rather than qualitative in nature; where there has been no fundamental passage from one type of state to another, but only evolution of the same type along unbroken lines. In contrast, a progressive form of Caesarism can be deemed to have existed in conditions where societies have been forced to advance in an epoch-making way; where innovations have been so numerous and of such a nature that they have represented a complete revolution, and where in effect the historical passage from one type of state to another has been the main result.

From the Gramscian perspective, therefore, the exact significance of each form of Caesarism can, in the last analysis, be reconstructed only through concrete history, and not by means of any sociological rule of thumb. To this extent, the ultimate and definitive verdict on Boris Yeltsin must, for the time being, be postponed. That Yeltsin himself would like history to view his Caesarist actions in a progressive light is not surprising. Asked to comment, in the middle of the December 1993 election campaign, on how he himself would describe the latest three-month period of rule by presidential decree, he replied in no uncertain terms that it represented the defining moment 'of the inglorious end of Soviet power'.[41]

This is also how intellectual supporters of the current need for a Caesarist solution would legitimize their stance. Igor' Klyamkin, for example, has often written of the capacity of the 'strong hand' [*silnaya ruka*] ultimately to create the conditions for consent and harmony out of the chaos that inevitably accompanies a fundamental process of transition.[42] Andranik Migranyan, too, has always stressed that Caesarism must be used as a means of creating the premises necessary for the ultimate passage to a fundamental democracy in Russia, and has likewise stressed that the only viable option open to the country in its current phase of development is either a progressive or a reactionary form of Caesarism.[43]

For other analysts, on the other hand, the current objective conditions in Russian society today make the whole Caesarist-type solution too risky to contemplate. The theoretical niceties that differentiate a reactionary form of Caesarism from a progressive form would never be able to materialize, given those specific conditions. In other words, then, any imposition of a long-term Caesarist solution, no matter how progressive it starts out to be, would always be susceptible to floundering in the old structures and would always end up playing the game by precisely the old rules.[44] As one newspaper editorial graphically put it during the height of the October 1993 disturbances: 'It is hard to believe that good can come out of this. You do not build [any kind of] democracy upon the smoking ruins of an old parliament. You do not cement freedoms by closing down dissident newspapers or censoring television. You do not bind the wounds of a far-flung nation with blood-stained bandages. The graphic scenes of [Yeltsin's victory in Moscow] come swathed with foreboding.'[45]

The Military in Politics

The image staring out from the television screen is powerfully evocative. An old-style military parade is taking place in the heart of the city. At the dignitaries' podium, taking the salute, is a middle-aged man, short, well-built, with greying features and a short, well-trimmed moustache. 'President' is his formal, official title, though all those close to him still refer to him as 'General': the rank he held as a serving officer. A military parade; a military man at the helm in his bemedalled tunic; a military conflict in full swing. The place is Chechnya, in the heart of the Caucasus mountains, shortly before the invasion of Russian troops; the man is General Dzhokhar Dudaev. And the question on many people's lips: Is this just a foretaste of what Russia as a whole can expect? Is the only viable option open to the country a civilian Caesarist President or a military Napoleonic President?

In their much-discussed almanac on the future of Russia up to the year 2010, one of the future scenarios portrayed by Daniel Yergin and Thane Gustafson is indeed a military takeover.[46] Painting a scene in which mob rule is rife, social and economic turmoil is everywhere, regionalism is becoming outright separatism and an ineffectual government is forced to take refuge in the provinces following daily political battles in Moscow, the last saviour of the country is the fictitious Russian Defence Minister, General Ivan Nikolaev. An Afghan war hero with strong patriotic views and a striking contempt for *all* politicians, Nikolaev sets about restoring order throughout the country using the entrenched military administration at his disposal, and eventually goes on to proclaim himself 'President for life' in conjunction with a small advisory junta, collectively known as the 'Defenders of the Russian Nation'. Rule is by decree and administrative edict only; the judiciary and the legislature are curbed, and local government is effectively quashed. The economy is run on a war footing; detention without trial and summary execution of 'traitors', 'enemies' and mafia-type criminals becomes an everyday experience, and the media report only what they are told to report by the army general placed at its head.

Given the label the 'Russian Bear' scenario by the authors, the new dictatorship is also portrayed as anti-Western and expansionist in nature, at least *vis-à-vis* the territory of the 'near abroad'. Ethnic Russian interests outside the Federation are now openly protected, and regions like the Crimea and the northern and western parts of Kazakhstan are eventually annexed to create a new Greater Slav Russian entity.

The fact that such a scenario seems so *plausible*, of course, is in large part due to the longevity of the crisis of instability and lack of any real sense of authority at the centre of the Russian political process. As Samuel Huntington made clear in his pioneering studies of military intervention in politics, if an effective political vacuum appears in a country that is also engaging in a fundamental transition or modernization process, then the tendency for the military to become increasingly politicized is very much strengthened.[47] The situation is also not helped by the fact that in present-day Russia there is a serious lack of any genuine democratic control mechanisms over the army.[48]

Similarly, the plausibility is also due in no small measure to the actual changing role of the Russian/Soviet military in recent years. After decades (if not centuries) of the military rarely, if ever, involving itself directly in politics,[49] it has recently been forced to play the most pivotal political role possible on two separate occasions in August 1991 and in October 1993; and in both cases it ended up being the ultimate '*arbiter* of the fate of one group of politicians as against another'.[50] And as if this wasn't enough, the degree of plausibility is also helped by the prominence of those individuals and commentators who are more and more convinced of its seeming inevitability. As Mikhail Gorbachev, for example, gloomily warned in late October 1994: 'The country is objectively being pushed into the abyss of a military-political coup, in a protracted spell of social vegetation and putrefaction.'[51]

Credible as the above scenario seems, however, one must nevertheless avoid being deceived by oversimplistic or superficial appearances. One thing that should certainly never be forgotten is that in both these cases of intervention the military itself, as an institution and organization, was bitterly divided by the specific role it was asked to perform. In August 1991 the presence of Defence Minister Marshal Dimitrii Yazov in the State Emergency Committee was blatantly insufficient to secure the loyalty of the vast majority of the armed forces, even in Moscow itself, let alone in other parts of the Russian Federation or the rest of the Soviet Union. The same can also be said of the other members of the Committee, who, with one exception (Vasilii Starodubtsev), had all previously enjoyed direct links with the armed forces or other sections of the military or security apparatus.[52]

In the very different circumstances of October 1993, meanwhile, fears over divisions in the ranks of the army led the Defence Minister, Pavel Grachev, initially to deny President Yeltsin the full backing of the army in his conflict with the Supreme Soviet. And although Grachev's hesitancy was eventually overcome following a direct order from the President (and Commander in Chief), it was nevertheless clear that even then not all elements of the army were prepared to enact the orders from their superiors. According to some reports, many members of the Defence Ministry Collegium were still reluctant to use force; several senior generals refused or hesitated to bring their troops into the centre of Moscow;[53] others actually went over to the ranks of the parliamentary forces, which already included prominent military figures;[54] indeed, according to Yeltsin's own version of events, despite all the last-minute assurances of loyalty from the High Command, there was so much mistrust of the army that ultimately the only really reliable forces were those from the Interior Ministry (MVD).[55]

Thus, 'kingmaker' it may well have been, but in the process of playing that role, few can doubt that the army significantly worsened the condition of its own internal cleavages – something to which the Chechen crisis in late 1994 also clearly attested. On the battlefield itself, for example, at least two senior military figures (General Ivan Babichev, commander of the western group of Russian forces in Chechnya, and Colonel General Eduard Vorobev, the first deputy commander of ground forces) refused point-blank to obey orders from the High Command. And again it was very noticeable that internal security troops ultimately proved far more reliable than regular army forces. Within the top echelons of the military establishment, meanwhile, serious divisions publicly emerged not only over the general handling of the conflict, but also over the very principle of military intervention in the first place.[56]

Given that these internal divisions are still very much apparent, this must clearly place severe limitations on the military's overall capacity to act as the last 'binding' force in a fractious, deconstructing society. Indeed, if anything, the nature of the stratification that has emerged inside the lower ranks of the army is an accurate mirror-image of the broader Russian social realm. As the military sociologist Yurii Deryugin has argued, while one section of the officer corps faithfully abides by all the old 'conservative' traditions of service in the army and is genuinely committed to staying there for life, another section views the army today as nothing more than a short-term stepping stone into some other, financially more lucrative, form of career. For them the military opens up possibilities for gaining access to capital, which they can then use to set themselves up in business; indeed, more time is actually spent in commercial activities than in combat training exercises.[57]

Similarly, while some are content with an undemanding, routine *apparatchik*'s life, others are more desirous of using their position in the military hierarchy to acquire contacts in the ever-burgeoning criminal underworld or in other forms of crime and corruption. According to the latest available figures, more than 2,000 reported crimes were committed by military personnel in 1993, with a further 600 reported in the first quarter of 1994.[58] Moreover, by autumn 1994 allegations of corruption and criminal activity had reached the highest echelons of the military establishment, bringing about the dismissal of the first Deputy Defence Minister, General Matvei Burlakov, who had previously been the chief of the Russian armed forces in Germany (long known as the main centre of military commercial clans – *voenno-kommercheskogo klana*).[59] And this, of course, is merely the social basis of stratification currently affecting the army. When one adds to this the clear-cut ethnic and political cleavages (which will be dealt with below), not to mention the generational differences in outlook, then one can appreciate the obvious hurdles any aspiring military putschist would have to overcome in his own organization, even before facing the broader consequences of his actions.

In such an atmosphere, then, it is small wonder that reported levels of morale are at an all-time low. In 1992, no fewer than 35,000 officers under the age of thirty resigned their commissions; and in 1993 the total number of resignations was even higher. Draft avoidance into the army is rife, as is desertion, with no fewer than two-thirds of respondents in one military poll openly approving of such action, or at least claiming to be 'indifferent' to it.[60] And again, the television pictures of thousands of young, poorly trained and poorly equipped conscripts mercilessly killed in Chechnya is hardly designed to improve those levels of morale.

Of course, all this does not prove that the military does not possess certain well-defined common aims and ambitions. It clearly does, and in its highest echelons it strives, in good corporatist, lobbyist fashion, to influence the civilian authorities to implement such ambitions. Such aims range from the more narrowly conceived desire to resolve the housing problem for troops returning from abroad and campaigning for ever bigger increases in the overall military procurement budget, to much broader ambitions in the foreign policy domain with respect to issues concerning the 'near abroad' and NATO expansion into Eastern Europe. Nor does it prove that there are no prominent, charismatic individuals in the ranks of the military who are clearly *desirous* of playing the Napoleonic or Caesarist role of the country's 'saviour' – individuals who truly believe themselves to be a unique force for establishing order, discipline and unity throughout the country, and believe that there is a strong residual degree of pent-up anger and frustration in the army that can be channelled to 'good effect'.

If anyone, for example, fits the description of the 'Nikolaev' figure portrayed above by Yergin and Gustafson, it is currently Lieutenant-General Lebed', the 'pseudo-renegade' commander of the 14th army unit, which since the collapse of the USSR has successfully defended the interests of ethnic Russian *pieds-noirs* in the Trans-Dniester region of Moldova. An Afghan war hero who fervently mistrusts all politicians; a tireless devotee of military leaders such as Pinochet in Chile, who is convinced that the concept of democracy in Russia has been so abused as to make ordinary people 'vomit', Lebed' has undoubtedly become a significant rallying point for many of the most disgruntled sections of the officer corps.[61]

Nevertheless, while the threat from the 'Lebeds' and other potential 'Nikolaevs' in Russia's post-communist society is an ever-present phenomenon, one must still not be too hasty in viewing the military takeover scenario as in any sense inevitable. Specific regional factors, such as those in Trans-Dniester or Chechnya, may well make their appearance on the public stage that much more explicit and prominent, but the national stage is a different theatre altogether. Similarly, while the military is undeniably an important factor in the current hegemonic context, the underlying struggle that is taking place at the moment is still more traditionally 'civilian' in nature. If a military man does make it to the Kremlin, it is more than probable that it will be through electoral politics rather than anything more sinister.[62]

To conclude the contextual survey of this and the previous chapter: it is thus clear that the existence of a *quasi*-civil society; an economic realm subject to perpetual chaos, depression and criminalization; *proto*-political parties; a weak sense of nationhood and statehood; a populist President prone to Caesarist solutions and a more politicized military hardly amount in total to the most optimal context in which to observe a genuine

Gramscian-based struggle for hegemony. That said, some basic conditions for such a struggle, I would contend, do exist somewhere in the chaotic haze that currently envelops Russian social, economic and political life; and there is at least some recognition by *most* – though certainly not all – the combatants engaged in a struggle for power in Russia today that it is in their ultimate interest to play by the rules of modern, hegemonic politics rather than the pre-modern absolutist rules. Certainly the alternative if they do not play by the basics of the hegemonic rules will be a continued catastrophe for the vast majority of Russia's citizens – a catastrophe that might even surpass the gloomy predictions of Russia's famous nineteenth-century poet Lermontov, when he wrote:

> A year will come for Russia, a dark year
> When Royalty no more their crown will wear,
> The Rabble who loved them once will love forget,
> For Blood and Death will richest feast be set;
> The fallen law no more will shield the weak,
> And maid and guiltless child in vain will seek
> For justice. Plague will ride
> Where stinking corpses fill the countryside,
> And flapping rags from cottages demand
> Help none can give, while Famine rules the land.
> Dawn on thy streams will shed a crimson light;
> That day will be revealed the Man of Might
> Whom thou wilt know. And thou wilt understand.
> Wherefore a naked blade is in his hand.
> Bitter will be thy lot; tears flood thine eyes,
> And he will laugh at all thy tears and sighs.

PART II

The Hegemonic Combatants

Westerners

Variety is disappearing from the human race; the same ways of behaving, thinking, and feeling are found in every corner of the world. This is not only because nations are more in touch with each other and are able to copy each other more closely, but because the men of each country, more and more completely discarding the ideas and feelings peculiar to one caste, profession, or family, are all . . . the same getting closer to what is essential in man, and that is everywhere the same.

Alexis de Tocqueville, *Democracy in America*

Defining the Collective Will

A theme that has been prevalent in virtually every serious analysis of recent events in Russia has been the emphasis on the idea that for some time now (even prior to the August 1991 coup and the official demise of the Soviet Union) the country has been standing at a new crossroads [*rasput'e*] in its history.

The use of the crossroads leitmotiv is, needless to say, highly symbolic. It implies, first and foremost, a need for movement in one direction or another, accompanied by an all-pervading sense of choice. This, in turn, implies, as is made clear in the official dictionary of the Academy of Sciences' Institute of Russian Language, that there might invariably be a sense of doubt, or at the very least hesitation, attached to such a choice. And on top of this the leitmotiv also conjures up a sense of destination, perhaps even destiny itself; and this sense of destiny is clearly orientated in geographical terms. Hence the path that Russia chooses has a fixed geographical point in view.

This sense of geographical destiny has likewise always played an important role in the Russian tradition, and it is for this reason, therefore, that in discussing the first of the hegemonic combatants in Russia today, a geographical reference point – the West – has been preferred to any other form of identification – radical, liberal, capitalist, and so on.

Russian intellectual understanding of precisely what the 'West' embodies, of course, has never been historically consistent. As Walicki has argued, in the middle decades of the nineteenth century, the Westerners [*zapadniki*] were clearly divided between the democrats (with their emphasis on citizen rights and the de-monopolization and de-legitimization of absolute state power) and the liberals, who were much more exclusively orientated towards the desirability of fostering the emergence of a capitalist economic system in Russia.[1] Moreover, later in the century the Westerners were to be joined by the radical democrats and ultimately by the early Marxists as well. In this sense, then, the West in Russian intellectual circles has always tended to signify different things to different people at different times. Transcending all these differences, however, all Westerners did at least share a basic conviction that Russia lagged far behind the standard form of Western civilization, and would therefore have to assimilate many aspects of the Western legacy if it was ever going to achieve a thoroughgoing modernization. The West, in other words, clearly personified (in all its different ways) *progress* and *development*, and was the one means of genuinely overcoming the more reactionary elements of Russia's past.

Here, then, in essence, is the heart of the Westerners' collective will – that common mode of understanding which for Gramsci was the essential prerequisite to the attainment of a cultural–social unity through which a multiplicity of heterogeneous aims could be welded together.

Russia, it is argued, has always essentially missed the mainstream of progressive civilization precisely because of its stubborn refusal to follow the Western cultural path. Rather than forlornly continuing to hope that a special Russian road might produce a better civilization than that of the West, it should simply be accepted that this road is in effect a constant 'dead end'; a cul-de-sac beyond which further progress is simply impossible. More significantly perhaps, the modern Westerners are also adamant that for all its roots in nineteenth-century Western modernity, communism as applied in Russia was simply another 'mistaken' attempt to traverse some unique Russian road to civilization. Now that that failure has finally been unmasked as well, the Western path must at last be accepted – not simply with reluctance, but with great enthusiasm; yet another attempt at a uniquely Russian approach would simply doom the country to backward oblivion in perpetuity.[2]

Before we can put some more detailed flesh on the skeletal bones of this collective will, it is important to bear in mind that the emergence of any new collective will out of the ruins of the former communist style of domination would inevitably have had a formative period of gestation. It is this period of gestation, then, that must concern us first.

Writing many years ago, the distinguished anthropologist Arnold van Gennep constructed a threefold schema of rites which analysed the process whereby individuals and groups experience a fundamental type of social (or other) transformation.[3] The first stage in this process of transformation is what van Gennep called 'separation', whereby an individual slowly begins to shed the traditional forms of identities which had previously formed his social make-up. This then takes the individual into a transitional phase where he has lost the orientations of the immediate past, but is not yet certain of his future social orientations; an in-between phase categorized by van Gennep as 'liminality'. Finally, the process of transformation is completed when a new social identity and role is acquired through a definitive process of aggregation or 'incorporation' of the values and symbols corresponding to one's new status.

While acknowledging the very different context of van Gennep's analysis, I think one can (admittedly with some degree of reinvention) perceive this threefold schema of transformation at work in the evolutionary process of the collective will of the contemporary Westerners in post-communist Russia. According to Vladimir Shlapentokh and Boris Kagarlitsky, two writers who have both made the study of intellectual development in Russia and the former Soviet Union their area of experise, the Gorbachev era and the subsequent emergence of a post-communist, pro-Westernization set of values and principles can likewise be divided into three distinct phases.[4]

In the first phase of evolution, roughly corresponding to the period 1985 to 1988 (though neither Shlapentokh nor Kagarlitsky would set these time periods in stone), one witnesses the emergence of a number of clear trends within the reformist movement. Firstly there is the rediscovery of what both writers would term 'liberal-socialist' or 'liberal-communist' ideas, dating back to the early to mid 1960s. These ideas included such things as a recognition of the positive virtues attached to a planned form of economy, rational principles of government, collectivism and equality. But there was also a basic recognition of the need to restore some semblance of autonomy and sovereignty to the individual; to modernize the official ideology and make it more amenable, if not accountable, to the requirements of a genuinely ascertainable public opinion; to create some semblance of a pluralist input into the mechanisms of government; and, most important of all, to liberalize the operational mechanisms of the planned economy by fostering such things as greater enterprise autonomy, and looking once again at the role of prices and material incentives.[5]

A second trend that emerged in this period, in conjunction with a return to liberal-socialist ideas, was a concerted effort formally to deconstruct any remaining vestiges of Stalinism in the system (symbolized at its best by films like Abuladze's *Repentance* and books such as Rybakov's *Children of the Arbat*).

Finally, a third major trend in this period has been characterized by Shlapentokh as the clear emergence of a 'closed strategy' by the reform intellectuals aimed at constructively supporting, rather than openly pressurizing, the Soviet political elite around Gorbachev; perhaps the best example here being the collection of articles published in the summer of 1988, entitled *Inogo ne dano* (There is No Alternative).[6]

In outlining the three main trends of this period, I do not intend to say by any means that there were no dissenters in the liberal camp who were clearly more predisposed right from the very outset to a process of Westernization which did not make allusions to liberal-socialist values, but was firmly supportive of an outright and immediate transition to Western-style liberalism and capitalism. One thinks, for example, of Larisa Popkova's article in *Novyi mir* in 1987, 'Where are the Pies of Plenty?', in which she accuses her liberal-socialist intellectual colleagues of engaging in half-truths;[7] or Nikolai Amosov's article in *Literaturnaya gazeta* in 1988 in which the values of individualism, egotism, inequality ('a strong stimulator for progress') and private ownership are all lauded over the old socialist allegiance to collectivism and egalitarianism;[8] or Vasilii Selyunin's powerful critique of Leninism and his strong espousal of Western-style capitalism in his May 1988 article in *Novyi mir*.[9]

Radical as articles like these were in their nonconformism to any kind of socialist allegiance (liberal or otherwise), it nevertheless has to be emphasized that during this first period of gestation of the collective will, such paeans to a capitalist-type Westernization represented far more the exception to the rule than an embodiment of the rule itself. Almost every time such an article appeared, a vociferous attempt was made to rebut the more radical elements of the ideas that were being espoused, as in some way 'premature', 'dangerous' or 'inappropriate' at that particular moment. In this manner, therefore, the dominance of liberal-socialist ideas among the reformers, combined with the closed strategy *vis-à-vis* the Gorbachev leadership and the limited nature of ideological deconstruction, was at least maintained until the latter stages of 1988.

In the second period of gestation, however, a fundamental transition away from liberal-socialist ideas towards the prevalence of *liberal-capitalist* ideas was very marked. Likewise, throughout this period, which lasted from early 1989 to the August 1991 coup attempt, there was also a much clearer indication of a far more concerted 'open' strategy of explicitly pressurizing the incumbent political leadership, as well as a far more thoroughgoing attempt to disaggregate the *entire* socialist and Marxist–Leninist ideological heritage of the Soviet system.

In his own, much broader analysis of Soviet intellectual development,

Vladimir Shlapentokh raises the important point that back in the days of
the first thaw of the 1960s, Westerners of the neo-liberal, capitalist variety
were not only few in number, but also much more readily succumbed to the
idea that their potential at that time was intrinsically very limited. During
these years there was an accepted, tacit consensus that Russia would not be
able to find its way back to a traditional form of capitalist development
(based on private property, etc.). It was precisely this consensus, it is suggested, that therefore gave extra impetus to the necessity to develop
liberal-socialist ideas, and what in effect amounted to an attempt to find
that ever-elusive Third Way. 'In the 1960s', writes Shlapentokh, 'the liberals, with their strong belief in the might of the Soviet state, clearly lacked
the imagination to envision a time when the General Secretary would
[himself] become the champion [of a very radical reform programme].'[10] It
was certainly this distinction, perhaps more than any other, that made the
transition from liberal-socialism to liberal-capitalism at all feasible in the
late 1980s and early 1990s.

A good illustration of the depth of the transition at this time can be
found in another leading collection of reformist articles, this time published in 1989 and intended as a follow-up to the *Inogo ne dano* collection.[11]
Entitled *Postizhenie* (Understanding), this new collection brought together
thirty-two intellectuals from a range of political, philosophical, economic
and sociological domains. Certainly the most striking thing about this
particular collection of reformist attitudes when it appeared was the way in
which the fundamental attributes of a free-market, capitalist economic
system had now been accepted. Consequently, the only remaining thing
left to debate, it appeared, was the extent to which the future orientation of
Soviet capitalism should be social democratic or liberal in nature.

Leading the liberal, openly Friedmanite camp was once again Larisa
Piyasheva (using her own name this time, rather than the Popkova cover).
In a fifteen-page essay Piyasheva once again refused to soft-pedal the lav-
ish praise she gave to the intrinsic benefits of private rather than public
ownership, and to the advantages of an individualist rather than a collectivist outlook. Moreover, Piyasheva now felt bold enough to push back the
frontiers of the entrenched defence mechanisms of the old order by sav-
aging those remnants of what she termed the system of compulsory
benevolence, and in the process particularly turned her attention towards
the need to create a 'self-supporting' Soviet citizenry *vis-à-vis* the provision
of education, health care, and all other forms of welfare;[12] what in the liberal West, of course, would be called 'commercialization', though as yet
this term had not definitively entered the lexicon of pro-Western
terminology.

Perhaps the other striking thing about the *Postizhenie* collection was the
extent to which a deep-seated anti-working-class bias had now also

emerged in the reformist camp. In contributions by Viktor Sheinis and Tatyana Zaslavskaya, for example, Soviet workers came across as over-pampered, backward, and the main social obstacle to economic regeneration; something which could now be achieved, they both contended, only by grasping the bull of labour rationalization (i.e. unemployment) firmly by the horns.[13]

The real significance of the kind of ideas given such prominence here was ultimately seen in summer 1990 with the emergence of the so-called 500 Days Economic Reform Programme. What this reform programme demonstrated more than anything else was that intellectual ideas that had arguably been on the fringes of the Soviet power elite had now entered the heart of the political establishment. Accompanying this intellectual transition towards a liberal-capitalist dominance, and indeed providing it with vast amounts of sustenance at the same time, was the ever-increasing de-legitimization of any remaining ideological vestiges associated, no matter how loosely, with the old order. The open attacks on Lenin, referred to above in the Selyunin article, now became ever more vociferous, as too did the attacks on all the fundamental principles of the entire socialist legacy.[14]

Moreover, marking this ever-deepening process of ideological de-legitimization and de-mythologization was the emergence of highly personalized recantations of the old ideological faith. One very prominent example of this *mea culpa* was Oleg Bogomolov's 1990 article in *Ogonek*, entitled 'I Cannot Absolve Myself from Guilt'; a clear retort to Nina Andreeva's infamous anti-*perestroika* piece of two years before in which she had announced that she herself could never forgo her principles. In a remarkable piece of expurgation, Bogomolov talks endlessly of the contemporary moral problem of repentance, atonement and purification that he, and others who had once belonged to the communist movement, must now perforce face up to. And concluding his article, he writes: 'It is time to stop swearing allegiance to the dogmas of the Marxist faith and to turn towards common sense, universal human experience and age-old moral precepts, which have never yet let people down.' Isn't this, after all, he asks rhetorically, the key to salvation and the only way out of our impasse?[15]

By the end of this second, transitional or liminal period of gestation, then, the Westerners of a more neo-liberal, capitalist hue were beginning to strike deep roots in all areas of Soviet social, political and economic life. As Shlapentokh has rightly emphasized, the whole cultural-ideological atmosphere of the country had been radically altered by fewer than one hundred committed intellectuals.[16] With all these successes in mind, however, and despite the preconditions for a thoroughgoing degree of Westernization, there was still a sense in which, prior to the August 1991 coup, serious doubts remained about the attainability of such a strong pro-Western vision for Russia.

Only *after* the defeat of the coup, therefore, could the Westerners enter a new phase of development in which their collective will would have the chance to blossom into full flower, unhindered at least by external constraints. Westernization, in other words, could now be fervently pursued by a new generation of intellectuals, not tainted at all with sixties-style liberal-socialism or third-wayism. Moreover, a new type of organic intellectual could now emerge, who would also have direct access to some of the highest positions of authority and leadership – not only in the hoped-for new civil society, but also in the new structures of political society itself.

It was the emergence of the 'Gaidar team' in the winter of 1991, of course, that best symbolized the growing maturation of the Westerners' camp. Gaidar himself, who eventually went on to become acting Prime Minister for most of 1992, had previously worked as Director of the Institute for Economic Policy in Moscow before his transfer to the heart of the new burgeoning political elite. Alongside him were a whole host of other young professionals who likewise, for the most part, had succeeded in transforming their careers from positions of intellectual authority to positions of outright political authority. Known collectively as the 'Young Turks' the group primarily consisted of Gennadii Burbulis, Sergei Shakhrai, Andrei Kozyrev, Aleksandr Shokin, Nikolai Fedorov, Evgenii Saburov, Mikhail Poltoranin, Anatolii Chubais, Andrei Nechaev, Vladimir Lopukhin, Aleksei Golovkov and Konstantin Kagalovskii.[17] As for the older breed of intellectuals who had so decisively paved the way for the new radical Westerners, many of them now either left the public domain entirely or were given background positions of influence in such institutions as Yeltsin's new Presidential Consultative Council;[18] a public show of gratitude, in other words, to those who had played a prominent part in the period of transition, but at the same time a clear recognition that something fundamentally new was about to be embarked upon.[19]

So it was under the formal leadership of the Gaidar team of key political and intellectual figures that the collective will of the Westerners was now able to develop a much more consistent and cohesive framework. As for the fundamental task facing them at this point in their development, this was perhaps best summed up by Gavriil Popov:

> . . . the most important thing [now] is to work out a minimum programme which would unite the main constructive forces in our society. Not to split, but to unite! You see – I will give you a simple example – we can argue about how many two-room or one-room flats there will be in a building and where the internal walls are going to be put, and so forth, but we all agree that we must build the walls and the roof of the building and the water supply facilities and

the roads near it, etc. So let us now stick to this group of issues, on which we don't have any disagreements. If we manage to get this short-term programme formulated and unite the forces which will back it up, then I think we shall fulfil the task now confronting Russia.[20]

Without doubt, the dominant theme that lies at the core of the Westerners' hegemonic strategy is the emphasis on individualism (that quintessential 'Western Idea', as Aleksandr Herzen once called it); or, more strictly speaking, an emphasis on the notion of *possessive* individualism. Individual initiative and individual advancement through the encouragement of 'natural' acquisitive and accumulative instincts is now seen as the primary form of human motivation, and its pursuance should be firmly rewarded with 'well-earned privileges' as distinct from the old privileges earned through nothing more than nepotism and subservience. Old-style collectivist values, meanwhile, must be deconstructed as a primary means of weaning individuals away from the former 'culture of dependency' and thus providing them with the freedom and space to pursue their individual aspirations in this new 'society of opportunity'.[21] Moreover, the fact that this will also engender a process of de-solidarization within entrenched social groups is also seen as a very positive outcome, both in terms of disaggregating potential opposition forces and in further encouraging a popular belief in the virtue of self-reliance.[22]

In a similar vein, the old collectivist 'illusion' of egalitarianism should be unmasked 'for the perversity that it is', and in its place a 'rationalized' form of inequality, aimed at broadening the scope of meritocratic productive privilege, should be encouraged. Distribution, in other words, must make a fundamental shift away from the old beneficent principle of providing 'a little to everyone'.[23] Indeed, it is only through this process of creating a highly stratified, indelibly consumer-orientated society that one can hope to replace the old stagnant economic system with a brand-new 'dynamic' one.

The cash nexus and private ownership, of course, are the ultimate rewards and the ultimate driving forces of the newly engendered acquisitive instincts. As regards the first of these, no group is perhaps doing more to foster the centrality of the cash nexus as the fundamental basis of social relations in the new post-communist Russia than the burgeoning ranks of the advertising sector. As one commentator has rather astutely commented, it is today's 'ad-men' in Russia who have taken on the traditional Leninist mantle of 'collective mobilizer' for those in the vanguard of forging a Western-style consumer culture.[24] Likewise, the cash nexus is also to form the basis from which the once rigid understanding of moral norms in Soviet and Russian society can now be broadened and liberalized; echoing the (in)famous assertion of Nikolai Shmelev back in 1987 that everything is moral which is economically efficient. Former 'illicit' pleasures, in other words, must now become accessible to those with the cash available to enjoy them as a means of providing further stimuli and incentives for economic advancement.[25]

As for private ownership, the principles behind the Westerners' drive here are very clear-cut. First and foremost, considerable emphasis is laid on the accepted Western understanding of private property as a natural and inalienable human right; something tacitly acknowledged in Russia since 1989. This has also invariably been accompanied, particularly after August 1991, by a much more concerted effort to associate this human right in ever more forceful terms as an essential precondition for individual freedom.

A second key legitimatory aspect of the new outlook on private property has been the emphasis on its potential for serving the cause of redistributive justice – the transference of property rights from supposedly undeserving to deserving social groups. This principle, for example, played a prominent role in a conference on de-statization and privatization held in the Kremlin in June 1991.[26] And once again, in the aftermath of the failed August coup, and especially in the light of the introduction of so-called 'voucher privatization', this notion of redistributive justice has been further extended to incorporate the idea that the whole Russian population are now being given back that which was rightfully 'theirs'.

Not surprisingly, the link between private property and the motivational requirements of a fully operative market system is now a well-established aspect of the Westerners' lexicon; as too is the correlation between private property and economic efficiency. Indeed, according to the well-known eye surgeon and entrepreneur Svyatoslav Fedorov, these two factors are also perfect illustrations of how the old communist notion of exploitation can be turned to capitalism's advantage. Speaking in his capacity as a member of Yeltsin's Consultative Council, he once remarked that whereas state ownership was now popularly associated in Russia with the exploitation of the hired worker, the fundamental benefit of capitalism was its capacity to bring the individual 'closer to his lathe and closer to the profit that he creates'.[27] Another aspect of the Westerners' justification of the benefits to be gained from the transition back to private ownership has been couched in specifically cultural terms. Writing in *Rossiiskie vesti* in April 1993, for example, President Yeltsin was keen to recall that at the turn of the last century, it was precisely the existence of a new class of private property owners that engendered what he called, 'that huge upsurge in Russian culture [at that time]'.[28] And last, but not least, much emphasis is also laid on the fact that the emergence of private ownership can also have the very great political advantage of representing the ultimate personification and guarantee of the death of the old order.

Another positive factor, often associated with the emergence of private ownership, is the way in which it can also help to create a 'responsible society', thus giving people a legitimate stake in the perpetuation of stability and providing a means by which state and civil society can best coexist, the one buttressing the other. And, of course, when the notion of civil society is used in this kind of context, it has invariably lost most of its fundamental political connotations and is seen instead as an exclusively economic category, virtually synonymous with the operational mechanisms of a market society, in which citizens are defined merely by their economic interests. In this way as well, a process is engendered whereby, as in the contemporary West, the attribute of democracy itself begins to assume greater economic, rather than strictly political significance. A civil society *qua* capitalist market society is seen as the absolute *sine qua non* for a system to be worthy of the 'democratic' label. Indeed, to borrow Marxist terminology, one can say that in such a situation, democracy has successfully become structurally bereft of the entire superstructural realm. Nor is this all. In this way as well, the *future* ambitions and dreams of the Westerners become very clear. Just as in the West they ultimately aspire to a condition in which politics as a whole can successfully be *de-politicized*; where citizen, for example, can effectively be reduced to consumer, and participation becomes nothing much more than consumption.

Another key aspect of the emerging collective will is the adherence to the idea of a *Rechtsstaat*: a law-based state which guarantees the rights of the individual and which, above all else, is a guarantee of the enforcement of contracts made in an advanced, civilized society.[29] As the writer Boris Vasil'ev made clear in an article in *Nedelya* in March 1992: 'the recent triumph of democracy in Russia is only an apparent victory. . . . [A definitive] victory will be achieved not when democrats or politicians from a variety of parties hold power, but when a structure has been created to support that power' – a structure, implied Vasil'ev, that must have a law-based state as its pivotal element, which can truly protect the incontrovertible interests of the individual both from other individuals or groups seeking wrongfully to encroach on those interests, and from future arbitrary rule imposed by the state.[30]

A final key aspect of the Westerners' collective will that certainly deserves mention is their desire (at least after December 1991) to gain international recognition for the new post-communist Russia as a traditional, modern European-style nation that has given up its imperialist heritage; something their nineteenth-century ancestors never sought to do.

As with all their principles, there is a strong sense of pragmatism to this aspect of the Westerners' value system. They are fully aware that if their project for the post-communist transformation of Russia is ever going to succeed, then it cannot do so in (splendid) isolation. By implication, they both openly recognize and openly desire the need for a fundamental degree of Western (financial) support, and they also recognize that one of the preconditions for this Western support must be their own acceptance of the disintegration of the former, force-induced Soviet geopolitical realm. This, in turn, demands that Russia must begin the process of defining a new role for itself in the international community on the basis of having established a brand-new form of statehood and identity. Grigorii Pomerants, a prominent cultural theorist and publicist within the ranks of the Westerners, has defined the task as follows. What is required is a clear-cut recognition that what we have recently witnessed is 'not the disintegration of the former Great Russia, but the emergence of a *new* Russian state'. In this way, he goes on, Russia can at last find a new image for itself and a new role to play 'in the future development of mankind'.[31]

One important consequence of this basic orientation of the Westerners has been their natural instinct, since the demise of the USSR, to favour a *re*active rather than a *pro*active stance in terms of Russia's relations with the other former republics of the Union (the so-called 'near abroad'), largely out of fear of bringing forth any accusations that Russia might indeed secretly continue to harbour 'imperial ambitions' in the region.[32] Similarly, there has been a concerted effort both to reassess and redefine the notion of *patriotism* in today's Russia. According to Arkadii Popov, for example (citing Leo Tolstoy), the old Russian nostalgia for the empire represented nothing more than a chaotic and totally destructive form of irrational patriotism that was the last refuge of political rogues. Deciphering the eruditions of such intellectual constructions as 'the spiritual-semantic peculiarities of Russian ethnicity'; 'the historical programme of the Russians'; and 'the gathering in of Russian lands', Popov likens them to speeches about mushrooms and strawberries rather than real, living people, most of whom, in the process of being 'gathered up' in the cause of Russian patriotism, were subsequently wiped out.[33]

For Marina Pavlova-Sil'vanskaya, meanwhile, patriotism today must not envisage territorial expansion but, rather, must concentrate on properly utilizing existing resources within the current confines of the Russian state.[34] In a similar vein, other Westerners have drawn attention to the advantages of a much smaller, non-imperialistic or expansionist Russia, arguing that the country's energies will be less wasted in having to sustain support in areas where Russia is not welcome, leaving it free to concentrate exclusively on genuinely trying to improve its own population's living standards. And this, in turn, is the route to finally establishing a much more coherent and modernized form of Russian nationhood; something that has never really existed in Russia, writes Boris Vasil'ev, simply because in the past no Russian was even conscious of where the borders of the state commenced and where they finished.[35]

Before moving on to look at the social base of the Westerners, attention, finally, should be drawn to two other crucial leitmotivs of their collective will, both of which emerged in the latter part of the Gorbachev era, and both of which underpin their whole hegemonic campaign. These two leitmotivs are, first, the conviction that everything the Westerners stand for represents an embodiment of tried and tested *universal values*, as distinct from the former, ethical relativism of Soviet Marxist dogma based on the prognosis of class.[36] And secondly, the struggle to attain hegemony for these universal values is akin to creating a *normal society*, as distinct from the abnormal, artificial society of the Soviet era.[37]

Certainly, the adoption of these two notions and their constant adumbration in connection with everything the Westerners are striving to create cannot help but be powerful and attractive magnets pulling people towards a Gramscian-type *common-sense* appreciation of the Westerners' project. As such, therefore, one must surely give credit where credit is due, and praise the tactical acumen of the Westerners here.

The Social Base of the Historical Bloc

For the Westerners in post-Soviet Russia, economic policy has essentially been underpinned by an allegiance to a 'shock therapy' form of transition which has had as its ultimate defining goal 'the rapid creation of a flexible and efficient market economy'. Following the dictates of such institutions as the International Monetary Fund and the World Bank (and a host of specialist research institutes from Harvard to the MIT and LSE), three broad tasks have been outlined as crucial to the achievement of such a market-orientated system.

The first task has been the 'liberalization' of the economy in such areas as commodity markets, currency regulation and foreign trade. Of primary importance here has been the lifting of centralized controls over the prices of most (though not yet all) goods and services,[38] as well as the cancellation of former restrictions on the growth of incomes in production sectors and in relation to commercial and brokerage activities. This has led to the burgeoning of a consumer market (especially in terms of private retail trade), and has also introduced new market mechanisms into the technical and industrial production process.

The second major task has been financial stabilization, with a specific emphasis on reducing the inherited state budget deficit; eliminating the huge monetary overhang of 'useless money'; restricting state credits to enterprises, and trying to stabilize the exchange rate of the rouble. Various measures have been proposed (and subsequently implemented) with these aims in mind, including drastic changes to the tax system; the imposition

of high export duties; and a reduction in military spending, state investments and social welfare programmes.

Third, and finally, the Westerners have also emphasized the need for
thoroughgoing institutional changes aimed at developing a genuine market
infrastructure. Above all, of course, this has brought about the need for a
wholesale privatization of state-owned property and resources. As several
commentators have pointed out, the phenomenon of privatization can
take a varied number of forms, and be understood in a plethora of ways.
The most common understanding of the term refers to the sale of state
property to private operators. Apart from this, however, it can also encom-
pass leasing arrangements, the transformation of state enterprises into
joint-stock companies, the creation of capital market institutions such as
stock markets and commodity exchanges, as well as the general transfer of
socioeconomic processes from the sphere of the state into the realm of civil
society.[39]

Since the early months of 1992 three major variants have been on offer
for those state enterprises slated to be part of the privatization process.
Each variant stipulates a different proportion of shares available to the
existing workforce and management of an enterprise (at no cost, a reduced
cost or the full selling price), as well as outlining the proportion of shares
that can be sold at public auction.[40] Perhaps more significantly, since the
autumn of 1992 every one of the 148 million residents of the Russian
Federation has been granted their own personal 'ticket to enter the market
economy' through the acquisition of a 10,000 rouble voucher (approximately 40 dollars in 1992 prices) for use in the privatization process.[41]

Notwithstanding the *populist* appeal of the voucher scheme, it is perfectly clear from even this very cursory account of their socioeconomic
ambitions just who was slated to be the main beneficiary and the main
social bedrock of the Westerners' cause. Speaking to the assembled parliamentarians at the sixth Russian Congress of People's Deputies in April
1992, President Yeltsin stressed in no uncertain terms that the only social
force that was capable of extricating the country from its crisis were the
new 'entrepreneurs'; hence the government was determined to give this
social stratum all the support and benefits it could offer.[42]

Nor was this kind of appeal to the new entrepreneurs an isolated, or a
new phenomenon. After all, in the immediate aftermath of the failed
August 1991 coup several newspapers regularly singled out the burgeoning
entrepreneurial elite, and the new business community in general, for
exclusive praise for its support of Yeltsin at that particular time; a form of
support, it was made clear, that included a significant contribution of
finances and organizational resources, as well as an emphasis on the fact
that hundreds of businessmen were there in the front lines of the barricades
physically defending the Russian parliament.[43] Moreover, although the

adopted privatization process did include significant preferential treatment for the old Soviet working-class employees of the enterprises, thereby perhaps mitigating the opportunities for a new entrepreneurial elite to accumulate vast amounts of state property on its own preferred terms, it was often implied, by the likes of Gavriil Popov (among others), that this was nothing more than a grudging acceptance that conditions were *not yet* ripe to ride roughshod over such entrenched interests at the behest of the entrepreneurs.[44]

Identifying 'the entrepreneurs' as the main social pillar of the Westerners is one thing. What this, in turn, raises, however, is a more pertinent set of questions, which demand some kind of response. Who, for example, are the new entrepreneurs? From which stratum in the old Soviet social structure are they emanating? Who else, apart from the entrepreneurs, firmly supports the Westerners and identifies their long-term interests and aspirations with their professed collective will? How solid is their social *institutional* basis in the developing civil society? And perhaps underpinning all of these questions is the following: Who, in short, will form the nucleus of the new Russian bourgeois class?

Looking first at the actual *size* of the new private sector, it has been calculated that at the beginning of the reform process in January 1992, 80,000 so-called 'new economic structures' were already in existence. Included within these figures were approximately 9,000 joint-stock companies, 3,000 associations, 200 concerns and more than 100 consortia. There were also 1,300 commercial banks, approximately 100 stock exchanges and some 50,000 private farms, all of which accounted for about 4 per cent of Russia's total capital stock and 14 per cent of the country's total output.[45]

By the middle of 1994 and the designated end of the voucher phase of privatization, a total of 106,000 enterprises had been successfully taken out of state control. Industry accounted for 28 per cent of these new forms of businesses; construction 11 per cent; transport and communications 5 per cent; and shops, catering and services 45 per cent.[46] Altogether this new non-state sector was now responsible for 62 per cent of the country's GDP.[47] In terms of the number of *employees* earning a living within the newly privatized sector, figures here tend to vary according to the type of categorization used. In some accounts, only figures for fully private enterprises are cited, whereas in others the much broader term 'non-state sector' is often used. Even the most conservative estimates, however, would suggest that by the end of 1994 no less than four-fifths of Russia's manufacturing workforce was employed in the privatized sector, and a total of 55 million people were officially registered as shareholders.[48]

Irrespective of which classification is used, of course, there is certainly no automatic assumption that employees who find themselves located in the new private sector can be labelled definitive advocates of the

Westerners' hegemonic struggle. Some evidence certainly does exist to suggest that these employees *might* have a material stake in supporting the Westerners' blueprint for Russia, because they enjoy higher salaries and better standards of working conditions. What evidence exists, however, is often scanty and contradictory, with some surveys occasionally finding better material forms of remuneration in a related state sector enterprise. Thus, until more data become available, one should perhaps reserve judgement on the extent to which private and non-state sector employees – for *material* reasons, at least – are as firmly behind the Westerners' hegemonic campaign as their employers.

Looking more closely at the nature and make-up of the burgeoning entrepreneurial class itself, one quickly realizes that this term can cover an enormously diverse range of activities and personnel in today's Russia.

On the positive side, a genuinely *new* social breed of business entrepreneur is slowly beginning to emerge – people with no real social or political connection with the old order, who clearly do have aspirations to operate in a civilized, competitive business environment and, just as importantly, do have aspirations to engage in the production of commodities that can genuinely benefit the national wealth of the country. Liberal newspapers, journals and television programmes on 'New Names in Business' now frequently highlight the careers of prominent businesspeople who fall under this category, in the clear hope of fostering a role-model image.[49]

One of the most common attributes of these positive role models is invariably their origins in the co-operative sector in the middle period of the Gorbachev era. In a detailed study of the co-operative movement up to the point shortly before the collapse of the old order, Anthony Jones and William Moskoff profiled the typical or average co-operative entrepreneur: overwhelmingly male, young (if an employee), middle-aged (35–50) if a head of a co-operative, and well educated, with most having been through higher education or a specialized secondary education. The vast majority, it was argued, had also held responsible positions in the state sector before joining the co-operative movement, often having been enterprise directors, heads of shops or departments, or engineers and technicians; very few, on the other hand, had been blue-collar workers.[50]

As for the reasons why they joined or initiated a new co-operative venture, Jones and Moskoff, citing a 1990 survey of 586 co-operators, reported that the desire to gain a higher income was far less important than the possibility of realizing an individual's creative potential, entrepreneurship and talents; and was also less important than the perceived need to break away from the existing administrative-bureaucratic yoke.[51] Similar findings have also been found by Igor' Bunin, who for several years has been the head of a sociological project investigating new Russian business entrepreneurship.[52]

While there is no denying the accuracy of such findings, there can nevertheless be no doubt that such profiling often gives, at the very least, a somewhat distorted overall image of the new Russian 'entrepreneur'. Above all, the findings considerably overlook the more *negative* features of this new entrepreneurial figure. One distortion, for example, is the clear undervaluing of the heavy involvement of the Communist Party in the co-operative movement. And certainly, if Michael Burawoy's research studies are anything to go by, there can be little doubt that former party functionaries represented, and continue to represent, perhaps the most crucial component of all of today's entrepreneurial class in Russia.

Citing in particular a study he had made of the situation in Syktyvkar, capital of the Komi Republic, Burawoy indicated that by the end of 1990, 'three-quarters of the party secretaries in local organisations were involved in cooperatives'. Co-operatives in effect, then, were not so much an indication of a brand-new entrepreneurial group striving to break free of the old placemen so much as 'new bottles for old wine'. 'The shift from Marxism–Leninism to sociology', he writes, thus 'obscured the continuity of function and personnel.'[53] Indeed, according to Vadim Bakatin, former Soviet Minister of Internal Affairs, as soon as the Party realized that its days of unassailed political leadership were numbered, instructions were issued at all levels 'to invest party money in commercial structures'.[54]

In a similar vein, another less positive role-model image of the new Russian entrepreneur, but a category nevertheless that is an accepted vital component of the burgeoning business elite, is the old-style black marketeer of the former 'shadow economy'. According to several estimates the number of people who had made their fortunes out of one kind of 'illegal' activity or another in these pre-reform years was anywhere between 30 and 100,000. Some of these, of course, have invested their fortunes in new private ventures and are now operating as genuine capitalist-style producers and managers. Many others, however, it has to be said, have joined the ever-burgeoning ranks of financial speculators; not producing commodities or work or a form of wealth that can be socially redistributed, but content simply to play the new stock markets.[55]

The emergence of a new private sector, as well as basic market mechanisms in the economy as a whole, also means the emergence of new personnel, groups and institutions to *service* this type of economic structure. In the course of three years, for example, more than 700 commodity exchanges employing thousands of brokers and dealers have sprung up in Russia to help service the development of a new type of wholesale market.[56] More than two thousand commercial banks have also been established, and in Moscow alone there are now more stock markets than there are in the whole of Western Europe. Trading houses and insurance companies are also being established in great numbers; and the introduction of voucher-style privatization has also necessitated a dramatic increase in the number of investment funds and agencies (550 by mid 1993).

As the number of people operating in the private sector, in one capacity or another, grows, so too does the institutional support base of civil society. Those connected with the aforementioned commodity exchanges, for example, have already established two powerful lobbying organizations in the form of the Russian Exchange Union and the Congress of Exchanges. Since 1988 the common interests of the co-operative sphere have had several representative organizations. In the autumn of that year, for example, the *Rossiya* Association of Co-operatives was formed under the leadership of V. Korchagin. Later that year the Moscow Union of Co-operatives was established, and in July 1989 the Union of Amalgamated Co-operatives was established, under the leadership of Vladimir Tikhonov.[57]

Another important group, which held its first congress in June 1990, is the Union of Leaseholders and Entrepreneurs. Led by Pavel Bunich, the Union at its outset claimed to represent over 11 million people working in more than 10,000 enterprises which had been converted into leased property. Moreover, as Peregudov, Semenenko and Zudin have pointed out, the Union has consciously striven 'for a leading role in the microcosm of private or semi-private business organisations which are now being born', and has also sought to campaign for the future prospects of the private business community.[58] Other significant interest-lobbying institutions worth mentioning are the Moscow Convention of Entrepreneurs (led by Konstantin Borovoi); the Union of Small Businesses of Russia (led by Nadezhda Shulyatyeva); and the Inter-Regional Trade and Banking Union (led by Konstantin Zatulin).

As we shall see below, Konstantin Borovoi has openly used his new-found economic interests to engage directly in political activity. The same is true of Konstantin Zatulin. As head also of the organization known as Entrepreneurs for a New Russia, he has been instrumental in forging a much more coherent and cohesive alliance between businessmen, trade companies, stock exchanges and private banks, and he has also made it abundantly clear that his organisation will consider providing financial support only to those political groups with absolutely clear political goals.

Perhaps the most significant of all the new business lobbying associations to have emerged in recent times, however, is the Association of Private and Privatized Enterprises. Established in April 1993, the constituent congress of the Association was attended by more than 1,000 managers from 80 different regions, united in their aspiration to promote their common interests and to secure far greater conditions of economic freedom and legality for the private sector. What gave the Association its undoubted primacy, however, was the fact that it was able to elect former Prime Minister Yegor Gaidar as its President.[59] Moving away from the strictly entrepreneurial basis of support for the Westerners, a number of other social strata and forces can likewise be counted as committed advocates and supporters of their hegemonic campaign.

Despite the growing numbers of entrepreneurs and expanding private-sector activity as a whole, and despite the Westerners' obvious commitment to expand this sector rapidly, large tranches of the post-Soviet Russian economy, of course, still remain dominated at this point in time by the state sector; a reality that the Westerners have been forced to face up to. Part and parcel of facing up to this reality has been a committed attempt to differentiate between various employment sectors in the hope of winning over vast numbers of people operating within certain specific spheres. If we take official statistics on wage differentials, we can perhaps appreciate the strategy of the Westerners here. Certainly, the first thing to bear in mind is the way in which much greater emphasis has been given to those engaged in material rather than non-material production. According to figures for August 1992, wages, on average, rose by 9.5 per cent in the former compared to a mere 0.7 per cent in the latter, with such sectors as health, education and culture coming off worst of all.[60] Within the productive sector itself, meanwhile, preferential treatment appears to have been given to a number of industrial branches, most notably to those in the oil extraction industry; in the gas industry; in non-ferrous metallurgy and in the coal industry. In all of these sectors wages are at least twice – often three times – higher than the average industrial wage in other sectors.[61]

What is most striking about these kinds of industries, of course, is the fact that they represent some of the most productive parts of Russian industry; they are all sectors which will have no problem whatsoever in finding a niche in the world market; and they all represent types of industrial production whose profit potential will make them very attractive to any future private takeover and to any future foreign involvement and investment. Given these advantages, therefore, it perhaps came as no surprise that when the main trade-union organization in Russia, the Federation of Independent Trade Unions (FITUR), came out firmly against the socioeconomic programme of the Westerners (despite having initially supported some of its broader aspirations), groups such as the Metal Workers' Union immediately broke ranks. In the words of its Chairman, Boris Misnik, metal workers could no longer be associated with an organization which stood in the way of a prosperous economic future and which ultimately would be reduced to representing the old entrenched interests of pensioners, housewives and children.[62]

This kind of reasoning – which, after all, is based on significant material advantages, not only in terms of higher wages but also direct access for workers to such things as foreign currency accounts and foreign consumer products – also perhaps explains just why it was that the miners, in the early period of the reforms at least, were so closely associated with the ambitions of the Westerners.[63] Indeed, so close was their association at this time that the miners from the Kuzbass were colloquially referred to as the *oprichniks*.[64] These were the special corps of bodyguards under Ivan the Terrible, and the analogy reflects the actions taken by miners on such occasions as the convening of congresses of People's Deputies in Moscow, where they often formed protective cordons for pro-reform deputies.

The independent trade union Sotsprof is another good illustration of the way in which workers in certain types of employment have regarded the pro-Western orientation in a favourable light. According to the ideologists of this particular union, it is much better for the worker when the free market and free enterprise dominate. The task of the union, therefore, should not be to disrupt the emerging system of free enterprise; it should simply concentrate on getting a fair, proportionate share of any new wealth created by the new economic mechanism in terms of higher wages.[65]

Another major social bulwark of the Westerners are their supporters within the intelligentsia. Mention has already been made of the vital role key sections of the intelligentsia played (and continue to play) in forging and popularizing the broad collective will of the Westerners' hegemonic campaign. Analysing the *motivations* of such intellectuals, of course, is an almost impossible task. Many of them clearly do believe, passionately, in the intrinsic positive attributes of a Western-style liberal capitalism, and associate these attributes with the ultimate personification of human progress. At the same time, however, one cannot help but consider other possible motivations as well. As Daniel Singer has astutely commented, the Western-orientated reformist intelligentsia of today is consciously aspiring to be tomorrow's *priviligentsia*. Economists, engineers, doctors, successful writers and journalists are all equally adamant that a vital aspect of any successful reform transition must be 'the transfer of privileges and power from the apparatchiks, whose main virtue was their faithful obedience, to [people like] themselves, whose main quality is allegedly their competence'.[66]

In any value system based on meritocracy, therefore, large elements of the intelligentsia will be in the forefront of the self-proclaimers of their value; and as the ones in the vanguard of representing the interests of a new emerging class, they will inevitably claim their own spoils in any victory for this class: privileges, power and, of course, property.

Finally, another indication of the *broader* social support base of the Westerners can perhaps best be found in an analysis of those situations where they have already been forced to test the popular attractiveness of their overall aspirations for a new Russia. In the aftermath of the April 1993 referendum, for example – which focused on the desirability of early parliamentary and presidential elections; support for President Yeltsin; and support for continuing radical socioeconomic reforms[67] – it was confirmed that the primary social support base for the Westerners' campaign came predominantly from younger, more educated parts of the population. Large-city and urban residents were also much more attracted to the Westerners than their small-town and rural counterparts. And, not surprisingly, in terms of occupational category, the main basis of support was to be found among independent entrepreneurs, managers and technical specialists. Categories least amenable to the Westerners, meanwhile, were the unemployed, pensioners and housewives.

Forging the Political Base of the Historical Bloc

In the Gramscian framework of a hegemonic struggle, the major significance of a historical bloc lies in the fact that it represents the mechanism by which the economic and political levels of existence can be most effectively sutured together. A socioeconomic class, as it develops from a narrow economic-corporate starting point, becomes progressively more powerful – not simply because of its position within the economic structure, but also because it is the purveyor of certain values, which, though certainly expressions of its experience in the world of production, are nevertheless able to become detached as images or projections possessing a well-structured *political* form. Depending on the attractiveness of such images, the dominant class will thus be able to attract to itself other social groups (over which it exercises leadership) as mutual power-seekers, potential power-shapers, and instigators of new cultural expressions. In a society embarking upon such a fundamental depth of transition as that currently envisaged in post-communist Russia, it inevitably follows that the process of forging such a political base for a new historical bloc will be very time-consuming, and will also be subject to enormous degrees of flux and change.

The turnover of individual new political organizations will be numerically phenomenal (as well as chaotic). As for those that manage to survive for any length of time, they will invariably find themselves waging a struggle on two key fronts, either one of which could lead to their demise. As a purveyor of a general set of value orientations in a time of transition and transformation, they will be faced with opposing political forces representing entirely dichotomous value orientations. And as one of a number of organizations *sharing* a broad common set of values, they will at the same time invariably be engaged in a struggle to be the one assuming the dominant *mantle* of that orientation. In other words, then, in the very process of trying to forge a strong political representative arm of an emerging historical bloc, constituent political groups of that bloc will constantly be at loggerheads with each other, until such time as a definitive form of political supremacy and political unity is attained.

As one participant actively engaged in these political struggles has astutely remarked, a political bloc of forces can best be likened to a platform in a railway station: 'As long as we are all waiting for the same train, we share a single purpose. When the train pulls in, we divide up. Some of us have comfortable seats; others have to sit in the corridor. And we all get out at different destinations.'[68] Such, then, is the nature of the political struggle in Russia today, and such is the problem of trying to forge a cohesive and powerful political base of any new historical bloc.

Looking specifically at the political base of the Westerners' hegemonic struggle, one can certainly say that there has been no shortage of parties and groups emerging in recent years, highly committed to advancing the Westerners' cause.

One such organization, which came into existence in November 1990 and has its roots in the liberal, reformist wing of the former CPSU, is the Republican Party of the Russian Federation (RPRF). For a long time, the Republicans seemed to be plagued by an underlying uncertainty regarding their own self-identity, which seriously threatened not only their long-term but also their short-term existence. Following their third congress in June 1992, however, the party leadership adopted a definitive line in support of the pro-Western orientation of reform, and for a time this appeared to provide them with a fresh lease of life.

In the aftermath of the congress, for example, the Party became a consistent supporter of the *fait accompli* of the USSR's disintegration, and keenly promoted the positive arguments in favour of Russia's new-found status as well as warning of the dire consequences of any attempt aimed at re-creating the old Union. Meanwhile, support for the priority of the personal freedom of every individual on the basis of private ownership now became a central plank of the Party's new programme of principles (also adopted at the third congress); in particular, the Party took the major initiative in encouraging the implementation of a much more deep-seated land reform (a position fostered, no doubt, by its increasing links with such organizations as the Association of Peasants' Households and Agricultural Co-operatives of Russia).[69]

Just as significantly, the Party also began to identify itself for the first time with a very specific social base, claiming that it had attracted a considerable degree of support from the newly emerging small and medium-sized businesses, and from those engaged in the services and trade sectors.[70]

Formal membership figures at this time remained low (at approximately 7,000), but with 65 regional branches to its name, a youth organization (known as the Russian Young Republicans Union) led by Vladislav Lebedev making an open pitch for new young entrepreneurs under the age of thirty-five, and with a high-profile party leadership encompassing the likes of Vyacheslav Shostakovskii, Igor' Yakovenko, Petr Fillipov and Vladimir Lysenko, the Party could fairly claim to be a not insubstantial political bulwark of the pro-Western orientation. In the period between the October 1993 uprising and the December parliamentary elections, however, the fragile unity that the Party had managed to attain for itself rapidly began to come unstuck. Following its fourth congress, different elements of the Party joined different electoral blocs, and as a consequence the singular identity of the Party was once again forfeited.[71] Further splits emerged, meanwhile, at the Party's fifth congress in June 1994, and by the end of the year a breakaway faction (under the leadership of Shostakovskii and Yakovenko) had formally left to create a brand-new political organization (in the guise of the Democratic Alternative Party).

Another party, closely linked with the Republicans – indeed, at one time it looked as though it might merge with them – is the Social Democratic Party of Russia (SDPR). It, too, according to its initial programme, was fundamentally committed to the radical privatization and marketization policies of the pro-Western orientation, and keen to help in the creation of a new Russian middle class. Moreover, its leaders openly admitted that they saw the role of social democracy in post-communist Russia as an inversion of the normal traditions of social democracy. Whereas the latter has historically engaged itself in the struggle to 'socialize' capitalism, the SDPR had no qualms at all at seeing its own task as the *capitalization* of socialism.[72]

Unlike the Republicans, of course, the Social Democrats brought with them a long-established tradition in Russian political life. In normal circumstances this should have stood the Party in good stead; certainly, few political organizations emerging out of the old CPSU were as keenly anticipated as the SDPR when it first came on to the scene in May 1990. If the evidence so far is anything to go by, however, this particular legacy is one that the present-day leadership would gladly have forfeited.

In congress after congress, deep-seated divisions within the Party have mitigated much of its underlying potential. For a time, these divisions were camouflaged by repeated public references to the fact that 'the strength of any social democratic party lies in its capacity to combine the seemingly uncombinable'.[73] At the fourth Party congress in May 1992, however, the fallacy of this rhetoric was finally unmasked, and in the months that followed a three-way split between the 'socialists' on the left, the 'centrists' in the middle and the 'liberals' on the right finally formalized itself when the first two groups effectively broke away to find new political homes.[74] This left the 'liberals' in command, but the price they have paid has been a heavy one. With a membership base reduced to fewer than 4,000; with two leadership changes within the space of several months and continuing doubts about precisely which social interests the Party should be most eager to articulate, the Party was clearly in desperate need of a radical facelift by the summer of 1993.[75] Moreover, as with the Republicans, subsequent developments have only tended to exacerbate the internal tensions, and by the end of 1994 the SDPR had likewise become a marginalized political organization.

A much more recent addition to the political base of the Westerners' cause – and, for that reason, a party which considers itself to be among the few genuinely new post-Soviet, non-CPSU-connected organizations truly orientated towards the evolution of a new Russia – is the Party of Economic Freedom (PEF). Set up in May 1992, the Party was initially co-chaired by two of the wealthiest businessmen in Russia today, Svyatoslav Fedorov and Konstantin Borovoi (who was also head of the Party's top decision-making council). As befits its name and its leadership, the in-augural conference was primarily attended by some 3,000 commodity brokers and representatives of other commercial institutions, all of whom expressed their commitment to fund the future activities of the Party directly, rather than relying on the more normal process of membership fees.[76]

Claiming initially to represent some 250,000 supporters (a clear exag-geration that was ultimately demonstrated by its inability to gain enough signatures of support to participate in the December 1993 elections), the Party leaders have boasted that their future potential base could consist of anything up to 40 million. What were termed 'citizens of the new economy' represent the primary base of support, though the Party has also cam-paigned strongly to win over progressively minded leaders of industrial enterprises, highly skilled workers and private farmers.[77]

At the Party's first congress in December 1992, and in speeches prior to the congress, both Borovoi and Fedorov made it absolutely clear that their Party's first allegiance was to the principles embodied in a normal func-tioning capitalist economic system. Any Russian government, therefore, would receive the full backing of the Party only provided that it could demonstrate a full commitment to putting these principles into practice. The then Gaidar government, it was argued, had certainly shown a great deal of enthusiasm for such principles, but many of the reforms needed to be freed from 'the weights of a half-measured approach'. Going on to specify what these half-measures were, they cited, in particular, the mis-takes that had been made in the government's budgetary policy, which had allowed inflation to increase through too much credit expansion, and had likewise imposed a highly oppressive and exorbitant level of taxation, thus killing the stimuli to production.[78]

In later speeches and interviews Borovoi, in particular, has also been highly critical of the continued levels of monopolism in the economy. He has criticized the slow pace of privatization as well as the economic logic behind the introduction of the voucher programme. He has vehemently attacked the reluctance of state enterprise directors to shed their excessive labour reserves and create a pool of unemployed labour which would both motivate those remaining in work and stimulate the development of new small-scale entrepreneurial activity in the service sector. And he has also expressed his concern at the lack of a really effective information and propaganda support base to buttress the popular legitimacy of the desired form of transition to a Western-style capitalist system.[79]

Apart from Borovoi and Fedorov (who has since gone on to establish his own political party), other luminaries of the party have at one time or another included Irina Khakamada (one of only a few women to have reached an authoritative position in the post-communist political scene) and Leonid Shpigel, who was imprisoned in the Soviet era for illegal economic activities, and who was closely connected with the Society for the Protection of Convicted Business Managers and Economic Freedoms.

If the likes of the above political parties have, in the course of recent years, represented some of the most significant component organizations within the emerging pro-Western mainstream, they are certainly not short of other new parties willing to associate closely with them. Three other groups worthy of mention are the Party of Free Labour, established in December 1990 and led by Igor' Korovikov; the Peasants' Party of Russia, established in September 1990 and led by Yurii Chernichenko; and the Free Democratic Party, led by Marina Sal'e, Lev Ponomarev and Igor' Soshnikov, which was established in May 1990 as a breakaway movement from Nikolai Travkin's Democratic Party of Russia.

Although all these parties have played a not inconsiderable role in articulating the broad aims of the pro-Western orientation over recent years, and have become fairly established political actors in their own right, certainly none of them would stake any claim to the potential to become a force that is strong enough to exercise *sole* political leadership in the current hegemonic struggle. What they have successfully done is *initiated* a process of articulating newly emerging social interests in post-communist Russia in the cause of a pro-Western type of transformation. What they all recognize, however, is that if this cause is to have any long-lasting hegemonic success, they themselves must become the *subjects* of a new, much higher synthesis of political articulation.

Right from the very moment when it was realized that the old domination of the CPSU was really and truly disintegrating, efforts have thus been made to try to create a much more cohesive bloc of political forces; a bloc of forces which might eventually emerge as a single, homogeneous political entity able to articulate a well-defined set of social interests and which might, therefore, be able to fill the vacuum that was left in the CPSU's wake. The ultimate ambitions, then, are clear. The attempts to fulfil these ambitions in practice, however, have been rather disappointing, to say the least.

One such bloc which aspired to exercise leadership over the vast array of forces comprising the Westerners' camp was the Movement for Democratic Reforms (MDR). This originally started out in the summer of 1991 as an all-Union organization whose leadership represented nothing less than a veritable 'who's who' of heavyweight ex-CPSU liberal reformers. Following the disintegration of the USSR in December 1991, the Movement's baton was taken up in Russia by two of its most prominent leaders, former Mayor of Moscow Gavriil Popov, and the Mayor of St Petersburg, Anatolii Sobchak. Designed, like its parent organization, to be a 'consolidator' and a 'synthesizer' of progressive forces, the Russian MDR (RMDR) hoped to be 'a free association of parties, organisations and individuals campaigning for a socially-oriented state with a market economy'.[80]

In its self-appointed task, however, the Movement has been an abject failure. While a number of prominent organizations refused outright to join its ranks, those that did join at the outset progressively became more and more disillusioned, and subsequently suspended their membership. Most notable here was the example of the Republican Party. The Party had already been a constituent member of the original Soviet version of the MDR; its leadership became highly sceptical of Popov's takeover of the Russian section and his increasingly authoritarian style. And following what appeared, to Vyacheslav Shostakovskii, to be nothing more than a stage-managed debate on the Movement's draft statutes at the constituent congress, delegates of the Republican Party formally suspended their membership – a measure that was subsequently endorsed at the Party's third congress.[81]

In effect, then, the RMDR has become just another *individual* component organization in the complex heterogeneous political domain. It has had some notable successes in campaigning for a brand-new Constitution to be introduced in Russia to underpin the desired socioeconomic and political transformation; and it has also been quite effective in articulating some of the essential concerns and needs of the new business elite. As a potential leader of a united, cohesive political bloc, however, its effectiveness has been minimal to date, and its potential in the immediate future looks no more promising, especially bearing in mind its very poor performance in the December 1993 parliamentary elections when it failed to cross the 5 per cent threshold in the Party list contest.

The one organization that really did look as if it had the potential to be the nucleus of a cohesive bloc of forces was the Democratic Russia movement. Formally established in October 1990, the movement certainly had what appeared at the time to be a number of very positive factors working in its favour.[82]

First, for example, it was able to bring together under a common political roof a vast array of interest groups (eighteen in total, most of which were representatives of the cultural sphere) and no fewer than nine individual political parties (comprising the Social Democrats, the Republicans, the Free Democrats, the Democratic Party of Russia, the Party of Free Labour, the Christian Democratic Movement, the Peasants' Party and the two versions of the old Cadets, the Constitutional Democratic Party/Party of People's Freedom and the Party of Constitutional Democrats). Secondly, it also brought together some of the most prominent reformist intellectuals of the time. Thirdly, in the Democratic Russia Foundation the movement had one of the best financial support structures outside the CPSU itself, which was also able to offer a vast range of information, expertise and organizational assistance. Fourthly, the movement also had one of the most reliable and effective information and publishing outlets in the guise of the *Democratic Russia* newspaper and the Democratic Russia Information and Publishing Association. Fifthly, it possessed a well-structured administrative set-up which quickly established itself into local and regional chapters throughout the Russian Federation. And last, but not least, after contributing the main support base for Boris Yeltsin's victory in the presidential elections in the summer of 1991, the movement also had a direct connection with the foremost executive political structures in the country.[83]

As is often the case, however, what appeared to be distinct advantages in the dying days of the communist era very quickly began to look decisively like *dis*advantages in the aftermath of the definitive collapse of that order. And as a consequence, in the months following the defeat of the August 1991 coup attempt, Democratic Russia's decline into something not far short of oblivion has been almost unstoppable.

First and foremost, perhaps, the movement has tended to suffer from the axiom that 'the sum of amorphous parts tends only to make up an amorphous heap'. As an opposition force able to preach a strong 'anti' programme, the movement was always bound to achieve a fairly high degree of popularity in its initial stages. But as a force able to provide a real sense of unity and identity around which a whole range of admittedly disparate, but nevertheless for the most part contiguous, forces could progress together, the movement has largely been a recognized failure.

Writing back in February 1991, a former leading intellectual doyen of Democratic Russia, Aleksandr Tsipko, openly warned his associates: 'The weakness of our democratic movement, which hasn't been either described or discussed yet, consists in the fact that the radical opposition hasn't yet really aspired to win over communism, speaking in the broadest sense of the word. But there's no chance for [a long-lasting] victory without this.'[84] It was a warning, however, that simply went unheeded.

An indication of the kinds of problem that have continually plagued Democratic Russia was nowhere better witnessed than at the movement's (perpetually delayed) second congress in November 1991. First, with the disintegration of the Soviet Union imminent, three constituent members – the Democratic Party, the Christian Democratic Movement and the Constitutional Democratic Party/Party of People's Freedom – announced their decision to split from Democratic Russia – not only because of the leadership's support for the Union's demise, but also because of their ratification of a commitment allowing for a 'unified, but *divisible* Russia', which carried the implication that Russia's own republics might possibly be allowed to leave the Federation by purely constitutional means.[85] A second contentious issue that emerged at the congress concerned recent developments in the construction of the movement's administrative and organizational structure. In the weeks and months prior to the congress a much more vertical and unitary-type structure had begun to emerge. In particular, so-called primary organizations had been set up at the workplace level, with each of them responsible for electing an executive co-ordinating council.[86] This, combined with a decision to change the rules of membership, led many constituent organizations to express their anxiety that Democratic Russia was perhaps following in the footsteps of the CPSU and preparing the ground for a form of one-party domination, which would be nothing more than an appendage of the state structure.[87]

With the continuation of this trend after the congress, a number of parties now felt that Democratic Russia was becoming too much of a political *obstacle* to the emergence of a genuine multiparty system in the country. As a result, in February 1992 the Social Democrats, the People's Party of Russia and the Peasants' Party (among others) likewise announced that they were suspending their membership.[88]

Perhaps the most contentious issue that emerged at the second congress, however, concerned the question of the movement's official relationship with President Yeltsin and his new government. Quite simply, the question at hand was: should Democratic Russia be transformed into a *de facto* presidential organization providing Yeltsin with virtual unconditional support, or should it be a movement of general aims and principles, which would thus allow it to pursue a policy of constructive criticism and opposition when necessary? It was a question that produced no clear, definitive answer at the November congress, and as such it has continued to plague the movement ever since.

By the time of the movement's third congress in December 1992 – which elected Gleb Yakunin, Lev Ponomarev, Ilya Zaslavskii, Grigorii Tomchenko and Galina Starovoitova as its co-leaders – it was already clear just how badly tarnished it had been by its perpetual divisions. With a registered support base now numbering no more than 200,000 (compared with a peak of 1.5 million); with all the major original constituent parties having left; and having failed to attract the support of new parties such as Borovoi's PEF, it was small wonder that one leading member (Ilya Zaslavskii) was wont to comment that perhaps after all the Russian democrats could unite only under very exceptional circumstances: defending themselves from tanks, underground, or in a forced-labour camp.[89]

Hegemonic Potential

In assessing the overall hegemonic potential of the Westerners, a couple of preliminary points must be borne in mind. First and foremost, it is crucial to remember never to underestimate the difficulties and the complexities of the hegemonic process itself. Formulating a new collective will and constructing a historical bloc are by no means easy or simple tasks. What we are therefore witnessing in post-communist Russia is merely the first phase of a process that could take decades to assert itself conclusively. With this in mind, then, the real question that needs to be addressed at this stage cannot go beyond the confines of considering how the Westernization project has fared *so far*, and its *potential* for future progress. Above all, we must remember that it is going to take far more than the occasional referendum or even election before one can pronounce the attainment of a much more decisive and definitive hegemonic triumph.

All this, of course, is itself dependent on the hegemonic process taking a *natural* course; and as we saw in the last chapter, there are serious doubts as to whether key members and supporters of the Westernization project are really imbued with a desire to play by the consensual rules of the hegemonic game.

Addressing the question of its achievements so far and its future potential, it must be made clear, of course, that the Westerners held many, if not most, of the key reins of power and wielded most influence on the decision-making process within the realms of political society in the crucial first period after the defeat of the August 1991 coup. If any group, therefore, warrants the description of being in the hegemonic driving seat it is the Westerners. Their opponents, initially at least, were much more in the position of potential *counter*-hegemonic forces.

What, then, can one say about their achievements and their longer-term potential? How close have they come to even *partially* realizing their aspirations, which for Ernest Gellner would be sufficient in itself to make us salute a veritable miracle?[90]

If one listens to the *optimists*, a number of positive observations can be made in their favour, especially if one is discussing the period *prior* to the elections of December 1993. It is contended, for example, that the beginnings of a real, cohesive social base supporting the wider aspects of the Westernization project can now be seen. If, at first, there was perhaps a tendency to over-rely on the social psychology of the undefined masses, this tendency did eventually evaporate. Now, the Westerners are perfectly aware of just where their real social support base lies, and they are doing everything they possibly can to develop and sustain this base. Indeed, as Boris Yeltsin himself has expressed it, there might not be a *classical* middle class in post-communist Russia as yet, but the number of entrepreneurs, private farmers and others who desire such a middle-class status is growing very quickly; what is more, this embryonic new class does at least have a state of mind, a set of desires and an overall world-view that is now sufficiently and adequately *represented*.[91]

Nowhere is this better indicated than by the fact that many new Russian entrepreneurs – both individually and from the perspective of the groups and associations they belong to – are increasingly becoming highly politicized. Mention, for example, has already been made of the organization known as Entrepreneurs for a New Russia (chaired by Konstantin Zatulin), and when the aforementioned Association of Private and Privatized Enterprises was set up in April 1993, its new President, Yegor Gaidar, made it perfectly clear that the Association would certainly take part in political activities, and would 'provide organizational and financial support to those political forces which stand for normal market legislation'.[92] In addition, more and more entrepreneurs, it is contended, are likewise becoming acutely conscious of their broader social role. Thus, for example, in attempting to raise the status and stature of the new entrepreneurial class, many have become patrons of the arts and have begun to invest widely in setting up grammar schools, hospitals, nursing homes, museums, as well as a whole range of charitable work.[93]

On the economic front, whatever the *performance* indicators might have been saying since the collapse of the old order, the optimists would similarly have no hesitation in laying claim to some considerable successes for the Westerners. Like it or not, for example, *structural* changes to the economy have gone so far now, it is contended, that there is little option but to try to make a capitalist system viable in Russia. Quite simply, the country's economy could not cope with another upheaval, either back to something like it was or towards something not strictly capitalist in form. Some of the precise contours of the capitalist system that will eventually emerge are, it is openly recognized, still an issue that can be fought over. But this is now all that is under serious dispute; the rest is irreversible.

Summing up the extent and depth of the changes, Keith Bush of the

Radio Free Europe and Radio Liberty organization has emphasized, in particular, the liberalization of nearly all prices; the unification of exchange rates; the reduction in currency and trade restrictions; the blossoming of the private sector; the explosion of entrepreneurial activity; the filling up of store shelves; the vanishing of queues; the renewed significance of money (with the notion of 'buying' replacing that of 'obtaining'); as well as the fact that enterprise transactions are now based on the normal mechanisms of contracting rather than on state plans or orders. Capping it all, writes Bush (with reference to a quotation from former Deputy Prime Minister Andrei Nechaev), 'the "market mentality" has [successfully] taken root in the minds of ordinary people'.[94]

As to whether the Russian people really do like these changes or not, the optimists can at least cite some evidence to suggest that the *acceptance threshold* of the ordinary citizen is relatively high, given the backdrop of actual economic decline during the initial period of transition.

A lot of the optimists' case here, it has to be said, rests on a rather dubious and very selective reading of polling information commissioned by various institutions. As this in itself, however, is such a predominant part of the modern rules of the political game, one should perhaps not labour this criticism excessively. One should nevertheless be a little wary. When *The Economist,* for example, boldly proclaimed at the end of 1992 that 'social science does not support the view that Russians are more hostile to free markets than other people are', and went on to cite a number of supporting indicators from 'the most extensive comparative research',[95] one was not directly informed that this research had been carried out as long ago as May 1990, when the full effects of the transition to capitalism had not even begun; that it had been carried out by telephone (almost certainly distorting the hoped-for cross-section of Russian respondents); that only Moscow had been included in the research; and that only 391 residents had been asked the questions in the survey.[96] So much, then, for the most extensive comparative research. Moreover, it is interesting to note the Russian attitude towards conducting polls. According to one sociologist (who was also a former President of the American Association for Public Opinion Research):

Polling was seen by our . . . colleagues not simply as a means of gathering information or monitoring developments in public opinion. Rather it was for many a weapon in the struggle to build and sustain democracy under conditions in which the success of liberalization programs and the emergence of civil society were by no means assured. Research practices were informed by norms of scientific objectivity, but the driving purpose of polling, initially at least, was as an agency in the *formation* of public opinion to support democratic reform.[97]

Looking, then, at more extensive polling carried out between 1991 and 1993, there is, as mentioned above, some indication of a relatively high acceptance threshold as regards the necessity for making the transition to a capitalist system, as well as a willingness to undergo short-term difficulties in return for the prospects of longer-term gains.[98] While none of the polls revealed a clear majority of respondents *positively in favour* of such things as price liberalization, increasing wealth disparities or the mass privatization of state-owned industries, the Westerners could nevertheless take *some* comfort from the fact that the more the reforms progressed in these areas, the *less antipathy* there was to them. And of course, when it came to the first real moment of decision in the April 1993 referendum, a majority of those who voted (53 per cent) did explicitly express an overall approval of the socioeconomic transition.[99]

If these represent some of the most *quantifiable* aspects of the Westerners' successes so far, and point up the degree of potential for hegemonic success in the future, there are likewise many other factors that the optimists would wish to cite in their favour.

One important point that one must not by any means downplay is the degree to which key elements of the media are either under the direct control of the Westerners, or are very supportive of their cause and their struggle. This applies (from an editorial point of view) to all the Russian broadcasting media, the news agencies and to the vast majority of those newspapers readily available through official street newsstands. A lot of this support, it has to be said, is very overt in its nature and as such, therefore, is barely different from the old CPSU-type domination; one illustration being the frequent interruption of television programmes on the *Ostankino* network in the run-up to the April 1993 referendum to allow time to broadcast appeals from Democratic Russia members in support of President Yeltsin.

In other instances, however, the support is much more subtle and much more orientated towards establishing an internalized acceptance of many of the aims and ambitions of the Westernization hegemonic project. One thinks, for example, of the need for most newspapers today to survive through advertising revenues and direct loans from business interests; the ability to establish private television and radio networks, which again are inevitably furthering the primary commercial and consumerist instincts of the Westernization project; and, of course, the ready availability (in most large cities, at least) of Western newspapers, television news broadcasts from the BBC, ITN and CNN, together with popular American soap operas and the like, all of which similarly buttress and sustain the broader aspects of the pro-Western orientation. In all these ways, therefore, the Westernization project can be boosted by a series of 'cultural-ideological injections'.[100]

Another phenomenon – working in the favour of the Westerners, and very consciously and assiduously being propagated through the information channels under their control – is the manner in which *their* 'victory' during the days of the August 1991 coup attempt has become almost *mythologized.* As Richard Sakwa has pointed out, there has been an attempt to engender a *maximalist* interpretation of the events of those days which has deliberately focused on the apparent popular mobilization of the Russian masses and the *revolutionary* consequences of the coup's defeat. Irrespective of its relationship with actual reality, a version of what took place in August 1991 has thus been moulded which amounts to a very astute exercise 'in a socially-constructed reality'.[101] Indeed, in effect, what the Westerners have done is to manufacture for themselves their very own 'storming of the winter palace', which can thus be used as a powerful legitimatory weapon.[102]

Closely associated with this is the creation of another popular perception that the *only* alternative to the Westernization project is a return to neo-communism, neo-Stalinism and/or neo-Bolshevism. As Gennadii Burbulis has expressed it, what exist in Russia at the present moment are two fundamental structures. There is what can loosely be called 'a party of reforms', and there is 'a party of revenge'. There is no centrism, or any other alternative, in Russia, 'and cannot be any in the next few years'.[103] As we in Britain know only too well from our own experience under Margaret Thatcher in the 1980s, the constant repetitive emphasizing of the claim that there is, in practice, no *real* alternative to the present course of change can often have its desired popular effect. This kind of mentality, of course, also prevails in many corridors of power in the West, and acts as a further incentive for Western governments and financial institutions to throw their full weight behind an orientation with which they would naturally have a lot of intrinsic sympathy in any case. What it does sometimes mean in addition, however, is their (over)vociferous support for a narrow group of individuals also associated with that orientation.

In either case, the day-to-day economic influence the West can now exert on Russia is an important factor in the country's hegemonic struggle, and the Westerners are clearly prepared to milk the direct and explicit support they receive from foreign governments and institutions like the IMF and the World Bank all they can get. Another important factor in any hegemonic struggle is the role and use of language; and this is certainly no less so in the current Russian context. Accompanying the transition to a Western-orientated socioeconomic and political condition in Russia has been the clear necessity to formulate a corresponding vocabulary to cater for this new set of conditions. And what this has meant in practice has been a thoroughgoing 'Anglicization' or 'Americanization' of Russian. Thus, for example, rather than using long-outdated Russian terms to describe some of the new functions and personnel in today's Russia – or rather than using existing Russian terms to invent a close approximation of these new functions – an existing English or American word or concept has simply been adopted in a suitably 'Cyrillicized' form.

A similar phenomenon is noticeable in the recent evolution of Russian slang, which is simply littered with English and American terms, transliterated directly into a Cyrillic form. On top of this, a newly published dictionary of contemporary slang also gives us a good indication of just how much the old linguistic and ideological norms of the communist period have now been turned on their head; one illustration being the invention of a new verb, *skommunizdit'* (literally, to communize) bearing the meaning of 'to steal' [*ukrast'*].[104]

Again, therefore, such linguistic developments all help to increase the depth of receptiveness of a pro-Western orientation. They make people constantly aware of the new Russia that is being built; they help them to internalize the requisite values and messages that are being conveyed; they also enhance the belief that Russian society has adopted the rituals of normalcy.[105] Last, but not least, there can be little doubt that in terms of all the *signs* and *symbols* which convey to the ordinary citizen just what their society is, or what it is trying to strive for, the Westerners are certainly already well down the road of hegemonic success. The sheer weight of advertisement hoardings where staid communist party slogans once stood, and the expansive visibility of giant Coca-Cola and McDonald's signs, conveying nothing less than an irrepressible sense of triumphalism, are symbols that no hegemonic competitor to the Westerners has been able to match.[106]

If this, then, represents the case of the optimists, what about the case for the pessimists? What factors have already militated, or perhaps might militate in the foreseeable future, against the attainment of a hegemonic victory for the Westerners?

Let us start with a couple of pieces of (self-) critical candour on the part of Yeltsin himself. First of all, in an address to a self-styled Congress of Intelligentsia at the end of November 1992, the Russian President bitterly lamented the fact that in the aftermath of the collapse of the old order, 'we still have a rather poor understanding of the in-depth philosophical meaning of what is happening to us and what is happening to Russia. I am convinced that whilst confrontation holds sway, progress here will be insignificant.'[107]

This rather indiscreet comment (considering the audience he was addressing) on the reformers' inability properly to define and, of course, articulate in a satisfactory way to the general public what precisely was happening in Russia and where they wanted to lead the country was followed by another piece of reproof in his April 1993 article in *Rossiiskie vesti* – written, appropriately enough, to outline his own vision for Russia. After again making a great point of emphasizing the fact that Russia had begun the transition to a 'normal state', Yeltsin asked whether people knew how to accomplish the transition. His reply, once again, did not instil great confidence, amounting to no more than a 'yes and no' and a confession that 'the ideology of this transition is *only just* being shaped'.[108] Yeltsin then went on to admit:

> What tortures me most is the mistakes we have made. The main one is that the first and decisive step towards real economic reforms was not reinforced with the requisite back-up. Not politically, socially or organizationally, nor with a sufficient theoretical base, nor in terms of personnel. Too much time, effort and attention were devoted to the tactics of political actions; often the tactics became an end in themselves.[109]

These quotations, then, from Yeltsin's own mouth (or pen) can, I think, help to form the backdrop to the pessimists' case, especially in the aftermath of the December 1993 elections.

Again, taking the economic realm first, even the optimists readily admit that among that segment of the population who have in the past indicated their broad support for the transition so far, the manner of their support is often very precarious indeed. Only a small proportion of it, it seems, is based on a really *positive* adherence to the reforms; the rest is based either on a greater fear of the possible alternatives or, at best, on some *reluctant* perception of the necessity of some such reforms. What is most worrying to the Westerners, therefore, is the obvious *fragility* of this kind of support and the possibility that it will wither away as the reforms begin to bite even harder; a fear exacerbated by the knowledge that the spectre of mass unemployment still has to be faced.

As for why there is such a lack of positive enthusiasm for the economic transformation, this can perhaps best be explained by looking at the major issue at the heart of the pessimists' case: the essential *nature* of the capitalist system that is actually being constructed in reality.

According to Michael Burawoy and Pavel Krotov, the optimists of the Western orientation have grossly exaggerated both the nature and the depth of economic transition in post-communist Russia.[110] They are certainly correct, they write, in their assertion that there has been a dramatic transformation in the old-style relations of exchange and distribution, brought about by such things as the freeing of prices, the development of a non-state sector and the fostering of a Western-type consumer culture, all of which is underpinned by the development of 'commercial structures'. This, however, is as far as Burawoy and Krotov are prepared to go. What certainly has not changed is the old type of *relations of production*, which are still, crucially, organized along the traditional matrix of a *redistributive economy*: a redistributive economy where 'monopolies retain their grip on the supply of crucial commodities, and workers continue to retain their hold on production'.[111]

For Burawoy and Krotov, then, the essence of these changes can in no way amount to a transition to a *modern* form of Western-style capitalism; nor can they even amount to the taking of the first essential steps down a road whose ultimate destination is a modern form of capitalism. What these changes amount to at best, they contend, is the emergence of a feudal or a *merchant capital* system, epitomized by an orientation to maximize profit through nothing other than trade; that is, 'by selling dear and buying cheap'. Far from radically transforming the nature of production, managers are simply attempting to maximize their returns on their existing lines. Moreover, 'like merchants of the early modern cities, Russian . . . managers advance their profits from trade through political regulation. [They] use close ties with governmental organs inherited from the Soviet order to protect their subsidies, credits, export licences and at the same time *stifle* [any kind of] *independent* capital accumulation.'[112]

Because of its intrinsic tendency, therefore, to buttress and sustain an existing form of production (which it grafts itself on to), rather than seeking to destroy what was previously there, a merchant capital system such as currently exists in Russia will do everything it can to *prohibit* the growth of a classical, autonomous bourgeois class, and will thus effectively *inhibit* the independent development of a modern, Western-style capitalist system. What you have, then, is 'commodification without capitalism'.[113] And this, by implication, leaves the current market ideology of the Westerners effectively playing the same role as that performed by Soviet-style Marxism–Leninism: 'obscuring the chasm between the grim reality of today and the promise of a radiant future'.[114]

A similar line of argument has also been taken by Simon Clarke. With the lack of competition in the new market circumstances; with the consolidation of old monopolies and cartels; with the failure to subject enterprises to any kind of law of value; and, once again, with no sign whatsoever that there has been any kind of fundamental change in the old-style social relations of production, Clarke is doubtful whether this represents even the most basic kind of capitalist system. 'To put the point aphoristically,' he writes, 'it is not the state which is privatising the soviet enterprise in Russia, but the soviet enterprise which is privatising the state.'[115] Consequently, within this new Russian enterprise one would be hard pressed indeed to see capital playing any kind of predominant role.

If we accept the logic of the analyses put forward by the likes of Clarke, Burawoy and Krotov, then it does, I think, highlight very clearly some of

the reasons why the popular support for the Westerners is currently perceived as so fragile. It also throws considerable light on the nature of much
of the supposedly 'new' entrepreneurial class that has emerged in recent
years. Certainly, if we follow Burawoy and Krotov's notion of the rise of a
merchant capital class, whose *raison d'être* is based on nothing more than
a desire to maximize profit through a trading policy of buying cheap and
selling dear, then I think it helps us to appreciate why many Russians are
apt popularly to associate privatization [*privatizatsiya*] with nothing less
than 'grabbing' [*prikhvatizatsiya*].

And who are the real merchant capital 'grabbers'? Well, even as staunch
a Westerner as Anatolii Chubais (who headed the privatization process
throughout its first decisive phase) could not deny that the primary beneficiaries of the reforms so far were probably members of the old
nomenklatura and the old shadow economic structures, a vast proportion
of whom had become some of the most influential bank managers,
company directors and *biznesmen* in the country.[116] And certainly no one
could possibly deny the obvious linkage between this new system and
organized crime. As was outlined in Chapter 1, it is often claimed that as
much as 40 per cent of Russia's production is now controlled by organized
crime structures, while virtually half of the country's domestic product is
based on criminal deals. And far from disclaiming the accuracy of these
figures, many Westerners would readily admit that these might be conservative estimates.

Quite clearly, then, these kinds of figures cannot help but do serious
harm to the overall cause of the Westerners and cannot help but leave
them extremely vulnerable to the charge that a new social elite is being
manufactured without any consideration of the means being employed,
just as long as they support the overall direction of change.

Moreover, as Burawoy and Krotov also highlighted, it certainly does
appear that the predominance of this kind of merchant capital approach is
having an inhibitive effect on the emergence of a more modern, civilized
form of capitalist system. Few genuine, aspiring capitalist entrepreneurs
can escape the tentacles of organized crime or of state officials who
demand 'payoffs' of one kind or another. And it is clear that the existing
monopolized corporations are having a lot of success in placing serious
obstacles in the path of those not willing to abide by the present rules of
the game. As Larisa Piyasheva scathingly remarked in a November 1993
follow-up to her infamous article of six years previous ('Where are the Pies
of Plenty?'), all the hopes and aspirations of the initial 'pioneers' of a capitalist transition in Russia have come to virtually nothing. Like naked
sheep in the freezing cold with no sustenance, she has written, the new private sector was told to fend for itself. One can hardly be surprised,
therefore, if instead of choosing to perish, they took on characteristics

more associated with a cross between a wolf and a fox. 'While the wolf thus began to rob the consumer, the fox undertook to pay off the state bureaucrat [*chinovnik*].'[117]

Similarly, as Nadezhda Shulyatyeva of the Small Businesses Association has also bitterly lamented (if not quite so lyrically), her members were close to ruin, among other reasons, because genuine forms of business were being prevented from getting to their feet, and this was being done deliberately.[118]

Once again, then, it was small wonder that President Yeltsin was forced to admit that serious damage had been inflicted on the formation of civilized market relations, and that this had created tangible negative images of Russia's new economic system, both domestically and in the eyes of the world community at large.[119] Negative images, moreover, that have hardly been helped by a new trend that first emerged in 1994 which witnessed the collapse of some of the country's largest commercial investment funds (such as Neft-Almaz-Invest and MMM), following highly dubious, if not downright illegal, practices of share issuing.[120]

Finally, before moving away from the economic realm, one should also note that whatever the debate about the Westerners' success or failure *vis-à-vis* its urban-orientated economic reforms, few can doubt that the success rate in the *rural* domain has been negligible almost to the point of non-existence. As many commentators point out, traditional Russian (and not just Soviet) values of collectivism and egalitarianism have retained much of their old grip, and new kinds of values, beliefs and attitudes have barely begun to be inculcated. Land reform in general has been laboriously slow and difficult, and in the view of one expert has never really been designed with the intention of destroying the old rural elite. Indeed, if anything, the opposite has been the case. Right from the outset the regime has deliberately sought to 'prevent the rise of a newly landed, powerful, rural elite' that 'could gain control of land, resources and capital flows' for fear that such an elite would become a *rival* rather than a partner of the liberal forces in Moscow.[121]

Such criticisms concerning the whole nature of the socioeconomic changes in recent years also help to explain, the pessimists would contend, just why there has been no success to date in developing a truly unified, cohesive political bloc. And it is here, perhaps, that we encounter the Westerners' biggest failure.

With the steady diminution in the influence of the Democratic Russia movement by spring 1993 – a diminution that was perhaps most encapsulated in a lengthy and scathing analysis penned once again by Aleksandr Tsipko in which he reiterated and expanded his earlier charge that the movement had singularly failed to transcend its original role of *destruction* of an old order into one of articulating the *construction* of the new[122] – the search for a new type of unified political movement began to dominate the political agenda more and more. In the words of Mikhail Poltoranin, the democratic movement was in serious danger of 'drying up like a stream in the desert in the heat', and it was therefore necessary, especially with elections forever looming closer on the political horizon, 'to breathe fresh life and infuse fresh blood into the movement' in order that the pro-Western groups could approach the elections with confidence.[123]

Those elections, of course, emerged more quickly than perhaps anyone had previously foreseen, and by the time of their announcement in late September 1993 three brand-new groups had appeared on the scene, professing an allegiance to the overall pro-Western cause: Russia's Choice (which was formally led by Yegor Gaidar), the Party of Russian Unity and Accord (led by Sergei Shakhrai) and a new political bloc led by Grigorii Yavlinskii. From the perspective of electoral aspirations, these three groups were also joined by the Russian Movement for Democratic Reforms. As with Democratic Russia, the RMDR had seen its influence decline dramatically over the previous two years, but unlike Democratic Russia it was still adamant that it would contest the elections under its own political banner.

The mere fact that four separate groups were contesting the elections under a common ideological roof was in itself, of course, not a very promising start to the campaign. Although some commentators did try to suggest that the hybrid nature of the electoral system that was chosen – part proportional representation, part first-past-the-post – might boost the Westerners' overall share of the vote because of the range of choice on offer, this was never really an argument that carried any significance with the contestants themselves. Throughout the campaign they openly alluded to the harm caused by their divisions, but no matter what efforts were made to overcome such divisions, all failed abysmally.

Assessing the primary reasons for the continued divisions within their ranks, one would have to say that personality clashes and individual political aspirations were far more important than outright policy differences. The latter certainly existed in some key areas – for example, over the nature and pace of privatization[124] – but these were never a match for the fact that each electoral grouping was essentially meant to serve the function of being primarily a springboard for individual political ambitions in future *presidential* elections. That such divisions proved ultimately detrimental to each and every one of them, however, was undeniable. All plans to co-ordinate candidates in the single-member constituencies repeatedly failed to materialize. As a consequence, in many instances there were often three or four pro-Western candidates not only standing against each other, but criticizing each other far more vociferously than their main ideological opponents. To make matters worse, the personal bickering between the individual personalities of each group seriously negated what could otherwise have been a vitally important factor in their favour: the increasing politicization of the country's new business elite. As events turned out, many of the new business elite that did participate in the elections ended up standing as *independent* candidates in protest at the self-serving nature of the political groups.[125]

Notwithstanding the fact that all the new electoral blocs could point to a galaxy of 'star names' lending them support, it was undoubtedly Russia's Choice that was the most prominent of the pro-Western groups, the one on which most hopes for electoral success were pinned.

Formally established in the summer of 1993, this bloc had been able to unite some of Russia's foremost government officials at this time with a whole series of socioeconomic interest groups and parties. Individuals associated with the movement, for example, included Yegor Gaidar (the bloc's chairman), Anatolii Chubais, Andrei Kozyrev, Sergei Filatov, Mikhail Poltoranin, Gennadii Burbulis, Sergei Kovalev, Ella Pamfilova, Sergei Yushenkov, Arkadii Murashov, Dmitrii Volkogonov and Petr Aven. Other constituent group members, meanwhile, included the Association of Peasant Holdings and Agricultural Co-operatives, the Association of Private and Privatized Enterprises, the League for Russian Progress, the Union of Entrepreneurs and Leaseholders, and the Peasants' Party of Russia, Democratic Union and, most important of all, Democratic Russia.[126] Once again, however, what appeared on paper to be a formidable gathering of individuals and groups designed to represent a stable, consistent and constructive movement firmly wedded to the cause of Russia's definitive capitalization and liberalization turned out very quickly to be nothing more than an alliance of convenience at best, and a shambolic confusion at worst.

Right from its outset the movement rapidly began to split apart at the seams. By the end of the first few weeks of electoral campaigning, no fewer than a quarter of its regional branches had failed to come up with a mutually agreed candidate, with grass-roots members of Democratic Russia in particular refusing to relinquish organizational control to a movement many likened openly to a 'pact with the devil'.[127] Elsewhere, many of its top-ranking candidates often appeared to be campaigning in an American-style primary, rather than in a contest with other political parties and blocs; and in general, as Anders Aslund was reluctantly forced to admit, most candidates (not only from Russia's Choice, it has to be said) did not even bother trying to win over the support of the general public; instead they simply lectured people 'like old-style communists'.[128]

Certainly the final outcome of the electoral contest represented nothing less than a political disaster for Russia's Choice. Having set themselves a minimum target of 30 per cent of the party list vote, they ended up with no more than 15.51 per cent (see Appendix 1). The four 'pro-Western' blocs as a whole, meanwhile, could muster only just over 34 per cent between them and, as mentioned above, the Russian Movement for Democratic Reforms even failed to pass the 5 per cent minimum threshold to be awarded parliamentary seats from their party list.

Speaking in the aftermath of the election results, Yegor Gaidar commented that the outcome was indeed 'a battle lost', but that the overall war 'can still be won'.[129] Even this analysis, however, has begun to look decidedly optimistic.

At a conference of Russia's Choice in February 1994, designed to lay the foundations for the movement's transformation into a formal political party, Democratic Russia rejected any attempt at unification of the separate constituent parts. Consequently, while the former established the Democratic Choice Party in June of that year, the latter 'retaliated' by turning itself into the Democratic Russia Federal Party shortly afterwards. Prominent individuals who had been associated with both organizations in the recent past were now forced to choose a single allegiance;[130] some even ended up opting for neither, choosing instead to establish yet more new organizations and affiliations. This was the case, for example, with Boris Fedorov (the former Finance Minister) who, at the beginning of the year, broke away from the parliamentary faction of Russia's Choice and, in the process, created a new faction known as the Liberal Democratic Union of 12 December[131] (which in itself was to be the basis of a new federal-wide political organization known as 'Forward Russia', created in early 1995).

The sense of deep frustration that all this has caused in many circles has barely been camouflaged. As Vladimir Zharinov and Tai Pel'she put it, the whole basis on which the pro-Western liberal parties need to find some kind of unity now had to be laid all over again.[132] This sentiment was echoed by Marina Sal'e,[133] who went even further when she claimed in spring 1994 that the whole of the liberal Westerners' philosophy had been defeated – a defeat, moreover, that had been largely self-inflicted by its incapacity to win the struggle for the *ethical* high ground in post-communist Russia.[134] And just to make matters even worse, this in turn revived all the old familiar doubts as to whether Russia was culturally ready for Western-style liberalism.[135]

The Westerners' post-election troubles have also been exacerbated by a number of other factors. Deep rifts, for example, have clearly emerged between some of the most prominent advocates of Westernization and the man they had always accepted as their foremost standard-bearer, President Yeltsin. The lack of any kind of committed presidential endorsement for Russia's Choice undoubtedly lay at the heart of this rift, which has since been considerably deepened by events such as the Chechen conflict (a matter which will be taken up in Chapter 7).

Within the broader political spectrum, meanwhile, Russia's Choice has also started to find itself more and more isolated. Following their own poor showing in the elections, the Yavlinskii bloc, the Party of Russian Unity and Accord and the Russian Movement for Democratic Reforms have all attempted to occupy the new centre ground that emerged after the elections by reneging on many aspects of the traditional pro-Western programme. At the second RMDR congress in January 1994, for example, the leadership was openly adamant that the time had come to reject 'the most dangerous measures of the Western reform model'.[136] And, not surprisingly, the outcome of the elections has had an equally serious deleterious effect on the cohesiveness and strength of the Westerners' social base of support. The heterogeneity of the social alliance that was constructed was always going to be difficult to maintain once concrete policies started to be implemented; indeed, even before the elections many groups, such as the miners and other skilled workers, which had previously lent their support to the Westerners, had begun to move into opposition.

In the aftermath of the election and the political defeat of the Westerners the degree of fragmentation has increased significantly, especially within the intelligentsia, where some of the most prominent defections have taken place. This – as we will briefly see below and in later chapters – has perhaps been most evident in the debates that have taken place concerning Russia's 'imperial' heritage and the desirability of its now wiping the slate of the past clean by pursuing a new non-integrationist, non-interventionist role in the Eurasian geopolitical realm. But in much more general terms, as Andranik Migranyan has reluctantly admitted, the overall attempt to mobilize the vast majority of the Russian intelligentsia behind the pro-Western orientation has simply not succeeded, and with the benefit of hindsight far too much energy was expended on the efforts to win over this particular social group *en masse*.[137]

In many other areas as well, the degree of control previously exercised by the Westerners has been seriously undermined. In the first post-election government that was established, Westerner designs on many key portfolios simply did not materialize. The premiership was retained by the centrist Viktor Chernomyrdin, and the head of the Central Bank (a post that the Westerners have long had ambitions to control) was retained by their long-standing opponent Viktor Gerashchenko. Indeed, by February 1994 only two recognized Westerners remained in the Cabinet: Anatolii Chubais and Andrei Kozyrev. Given the nature of the new government, it was also not surprising that Prime Minister Chernomyrdin now felt emboldened to announce the definitive end of 'shock therapy' economic reforms – or what he euphemistically called 'the end of market romanticism': an announcement most cogently symbolized, perhaps, by the resignation of all leading Western advisers to the Russian government.

Pro-Western influence in the regions, meanwhile, has likewise looked increasingly fragile. Right from the beginning of the post-communist transformation, large swathes of the Federation have consistently been identified as strongholds of resistance to the kind of reforms the Westerners have wished to implement; something that is particularly apparent in the territory that stretches from the southern agricultural regions of European Russia to the heavily industrialized regions of the southern Urals.[138] And once again, in the aftermath of the December 1993 elections, the regional strongholds opposed to Westernization have either increased or strengthened their existing base of support. In a whole series of local and regional elections throughout 1994, for example, pro-Western forces were not so much defeated as annihilated by their political opponents.[139]

Last, but not least, pro-Western influence on many aspects of foreign policy has also dwindled fast, most noticeably in the sphere of relations with the other former republics of the USSR. Pro-Western ambitions for Russia to be rid of its 'imperialist' legacy have been sharply challenged by increasing pressures to treat the territory of the former USSR as a special sphere of Russian influence and, in particular, to view the defence of Russia's new diaspora in these countries as a legitimate *casus belli*.

Leading the challenge here has been the Russian military establishment which, according to most commentators, has long resented the disintegration of the old union structure and has also by no means been convinced by the Westerners' arguments that Russia would be better off in isolation from the rest of the CIS, or should at least not positively seek to carry out measures which would produce any kind of effective reintegrationist tendencies.

In the aftermath of the military's (clearly reluctant) role in quashing the October 1993 parliamentary rebellion, it was clear that the political regime owed the military a large debt, and for many observers elements of that debt were called in throughout 1994 – nowhere more so than in the military's new-found ability to involve itself directly in such areas as Tajikistan, Moldova, Georgia and Azerbaijan, where it increasingly played the role of propping up Geidar Aliyev's autocratic rule. The whole issue, then, of Russian imperial ambitions has simply refused to go away, and the longer it has stayed around, the more it has begun seriously to divide the ranks of the Westerners. On the one hand, for example, Yegor Gaidar cited as one of the main reasons for his resignation from the government in January 1994 the decision to consider establishing a formal economic union between Russia and Belarus. On the other hand, many other pro-Western liberals have begun to acquiesce in a more nationalist-orientated foreign policy; viewing it, in effect, as an expendable part of their overall cause in order to court greater short-term public support. Indeed, as Viktor

Bondarev astutely put it: 'If you listen to [the speeches of many pro-Western liberals today] it is difficult to tell them apart from the most active "patriots".'[140]

The ultimate dilemma here, then, is clear. If a liberal Russian state is to be constructed in the long term, it cannot possibly be constructed on the foundations of imperial-type responsibilities; the political and economic costs of maintaining such an empire would simply involve too much coercion. On the other hand, what kind of state, and in particular what kind of influence, can Russia have in the international domain if it voluntarily gives up its control over its former hinterland?[141] This dilemma is far from being resolved in any definitive way, though Roman Solchanyk is right, perhaps, when he asserts that it will be the *Russian–Ukrainian* relationship that will ultimately prove to be the acid test of Russia's (and the Westerners') ability to accept a genuine post-imperial political vocation.[142]

Before concluding our analysis of the Westerners' hegemonic potential, one final issue must be addressed. Underpinning the whole hegemonic struggle in Russia today is a cultural struggle for the heart and soul of the nation. For the opponents of the Westerners, it is precisely here, in the cultural sphere, that the real Achilles heel of the Westernization project can be found. Perhaps no one has summed up this underlying weakness running through the Westerners' project more cogently than Boris Kagarlitsky:

> Western society took shape without any need for such a concept as 'westernization'. For any western society progress involved an affirmation of the national culture, not a rejection of it. The historically developed state structures of Europe and the USA, with all their strengths and weaknesses, were not forced on to society from above or from outside; they were the product of the natural development of society itself. . . .
>
> The Westernist orientation of the regime today is a clear testimony to its crisis and marginalization. The state authorities were just as marginalized in post-Petrine Russia, in the times of Anna Ioannovna, Anna Leopoldovna, Yelisaveta Petrovna and even Catherine the Great. These were regimes isolated from society, profoundly hostile to the majority of the people and to the people's traditions and history.[143]

As we shall see in Chapter 6, Kagarlitsky has his own prescriptions of what the people's traditions in Russian history fundamentally amount to. In this, however, he is by no means alone, and it is these alternative formulations of Russia's cultural exceptionalism which have traditionally posed the bigger counter-hegemonic threat to the Westerners.

Russophiles

*Attempts to 'Europeanize' Russia can be compared to the labours of
Sisyphus: every attempt to roll the 'European stone' up the 'Russian
mountain' by the gigantic effort of the whole nation ended with it rolling
back downhill crushing and devastating everything in its way.*

Elgiz Pozdnyakov, 'The Soviet Union: The Problem of Coming Back
to European Civilization'

Defining the Collective Will

If the contemporary Westerners date their revival back to the liberal thaw
of the early 1960s, the contemporary Russophiles owe their revived intellectual prominence largely to the anti-liberal, anti-Western backlash that
set in after 1968. This immediate 'pre-history' of the contemporary
Russophiles has been dealt with at length by a number of writers and
specialists and will not, therefore, concern us here.[1] Suffice it to say that in
the post-Khrushchev era, Russophilia was very much the *acceptable* face of
'opposition', often receiving considerable tacit support from inside the
top echelons of the Soviet political establishment.[2]

On looking through the specialist literature on Russian nationalism (or
what I prefer to call 'Russophilia') in the last years of the Soviet era, one
is often faced with a minefield of heterogeneous labels and currents.
Depending on the author, one will invariably come across references to a
whole series of specific tendencies ranging from 'traditionalists' and
'nativists' to 'statists', 'conservatives', 'fundamentalists' and 'patriots', all
of which possess deep-seated roots in an equally varied range of intellectual ancestry. Valid as some of these distinctions undoubtedly were (and
still are), one nevertheless felt that the attempt to categorize in this way was
often excessively clinical; in short, some of the distinctions used were far
too neat and far too clean. Some major specificities aside, many of the

different currents were clearly interconnected by a great many shared ideas, not to mention a shared personnel. Boundaries between them were constantly shifting and constantly being transcended (or in some cases, constituted afresh). For this reason, I propose at this stage to bypass the distinguishing labels that have traditionally been used, and will instead discuss key ideas under the single, all-encompassing rubric of Russophilia. Any remaining contradictions and incompatibilities of the different component parts who advocate a Russophile approach will be dealt with in greater detail later in the chapter.

To put it another way: what we are dealing with here in this opening section is a set of fragmented and very general self-conceptions. It is the task of sociopolitical, hegemonic-aspiring forces to try to give concrete and specific meaning to these conceptions, which will unite large numbers of people behind a common project. There are, however, two groups that must be singled out for their uniqueness right from the start: the so-called 'liberal nationalists' and the 'national Bolsheviks'. The liberal nationalists, encompassing the likes of Dmitrii Likhachev and Sergei Zalygin, have, for the most part, been forced into the Westerners' camp. What we are dealing with in this chapter, therefore, is the notion of Russophilia as a counter-hegemonic project; or, to quote Yanov's time-honoured phrase, Russophilia as 'a rallying point of counter-reform'.[3] As for the national Bolsheviks – those communists who have openly embraced the cause of Great Russian nationalism – it is their attempt to seek common ground with the Russophile mainstream (somewhat reminiscent of the *Smenavekhovtsy* after the 1917 Revolution) that has been one of the most characteristic features of the whole post-communist political scene. How successful this attempt at amalgamation has been is, to a large extent, the central, definitive question of the current chapter.

The starting point of the Russophiles' collective will is the contiguous theme of Russia's distinctiveness [*samobytnost'*], combined with a virulent anti-Westernism. Following a historical, intellectual trend which dates back to some of the Slavophile ideas of the mid nineteenth century, all the major aspects of Western civilization are analysed in highly denigratory terms. Western-style individualism, for example, is correlated with a very decadent form of narcissism, which will always subject the individual to a life of isolation and loneliness. Western-style freedom, argues Igor' Shafarevich, possesses as much substance as 'a spoonful of sugar stirred in a cup of tea'.[4] It is as false as it is immoral, and Russia should always avoid its 'narcotic effects'.[5] And as for Western-style democracy, this is invariably considered to be the last illusion of the Russian intellectual[6] and, according to Aleksandr Dugin, 'can only ever end in disaster, since it is the direct path to the dictatorship of materialistic, plutocratic oligarchies'.[7]

Above all, it is the Westerners' supposed rational belief in a form of universalism that strikes at the heart of Russophile contempt. The notion that Russia has no choice but to follow in the wake of a set of universal principles and categories determined by the more technologically advanced nations of the West is seen as totally anathema, let alone disparaging, to the perceived cultural exclusivity of Russia's national, historical evolution.[8]

At the heart of this belief in Russia's exclusivity and distinctiveness lies the concept of *unity*; a virtue without parallel in Russophile thought which finds its expression in all manner of ways. It is the quintessential attribute, for example, in the Russophile belief in the *narod*, a qualitative categorization of the uniqueness of the Russian people. It is likewise at the centre of the Russophile notion of *pochvennost'*, the intrinsic intimate bond that all Russian people are meant to have with their native soil.[9] And it also figures most prominently, of course, in the perpetual glorification of the unified collective over the atomized individual, that constant search for an organic harmony, which has likewise witnessed the prominent re-emergence of the old Orthodox belief in *sobornost'* (either with or without its specific religious undertones). It is certainly this attribute of *sobornost'*, for example (a term basically denoting the organic synthesis of multiplicity and unity), that comes across most strongly in the popular literature of the so-called village prose writers [*derevenshchiki*], most notably in their idealistic portrayal of the organic community which is the embodiment of the traditional Russian village. And this is invariably contrasted in their works with the loss of a sense of community wherever 'alien' values of possessive individualism predominate; the latter being traditional Russia's greatest enemy.[10]

As for the ultimate institutional embodiment of this longed-for unity, this can most often be found in the Russophile conception of the state. To talk of the pivotal role of the state in Russophile ideology is not enough. One almost needs to rely on quasi-mystical language to express the feelings most Russophiles have towards it. The 'worship' of the state and the 'cult' of the state are expressions which more readily come to mind here.

Resounding with the echoes of ideas very familiar in the interwar years in Italy and Germany, the state is portrayed as the ultimate incarnation of a nation's and an individual's well-being. As Eduard Limonov has commented, for example, in his 'Manifesto of Russian Nationalism': 'everything that is good for my state is good for me. The state is above everything. Nothing matters but the state.'[11] From here, of course, it is but a short step to an open advocacy of authoritarianism, which likewise features prominently in much of the Russophile literature.[12] Intertwined with this statist ideology is an understanding of patriotism as nothing less than a *duty* to serve the state, even to the point of sacrifice. For many Russophile writers, no other nation in history has been able to secure such

unfathomable devotion to the state and the Motherland as Russia; hence
this is another factor which accounts for its distinctiveness.[13]

Needless to say, given such a conception of the state, the autonomous
life force of a civil society mediating between the state and social interests
of one kind or another is viewed as totally anathema. There can be no
interests outside of the state, nor can there be any associational barriers.
For many Russophiles, however, this does not necessarily mean to say that
democracy is equally anathema to the distinctive Russian way of life.
According to Aleksandr Dugin, one of the Russophiles' foremost metaphysical philosophers (who has drawn heavily on the writings of key
European ideologists of the 'New Right' such as Alain de Benoist, Carl
Schmitt, Julius Evola and Arthur Möller van den Bruck), Russia has traditionally been inclined towards an 'organic' form of democracy; and it is
this conception of democracy, rather than a liberal-based conception, that
should guide the country's post-communist transition. For Dugin, the key
attribute which underpins an organic form of democracy is 'brotherhood';
and such brotherhood, he writes, is possible only in a homogeneous society
composed of true citizens. What distinguishes a true citizen from a non-cit-
izen, we are told, is the extent to which an individual is connected to a
specific society by ties of history, blood, religion and politics:

> An organic democracy must qualitatively distinguish between citizens and non-
> citizens, relegating to its periphery those who have only a secondary, fortuitous
> or remote relation to the organic unity of the people. . . . Such democratic [sic]
> discrimination is absolutely essential to the preservation of homogeneity, which
> in reality is always under the threat of interference by ethnic, religious, economic
> and cultural minorities (slaves, vagrants, sectarians, emigrants, etc.) which can
> fracture a people's organic unity in the event that they are granted equal rights
> in its government. . . . [Without the distinction between citizen and non-citizen]
> organic democracy would immediately turn into either anarchy or tyranny.[14]

Citizens comprising an organic unity, continues Dugin, are imbued not so
much with a sense of national consciousness so much as a 'collective
unconscious'. This is likened to a 'social soul of the people, on which its
sacred, historic memory is imprinted, and which has preserved since antiq-
uity the psychic archetypes of Tradition in the form of enigmatic symbols,
vague images and typical dreams'.[15] In other words, a people's understanding of its own heritage is unconsciously defined through its folklore
and legends, and for as long as this predominates the people will be apt to
want a strong, renowned and courageous ruler to give credence to their
heroic images.

In an organic democracy, people want above all to respect their leaders
and admire them. They want leaders who are not like most ordinary
people, and part and parcel of a people's collective unconscious is to love

greatness and be capable of recognizing and choosing it (hence the 'demo-cratic' component) when it appears before them. This condition can be attained, however, only for as long as the collective unconscious retains priority over individual opinions.

Distinguished as it is by its long-standing contemplative abstraction from the rationalistic individual, its metaphysical qualities, its collectivism, communalism and 'anthropological pessimism', Russia has, by and large, we are informed, retained its sense of collective unconscious, irrespective of its radical changes in outward ideology over the decades. Westernization, however, offers a far more serious threat to the collective unconscious than did communism, argues Dugin. While liberalism contains absolutely nothing that could be mistaken for the expression of the genuine organic democracy that accords with the ancient archetypes of Russia's collective unconscious, the communist system did at least partake in some of its characteristics. 'It sometimes seemed', concludes Dugin,

> that the people was really 'participating', really deciding, really living in the vast construction projects, in the bloody and cruel, but Patriotic wars, and in a com-mon national pride in the knowledge that, even in this loathsome twentieth century, we Russians had been able to turn away from the world plutocracy and had chosen noble poverty over suspect abundance [and] physical suffering over the psychological terror of liberalism. There was something of organic democ-racy in Russian socialism. Our people is too great, too spiritual and too organic to have fully identified with a provocative, anti-national, false doctrine.[16]

Another aspect that underpins the vast majority of Russophile writings is a considerable belief in Russia's messianic destiny. Again, this can take various forms. In one sense, it provides new life to that centuries-old belief that has tended to equate Moscow with the Third Rome.[17] In another sense, it gives fresh credence to Berdyaev's more modern formulation of the so-called 'Russian Idea', which cherished the notion of Russia's destiny as a chosen land, which possessed enormous moral and spiritual superiority over the West, and whose mission it was to 'save' the West from its increas-ing decadence.[18] As Shamil' Sultanov has contended, for example, the current consumer-orientated phase of Western civilization represents its ultimate stage of cultural development. Such a 'decadent, hypocritical and atheistic civilization', he insists, 'will either lead to global apocalypse or give way to another, alternative trend based on . . . a fundamentally new attitude towards spiritual and sacred creative work and on a return to the archetypal traditions of humanity'.[19] There is simply no avoiding the final and inevitable clash between these two alternatives, and ultimately there can be only one outcome, writes Yurii Borodai: 'The future belongs not to the West but to the East.'[20]

More usually, however, the messianic tendencies in Russophile ideology are most closely associated with very clear-cut *imperialistic* ideas. For Russia, it is contended, the imperial idea is a natural outgrowth of its own very existence. As Aleksandr Prokhanov has remarked, for example, it is only as an empire that Russia has traditionally been aware of its deep, fundamental *raison d'être*.[21] And for Prokhanov, as indeed for most Russophiles, little distinction is drawn between the pre-revolutionary and the Soviet versions of the empire. Meanwhile, according to Aleksandr Vodolagin, Russia's mission is nothing less than the gathering in of new territories and peoples, the search for a new sky and new land, so as to create a new kind of unified human community unparalleled in the history of mankind.[22] In other words, Russia is either a great power [*derzhava*] or it is nothing.[23] The traditional strength of the Russian state, as we have already seen, is ultimately what epitomizes this great-power status, but for the most part in Russia's history it has been a state which has conceived of no restrictions at all on its possible extent. It was thus left to Aleksandr Dugin to draw the necessary inference of such beliefs:

> The creation of the Russian empire, which lasted for eleven centuries, devoured a great number of human lives. People died for their national, imperial and geopolitical interests. It is [therefore] necessary to fight and die in order to preserve our empire.[24]

Such desires to locate Russia's very *raison d'être* in a messianic *derzhava*, however, fall a long way short of the present reality of the post-communist inheritance; and this in itself, therefore, goes a long way towards defining key aspects of the Russophiles' collective will.

First and foremost, a good many Russophile writers cannot detach themselves from the idea that a great tragedy has befallen Russia, which has led to the humiliation of its people. As Aleksandr Kazintsev has written:

> Look at the great Russian people [today]. In the past the mere mention of their name used to destroy the walls of impregnable fortresses. Now they are defeated by Lilliputians. . . . We have lost our identity: the notion of 'Russians' has become an empty sound without any meaning.[25]

Similar sentiments pervade most of the theoretical writings, as well as the political programmes, of the Russophile groups. The current boundaries of the Russian Federation are denounced as 'an unnatural formation', and much is made of the potential of even this 'bastard' offspring of Russia to disintegrate into minuscule entities, therefore giving rise to that supposedly perennial Russian fear – anarchy and chaos.[26]

Xenophobia (a traditional element of Russophile thought throughout the ages), combined with a need to uncover 'hidden conspiracies' and find 'scapegoats' for Russia's apparent decline into oblivion, are also common elements in the Russophile creed today. Most notably, of course, that long-standing bogey anti-Semitism has been unleashed with renewed vigour. Igor' Shafarevich, for example, arguably one of the foremost theoreticians of an anti-Semitic creed, and author of what is often regarded to be a genuine Russian equivalent of *Mein Kampf* ('About Russophobia'), has long equated the Westernization project of Russian liberals with a formal and well-prepared Jewish plot, aimed at undermining Russia's unique existence.[27] As for the litany of other 'crimes against Russia' associated with Jews (and Masons) by Russophile writers and activists, space (fortunately) precludes a detailed examination. Suffice it to say, as Shlapentokh has pointed out, that anti-Semitism has become 'a sort of shibboleth that allows [most Russophiles today] to recognize one another'.[28]

Having examined the main components of the Russophile collective will in post-communist Russia today, it seems pertinent at this stage to take just a short step back in time to draw attention to the following salient question: to what extent were elements of the Russophile project the motivating force of the August 1991 coup attempt? In some ways, of course, this phrasing of the question is perhaps too stark, for it can be said right from the outset that the coup was *not* a Russophile-sponsored event. And by this I mean two things.

First, it has to be acknowledged that today's Russophilia is, in many important respects, a very different kind of phenomenon to what it was while the Soviet Union still existed. Quite clearly, the disintegration of the Soviet Union – and, just as importantly, the disintegration of the Communist Party of the Soviet Union – has had an enormous impact on the Russophile movement and on the project it espouses. Since December 1991 it has had to respond to a totally different set of circumstances, and that has inevitably changed its appearance significantly. In short, then, one simply cannot transpose today's Russophilia back to the days of August 1991.

Secondly, one can also state very clearly that the coup leaders did not belong to – nor for that matter did they have – what could be called close, integral connections with Russophile or associated groups. Their allegiance (and it is debatable whether one can really use this term) was, if anything, to certain key sections of the Soviet establishment (primarily, of course, the KGB and the other security organs), and their one well-defined aim was simply to preserve the Union and the power of certain sections of the *nomenklatura* that controlled the key levers of influence in that Union.

At no stage was there a direct attempt (perhaps because of time factors or perhaps for other reasons) to make even an informal kind of alliance with the Russophile or broader 'patriotic' groups then in existence, or to bring key members of these groups into the inner circles of the SCSE (State Committee for the State of Emergency) framework. Nor was there any indication of any kind of even basic organizational co-ordination.

It is certainly possible, as Richard Sakwa has conjectured, that if there had been a more formal alliance between the '*gekachepisti*' (the putschists) and the patriots (who, after all, he asserts, were their 'natural allies'), then the potential of the attempted coup might well have been more powerful.[29] This, however, did not happen, and such a conception must be left in the realm of conjecture. Moreover, while on this particular matter, it is also interesting to note the mixed reaction to the coup by some of the patriotic groups and their leaders. While some did express their immediate and absolute support,[30] many others were either ambivalent at best (no doubt because they too were taken completely by surprise and therefore preferred to adopt a wait-and-see kind of approach), or were explicitly *hostile* to the coup right from its initial stages. And there is certainly no shortage of explanations for such ambivalence or hostility. One must remember, for example, that many 'patriots' simply did not trust the leading members of the SCSE; others, meanwhile, were concerned at their obvious lack of organization and co-ordination, and by their abject failure to have constructed any kind of concrete, cohesive support base for their aims; while many others simply felt that the putsch was far too premature, as well as far too benign and limited.[31] As already mentioned, therefore, for these two key reasons, one is certainly correct in saying that the coup attempt was not a Russophile-sponsored phenomenon.

This, however, is by no means a complete answer to the question that was asked. Despite the force of the above two arguments, there is certainly a lot of compelling evidence to say that the *legitimatory* and *mobilizationary* discourse that was used by the coup leaders during their seventy-hour existence undoubtedly bore a much greater resemblance to Russophile ideas than it did to any other form of ideological discourse, *including* traditional aspects of Soviet-style socialism. Many Western commentators were either very late in appreciating or giving credence to this fact, or, in some cases, simply chose to ignore it. Andrei Kozyrev, however, Russia's first post-communist Foreign Minister (and leading Westernizer), has stressed the point forcibly. In an interview in *Izvestiya* in summer 1992, he argued:

> Last August the people reaffirmed their choice by refusing to submit to the SCSE. Incidentally, there was nothing at all in its platform about communism and it was identical to what the national patriots are proposing now. The people rejected this option, but efforts are again being made to impose it.[32]

It might be claimed, of course, that as a key participant in Russia's ongoing political struggle, Kozyrev (and many others as well) are perhaps prone to manipulate the events surrounding the coup attempt in a selective way,

depending on the audience they are addressing and on the biggest perceived threat to their own political aspirations at that given point in time.
This note of scepticism aside, however, there is, as already emphasized, a
good deal of more than circumstantial evidence to give credence to the sentiments voiced by Kozyrev.

Undoubtedly, the primary evidence for making this claim can best be
found in a comparative analysis of some of the documents issued by the
SCSE with some of the documents, articles and platforms published by
patriotic and Russophile-inspired groups in the weeks immediately prior to
the outbreak of the coup. By far the most noticeable comparison is that
between the 'Message to the Soviet People', published by the coup leaders
in the early hours of the morning of 19 August 1991 and the appeal entitled 'A Word to the People', which was published a few weeks earlier, on
23 July, in *Sovetskaya Rossiya*.

At the time of its publication the *Sovetskaya Rossiya* appeal was clearly
recognized as a political testament of ultra-conservative, Russian
nationalist forces. Its underlying themes were threefold. It was clearly anti-
Western in spirit, if not in substance, in its vilification of those in positions
of power who did not love their country, 'who fawn on foreign patrons and
who seek advice and blessings across the seas'. It talked of intentionally
destructive activities conjured up by pompous foreign masters and singled
out, in particular, the designs of greedy, money-grabbing capitalists. It
likewise made a strong denunciation of *perestroika* as a concept that
invoked Western traditions of democracy which had simply resulted in
the empowerment of 'frivolous and clumsy parliamentarians' who had
brought about the enslavement of the people and 'divided the tormented
body of the country into portions'. In contrast, the army was glorified as
the one remaining institution that retained the potential of providing a
much-needed sense of unity and harmony to society, and could act as a
'bulwark to all the healthy forces' remaining therein. Finally, a good part
of the appeal was nostalgic in its tone. It constantly warned of the
'unprecedented tragedy' that was befalling the country, and talked of the
accompanying need to preserve the old traditions and prevent a once great
state from dying and from 'plunging into darkness and oblivion'. It also
clearly implied that the 'great state' in question was Russia; or, to be more
exact, the old notion of Holy Russia.[33]

Of the twelve signatories that put their name to the appeal, three were
(and still are) prominent Russophile writers and intellectuals: Aleksandr
Prokhanov, Yurii Bondarev and Valentin Rasputin. They were joined by
two high-ranking army officers, General Valentin Varennikov (who was
part of the delegation that visited Gorbachev in his Crimean *dacha* on 18
August) and Colonel General Boris Gromov (deputy Minister of the
Interior). And most significantly of all, the signatories also included two

individuals not previously associated in such high profile with right-wing patriotic forces, Vasilii Starodubtsev and Aleksandr Tizyakov; and it was these two, of course, who later went on to be outright instigators of the State of Emergency Committee.

As for the SCSE's own 'Message to the Soviet People', this not only mirrored most of the statist, patriotic, collectivist and anti-Western sentiments contained in the *Sovetskaya Rossiya* appeal, it also reiterated most of the ideas virtually in the same order and in the same kind of language.[34] In addition, it threw in a few other significant points of principle of its own. It castigated, for example, the sharp decline in the population's standard of living, which had been due to the past few years' flourishing of officially sponsored black-market and speculative activities. It strongly attacked all the recent 'incantations' concerning the interests of the individual and a concern for his/her supposed human rights (i.e. from a Western point of view), which had ineluctably led to the degradation of the Soviet citizen, an encroachment upon his real rights and opportunities, and had ultimately driven him to despair. And it also shot a broadside at the Western-style moral decadence that had infected the country in recent years, emphasizing the fact that 'Never in the history of the country has the propaganda of sex and violence had such a scope, threatening the life and health of the future generations.' 'Millions of people', it went on, 'are demanding the adoption of measures against the octopus of crime and scandalous immorality.'[35]

Granted, then, that one can perceive a clear-cut relationship between some of the broad contemporary themes of the Russophile project and the kind of rallying calls that were utilized by the putschists (who can perhaps best be termed 'sympathizers' of the Russophile-type approach), what, if any, conclusions can be drawn from the rapid defeat of the coup, which might have a bearing on the current hegemonic potential of the Russophiles?

To draw a neat equation between the failure of the coup and the popular discrediting of the few basic ideas to which it gave credence would, I think, be far too presumptuous. In other words, Kozyrev was clearly exaggerating when he made this implication in the above-cited quotation. The coup failed for many more significant reasons than the kinds of ideas to which it tried so tentatively to give popular expression. The weakness and indecisiveness of the leaders; the total disunity within the organizations in whose name the coup was launched; even their unwillingness to sanction an early demonstration of brute, physical force, to name just a few reasons among many, were all factors that were more substantial in undermining the coup than their supposedly 'unpopular' ideology. Indeed, the very notion that the coup leaders possessed an 'ideology' of any sort is also totally inaccurate. They may have been 'sympathetic' to the Russophile, patriotic cause, but they were certainly not imbued with anything like a really coherent ideological vision that could bind them all together and act intrinsically as a basis from which they could reap vast swathes of support among key sectors of society.

All in all, then, one certainly cannot draw any definitive conclusions concerning the failure of the coup and its related effect on the hegemonic potential of today's Russophiles. And on top of this, one also has to remember that it was President Yeltsin's very own propagation of an explicit *Russian* patriotic sentiment that helped to mobilize a significant element of Moscow's population actively to counter the coup.[36]

Perhaps the real lessons that can be (or at least *need* to be) learned from the coup have been best summed up by Sergei Kurginyan. Kurginyan, it should be pointed out, is an important, if extremely contradictory, figure within the intellectual ranks of Russophile supporters, whose background and biography will warrant much closer scrutiny a little later on. Suffice it to say for now that he is a consistent advocate of a State-of-Emergency-type solution ('I was, I am and I will be an ideologue of an emergency situation'),[37] who nevertheless took an ambivalent view of the August coup attempt, sympathizing with the broad motivations of the leaders, many of whom were his personal friends, yet ultimately renouncing the unconstitutional methods they adopted.

Three factors, periodically cited by Kurginyan as contributing to the downfall of the coup and from which lessons must be learned, merit particular attention. First, he has argued in very forthright terms that if a State-of-Emergency-type situation is to achieve any success, it must be based on a coherent set of principles and ideas; it must have an identifiable social support base already in place; and it must have at hand a well-thought-out programme of policies to implement immediately and, if necessary, ruthlessly.[38] Secondly, in Kurginyan's own words, '[another] lesson of the putsch consists in the fact that the "social tissue" [of society], as a self-constituted phenomenon, even when it lacks strength and structure, can still manage to avenge itself on those who do not understand or deliberately ignore the principles of its internal construction'.[39] Finally, the putschists, Kurginyan has contended, were ultimately far too imbued with the ideas of the past. What they failed to understand was the necessity of developing a strategy and a set of ideas (not necessarily new in themselves, but at least formulated anew) that could take Russia into the twenty-first century.[40]

The Social Base of the Historical Bloc

It is often said that Russophile ideas are far more impressive, influential and evocative as a literary genre than as a form of direct social and political

comment.[41] The significance of this statement, I would contend, is even
more apparent when it comes to assessing the *economic* potential of
Russophilia.

As an 'anti' movement, Russophilia certainly carries a degree of socioeconomic weight. Given the conditions of Russia's economic situation
following the demise of the Soviet Union and the command-administrative
mechanisms of the old order, the potential for any opposition force to
'plug into' the discontent faced by millions of ordinary people in their
everyday struggle for survival is not in itself a difficult task. And with the
Russophile theorists' ability to draw a direct correlation between economic
degradation and 'alien' Western values being imposed on Russia, there is
always going to be a highly attractive 'market' of dissent for the
Russophiles to exploit to the full.

They can always, for example, capture the attention of an audience by
their advocacy of a deliberate conspiracy to transform Russia into nothing
more than a raw-materials appendage for the developed capitalist world.
They can remind people that Russia has been turned into an experimental
laboratory for the observation by the West of certain economic principles
that they themselves never dared apply in such a 'pure' form. And they can
point to the fact that with the rouble so worthless against the dollar and
the mark, it would take very little Western capital effectively to buy up
most of Russia's industrial capacity, lock, stock and barrel, at almost piti-
fully low prices.

When it comes to forging a much more positive, distinctive programmatic alternative of their own, however, it appears that this is a totally
different 'ball game'.

For a long time, the only really recognized economic theorist of the
Russophile camp was Mikhail Antonov, who rose to some degree of public prominence back in the Gorbachev era as a member of the prestigious
Institute of World Economics and International Relations (IMEMO) and
Chairman of the self-styled Alliance for the Spiritual Rebirth of the
Fatherland.[42] But the substance underlying Antonov's ideas was always
very flimsy. Being a supporter neither of the free market nor of the command economy, Antonov instead advocated an alternative
nationalist-based co-operative movement which would be underpinned by
a very strong set of moral and spiritual principles. Close links with the
West, he argued, would be tantamount to a form of 'capitulation' and
submission, and would also lead to a form of consumerism in Russia
which would be nothing less than 'unpatriotic'.[43]

At the heart of Antonov's philosophy was the twofold desire to turn
the economy away from the normal motivations of quantitative growth
and profitability towards improving the 'quality of life' through such
means as improved spiritual and physical health and more free time;

above all, considerable stress was laid on producing alternative economic programmes that would pay greater attention to the preservation of nature.[44] More recently, Antonov has also taken up the cudgel of warning of the dire consequences for the Russian Orthodox Church should the process of Westernization and capitalization continue unabated. A worker who is an Orthodox believer, he has argued, is simply of no use to the capitalist, since he refuses to believe in the power and esteem of money and wealth. As such, therefore, 'the Western capitalist needs a worker who tries to earn more in order to be able to consume more . . . I [therefore] foresee that repression of the Orthodox Church will begin shortly'.[45]

Antonov's ideas aside, the one really genuine attempt to provide a serious framework for Russophile tendencies has been most closely associated with the figure of Sergei Kurginyan and his research institute – the Experimental Creative Centre [Eksperimental'nyi tvorcheskii tsentr], set up in 1989 by a decree of the Council of Ministers. The aim of the centre is to bring together prominent young researchers from across the entire range of academic disciplines, in order to act as some kind of forecasting institute, making use of some of the latest computer technology.[46]

During its first couple of years, the centre was fêted by a number of prominent conservative political figures. It received considerable support, for example, from the Ryzhkov and Pavlov governments at this time, up to and including a governmental decree directing key ministries to liaise closely with the centre.[47] Apart from its headquarters in Moscow, there were also branches in Leningrad, Novosibirsk and Zaporozhe, and by early 1990 no fewer than 100,000 qualified personnel were contracted in some form or other.[48] As for Kurginyan himself, he came to prominence largely as one of the co-authors in 1990 of a widely publicized book entitled 'Post-Perestroika', which, among other things, analysed the deleterious effects of the emergence of a new criminal bourgeoisie in the former Soviet Union.[49] Shortly after the book's publication in January 1991, a political club of the same name was established. According to rumours, a copy of 'Post-Perestroika' was found on Kryuchkov's desk (the former head of the KGB) when he was arrested on 22 August 1991 for his part in the anti-Gorbachev coup, and was predominantly perceived as being a key ideological source for the implementation of the coup. Kurginyan's response when pressed on this matter, however, was simply to say that the book was so overwhelmingly popular that it probably could have been found on everyone's desk at that particular time.[50]

Often referred to as a latter-day Rasputin or a post-communist Cagliostro, because of the nature of his work at the Experimental Creative Centre, Kurginyan emerged as one of the strongest critics of the Shatalin–Yavlinskii '500 Days' economic plan for the introduction of a market economy. He has also long been a prominent advocate of a

Chinese-style authoritarian modernization, which would seek to pursue a process of economic reform unencumbered by the political niceties of democratization.

In many of his interviews the influence of Pierre Teilhard de Chardin is frequently cited, and this is often apparent in many of his essays and articles. Kurginyan has an absolute conviction that *cultural* phenomena are a primary determinant of socioeconomic and political life. He is convinced of Russia's intrinsic attachment to an Eastern, traditional type of social formation, and he once lambasted the Gorbachev approach to Westernization (underpinned by a desire to 'return to Lenin') as sheer 'intellectual cretinism'. The dichotomies and antagonisms of the struggle between communism and capitalism, he has written, are nothing in comparison with the dichotomies 'East–West' and 'Culture–Civilization'.[51]

Since the collapse of the old Soviet order, Kurginyan has consistently argued that the only thing that can save Russia from its current interminable decline into a 'Fourth World' entity is a 'neo-conservative alliance' which would be based on three things: patriotism, statist democracy, and what he terms 'white communism'. As for the main specific goals of a neo-conservative orientation, these consist, he writes, in a specific form of economic liberalization, a modernization of production and the upholding of traditional values (with the likes of Reagan, Kohl and Thatcher perceived as clear-cut role models for just such a Russian neo-conservative project).[52]

According to Jeff Gleisner, Kurginyan's socioeconomic ideas are mainly predicated on three key intellectual sources: Frankfurt School Marxism, post-industrialism and 'Managerial Bolshevism'.[53] Of these, it is his convictions in a right-wing form of post-industrial technologism, combined with a belief in post-industrial environmentalism, that have emerged predominantly in his post-Soviet work. The basis for these beliefs as first outlined in an interview with *Sovetskaya Rossiya* at the beginning of 1990, and they have subsequently been developed in a whole series of publications.[54] If we take a general overview of these writings, Kurginyan's blueprint for Russia's post-communist economic development – what he himself likes to call a truly viable 'third way' – would look something like this. What is needed to create a post-industrial system is first of all the centralization of resources; primarily so that new technology is not wasted on unnecessary causes. Centralization will also increase the intellectual potential that is so vital in any transition to and smooth functioning of a post-industrial system.

The key to the whole process is the creation of what Kurginyan calls 'production mega-structures of a new type', together with 'free intellectual zones'. These are not zones founded on commercial or hard-currency principles, but genuine zones of intellectual creativity geared towards the maximization of the country's material, financial and informational resources.

In the first stages of the transition, of course, a considerable amount of technological resources would have to be imported. Whereas in the past the Soviet system's policy on imports was haphazard and largely spontaneous, Kurginyan insists that a better strategic approach should be adopted which would have concrete aims in mind and which would concentrate on specific pivotal areas. By this means a new technological base could be established, and from this a 'technological chain' would be promoted (with each 'link' in the chain encompassing something in the region of 20,000–30,000 individuals).

Workers associated with the new technologies should be given every priority; in particular, they should be encouraged to work in the right kind of spiritual and physical environment.

When it comes to the new 'megastructures', these should consist of the healthiest parts of the country's industrial and production sector; backward elements which have been subsidized by the healthier sectors in the past must be broken away. A 'megastructure' would in effect be a 'super-company' which would come under direct state control. There would be no separate ministerial tutelage, as in the past, whereby each ministry effectively conspired against the other. The super-companies, needless to say, must have absolute priority over state resources. Moreover, the chain of command must be simplified and made efficient and effective; strict lessons, in other words, must be learned from the overbureaucratization that afflicted the old Soviet command-administrative structure.

Finally, underpinning everything to do with the super-companies and the free intellectual zones must be a sense of patriotism, duty, national honour and pride. The unique 'imperial spirit' of Russia must be re-created as an essential prerequisite of success. There should certainly not be a sense of inferiority instilled in people *vis-à-vis* the supposed achievements of the West in recent decades. Instead, Russian achievements of the past must be honoured and glorified (including the positive achievements of the Soviet era) and a sense of Russia's mission and destiny must be fostered. Above all (and this, for Kurginyan, marks the distinguishing element of a proposed Russian route to post-industrialism, in contrast with the Western route), the aim should always be to harmonize technological resources with the cultural and environmental specificities of the country. Technology, in other words, must not be used, as it is in the West, to tear asunder the cultural roots and cultural legacy of the country.

Clearly, then, if there is another model to which we could seek to compare Kurginyan's ideas, it would almost certainly be the Japanese/South Asian model of development. Japan, in particular, is often cited by Kurginyan and a whole host of other Russophile writers as a society which

owes its success to the fact that it has built up a post-industrial technological base, unequalled in the rest of the world; and, just as importantly,
has successfully overcome any residual contradiction that there might have
been in basing a process of rapid technological advancement on a well-
defined sense of national and cultural tradition.

Critics of the Kurginyan/Russophile approach to the economy, and in
particular its stress on a set of well-developed corporate principles, would
also cite Mussolini's Italy as another potential role model; an analogy that
possesses a lot of substance, of course, not only from the economic perspective. Perhaps, though, Aleksandr Buzgalin is more correct when he
stresses that the search for *any* analogous comparative model to the
Russophile approach ultimately risks the danger of blinding one to the fact
that the real impetus behind it is the simple desire on the part of certain
key sections of the old Soviet elite to preserve, or even enhance, their old
dominant status in a new guise.[55] In other words, Buzgalin would want to
apply the time-honoured question to the Russophile approach (as he
would to any other approach); namely, *cui bono* (who benefits?).

And of course, there can be no doubt that the answer, in relation to
Kurginyan's economic model, would be: the old Soviet Military Industrial
Complex (MIC). What Kurginyan has done is effectively to produce a glorified model based on the founding principles (if not practice) of the old
Soviet MIC. And what he would most like to do is to preserve the old
privileges and special provisions given to the MIC, but base those privileges on a different set of ideological/motivational reasons. As he himself
is not afraid to make perfectly clear: as the one sector that has been given
privileged access to new technologies already, and as a sector that is
already imbued with the virtues of centralization and a close relationship
between production and intellectual resources, the MIC would, of course,
make an ideal base for a transition to a genuine post-industrial system.[56]

Before leaving Kurginyan's ideas, one point needs to be stressed.
Although most Russophiles acknowledge Kurginyan as their foremost
economic theorist and give him considerable credit for his attempts to
develop an alternative economic programme, far from all his ideas have
been universally greeted in the ranks of the Russophiles. A frequent com-
plaint is that his ideas are often far too forward-looking and 'futuristic';
they amount, in effect, to a form of 'technological fundamentalism',
founded on what has been described as a new 'intellectocracy', all of which
are traits not overwhelmingly recognized as being positive in many
Russophile circles.

While the elite of the Military Industrial Complex represents one of the
possible social bedrocks of the Russophiles' bid for hegemony in post-
communist Russia, other social/interest groups have likewise been courted
with equal vigour. Mention should first of all be made here of the

Russophiles' attempts to attract the support of the army, attempts that long predate the collapse of the old Soviet order.

Back in 1989, for example, the Defence Ministry-financed *Voenno-istorichesky zhurnal* started to carry a series of articles by the well-known Russophile thinker Karem Rash, under the collective title 'Army and Culture'.[57] Under the notional guise of supporting a de-ideologization of the Armed Forces away from the traditional communist dogma, Rash made it perfectly clear that his primary aim was in fact to pave the way for a *re*-ideologization under a new set of motivational criteria. According to Rash, only the army remained in these troubled times as the embodiment and expression of all the progressive national, cultural and political traditions of Russian statehood. The soul of Russia was in the army's hands, and only it could defend the state from the ever-growing threat posed by such alien values as egoism, separatism and anti-state individualism.

Rash was also joined at this time by the powerful and evocative writings of his fellow Russophile thinker Aleksandr Prokhanov. Arguing, like Rash, that the army was the 'last receptacle of national identity', and was also the only force that had managed to emerge from the 'stagnation period' with its historic tradition of virtue intact, Prokhanov was adamant that winning over the army would ultimately provide the key to Russophile success.[58] 'Our army', he wrote, 'is an expression of the people's life, popular ideology and consciousness.' 'The paragon of the merchant, rock star or political manipulator', associated with the Russophiles' enemies, would never be able to replace the popular sense of affection and honour that was traditionally reserved for 'the warrior, the defender, the martyr for the people and for society as a whole'. The army, then, had the equivalent of a mission once fulfilled by the monasteries in times of invasion and expansion. Its barracks would be a shelter from death, from devastation and from famine. 'In conditions of [inevitable] civil chaos,' wrote Prokhanov, 'only the army will have the strength to protect [the people], to preserve the seed corn of future progress, to defend the values and sanctums so that when the troubles pass, they can be returned to life.'[59]

Messages exactly like these, or very similar in tone, have been a constant feature of Russophile writings throughout the period since 1989; indeed, prior to the events in Moscow in late September/early October 1993, it was widely believed that the Russophiles had, by and large, been very successful in garnering a considerable degree of support from within the top echelons and the ranks of the army. Nor was this just idle speculation on the part of observers. There really did appear to be very good grounds for making such an assumption. Many of the stated aims and goals of the military hierarchy did seem to coincide much more with the stated ambitions of the Russophiles than with those of the Westerners, and this was often reflected in the findings of many, if not most, sociological surveys of army attitudes at this time.[60]

Of course, in the light of the outcome of the events in September/October 1993, many assumptions about the depth of army support for Russophile opposition groups have had to be somewhat revised. Whatever the nature of army support for Russophile tendencies, it was nevertheless apparent that when 'push came to shove' the military hierarchy turned out to have its own *independent* agenda, and it clearly felt that that agenda would be better promoted and better served by buttressing the existing (weak) power structures already in place, rather than risking everything in a dramatic showdown. Not for the first time (and certainly not for the last time), events therefore demonstrated just how dangerous and risky it is for an opposition to (over)-rely on the military as a key social bulwark for their broader ambitions; especially when it comes to the point of attempting a spontaneous armed insurrection against the incumbent state authorities.

In addition to the army, the other major institution that the Russophiles have been eager to win over to their cause has been the Orthodox Church. As with the army, Russophile thinkers instinctively tend to associate the Orthodox Church as being the main purveyor and life force of all the traditional values of Russian society and statehood that they themselves hold so dear. Where the army is seen as the physical defender of the country, the Church is often given the task of protecting the country's unique spiritual attributes.

As in most other institutions, the collapse of the old Soviet order has unleashed a vigorous struggle both inside and outside the Church hierarchy for control over its future orientation.[61] And while they do not disclaim the oft-repeated assertions by many of its top leaders (including Patriarch Aleksei II) that it wishes to remain absolutely neutral in the current climate of political struggles, the Russophiles are clearly confident that the advantage lies with them.

Looking at some of the main concerns that have tended to preoccupy the Church since the collapse of the old order, the Russophiles do at least have some cause to view the church as a natural partner. For one thing, the Church leadership has clearly been worried by the extent of the competition it now has to face from other religious denominations that have recently been making their mark in Russia. Many of the representatives of these denominations (which include Protestants and Catholics, as well as the more evangelical religious sects) have been accused of proselytization by the Orthodox Church, and of spreading non-traditional, alien cultural-spiritual values to the Russian heartland.

Supported by Russophile activists both inside and outside the Church hierarchy itself, attempts have thus been made on behalf of the Orthodox

Church to impose legal restrictions on the activities of foreign missionaries and religious groups, geared towards maintaining and guaranteeing Orthodoxy's religious hegemony. Such moves, however, have been treated circumspectly by many pro-Western forces – not only because of their concerns to be seen upholding Western-type principles of religious freedom and human rights, but also because such proposals have caused a lot of consternation in Western countries themselves (especially, of course, in America), where such groups and sects tend to originate.[62]

It is not only the problem of increased competition from outside the realms of Orthodoxy, however, that has concerned the Church hierarchy in recent years. There is also a perceptible threat to its own internal unity, posed by such counterparts as the Russian Orthodox Church Abroad (and its Free Russian Orthodox offshoot in Russia itself), as well as by the so-called True Orthodox Church and a number of Orthodox schisms originating in Ukraine. And once again, leading Russophiles have been eager to be seen to be lending their support to the Moscow Patriarchate in these difficult times.

Thirdly, and more generally, the Church has increasingly expressed its concern at the depth of the 'spiritual vacuum' that seems to be pervading Russia's post-communist transition, and the extent to which the Westerners seem unable to fill this vacuum.[63]

Finally, there can be little doubt that in many aspects of its beliefs, the Church does intrinsically embody many of the values professed by the Russophiles; creating, in other words, a natural sense of shared affinity between them. First and foremost, this applies to their mutual acceptance that Russia personifies a unique spirit of collectivism that sets it far apart from other countries. It also incorporates their mutual affinity towards the concept of *sobornost'*, in both its religious and its more political form, which eschews a divisive kind of pluralism that does not seek to provide an all-encompassing form of unity and harmony. And there is also some degree of support from within certain sections of the Church for the anti-Semitic and messianic beliefs of Russophilia. On the anti-Semitic front, for example, Metropolitan Ioann of St Petersburg and Ladoga is generally viewed as the Church's foremost purveyor of such ideas, with his regular references to the notorious 'Protocols of the Elders of Zion' and an underlying Jewish conspiracy for world domination (though he is by no means alone within the Orthodox hierarchy).[64] As for Russia's messianic duty to overcome the 'deified idols of modern day western consumer societies', Vyacheslav Polosin (an archpriest and a leading member of the Russian Christian Democratic Movement) has perhaps recently emerged as one of its most literary exponents. In an interview with *Megapolis-Express* he asserted in no uncertain terms that 'the age of pure rationalism and individualism' is finally nearing its death throes. In its place, he argued, 'an age of intuition and insight is approaching', and it was Russia's duty to ensure the victory of this new age: 'Russia must become a country with a new social structure, which will be of a higher order than the western pseudo-heaven that shallow people extol.'[65]

Strong as the natural affinities are between Orthodoxy and Russophilia, however, one should nevertheless be aware of a number of factors that have so far prevented a close alignment between the two forces.

First, the instinct of the Orthodox Church, like that of the army, has always been to support the incumbent state authorities; and it must also be remembered that the Westerners have themselves been assiduously courting the Church through such influential means as the financing of a large church construction programme, as well as giving the Church much more autonomy over its own financial affairs. Secondly, few can doubt that the Church hierarchy is keen to rid itself of charges of collaboration with Soviet-style communism; and to this extent, it is often recognized that the Westerners do in fact represent a much greater break with the communist past than do the Russophiles. And thirdly, the Church cannot be seen to be ignoring the desires of many ordinary people to improve their basic material conditions of life; and since such material desires are openly associated with a Western type of economy and civilization, the Church has to do a careful balancing act in upholding the virtues of traditional Russian values, often in conjunction with a greater orientation towards other aspects of the Western way of doing things.[66]

Perhaps the most remarkable aspect of the attempt to win over the Orthodox Church to the cause of Russophilia, however, has been the lengths to which the post-CPSU national-communist (or 'national-Bolshevik') wing of the Russophile tendency has also been prepared to engage in the most enormous number of ideological *contortions*, designed to make a political alliance with the non- (or even *anti*-) communist wing of the tendency that much more viable.

When the collective will of the contemporary Russophiles was analysed in the previous section, emphasis was placed on the broad ideas and beliefs which united, for the most part, a great many heterogeneous strands of Russophilia. Beneath the surface appearance of unity, however, there has always lurked a degree of contradictoriness that many Russophile strands and groups have found hard, if not impossible, to overcome.

One of the major contradictions, or forms of incompatibility, which have often divided the Russophiles has concerned the difference in attitude towards the place of religion in general, and Orthodoxy in particular, in their overall belief system. At the one extreme stand the 'traditionalists' who have always looked to religion and Orthodoxy as the main foundation of Russia's uniqueness and the main hope of Russia's future salvation; at the other stand the national-communists and their traditional affinity with atheism. Consequently, whatever else might have united these two groups in a spirit of collective affinity, the gulf that lay between them on the issue of religion has nearly always tended to predominate.

In the new conditions of *post-communist* Russia, however, that gulf has suddenly started to look perceptibly more shallow and more narrow; and it is the national-communists who have done most of the 'filling' and the 'bridging'. One of the first indications that a change of attitude was occurring in some sections of the old CPSU on the question and importance of religion was to be seen in the aforementioned book 'Post-Perestroika'. What emerges from this work is a fundamental belief in the *spiritual* basis of communism. The close affinities between religious belief and communism are frequently alluded to (albeit in a surreptitious way), and far from being seen as a contradiction or even a weakness, they are instead highlighted as a powerful source of communism's potential *renewal*.[67]

At first, the tendency among some commentators was to portray this 'sudden' closer realignment between communism and religious conviction as nothing more than an astute tactical or pragmatic move on the part of the anti-Western forces inside the CPSU. It soon became apparent, however, that something more substantial was emerging. Even some of the most die-hard, orthodox communist ideologists – such as Richard Kosolapov, the former chief editor of the journal *Kommunist* – were now prepared to utilize the mystical language of religion to justify the special mission of the Russian people and their 'organic ideals' of a collectivist way of life. Indeed, Kosolapov was even prepared to make full use of the notion that the Russian people have been 'chosen' to suffer at the hands of others in their strivings to fulfil their spiritual, collectivist destiny.[68] Moreover, for Kosolapov, Leninism is not the antipode of Christianity; it is ultimately the saviour of all its long-standing humanist ideals.[69]

The writer Ivan Vasil'ev has also made a similar point. The ultimate aims of communism and Christianity are in all essentials virtually the same, and the ultimate role model for communism must always be the figure of Christ.[70] Meanwhile, according to Gennadii Zyuganov, the leader of the re-formed Communist Party of the Russian Federation in spring 1993:

> The Socialist Idea is a centuries-old phenomenon and has always been viewed as an idea encompassing social justice. In all world religions the love of one's fellow human beings has been a key postulate. Humanity has always intuitively orientated itself towards this basic truth. Jesus Christ, who defended the best moral values of humanity, was crucified for his beliefs in a fundamental social justice. We have our own roots in the most important moral values of the Russian Orthodox Church and for that reason we must give full credence to our roots and the long-standing tradition of collectivism.[71]

Such ideological contortions by the national-communists have clearly had an impact on certain sections of the Church hierarchy. Back in spring 1991, for example, the priest Dmitrii Dudko wrote openly of the fact that communists and Orthodox believers had finally found each other 'at the crossroads leading to Golgotha'. Communists, he argued, were in many cases believers 'through the back door' to the extent that they also put their faith in an ultimate future salvation. In present-day conditions, he argued, communists and Christians were the only ones who fully realized and appreciated Russia's spiritual mission. It is therefore clear 'that communists and believers must find a common language to express their beliefs and they must join with one another in the common struggle'. Believers who have suffered at the hands of the communists must be prepared to forgive. 'One must simply believe in God and Russia. This cannot be rationally explained, [but then] Russia is an irrational country.'[72]

Quite clearly, then, a *potentially* large social base for the Russophiles does exist in contemporary Russian society; especially when one considers the additional important factor of the depths to which many elements of society have become 'lumpenized', marginalized or dispossessed through the collapse of the old order and the imposition of a more Western-orientated socioeconomic structure. Indeed, not for nothing has the concept of 'lumpenization' become one of the most constant features of Russophile literature in the period since the failed August 1991 coup.[73] As always, however, developing this potential social base into a strong, cohesive force of opposition is dependent upon the creation of a viable political unit of some kind. And it is this that the Russophiles have always had most difficulty with.

Forging the Political Base of the Historical Bloc

As with the Westerners, residual problems of political organization certainly do not stem from a *shortage* of groups or 'parties' willing to associate themselves with the broad aims of the Russophile approach and cause. If anything, the opposite is more accurate. There have simply been too many groups established in the post-communist period; and as all of them have tried to carve out an autonomous niche for themselves in the new political environment in Russia, so this has worked against the necessity of constructing a really viable, coherent and cohesive single bloc of forces.[74]

It is not just numerical extravagance, however, that has dissipated the political strength of Russophilia. As I hope I have demonstrated throughout this chapter, the very nature of the Russophile collective will and its emphasis on the supremacy of Russia's cultural uniqueness does not lend itself to a fixed identity on the traditional left–right ideological spectrum. This has consequently meant that a whole plethora of totally disparate forces have sought to personify the Russophile cause, thereby seriously complicating the overall search for unity and cohesion. Not for nothing has the politics of Russophilia been popularly portrayed in the Russian media as the 'Red–Brown' (or, from a different perspective, harking back to the days of the Civil War, a 'Red–White') orientation. Such is the breadth of Russophilia's potential allegiance.

It is certainly not for want of trying, however, that no genuine political cohesion has really been established. Starting with the republican parliamentary elections in the former Soviet Union in the spring of 1990, which witnessed the creation of a Bloc of Social-Patriotic Movements uniting ten different Russophile organizations at this time,[75] various attempts have been made to achieve that ever-elusive viable form of unity.

In summer 1990, for example, following what turned out to be a near-disastrous electoral performance by the 'Social-Patriots',[76] combined with a rather weak peformance by the conservative-nationalist elements within the CPSU, an organization bearing the name of the Centrist Bloc was established. Representing at its height a total of more than forty (micro) 'parties' and groups, its main significance stemmed from its explicit and very close association with conservative elements inside the ruling CPSU, the KGB and the armed forces. Determined at all costs to counter the growing influence of the liberal Westernizers, and stressing their allegiance to the maintenance of a strong, Russian-dominated USSR, five groups in particular provided momentum and a sense of continuity to the bloc: the Russian People's Front, led by Valerii Skurlatov; the People's Constitutional Party, led by Sergei Volkov; the People's Information Party, led by Ivan Yuzvishin; and two organizations bearing totally erroneous names in view of their political convictions, the Sakharov Union of Democratic Forces, led by Vladimir Voronin; and the Liberal Democratic Party of Vladimir Zhirinovsky.[77]

As events turned out, the Centrist Bloc managed to survive for less than a year before once again breaking up into various component parts. While most of the groups, however, slithered back into the oblivion whence they had originated, Zhirinovsky's Liberal Democratic Party somehow contrived to emerge with a significantly enhanced recognition. We should therefore make a short digression to focus more specifically on the emergence on the post-communist political scene of this key force.[78]

Originally constituted in March 1990, the party at first claimed to uphold the pre-revolutionary traditions of established liberal organizations such as the Cadets, the Octobrists and the *Trudoviks*.[79] Suspicion about such claims, however, quickly surfaced after it became apparent that both the party as a whole, and Zhirinovsky in particular, were openly being defended and buttressed by certain elements of the old CPSU and KGB apparatuses – charges that have persisted and increased in line with the party's ever-growing prominence.[80]

In the aftermath of a long-standing struggle for absolute supremacy of his party, Zhirinovsky immediately moved to dispel any doubts as to where it stood. Openly admitting that his party's misplaced original public adherence to classical liberal democratic values was a 'gamble', he now made no attempt whatsoever to hide the fact that it supported a rigid authoritarian approach to the problems besetting Russia and the once 'glorious empire'. From now on, it was emphasized, the party would seek to appeal to the alienated youth of the country, the 'new poor', as well as to those sections of the new economic elite which had long recognized the paramount need for order and stability.[81]

Few can deny that during his period of leadership of the Liberal Democrats, Zhirinovsky has astutely carved out quite a 'colourful' reputation. He has consciously sought to portray himself as an arch-defender of Russian national interests, and has quickly learned the benefits of the addage that for a politician all publicity, including *bad* publicity, helps to promote the cause one is trying to purvey. To that extent, he is always prepared to be deliberately provocative and shocking, in order to keep himself in the public eye.[82] Without doubt, the real turning point in Zhirinovsky's political fortunes can be traced to his candidacy in the June 1991 presidential elections. As a still relatively unknown public figure, and as someone who was frequently vilified and ridiculed from many quarters for some of his extreme Russophile positions, he nevertheless emerged with a more than creditable third place behind Yeltsin and former Soviet Prime Minister Ryzhkov, with a poll of 7.8 per cent (representing some six million Russian voters).[83] As for his fortunes following the elections, perhaps nothing personified the success he had built for himself better than the fact that a great many articles on him in the Russian press – whether favourable or not – were frequently prefaced with the acclamatory title 'the Zhirinovsky *phenomenon*'; and not for nothing did commentators start openly to equate his charismatic potential with that of Hitler back in the days of the Weimar Republic.

Long before the December 1993 elections gave him a world stage to perform on, then, Zhirinovsky had already stamped his personal mark on post-communist political life. Quite whether this has helped or hindered the broader political cause of Russophilia, however, is another matter entirely. While Zhirinovsky has often tacitly supported the efforts of other groups to coalesce into a broader and more effective political bloc, he has never really been a key player in the alliance-building process following the collapse of the Centrist Bloc. Two factors, it seems, have come into play here. First, there has undoubtedly been a lot of residual mistrust of

Zhirinovsky from other sections of the Russophile camp. His style and manner have always singled him out as a 'special force'. He is not by nature a 'team player', and there are clearly those in the Russophile camp who would not be willing to associate themselves with, let alone subordinate themselves to, the likes of such an individual. Secondly – and again this follows on from Zhirinovsky's character – there has clearly been a strategy on his part to play a 'long game'. Following the June 1991 presidential elections, there was undoubtedly a sense in which he felt that he and his party now had everything to play for in the political climate enveloping Russia. Given time, he adamantly believed, it was he who would inevitably emerge as the natural, undisputed leader of the Russophile, national-patriotic cause, and his own party would be the natural base of Russophile political aspirations. Until such a stage of recognition could be reached, it would be much better to remain somewhat aloof rather than be prematurely submerged in some kind of grand alliance.

With the collapse of the Centrist Bloc, the next organization that was left to pick up the pieces of coalition-building was *Soyuz*, a force that had started out as a parliamentary faction in the Soviet Congress of People's Deputies but which, at its second congress in April 1991, took the decision to transform itself into a much broader mass movement.[84]

For a time, *Soyuz* really did begin to look as though it was going to be the basis of a powerful and effective political force. It had a high-profile leadership (thanks to the activities of the so-called 'black colonels', Nikolai Petrushenko and Viktor Alksnis); its links with conservative elements of the CPSU and KGB were very strong; and after its second congress it had a recognizable programme of aims and ambitions orientated specifically to the preservation of the Soviet Union as an integral state. None of this, however, proved in the end sufficient to prevent it from fracturing at the seams at the time of the August 1991 coup. As a consequence, *Soyuz* was effectively doomed to oblivion long before the eventual break-up of the Soviet Union totally deprived it of its primary *raison d'être*.

With the remnants of *Soyuz*'s former potential scattered in ruins, it became increasingly apparent that nothing less than a total realignment and revamping of the political base of Russophilia was now needed. This was emphasized even more with the failure of the *Nashe* movement – a coalition of national-patriotic forces under the leadership of Aleksandr Nevzorov (a well-known television personality in St Petersburg), Viktor Alksnis and Sergei Kurginyan – to make any kind of significant impact at all.[85]

This process of realignment was several months in the making, and its final outcome witnessed the creation of several new organizations. In late December 1991, for example, the founding congress of the Russian All-People's Union [*Rossiisky obshchenarodnyi soyuz*] – henceforth RAPU –

took place in Moscow. Under the overall leadership of the young but already prominent Russian parliamentarian Sergei Baburin, the Union professed its strong allegiance to a number of key Russophile causes, among which were an espousal of a 'people's' form of democracy, quite distinct from a Western-style liberal democracy; the promotion of social justice, which thereby excluded a Western model of strict private ownership; a conviction of the superiority of collectivism over individualism; and last, but not least, a duty to defend Russian patriotism and promote the cause of a strong form of Russian statehood not only *vis-à-vis* the internal nature of the Russian Federation, but also in relation to Russian state interests in the rest of the territory of the former Union.[86]

The emergence of Baburin as one of the foremost political figures supporting the Russophile cause was extremely significant; not least for the fact that his political career had originally been launched under the auspices of Democratic Russia. Baburin's switch of allegiance, however, was by no means an isolated incident at this time. Also in attendance at the RAPU congress were the leaders of a number of other organizations, which only a few weeks earlier had been constituent members of Democratic Russia. The most prominent of these were Mikhail Astaf'ev, head of the Constitutional Democratic Party – Party of People's Freedom and Viktor Aksyuchits, leader of the Russian Christian Democratic Movement.

Although neither organization formally joined RAPU, their participation as observers certainly indicated where their new sense of allegiance lay;[87] indeed, it was the leader of the Christian Democratic Movement, Aksyuchits, who was primarily responsible for organizing an even bigger gathering of national-patriotic, Russophile forces some three months later, in February 1992. Held under the official title of The Congress of Civic and Patriotic Forces of Russia, the February 1992 meeting witnessed the largest open gathering of Russophile forces hitherto seen in Russia for many decades. Apart from the Christian Democrats and the Constitutional Democrats of Astaf'ev, more than a thousand delegates from forty-eight regions of Russia were in attendance, representing such diverse groups as the Cossacks and Orthodox religious brotherhoods, as well as a whole range of bizarre-sounding movements, conjuring up images of a long-lost Russian national identity.[88]

While most of the media attention focused on the uninvited antics of Dmitrii Vasil'ev and his colleagues from *Pamyat'* – a far-right, extremist organization that virtually no other Russophile-orientated group has dared to associate with openly[89] – a number of concrete issues of significance did emerge from the meeting. For one thing, it provided a public platform for the then Vice-President, Aleksandr Rutskoi, to *re-establish* his own Russophile credentials, notwithstanding his political allegiance to the supposedly different cause of centrism, a factor that was to have an immense political knock-on effect.[90] And for another thing, it gave rise to another new organization, the Russian People's Assembly, RPA [*Rossiiskoe narodnoe sobranie*], which further cemented a number of new ties that were beginning to be established at this time. Aksyuchits became the official leader of the Assembly; he was joined by Astaf'ev, Nikolai Pavlov (of RAPU) and the prominent Russophile artist Vyacheslav Klykov. Other constituent members of the governing central council, meanwhile, included representatives from the National Republican Party of Russia, the Russian Party of National Rebirth, the Russian Party of the Monarchist Centre, the Russian Union and the Cossacks Union.[91]

In principle, at least, the RPA insisted that it represented a more moderate form of Russophilia, which would therefore mark it out as the key constitutional opponent of the Westerners. In practice, however, its self-professed moderation became harder and harder to define in any real, concrete sense.

At about the same time that the RPA was making its appearance on the political stage in Moscow, yet another 'patriotic congress' was being organized in the city of Nizhny Novgorod. Out of this emerged the Russian National Council, RNC [*Russky natsional'nyi sobor*]; an amalgamation of a whole range of minuscule associations from across the Federation under the combined leadership of the former KGB officer Aleksandr Sterligov, retired army general Albert Makashov, the village prose-writer Valentin Rasputin, Gennadii Zyuganov of the Russian Communist Party and Aleksandr Barkashov from the organization Russian National Unity (a breakaway section of Vasil'ev's *Pamyat'*).[92] The Russian National Council was always far less ambivalent than the RPA about its attachment to supposedly 'moderate' Russophile goals. A vociferous supporter of the superiority of Slav values (e.g. *sobornost'*) over and above those of Western-style human rights, and vehemently anti-Semitic in its pronouncements, the RNC openly eschewed constitutional political norms in favour of a more forthright form of attack on the pro-Western forces of opposition (by means of such things as 'red brigades' or a 'movement of Russian national resistance').[93]

Within the space of three months, then, no fewer than three new coalition forces, professing their allegiance to broad Russophile goals, had managed to emerge on to the political scene. From an overall ideological perspective there was little to choose between the three groups. What kept them apart were some obvious personality clashes and some specific disagreements over the minutiae of policies, together with a number of differences concerning the nature of the strategy that needed to be pursued in the new political climate.

As for the latter, one issue above all others had consistently led to heated argument and division, both within and between their respective ranks, and that issue concerned the stance they should adopt towards the nationalist wing of the now fragmented (and at this stage, *banned*) communist movement in Russia. This was by no means a new issue of debate among them. From the moment it became apparent that the CPSU was losing control of the reform process that it itself had initiated, and especially from the moment when clear-cut factional divisions had emerged within the CPSU, thereby fostering the creation of a much more conservative-orientated *Russian* Communist Party organization, Russophiles of all different hues and persuasions had been faced with the dilemma of whether or not to seek a coalition with the national-communists.[94]

At heart, they had to choose between three possible options: a commitment to *non-co-operation* at any price for fear of being subsumed once again under an ideological force that made an allegiance to Russophile causes a mere subsidiary of its other ambitions; a commitment to *co-operation* at any price in the recognition that the ultimate goal was the defeat of the Westerners, and that anything that took their place could not possibly be inferior; and finally, a commitment to co-operation *on condition that* Russophile causes predominated over any remnants of communist ideology not conducive to that cause.

Of the three options available, it was the third option that ultimately emerged as the most favoured approach; although it has to be said that the degree of consistency to any of these approaches by various groups was always rather minimal.

The overall tone of the new relationship *vis-à-vis* the national-communists was perhaps best summed up in some of the speeches of the more moderate Russophiles at the Congress of Civic and Patriotic Forces in February 1992. Such was the nature and depth of the anti-Russian and anti-state policies being pursued by the Westerners, it was argued, that there was little option but to amalgamate the common strands linking the mainstream Russophiles with the national-communists. A lot of their policies and their general outlook made such an amalgamation both attractive and inevitable, although the ultimate onus of responsibility would be on the communists to prove their genuine commitment to those shared causes. In short, there had to be a definitive line of demarcation between national-Bolshevism and communist-Bolshevism.[95]

The first real indication that a concrete, formal basis for co-operation had indeed been established emerged at the beginning of March 1992. Under the auspices of the Russian All-People's Union, a conference was organized which finally brought together under one roof the whole range of non-communist Russophile tendencies and some of their main communist fellow-travellers, represented by the likes of the Communist Party of the Russian Federation (which considered itself the main successor to the Soviet-era Russian organization), the Russian Communist Workers Party (whose leadership included such luminaries as Richard Kosolapov, General Albert Makashov and Viktor Anpilov), as well as a number of smaller pro-communist groupings such as the United Front of Russian Workers.[96]

Following the conference, a formal programme of aims was drawn up, bearing the title 'Justice, Nationalism, Statehood and Patriotism', which committed its sponsors, among other things, to overcome any residual differences that had previously separated the disparate forces of the 'Left and Right' opposition.[97] Moreover, to buttress this call for unity a formal joint Council of Opposition Movements was created, charged with the specific task of paving the way for the ultimate establishment of a unified organizational structure that could represent the fullest range of Russophile ambitions.

A month later, in April 1992, the first fruits of this new commitment to overcome the traditional hostilities between the 'Whites' and the 'Reds' in an effort to save nothing less than the 'heart and soul' of Russia, was witnessed in the creation of a brand-new *parliamentary*-based bloc, known as Russian Unity. Led by Sergei Baburin, the bloc united five previously distinctive neo-communist and nationalist factions, and immediately became the largest and strongest force in both the Supreme Soviet and its parent institution, the Congress of People's Deputies.[98] Throughout the summer of 1992, efforts continued apace in a whole range of different forums – not least at this time on the streets of Moscow itself[99] – to construct an *extra*-parliamentary force to mirror that of Russian Unity. In September, a formal political declaration of the left and right 'united opposition' was agreed upon,[100] and in late October a constituent conference was finally convened to confirm the establishment of a brand-new organization, the National Salvation Front (NSF).[101]

Amalgamating a vast range of groups and parties, the National Salvation Front represented the Russophiles' most serious attempt to achieve a genuine basis of political unity and cohesion. Indeed, there was no better indication of the depth of the perceived threat posed to the pro-Western forces than the fact that President Yeltsin felt compelled to prohibit the Front on spurious grounds immediately after its inaugural congress, a move rescinded in February 1993 by a verdict of the Constitutional Court.[102]

Certainly, few would deny that at the time of its foundation the NSF posed a very real and serious challenge, and that Yeltsin had every reason to feel threatened. A simple perusal of the names gathered together in its Political Council and those lending it their firm backing and support was enough in itself to provide it with an aura of oppositional strength not witnessed heretofore: names such as Astaf'ev, Baburin, Makashov, Zyuganov, Ilya Konstantinov, Nikolai Pavlov, Valerii Ivanov, Nikolai Lysenko, Valerii

Smirnov, Gennadii Sayenko, Viktor Alksnis, Aleksandr Prokhanov, Igor' Shafarevich, Eduard Limonov, Valentin Rasputin, Svetlana Goryacheva, Aleksandr Nevzorov, Richard Kosolapov, Eduard Volodin, Sergei Kunyaev, Yurii Sidorenko, Sazhi Umalatova, Vladimir Isakov, Sergei Mikhailov, Stanislav Terekhov, Vasilii Belov, Aman Tuleyev. In short, a veritable 'who's who' of leading Russophile thinkers and political activists from the past three years or more.[103]

Even the eventual non-affiliation of Viktor Aksyuchits's Christian Democratic Movement and Aleksandr Sterligov's Russian National Council did little to detract from the overall appearance of the Front's underlying strength;[104] and few, therefore, would have countermanded the claim, made by one journalist in the pages of *Sovetskaya Rossiya*, that here at last was an opposition force which had surmounted past differences 'in the name of saving the Fatherland', whose basis of concord and agreement could well possess a significance far into the future.[105]

Without doubt, of all the forces that came together under the common auspices of the National Salvation Front, it was the newly established link with the main Communist Party of the Russian Federation that was the one with the most significance attached to it. It was left to Astaf'ev, speaking to the assembled delegates at the inaugural congress, to provide the basic logic to the new form of co-operation. 'What people think of the October Revolution of 1917', he insisted, had now become largely 'academic'. 'Just as the French can differ over Napoleon's role, but still not forget their national interests, so here people of the Left and Right need not be enemies.'[106] The underlying importance of the new formal linkage, however, went well beyond the confines of transcending ideological differences of the past. What the Communist Party, even in its formal condition of illegality, had to offer any prospective partner or ally was a well-oiled organizational structure encompassing the whole territory of the Russian Federation, which was unequalled by any other political force, irrespective of the 'camp' they belonged to.

If the National Salvation Front could have open access to this organizational set-up, then clearly its position would be strengthened. This, however, depended on two obstacles being overcome. First, at the moment when the NSF was first established, the Communist Party was still officially subject to President Yeltsin's post-August 1991 ban; secondly, assuming that the ban was rescinded, it depended on a new leadership being elected which would give formal backing to the new alliance with the mainstream Russophile forces, which had been forged by certain key individual figures, most notably Gennadii Zyuganov.

As events turned out, of course, both obstacles were indeed resolved very satisfactorily in the National Salvation Front's favour. In late November 1992, the Constitutional Court voted in favour of allowing the

Communist Party to re-establish itself as a legitimate political force; and in February 1993, at its re-foundation congress, the assembled delegates unanimously elected Zyuganov himself to the foremost leadership position.[107] As one commentator thus put it, in one fell swoop the prestigious 'generals' in the National Salvation Front were now handed a mass rank and file on a plate; a rank and file, moreover, that came equipped with half a million branch offices, one in virtually every town and city in the country.[108] And just to make the linkage with its Russophile allies absolutely clear, the new programmatic statement of the Communist Party, drawn up at the congress, stressed categorically that its 'top priority' was 'the creation and consolidation of a political alliance between communists and all progressive and patriotic forces opposed to the pseudo-democratic regime which has brought the country to the brink of national catastrophe. . . . The key unifying idea of Russian communists at the current historic time is the idea of patriotism. . . .'[109]

It was not just from an organizational-administrative point of view, however, that the prospects for the NSF looked considerably better than those of any of its Russophile predecessors. From a policy point of view as well, a genuine attempt appeared to be made to focus specifically on those issues that united the different strands of the Front; and every effort was made to articulate those issues to the maximum possible effect, in terms of building up a really viable social base of support.

Starting with the September 1992 Political Declaration and continuing with numerous policy statements afterwards, three issues in particular stood out as embodying the Front's creed. First, there was a consistent emphasis on the need to preserve Russia's state integrity at all costs, in conjunction with a messianic unificatory role on the Eurasian landmass that had previously defined the territory of the USSR. Secondly, there was considerable emphasis in all the programmatic statements of the NSF on the concept of 'social justice' and on the desirability of restoring the system of strong state social guarantees, 'which were an inalienable part of the way of life of all [the] country's citizens during recent decades'. A well-entrenched right to work, housing, rest, education and health care formed the core basis of the NSF approach here, and these issues were also inextricably linked to the regeneration of the Russian state and its pivotal role *vis-à-vis* society. And thirdly, few opportunities were lost in focusing on the spiritual-traditional degeneration that had been inflicted on Russia following the Westerners' attempts to commercialize all aspects of culture. A historical impasse had been reached, it was often emphasized, in which the whole of society was in danger of being mired in a state of total demoralization.[110]

With its official registration finally approved by the Justice Ministry in late March 1993, the NSF convened its second congress towards the end of

July that year. As a result of its ever-closer affiliation with the communists (as well as signs of an increasingly vociferous campaign against what it saw as a 'Judaeo–Masonic conspiracy' engulfing Russia), three of its original co-chairmen (Baburin, Ivanov and Pavlov) and three constituent organizations (RAPU, the Party of Russian National Renaissance and the National Republican Party of Russia) withdrew their membership of the Front.[111] Even this setback, however, did little to dampen the perception of its overall political potential. Indeed, as a number of commentators pointed out, the primary effect of the resignations, ironically enough, appeared to be the emergence of a leaner, fitter, more compact and coherent organization. While the decision-making Political Council was renewed with a new batch of high-profile leaders, a much stricter form of internal discipline (akin to communist-style democratic centralism) was imposed on the rank-and-file membership, and this clearly had the impact of strengthening the overall effectiveness of its administrative organs.

By early autumn 1993, then, the NSF – on paper, at least – looked very well placed. With the likelihood of early elections looming ever closer on the political horizon, some opinion polls suggested that it had garnered a respectable solid base of support for itself, and provided it could stay together until the elections, it would be the obvious 'magnet of attraction' for other like-minded groups.[112] Events, however, changed radically once Yeltsin abolished the old Supreme Soviet in September 1993. The leadership of the NSF, quite logically and to no one's surprise, came out with strongly-worded protests against the presidential dissolution. Unfortunately, though, for its own fortunes, it did not restrict its protests to words alone. When the moment of decision was reached to counter Yeltsin's actions with an attempted uprising in support of parliament, many of the leaders of the NSF led the call to arms. With the rebellion's defeat on 4 October 1993, following the destruction of the parliamentary building itself, the NSF was one of the first organizations to be banned under the ensuing State of Emergency, decreed by the victorious Yeltsin.

As with *Soyuz*, then, back in August 1991, any residual capacity that the NSF might have had of being a strong political articulator of the Russophile cause and its many divergent strands was shattered by its response to a *coup d'état*. The fact that on this occasion the coup was at least not of its own *initial* making was ultimately of no help to its overall cause.

Hegemonic Potential

In the immediate aftermath of the October 1993 uprising the hegemonic potential of the Russophiles, to all intents and purposes, appeared to be negligible. Certainly in the build-up to the December 1993 elections, which were called immediately after the dissolution of the old parliament, few commentators would have given the Russophile forces much cause for optimism.

The ban on the National Salvation Front was formally lifted by the Justice Ministry in late October, but they were not given permission to campaign or participate in the elections themselves. The one attempt to unite different tendencies – the so-called 'Fatherland bloc', which was an amalgamation of the Socialist Party of Workers, the Union of Cossacks, the pro-monarchist Union of Russia's Renaissance (led by Dmitrii Rogozin) and the statist Union of Oil Producers – failed to get the requisite number of signatures in order to be able to compete in the election proper. A similar fate befell the Constitutional Democrats led by Astaf'ev (who was now joined by such Russophile luminaries as Igor' Shafarevich and Aleksandr Nevzorov); the Russian Christian Democratic Movement led by Aksyuchits; the National Republican Party of Nikolai Lysenko; and Sergei Baburin's RAPU.

This left just three organizations in the campaign that could broadly or loosely be said to have belonged to the Russophile wing. Of these, the Communist Party of the Russian Federation under Zyuganov's leadership was allowed to enter the electoral race only some several weeks after the rest; and all indications were that it was badly split between those who wanted to continue giving predominance to Russophile causes and those who wanted to revert to more 'normal' socialist-orientated policies and aspirations.[113] The Agrarian Party, led by Mikhail Lapshin (which also included Vasilii Starodubtsev, Vladimir Isakov and Valentin Rasputin on its list), had been established only in February 1993, and although it had strong connections with the Communist Party and clearly had access to the latter's administrative structures in the towns and regions across the Russian Federation, few commentators believed that it would be able to make a significant electoral impact, given its short history. As for the third force, Vladimir Zhirinovsky's Liberal Democratic Party (LDP), most commentators had expectations that it would pass the five per cent hurdle in the proportional party list element of the electoral contest, but even the most optimistic (or, depending where commentators stood, 'pessimistic') prognosis was that it would achieve no more than eight, maybe ten, per cent at most of the overall vote.[114] There was also the fact that key Russophile newspapers had also been banned following the outcome of the October uprising. The *Den'* newspaper, edited by Aleksandr Prokhanov, was prohibited altogether, and although Prokhanov was instrumental in setting up a new newspaper called *Zavtra* (Tomorrow), the first edition of this appeared only a few days before the election was held.[115] *Sovetskaya Rossiya*, meanwhile, was allowed to reopen only after the ballot had taken place; and *Pravda* managed only a handful of pre-election editions.

The apparent gloom surrounding the Russophile cause was not lightened by the recognition that different Russophile forces, most notably the NSF, had clearly failed to exploit a good potential opportunity following President Yeltsin's initial dissolution of the old Supreme Soviet in September 1993. They had totally failed to maximize their substantial parliamentary majority, and to turn Yeltsin's unconstitutional dissolution of parliament to their popular legitimate advantage. They had likewise failed to exploit immense regional grievances at the new mood of centralization that seemed to be embodied in many of Yeltsin's actions at this time. They were not able to capitalize on the residual degree of popular support that had hitherto been shown to exist within certain elements of the military hierarchy. If some reports are accurate, they had also been deliberately *duped* into instigating violence on the streets of Moscow at a time when such a move clearly favoured their opponents.[116] And perhaps more than anything, they had totally forfeited a situation where the political momentum of support for Russophile tendencies had reached a new benchmark at this time. This was especially noticeable following the defections of Ruslan Khasbulatov (the Supreme Soviet Chairman) and Aleksandr Rutskoi (the Vice-President) from the centrist camp around the time of the second congress of the National Salvation Front.

In an article entitled 'The Russian Idea' in *Rossiiskaya gazeta* in June 1993, for example, Khasbulatov revealed, for the first time, the full extent of his anti-Western ideas, while at the same time praising to the full the mystical virtues that had always held Russia's unique cultural experiment together; a clear indication, as he himself openly admitted, that his political allegiance now lay with the NSF.[117] For Rutskoi, meanwhile, increasing disillusion with the centrists (of which he was the nominal head) finally convinced him that more political capital could also be made out of a closer alignment with the Russophiles. In an interview with *Pravda* in September 1993 (shortly after the parliament had been dissolved) he now admitted that centrism was too often a political cover beneath which certain politicians were too readily prepared to shelter, until such time as a victor had emerged and one could hang on to their coattails.[118] And shortly afterwards, in an interview with the Interfax news agency, his criticism became even more scathing. Centrism, and the individuals most popularly associated with this line, were now to be seen as his most vile opponents. 'I will have no common road with these people,' he fumed. 'History will show them for what they are.'[119]

The depth of defeatism and pessimism among the different forces of the Russophiles, however, clearly transcended the specificities of the situation that had emerged in the post-October uprising period. On the political front, events at this time merely seemed to confirm what many analysts had always assumed: that the National Salvation Front was too much of a 'political salad' ever to have been the basis of a real, cohesive, viable, organic and constructive political organization. At the very most it could be said to have represented a 'marriage of convenience'.[120] On the economic front, meanwhile, the lack of a clear-cut economic programme, in contrast to that of the Westerners, had clearly contributed to the failure to attract the kind of solid, cohesive social base of support that could be relied on in politically important, defining moments. And underpinning all these issues was the overriding impression that there were simply too many doctrinal incompatibilities separating the different elements of the Russophile camp.

Despite the genuine efforts of many high-ranking communist functionaries, for example, to place a new credence on the role of religion and the place of the Orthodox Church in the emergence of a new post-communist Russian civilization, many other Russophile tendencies viewed such ideological contortions with immense scepticism and suspicion. Elsewhere, meanwhile, a good many Russophile segments were also strongly inclined to reject any form of unity which granted Orthodoxy religious supremacy, since they felt that this also was in essence a non-Russian religion, which should be replaced by a return to old Russian pagan faiths.

Away from the domain of deep-seated religious schisms, substantial differences as regards the weight of emphasis that should be given to the state on the one hand, and the nation on the other, have separated many Russophile groups. Whereas for the statists, the traditional emphasis on the all-powerful Russian state has always embodied the ultimate source of protection for the Russian people, and should therefore be seen 'as the most genuine expression of the Russian nation', others have preferred to emphasize the more 'culturalist' supremacy of the nation as against the state. The imperialist element of Russophilia has nearly always been predominant; nevertheless, one should not downplay the vehement opposition to this particular line expressed by Russophile 'isolationists' or 'nativists'; another factor which has often militated against any fundamental degree of unity within the overall ranks of the Russophiles. For the latter, in particular, a nation is best seen as an organic unit in its own right which intrinsically acts as a (spiritual) bond uniting its people. An empire, by contrast, is nothing more than an ill-defined ad hoc conglomeration, intrinsically held together by nothing more than force and naked aggression. The two entities, nation and empire, are therefore perceived as totally incompatible.

Within the specific context of the post-communist period, significant differences have also emerged over many different attitudes *vis-à-vis* the *Soviet* period of Russian history, the role of Marxist–Leninist ideology, and, in particular, the attitude that should be taken towards Stalin. For many 'mainstream' Russophiles Marxism-Leninism (even in its Stalinist form) was just as much the embodiment of Westernization as the current neo-liberal project.

While most Russophiles are united by the need to pin blame on someone or something for what they see as Russia's recent decline, there are nevertheless innumerable sources of disagreement and disunity as to who should bear primary responsibility. Many Russophile groups, for example, have found it impossible to co-operate with those who have adopted anti-Semitism as one of the main planks of the Russophile creed. Yet another area of serious dispute has concerned a range of issues on questions of social and class allegiance. For the most part, national-communists have continued to rely firmly on the urban workers, while other Russophile groups prefer to focus almost exclusively on the pre-modern attributes of the agrarian peasants. At the same time, most non-communist Russophiles would in any case take serious issue with the notion of *class* identity representing the central definitive plank of social development, preferring instead to place far greater emphasis on cultural or ethnic-genetic factors.

Fundamental differences have similarly emerged over the issue of privatization. While the vast majority of Russophile tendencies perceive the mass industrial privatization programme as an intrinsically negative phenomenon, serious divisions have emerged between those who would like to see the restoration to supremacy of the *private* farmer, as against those who vehemently defend Soviet-style collectivization. And last, but not least, the modern spectre of fascism as an ideological force suitable for Russia's sociocultural and geopolitical rehabilitation has also caused many a significant rift in the ranks of many Russophile groups and leaders. A good illustration of this can be found in the pages of *Den'* in early January 1993, which featured a heated exchange between Sergei Kurginyan and Aleksandr Prokhanov.[121] While the former was highly critical of some sections of the Russophile camp which had begun 'flirting with the black poodle', and was adamant that he would not continue to participate in scholarly discussions of a Russophile-orientated third way, 'if Adolf Hitler [continued to be] named as the ideologist of that third way', the latter retorted that such accusations of fascist sympathies were far too simplistically imbued with the 'clichéd, drearily propagandistic manner that Soviet people have gotten sick of for the last four decades'. After all, continued Prokhanov, whatever had been carried out in the past in the name of fascism was nowhere near as brutal as even the most recent actions of liberal ideology (he had in mind 'the annihilation of 100,000 Iraqi women and children' during the Gulf war; or the fact that 'it is liberal ideology that is to blame for a colossal tragedy – the destruction of the USSR, which is giving rise to continual bloodshed that will know no bounds'). Dealing directly, therefore, with Kurginyan's demand for a purge of fascist elements from the Russophile cause, Prokhanov was equally adamant that this should be resisted at all costs.

Given all these negative factors that appeared to militate against any substantial Russophile showing in the December 1993 elections, the obvious question that needs to be asked is: Why, in reality, did the aforementioned three Russophile-orientated groups poll so strongly in the elections (between them they polled more than 43 per cent)?; and: Where, in particular, does the electoral success of Zhirinovsky's Liberal Democratic Party (which polled 22.92 per cent) leave the Russophile (counter-) hegemonic cause?

In the immediate aftermath of the elections, virtually all analysts were agreed on one thing: the strong showing of the Russophile groups represented a clear *protest* vote against the radical pro-Western reforms of the previous two years. And of course, there were many things to protest about, not least the depth of economic recession and social deprivation; the high levels of crime and disorder; and the loss of Russian national status and pride – all of which were the predominant themes of the three participating Russophile groups.

To understand the support for the Russophile groups *solely* from the perspective of it representing some form of negative-orientated protest, however, would, I think, be very misleading. After all, there were many other protest options available to voters in the form of self-proclaimed centrist parties, as well as among those groups in the pro-Western camp itself, who nevertheless campaigned for a slower and less harsh approach towards reform. In other words, therefore, the electoral success was also due to the fact that there clearly exists a solid, residual base of support for Russophile ideas that positively appeals to certain sections of society. As Liliya Shevtsova, herself an ardent supporter of the pro-Western orientation, was forced to admit:

> . . . since early 1992 the national 'patriots' have scored many victories. And first and foremost I mean by this the creation in Russian society of an atmosphere of chauvinism, together with the emergence of an explosive combination of feelings: on the one hand, nostalgia for [Russia's] former greatness . . . , and on the other hand, the feeling of defeat and of the destruction of statehood. Even some sincere democrats and liberals . . . cannot escape the oppressive influence of this ideological mixture.[122]

Other factors clearly assisted the electoral cause of the three participating groups. They all possessed very good administrative structures throughout the Russian Federation which clearly helped them to get their supporters out on the day of the election. All their respective leaders were deemed, even by their opponents, to have run effective campaigns, especially as regards their performances on television. All three groups were acknowledged to have been assisted by the fact that other Russophile-orientated groups were not standing in the election, which therefore meant that there was less of the vote to split. And on top of all this, those Russophile groups that had been excluded from the election did in the end urge their members to support those parties and individual candidates closest to their own ideological perspective.

Zhirinovsky, meanwhile, was also recognized to have gained enormous benefits from the fact that he had remained neutral during the October uprising and the military-backed destruction of the old parliament, thus buttressing his party's self-professed claim to be a genuine 'third force'. By far the most important question given the outcome of the election, then, concerns the ultimate significance of Vladimir Zhirinovsky's emergence as the ascendant force on the Russophile wing of Russian politics. To what extent can this be seen as a genuinely positive outcome for the (counter-) hegemonic cause of Russophilia?

Any answer to this question would almost certainly have to be couched in largely negative terms. Although the 'Liberal Democratic Party' which he heads has, by all accounts, a solid, reliable and even 'respectable' membership structure, which is clearly able to raise, by one means or another, huge financial resources,[123] there are nevertheless large doubts about the strength of cohesion within certain elements of the party, not to mention doubts concerning the long-term stability and allegiance of many sectors of the electorate that ultimately voted for him and his party.

Let us look at the latter issue first. According to one post-election survey, conducted by Yurii Levada of the All-Russian Centre for Public Opinion and Market Research, the overwhelming base of Zhirinovsky's support came from two very specific, if different, male-dominated sectors. First, there was a good deal of support from what can be termed the old Soviet working class; that is to say, people who are middle-aged or older, mostly from the cities in the Russian heartland, with average skills and average wages acquired from state-run industries, who were very worried about their future prospects and anxious about the growing crime figures and the loss of the country's former great-power status, and preferred strong to weak government. In other words, then, people who defected from the communists, largely because of the populist and nationalist appeal of Zhirinovsky himself. And secondly, there was also a large degree of support from the younger generation, who likewise were drawn to the novelty effect of the party's and the leader's appeal, and the sense in which it represented the most explicit kind of protest vote.[124]

Of most interest in the survey, however, was the finding that up to one-third of those who voted for the Liberal Democrats indicated that they had made up their minds only on election day itself, and they were already having some regrets about their choice in the aftermath of the outcome. This clearly implies, then, a great deal of volatility in the electoral base; a volatility, moreover, that may not stand up to the more critical public scrutiny of Zhirinovsky and his LDP.

Turning to the issue of the cohesion inside his own party organization, no one can doubt that Zhirinovsky wields almost dictatorial control over the wider party apparatus. As Sergei Putin, head of the party's ideological department, once expressed it: 'The LDP is the party of a leader. If there is Zhirinovsky, there is a party; if there is no Zhirinovsky, there is no party'[125] – an image that could not have been made more apparent to anyone observing the proceedings of the party's fifth congress in April 1994.

When it comes to the issue of the LDP *parliamentary* faction, however, a totally different picture emerges. Speaking shortly after the election results had been announced, Andrei Zavidia, Zhirinovsky's former running mate in the June 1991 presidential elections, argued that the new LDP parliamentary faction would quickly disintegrate under the weight of its own contradictions. Possibly up to half of the faction, he insisted, would have equally strong affinities with the Communist Party; up to a quarter would be more inclined to support the neo-liberal reformers of Russia's Choice; and the rest would remain independent of any direction given from above, be it from Zhirinovsky or anybody else in the party hierarchy.[126] Although this is something of an exaggeration, Zavidia's predictions have indeed partially materialized, and it does appear that the 'debt of gratitude' that many members owe to Zhirinovsky is not altogether strong enough to outweigh other interests and allegiances that many of them clearly have.

In mid February 1994, for example, Viktor Kobelev (designated as the 'number two man' in the party and 'Labour Minister' in the 'shadow Cabinet') and Aleksandr Pronin (the party treasurer) announced that they were resigning from the LDP faction in protest at the extremist antics of their party leader.[127] Later that month they were joined by Vyacheslav Marychev, the head of the St Petersburg branch of the party (who had appeared in third place on the electoral slate).[128] And in early April the head of the Orenburg branch of the party, Vladimir Borzyuk, and the Chairman of the Udmurt regional association, Vladimir Novikov, likewise announced their departure from the Duma fraction, with both of them again highly vocal in their criticism of Zhirinovsky's populist demeanour, which was negatively affecting the party's ambitions to be a serious political force.[129]

What most underpins the doubts about Zhirinovsky's long-term political potential, however, is the fact that neither he individually, nor his party collectively, possesses the capacity to act as a serious nucleus around which the disparate Russophile forces can unite. Earlier on in this chapter it was stated that Zhirinovsky automatically assumed that at some point in time all the other leadership contenders for the national patriotic wing of Russian politics would bow to his supremacy. Contrary to many expectations, that moment did not arrive in December 1993, and it is looking increasingly unlikely that it will arrive in the foreseeable future. Neither Zyuganov's Communist Party nor Lapshin's Agrarian Party, despite their close position on many significant issues, have openly dared to associate themselves with the Liberal Democrats for fear of the immense internal splits that such a move would unleash. While it was one thing to be closely allied with other Russophile-orientated groups within the framework of the National Salvation Front, it appears that it is another thing entirely to be seen as a strong partner of an organization which is openly perceived to have neo-fascist leanings. A similar degree of circumspection also prevails within the ranks of other Russophile groups, such as RAPU and the Constitutional and Christian Democrats. More importantly, in the aftermath of Aleksandr Rutskoi's release from jail in February 1994 (which owed much to the efforts of Zhirinovsky), the two foremost contemporary embodiments of a Russophile orientation have since found it virtually impossible to work together in any kind of constructive way.

When Rutskoi, for example, announced his intention of creating a new political alliance in the guise of Accord for Russia in March 1994 (which was supported by Zyuganov, Lapshin, Prokhanov, Konstantinov and many others), Zhirinovsky not only took this as a sign of offence and ingratitude towards himself, he also publicly denounced the new organization as a movement led by people who had done nothing but humiliate Russia and 'whose hands were stained with blood'. In retaliation, Rutskoi publicly charged Zhirinovsky with being nothing less than 'a clinical case' and a psychopath; echoing, in turn, similar public denunciations made by Aleksandr Solzhenitsyn both before and after his return to Russia in May 1994.[130]

In short, then, rather than clear what has sometimes seemed like a permanent fog that has enveloped the national patriotic wing of Russian politics since 1991, Zhirinovsky's success has made it even denser. For most of the disparate forces of the Russophile persuasion (with a few exceptions),[131] Zhirinovsky has clearly become an embarrassment. The question is can the Rutskois, the Zyuganovs, the Baburins, and company ultimately afford to ignore him? All this, of course, is not to say that even in isolation Zhirinovsky will not continue to go from strength to strength with his populist crusade. After all, his crude demagoguery during the December 1993 election campaign – with his dreams of a new Russian Empire, his calls to shoot criminals on the spot, and his regular use of some of the most banal sexual imagery imaginable – paid high dividends. Nevertheless, whatever he achieves in the future (and, of course, his real aim is to capture the Presidency, especially now that the constitution grants the President virtual absolute power), it is almost certain that it will not be a political success based upon the criteria of modernist hegemony as defined in the Introduction to this book.

In his important study entitled *Warrant for Genocide*, Norman Cohn refers to

> a subterranean world, where pathological fantasies disguised as ideas are churned out by crooks and half-educated fanatics for the benefit of the ignorant and superstitious. There are times when this underworld emerges from the depths and suddenly fascinates, captures, and dominates multitudes of usually sane and responsible people. . . . And it occasionally happens that this underworld becomes a political power and changes the course of history.[132]

It is precisely this kind of image that springs to mind when one thinks of a Russia dominated by the likes of Vladimir Zhirinovsky and his Liberal Democratic Party.

Centrists

Thus there are three dispositions, two of them taking a vicious form (one in the direction of excess, the other of defect) and one a good form, namely the observance of the mean. They are all opposed to one another, and the mean is opposed to both extremes.

Aristotle, *The Nichomachean Ethics*

Defining the Collective Will

If the Westerners and the Russophiles can trace their cultural-ideological ancestry back over the course of many decades (if not centuries) of Russian history, the roots of centrism are much harder to define. For that reason it is without doubt a far less self-assured, less self-confident orientation in the current hegemonic struggle.

Periodic efforts to create some form of analogy between centrism and the abiding Russian search for a Third Way have certainly attempted to provide it with stronger cultural foundations; though given the struggle to assimilate the Third Way identification among other hegemonic combatants, these efforts have so far borne little fruit. Other attempts, meanwhile, to fabricate for itself a deep-rooted sense of *theoretical* continuity have also encountered a good deal of resistance. The repeated references to the self-styled centrist heritage of nineteenth-century intellectuals such as Boris Chicherin, or politicians such as Petr Stolypin, do bear some credence in reality, but in both cases the legacy is highly contested.

For most commentators, therefore, this leaves centrism firmly rooted in the contemporary age. While this is no bad thing in itself, it does leave it frequently open to allegations of fickleness [*flyugerstvo*] or, worse still, 'opportunism', which it has always found hard to overcome. Like the double-faced Janus, with which it is often compared, centrism can often denote hypocrisy and insincerity. At the same time, the Roman god of the same name was also symbolic of a gateway to a new world and a new beginning. Centrism's success, therefore, clearly depends on its ability to portray itself as the incarnation of the latter rather than the former. In contrast to the historical search, the contemporary origins of the centrist orientation are certainly not hard to track down, emerging as they did in the twilight of the Gorbachev era. In what precise manner the term was used by this 'first modern centrist' (as Vladimir Mironov has called Gorbachev)[1] is, however, a matter of some debate and not a little controversy.

Writing in 1992, following the downfall of Gorbachev, one analyst, Professor V. Tikhomirov, outlined three different ways of understanding the phenomenological construction of centrism.[2] First, he argued, it could be used as a distinctive political-ideological tendency; secondly as a locational position in a given political spectrum at any given point in time; and thirdly as an instrument of political activity embodied in consensus politics. For Tikhomirov, the Gorbachevian use of the notion of centrism was only ever restricted to the latter two notions. At no point did the former Soviet leader ever attempt, or desire to attempt, to formalize a new set of ideological conceptions around the centrist label. This, Tikhomirov seems to imply, was the root of Gorbachev's problems at this time. Given the lack of a firm ideological foundation, it was also the basis for a very *manipulative* use of the remaining two facets of centrism.

This 'manipulation' is well brought out in Gorbachev's first detailed speech adumbrating the benefits of a centrist approach. In an address to Communist Party activists in Belorussia at the beginning of March 1991, he was adamant that centrism must become the dominant political orientation, given the situation developing in the country.[3] Going on to interpret the importance of the centrist approach, he asserted that it could not possibly occupy any kind of rigidly fixed position but must, rather, be an open political space 'conditioned by the dynamics of the political process itself'. It was an approach that intrinsically found unacceptable 'the adventurism of forces that call themselves radical', being instead the embodiment of even-handedness and 'political common sense'. Above all, he argued, the main tenet of centrism was the idea of civil and national harmony. And how was this national harmony to be understood? It was to be understood, argued Gorbachev, in the continued dominance of the CPSU, which even at this late stage he still believed had the potential of becoming the main integrative factor of the centrist approach. Indeed, for Gorbachev, this was nothing less than an embodiment of the most 'patriotic nature' of the only kind of 'realistic centrism' that could possibly exist.

With such a manipulated – not to say reductive – interpretation of this new Soviet phenomenon of centrism, it was small wonder that many commentators quickly came to equate it with little more than a political vacuum, a space guaranteed to speed up the unstoppable collision of diametrically opposed forces either side of it. Indeed, for Leon Onikov, the August 1991 putsch was nothing less than a just retribution for the political illusions of centrism at this particular time.[4]

In the aftermath of the outright failure to secure the dominance of a centrist orientation with little or no genuine *locus standi*, it is perhaps not surprising that those who continue to believe in the positive benefits of centrism in Russia today have attempted to provide it with at least some semblance of political-ideological cohesiveness and coherency. The notion of centrism as a specific, contextual, locational position and an instrument of consensual politics, as we will see, is still an important part of its creed; as, too, is its Gorbachevian assertion of being the epitome of good common sense; but it is possible now to identify a fairly clear-cut infrastructure of values and beliefs which act as a firm complement to these other aspects. What is also noticeable is that it is intellectuals close to Gorbachev (or, more usually, from within the Gorbachev Foundation) who have been responsible for elaborating a much more specific and consistent understanding of a centrist *Weltanschauung*.[5] Quite whether this continued close association between Gorbachev and centrism is a help or a hindrance to its overall cause will be touched upon later.

According to Vasilii Lipitskii, centrism should not be understood as 'a geometrical notion presupposing [a static] equidistance from the flanks'.[6] Instead, its content is very much determined by the most dominant trends impacting on society's development. Given this framework of understanding, it is possible to highlight a number of primary features of the post-Soviet centrist project. It is also possible to identify one overriding common factor that links these features together into some kind of hoped-for organic unity: the consistent emphasis on the notion of *conciliation* [*primirenie*].

The first and most important feature of contemporary centrism is an emphasis on the conciliatory role that must be performed by the state. The significance and centrality of this issue have never been better summarized than in a research document published by the Gorbachev Foundation (under the chairmanship of Professor Valentin Tolstykh), which was charged with the task of formulating a concrete 'Centrist Project for Russia' in the run-up to the December 1993 elections:

> The essence of the problem of centrism in its Russian variant consists in the fact that from an ontological and metaphysical starting point, it has an obligation to the idea and destiny of statehood, to the defence of Russia and to its social, historical, national and cultural identity.
>
> This is the starting point and the most general basis for the emergence of centrism as an ideology and a set of concrete political ideas. Russia possesses

only a minuscule tradition of parliamentarianism and party political struggle. Here in Russia centrism, in distinction to the West, has come into existence not as a result of the development of proper party relations and struggles, but as a response to the dangers faced by Russian statehood; even to its continued existence.[7]

For Tolstykh and his co-researchers, there is a firm conviction that Russia will never be able to free itself from its tradition of statism. As a result, the Westernizers' goal of an autonomous realm of civil society of the type that exists in bourgeois liberal democracies lies beyond its capacities. The Russian model of the state, however, is no inferior phenomenon, provided that it exists as a 'social state' with a well-defined responsibility for the welfare of its citizens. To this extent, the communitarian tradition of *Gemeinschaft* is still valued above that of the more individualistic *Gesellschaft*.

The state, not surprisingly, must be the entity binding the nation together and making it strong. The precise manner in which it achieves this task is never fixed; and here Chicherin's formula 'the less unity there is in society, the more there must be in the state' is one to which many centrist theoreticians would happily adhere. This is also the basis of the centrists' critique of their two major hegemonic rivals and their respective approaches to the state. As for the centrist interpretation of the Westerners, the main charge here is the conviction that their opponents have deliberately gone out of their way to destroy the whole fabric of the state in the misguided assumption that it will be possible to build some kind of brand-new edifice out of the rubble. This, it is frequently argued, is an attitude akin to nothing less than 'neo-Bolshevism'. If Russian history has demonstrated anything, it is precisely the contrary argument. The belief that a system can somehow be razed entirely to the ground so that only then can work begin on creating something new out of the debris is not only theoretically fallacious but, more importantly, is currently proving once again to be absolutely ruinous in practice.[8]

For the centrists, then, the basic demand made of the Westerners is a genuine recognition on their part that the collapse of the former USSR has in turn posed a serious challenge to Russian statehood itself, the negative consequences of which might ultimately end up undermining Russian statehood completely.[9] First of all, it has weakened the traditionally strong interventionist role of the state, which is undoubtedly one of the most central tenets of the centrist orientation; and this in turn also implies that the state institutions themselves have now become weak and vague in the post-Soviet set-up. Secondly, they would also point out that the collapse of the USSR has also had serious negative consequences in terms of clearly *accelerating* Russia's own centrifugal tendencies. Autonomous national entities within the Russian Federation have learned the lessons of the USSR's collapse, and because there is no real authoritative state structure in existence at the centre, they are both finding it easy to resist the will of Moscow, and in many ways are tacitly being encouraged to break away from the centre precisely because of the perceived weakness, ineffectiveness and confusion pervading the central institutions of power.[10] Likewise it is further contended, in clear contraposition to the Westerners, that no amount of Western support and assistance for a brand-new conception of what Russia now stands for can provide Russia with the same kind of viability it has traditionally gained in the past during the days of the Empire and the USSR. This is not by any means (and in distinction to the Russophiles) an a priori hostility or antipathy to the West and the civilization it embodies. It is, however, a firm recognition that the stronger the perception grows that Russia is today totally dependent on the West for its very continued existence, the more Russia will itself be undermining everything it has traditionally stood for.

As for the Russophiles, the centrists' main reproach here is that while they too, for the most part, adhere to a strong belief in the pivotal importance of the state, they are nevertheless far too zealous in their support for a specifically *totalitarian* approach. If centrist theoreticians are to be believed, what best epitomizes the centrist understanding of the state is a more typical Hegelian approach, whereby the state's fundamental task is one of conciliation of *autonomously* demarcated private and public spheres. In other words, it is not its task totally to 'swallow up' everything outside it.[11] Another specific aspect of the centrist approach to the state lies in its ability to act as the ultimate mechanism of conciliation between past, present and future. For Tolstykh, ties with the past and the importance of sustaining living traditions are vital aspects of the overall centrist *Weltanschauung*, and it is the state, more than anything else, that can truly embody a genuine sense of continuity.[12] Moreover, as Leon Aron has pointed out, given the intense condition of 'political anomie' that Russian society finds itself in today – a social condition analogous to 'a state of mind of one . . . who has no longer any standards but only disconnected urges, who has no longer any sense of continuity, of folk, of obligation . . . [who is] responsive to no one [and who] lives on the thin line of sensation between no future and no past'[13] – one can understand the pivotal importance of this allusion to the state as a bridge of memory between yesterday and today and a bridge of hope and anticipation between today and tomorrow.

Moving away from the exclusive realm of the state to the realm of society as a whole, it is clear that the main aspect of the centrist approach here is a fundamental attachment to the notion of social partnership. The specific *socioeconomic* consequences of this belief will be developed in far more detail below. It is, however, an aspect of their approach that has far-reaching consequences. According to Tolstykh, one of the most difficult questions for Russian centrism concerns the manner in which one can organically unite the natural and the social 'instincts' of the people with the goal and the task of constructing a genuine democratic society and a state based on the rule of law. Although he is not optimistic that this task will ever be fundamentally resolved, Tolstykh is nevertheless adamant that the one and only mechanism available here is the promotion of a wide-ranging 'social contract', aimed at encompassing all the major social, religious, ethnic, regional and, if possible, political interests in society.[14] Very much on the lines of Western notions of corporatism, the main emphasis here is clearly on the need to maintain social stability and avoid conflicts at all costs. Any notion of some kind of 'invisible hand' performing such a function is frequently dismissed in the most derisive terms, often as simply analogous to Hobbes's portayal of an anarchic condition in which a war of all against all inevitably ensues.[15]

However, corporatism, as we know, comes in many different guises and forms, and the precise nature of centrist corporatism in Russia is not always easy to fathom. The theoretical discussions clearly indicate a preference for a 'liberal' or 'consociational' type of corporatism, with countries such as Austria or Sweden being the main role models. Given the actual conditions in Russian society today, not to mention the centrality of the state in centrist ideology, one can at least understand the centrists' opponents' accusations that their real model in practice is more likely to be Mussolini's Italy in the 1920s and 1930s.[16]

Given the perceived fragility of Russian statehood – and, for that matter, a real sense of what Russia's national identity amounts to in the post-Soviet context – it is perhaps not surprising that centrist ideology, not unlike that of its main competitors, also focuses very much on Russia's present-day geopolitical status, hoping that by this means a concentration on such issues can in some way 'help Russia to become Russia'.

Mention has already been made of the centrist view that the disintegration of the USSR has had enormous negative consequences for the internal stability of Russia. Going beyond this, I think one can also say that a great deal of what the centrist orientation has come to stand for in recent years stems *explicitly* from its strong emphasis on Russia's position in the wider world. An essential feature of the centrist orientation here undoubtedly hinges on its stance towards Russia's relations with the so-called 'near-abroad' countries that formerly made up the USSR. As on many other issues, the self-professed centrist line is the attempt to claim a position somewhere between reformism (in this context denoted as 'isolationism') and restorationism; though few can doubt that on this issue, at least, the pendulum is very much weighted in favour of the latter rather than the former.

At the very heart of the centrist orientation is a strong conviction that once again history has demonstrated that Russian statehood is strong and most viable only when it is associated with some kind of unificatory, conciliatory role on the entire Eurasian landmass that has traditionally defined its territorial sphere of interest. That is to say, without this search for something bigger than itself, Russia as an entity *in itself* has no meaning. Expressed in practical terms, then, this amounts to a fundamental belief that the present-day framework of the Commonwealth of Independent States must be considered merely *transitional* in nature and form.

The utilization of the 'Eurasian' label here is very instructive; indeed, a number of commentators have openly drawn a clear analogy between contemporary centrism and the early-twentieth-century emigré school of Eurasianism [*evraziistvo*], associated with the likes of George Vernadsky, Nikolai Trubetskoi and Petr Savitsky.[17] On one level this analogy is slightly confusing, given the radical and instinctive anti-Western sentiments of the original *evraziitsy*; something that is certainly not reciprocated among most centrist theoreticians and politicians. On another, more *cultural* level, however, the analogy is well made. Underpinning both is the primary notion that Russia is neither Europe nor Asia, but an assimilation of both of them together; a 'unified geographical world unto itself' which is the embodiment of an autonomous cultural-historical phenomenon. Anthropologically as well, Eurasia represents a single entity, and the different peoples inhabiting this realm today are nevertheless part of a common 'symphonic personality' – members of an 'assimilated stock', to use Chkheidze's well-known description.[18]

As for the prototype of this concrete, distinctive Eurasian culture, this issue has been widely addressed by Sergei Agadzhanov. The essence of Russia's juxtaposition between Europe and Asia, he has argued, is its centuries-long adherence to a non-ethnic-orientated mentality. In conjunction with military, political and other measures, this furthered the transformation of the old Empire into an association of many ethnic groups, based more on mutual interests than on the type of exclusive nationalism that was the epitome of European statehood. Although the official doctrine of Tsarism divided its subjects into 'aliens', 'natives' and 'itinerant nomads', the more distinguishing features of Russian statehood, he has argued, appeared to have no basis of ethnocentrism, but were instead based on the concurrence of national and political borders. Rather than weakening the Empire, the ethnic diversity strengthened it and assisted its economic, social and spiritual image, as well as its religious-confessional image. On the basis of his own detailed studies, therefore, Agadzhanov is adamant that what was objectively conceived was a new original civilization and culture, one that can rightly be called a 'Eurasian culture'.[19]

Agadzhanov aside, arguably the most lucid correlation between today's centrist approach and the Eurasianist cultural legacy has come from Sergei Stankevich. In a highly controversial article in *Nezavisimaya gazeta* at the end of March 1992 (at a time when he was still a State Councillor in Yeltsin's Presidential Administration), Stankevich was very forthright in his conviction that post-Soviet Russia's hitherto exclusive pro-Western orientation constituted a fundamental mistake of historic magnitude.[20] 'Russia's mission in the world', he argued, was 'to initiate and support a multilateral dialogue of cultures, civilizations and states. Russia the conciliator, Russia connecting, Russia combining' needed to be the essential leitmotiv. 'A charitable state, tolerant and open within the limits drawn by law and goodwill, but formidable beyond these limits. A country imbibing West and East, North and South, unique and exclusively capable, perhaps, of the harmonious combination of many different principles, of a historic symphony. Such is my vision of Russia in a renewed world.' This, for Stankevich, was Russia's perfectly natural role, a role defined by its essential 'dualistic' nature. Russia, he went on, 'has always bifurcated and acted as an opponent to herself in order subsequently, negotiating a chain of ordeals, to reach an accord with herself. It is pointless to complain about the nature of this historical destiny. It is [simply] important for everyone who ventures to speak on Russia's behalf to listen closely to the voice of her essence.'[21]

Given the basic, restorationist outlook of the centrist orientation here, perhaps the inevitable question that needs to be asked is: how is centrism different from Russophilia on this particular issue? Any answer to this, it goes without saying, depends on how generous you are in the kind of motivations you ascribe to the often subtle nuances of the centrist approach. For the most part, however, one can certainly say that the *tone* is different, if not always the substance.

First, for example, most advocates of centrism vehemently deny the necessity for any kind of force in the reintegration process that must take place in the Eurasian realm; instead a negotiated process will suffice, largely because of the *objective* conditions that will make this process of reintegration inevitable. Aspects invariably cited here focus not only on the impossibility of the other non-Russian republics of the former USSR being able to construct any kind of viable national form of statehood, but also on the impossibility of Russia likewise establishing a form of national statehood akin to traditional European experience.[22] On top of this, there is considerable emphasis on the supposed common *genetic* heritage of the different peoples of the Eurasian realm, as well as a conviction that by its very existence the new Russian diaspora will invariably 'encourage' (by one means or another!) reintegrative tendencies.[23]

A second difference stems from the nature of the centrist embodiment and interpretation of the whole Eurasian phenomenon. Many Russophile thinkers have likewise assimilated the heritage of this vernacular, but have put it to totally different use. For the likes of Aleksandr Prokhanov, Shamil' Sultanov and many others, the concept is the epitome of Russian expansionist desires, and of a virulent form of anti-Americanism. The vision here is one of Eurasia *against* America, with the latter perceived as the intrinsic 'enemy of mankind' and 'a Carthage that must be destroyed'. Eurasia is the repudiation of everything that America stands for, and it must be the force which breaks 'the serpent's coils' which have been fastened around not only the unique Russian civilization, but the whole of European civilization as well. A Eurasia that stretches from Vladivostok to Dublin is the expressed ambition here, and it is Russia's divine task to be used as a battering ram capable of kicking America out of Eurasia by isolating and humiliating it, and thus depriving it of its world-power status.[24]

In contradistinction to this avowedly imperialistic mentality of many of the Russophiles, the centrists' identification of themselves as 'enlightened nationalists' does at least have some substance to it; and as emphasized above, it is clearly less ethnocentric in comparison with much of the Russophile orientation. Likewise, the xenophobia and explicit anti-Semitism or 'scapegoating' of the Russophile approach is conspicuous by its absence.

Finally, one should also note the centrists' own desire to distinguish the 'mission' that they perceive Russia possessing in the Eurasian realm from the ingrained messianism which is such a predominant feature of Russophilia. According to a number of prominent centrists, 'the key part of Russia's new mission in the world is to prevent, with the assistance of the world community, the transformation of the territory of the former Soviet Union into a geo-strategic hole, radiating instability and wars, ultimately threatening the very existence of mankind'.[25] In other words, the 'mission' is ascribed to Russia as much out of negative, preventive necessity as out of positive, affirmative desires. It is also the platform, according to many centrists, from which Russia can perform the much-needed task of providing an essential bridge between Europe and Asia, with the conciliatory leitmotiv once again being paramount here.[26]

Notwithstanding the differences between centrists and Russophiles, one should nevertheless be at least a little wary in understating the commonality of their approach to Russia's ambitions in the Eurasian realm and their firm objections to the demise of the USSR as an integrated state structure. Nor should one downplay their virulent opposition to the Westerners who instigated the disintegration of that structure.

For Aleksandr Tsipko – a leading intellectual figure in the opposition to communist power who has since gone on to become an influential doyen of the centrist orientation – the Westerners' come-uppance is an inevitability:

For as long as people believe that the USSR was not Russia and not their homeland, but some kind of 'empire', a remnant of history, the [Westerners] will be successful. But when sane ideas return to people and when they begin to understand that no idea is worth the crucifix of their state, that today not one people in the world has sacrificed their national interests, that in general, national masochism is not a better method of achieving authority, then the influence of the [Westerners] will come to an end.[27]

The real weakness of the Westerners' orientation, as far as Tsipko is concerned, consists in the fact that they refuse to believe in the absolute values of such things as state and nation. The consciousness of these people is inhibited by the kinds of belief they have, so that they cannot articulate these notions aloud in their positive sense. In their present condition, he has written, they cannot transcend those borders which partition their ideological consciousness from the supposed values of civil society and European democracy. 'They stand rooted to the ground in front of the river of national life, and they are afraid to enter it.'[28] Similar thoughts have been expressed by Sergei Karaganov, another Yeltsin adviser (and a key figure in the influential Council for Foreign and Defence Policy), whose intellectual orientation towards a centrist position has also been noticeable in the aftermath of the initial experience of Russia's post-Soviet transition. For Karaganov, the road to modernity in Russia must follow the signposts of nationalism and statism – not purely out of necessity, but out of some sense of desire as well.[29]

A final point that needs to be mentioned about the centrists' collective will, and one which once again brings us back to the pivotal notion of conciliation, is their clear desire to synthesize the cultural exclusivism of their opponents' orientation. An early recognition of the importance of this was given by Oleg Rumyantsev, long before he himself became a prominent political advocate of centrism. According to Rumyantsev, if Russia was rightfully to take its place among the countries of the civilized world, then nothing less than a cultural renaissance was needed; and the essence of this cultural renaissance should be the attempt 'creatively [to] unite the two main ideological and political positions that have historically divided our country: the Westerners and the Slavophiles'. Only by means of such a unification or synthesis could Russia avoid a 'fruitless and debilitating internecine struggle', and hope thereby to overcome the abiding 'Russian problem'.[30]

The tone of Rumyantsev's warning here is strongly reminiscent of Marx's dictum that history often tends to repeat itself, but only in so far as what was tragedy the first time round returns as farce the second.[31] That being so, however, the task facing centrist theoreticians in this cultural domain is simply enormous. It also once again leaves them vulnerable to accusations of amorphousness, vagueness and outright rootlessness. Nevertheless, it does remain a crucial component of their collective will, and there is some (self-) belief that the attempted cultural synthesis of their two major opponents will be able to strike a resonant chord among the Russian population. Certainly this is the prevailing perception of the aforementioned Centrist Project for Russia, drawn up by Valentin Tolstykh and his fellow researchers at the Gorbachev Foundation. Rarely a moment goes by without some kind of exhortation that while they uphold the traditional values of Western civilization (in the form of a market economy, a law-based state and an open society), the centrists are nevertheless convinced of Russia's cultural-civilizational distinctiveness [*samobytnost'*], which therefore demands that care be taken with experimentation which might override the country's historical traditions and special patterns of evolution. Vague it might well be, but Tolstykh vehemently disclaims any fundamental contradiction. As the concluding passage of the Project boldly asserts:

> Russian centrism can fulfil its historical role and function if the process of the transformation and the renewal of Russia is carried through on the basis of her past evolution, assuming features of genuine reforms free from any imposed actions or alien processes of transformation; if a genuine coalition is found, if compromises are made in the country's modernization, dictated by her national interests and supported by a mass basis of the population encompassing the widest social interests. This will happen . . . only provided that the government bases its actions on an all-national basis of agreement and unity, and not on sectional interests that it would prefer to favour.[32]

The Social Base of the Historical Bloc

According to Nikolai Kulikov, 'a centrist, above all else, is not a radical'.[33] Centrists abhor the notion of 'change for change's sake'; they look sceptically on the promotion of practice being derived from some kind of pure theory, and they have an in-built hostility to rapidity taking precedence over gradualism – especially a gradualism firmly rooted in accumulated, empirical knowledge. If we add all these attributes to the pivotal notion of conciliation referred to above, then it is already possible to appreciate the main features of the centrist's socioeconomic programme for stability and recovery in post-Soviet Russia.

If we look first of all at their economic plans, a number of detailed programmes have been promoted in the past few years, which indelibly bear the stamp of centrist influence.[34] The range of personnel and research institutes associated with these programmes also clearly signifies a broad base of intellectual support for many centrist-orientated ambitions.[35] Indeed, not for nothing has President Yeltsin, even at the height of his pro-Western orientation, frequently acknowledged that the plans of the centrists represent some of the most complete and thorough programmes on offer in the post-Soviet transition.

An important leitmotiv for the basic self-understanding of centrist economic thinking has been well summarized by Arkadii Vol'skii. Speaking to the assembled delegates of the Russian Union of Industrialists and Entrepreneurs, of which he is Chairman, he stressed on more than one occasion that:

> We believe that we must take all that is of benefit to Russia from all the existing market economy systems in the West and East. The Russian insignia has always borne the symbol of the two-headed eagle: one head is turned to the West, while the other looks to the East. There is a profound meaning in that.[36]

As with their overall ideological approach, the primary emphasis of the centrists' economic thinking is the firm conviction that any transition to the market (to which, as a matter of principle, they are more than prepared to give their support) should nevertheless be firmly regulated by the state. Part of the justification for this stems from their belief that the economy cannot be treated separately from the cultural specificities of the country. Given the long-standing tradition of state intervention in the economy, it would be pure folly to remove what is often seen as the economy's 'lifebelt' in order to gauge what will swim and what will sink.

Another justification stems from the fact that in view of the regional disparities of economic development in the country, not to mention the ethnic-cultural variety, the state must play a prominent interventionist (i.e. 'integrationist') role. More specifically, it is often argued that the state has 'no choice' but to continue to be the primary actor in economic life and the whole restructuring process, given the depth of production concentration in the country (particularly as regards the military–industrial complex). Without a strong role for the state, whole regions could otherwise be faced with virtual hundred per cent unemployment should enterprises not find a niche in the new free-market arena. Last, but not least, considerable emphasis is also placed on the state's capacity to oversee a co-ordinated investment policy in key areas of the economy's infrastructure, without which other aspects of economic development would simply not be feasible.

When it comes to attaining some kind of economic *stabilization* for the country, the primary emphasis here is on reversing the slump in production and halting the slide towards de-industrialization brought about, so centrists would claim, by the deliberate shock-therapy tactics of the

Westerners – tactics often likened to 'simplistic primitivism' and 'excessive economic Darwinism'. In similar fashion, the centrists are also adamant that Russia must not be reduced to a mere raw-materials appendage, servicing the most developed economies of the West (what they have dubbed the 'Kuwaitization' scenario).

As for the more fiscal–monetary aspects of stabilization the centrists, in sharp distinction to the Westerners, strongly favour soft rather than hard budgetary constraints. The ready availability of loans and subsidies to sustain enterprises from banks and government is a constant feature of all the centrists' proposals, as is their desire for enterprises to be made exempt from taxation on profits where they are subsequently reinvested, and for depreciation payments and fixed capital to be fully indexed. Repeated accusations of hyperinflationary tendencies in their proposals, meanwhile, are normally rebuffed on the basis that other aspects of economic stabilization are ultimately far more important. Massive declines in production capacity, for example, coupled with mass unemployment in highly skilled labour sectors, would almost certainly cost the country far more.[37] This is not to say, however, that anti-inflationary measures are not a factor in the centrist economic outlook. One constant feature is the proposal for price rises to be annually checked by cartel agreements between government, trade unions and entrepreneurs. And as a last-resort measure, centrists are also not averse to imposing price and wage freezes where necessary.

If this looks suspiciously like a return to key elements of the old Soviet economic order, it is not something that preoccupies the vast majority of centrists. Words like 'return' and 'restoration' vis-à-vis aspects of the old Soviet system – not to mention explicitly Soviet-inspired terms like 'control' and 'regulation' – unashamedly litter the texts of centrist-inspired programmes. The subsidization of key food items and medicines; long-term price controls in such sectors as fuel and energy; controls on supplies and distribution through state-controlled syndicates (akin to the old Soviet institution Gossnab); and the reintroduction of state orders in certain crucial, core areas of the economy are likewise long-established centrist principles.

Another aspect of the centrists' restorationist ideas is their promotion of production institutions largely defined by their economies of scale. What this would essentially amount to is the creation once again of huge vertically integrated concerns (similar to the old industrial associations of the Soviet era), whereby different enterprises would be amalgamated to handle all the successive stages of production from the extraction of raw materials to the final commodity output. Any criticism, meanwhile, of their restorationist tendencies, especially from Westerners, is often met with the retort that centrist 'pragmatism' is better than dogmatic ideological exclusivism, which all too often underpins the Westerners' approach.

On the issue of privatization, the essence of the centrist orientation here is that it should be considered much more as a means, rather than an end in itself (again, as it so often is for the Westerners).[38] As a means of enhancing productive potential and efficiency, and the *collective* rights of those who have actually staffed the factories and the enterprises, privatization is to be supported. For the centrists, however, the intrinsic problems associated with privatization cannot be ignored or lightly dismissed. If a major consequence of the process is a further destruction of the manufacturing potential of the country; or if speculators and asset-strippers, motivated by the desire to secure a quick profit irrespective of any long-term considerations for the enterprise, become the main beneficiaries of changes in ownership; or, worse still, if it leads to an increasing 'criminalization' of the economy, then privatization should not be pursued. In other words, the appearance of irreversibility that so appeals to the pro-Western supporters of 'privatization at all costs' is far from being a worthwhile justification for the centrists. And not unconnected with this is an equally strong conviction that widescale unemployment and an uncontrolled labour market should be fundamentally opposed.

In the sphere of agriculture, there is once again a strong emphasis on the twin themes of continued state subsidies and the maintenance of socialized forms of farming. And last, but not least, the centrists are also adamant that there must be strong protectionist measures to ward off excessive foreign competition through means of high tariffs, etc. National, rather than foreign, capital must be the basis of any future economic growth, with the main priority being the strengthening of the domestic productive basis, not satisfying short-term consumer demand through excessive imports. According to Vol'skii, in the event of Russia's economy being transferred to a regime of full openness on the world's market, no more than 16 per cent of its productive capacity would be able to withstand the ensuing competition; and nearly one-third of its manufacturing base would immediately go bankrupt. This, in turn, would inevitably increase the serious social divisions already plaguing society. While those employed in the more lucrative (raw-materials) sector of the economy would be able to reap the rewards of high wages and other privileges, the rest of society would be reduced to standards of living approaching Third World levels. Given these conditions, it is further argued that priority must perforce be given to maintaining strong trading relations with the countries of the former USSR by means of a well-worked-out and co-ordinated credit and finance policy.[39]

In the search for role models in the centrist approach, some commentators have argued that the basic overall strategy bears not a little resemblance to the policies and ideas associated with the Tsarist Economics minister Sergei Witte back in the early years of the twentieth century.[40] More frequently, however, it is the Chinese experience of economic reform that is slated as being the main influence on the centrist outlook. To some extent this close affinity with China is not surprising, given the fact that a good many of the centrist economic theoreticians have a strong first-hand knowledge of the country; some of them were even educated there. The focus on China is also not surprising given the undoubted success of Chinese economic policies in recent years – a level of success which would look favourable in a comparison with most countries of the world, and one which, in comparison with Russia, looks like a veritable economic miracle that most ordinary Russians can only look at with increasing envy.

Arkadii Vol'skii, in particular, is a tireless devotee of the Chinese approach, and rarely misses an opportunity to extol its virtues, and hence also to lambast the gross mistakes hitherto made by the Westerners. Interviewed in autumn 1992, for example, he pointedly stressed that the main reason he went on so much about the Chinese experience was simply because reforms there 'have been carried out without a drop in the population's living standards, while in our country we have simply postulated the notion that reforms demand sacrifices. Who said so? Why is it that the sacrifices have to be borne by the population and not by the theoreticians, whose incompetence and lack of practical understanding have brought the economy to ruin?'[41]

And certainly, if John Ross (a Western economist based in Moscow) is to be believed, the centrists have every right to look longingly at their eastern neighbour. According to Ross, the central feature of China's success has been the adoption of a reform strategy that fully recognizes the specificities of its own indigenous economic (as well as sociocultural) structure, and uses this positively as its launching pad, rather than relying (as Russia has done) on an approach that has been wholly dominated by Western patterns of development, influence, and not a little self-interest as well (especially in its desire to see Russia pursue an export-orientated growth which will give Western access to its oil, but will make most other parts of its industrial base totally unviable).[42]

When it comes to identifying the main social base of the centrist orientation, arguably the best working definition here has been provided by Michael McFaul. The primary *raison d'être* of Russian centrism, he has argued, stems from its claim 'to represent individuals and social groups advantaged by the *old* Soviet socioeconomic system who then sought to secure a *new* political and economic role in Russia's post-communist society'. These, then, were groups which did not essentially seek a restoration of the Soviet *ancien régime*, but did nevertheless have 'material and organisational stakes [arising out of the old order] which they sought to secure and defend'.[43]

As McFaul goes on to state, the basis of the 'centrist' identity from a social perspective stemmed largely from the fact that the centrists had one foot in the past and one in the future – unlike their two main hegemonic rivals, who sought to represent either the new interests of exclusively new identities (i.e. the entrepreneurs and middle-class base of the Westerners) or the old interests of exclusively old identities (i.e. the Russophiles). McFaul is also adamant that given the very nature of their predetermined status and identity within the old order, these were groups which clearly had – in the short term, at least – both a better understanding of their interests and greater access to a whole series of resources.

Although McFaul's postulation is by no means universally accepted, the two social groups that he singles out as embodying the backbone of centrism are unanimously recognized as the core social base of that orientation; those two groups being the vast proportion of state enterprise directors and key sectors of the industrial workforce.

For Michael Ellman, in contrast to McFaul, a better – and certainly simpler – conceptualization of centrism, based on a recognition of the centrists' main social base, would be to say that the orientation appeals mostly to society's 'losers'.[44] This also has its merits, though following McFaul here I would suggest that it is too easily dismissive of the *positive* aspirations of these social groups *vis-à-vis* the whole process of transition. In other words, there is clearly a desire on their part to accumulate a series of 'net gains' that will ultimately outweigh their undoubted 'net losses'.

Turning to the first of these groups, the directors of state enterprises, the sense of 'loss' to which both Ellman and McFaul have alluded is certainly apparent in a number of different ways. In a 'narrow' sense, for example, few can doubt that the period of radical shock-therapy reform during the initial period of the post-Soviet transition, with its emphasis on the withdrawal of state subsidies and other hard budgetary constraints, and so on, clearly disadvantaged many state enterprise directors and their capacity to operate in any kind of effective manner. It is in a more 'general' understanding of this sense of 'loss', however, that one perhaps truly starts to appreciate the current position of this social group. According to Vitalii Mashkov, no other social stratum in the former Soviet Union did more to initiate and sustain the process of *perestroika* after 1985 than the directors of state enterprises, and their reasons for doing so were perfectly rational. Having often accumulated vast resources under Brezhnev, they were keen to enjoy the fruits of their gains. This they were unable to do, however, given the constraints of the old system. Their aim, therefore, was always to try to jettison those elements of the old system that held them back, and set up in their place a more market-orientated system that they alone would control. For a time, everything went swimmingly – until the arrival, that is, of the shock therapists and their aspirations to a fundamentally different kind of economic strategy.[45]

A similar line of argument has been put forward by Simon Clarke. What many state enterprise directors fundamentally wanted, he has contended, was far greater degrees of autonomous control over their enterprises. To this extent, they were perfectly happy to see the disintegration of the old-style command-administrative system and a thoroughgoing de-ideologization of the system – both aspects of which gave their enterprise a new kind of autonomous juridical status. What they were certainly less keen to see, however, was the transfer of their enterprise to any kind of *outside* control in the form of *new* owners of that enterprise.[46]

It was certainly this aspect of the Westerners' privatization proposals that worried them most. Having fought so hard to establish their independence from the state under Gorbachev, enterprise directors were clearly not going to give up their new sense of control without a fight under Yeltsin. And as Clarke goes on to point out, it was precisely *control*, rather than direct, personalized ownership, that always guided their actions here. The possibility of enterprise managers themselves being in a position to 'expropriate' their enterprises for their own personal benefit was always highly unrealistic, at least on any *significant* scale. For all that they had gained substantial benefits under the old regime, they themselves tended not to possess the capital needed for expropriation. Meanwhile, attempts to raise the capital from other sources would simply leave them susceptible once again to outside control. And in any case, ownership also implied ultimate *responsibility* of a kind that had never previously been part of their understanding of what control entailed.

This sense of the enterprise being rightfully 'theirs' (i.e. the directors') is also something that has featured prominently in all post-Soviet economic debates. Arguments invoking the amount of 'energy' that these directors have 'invested' in their enterprise over the years are common. And as Vitalii Naishul', a prominent young pro-Western economist, has often pointed out, enterprise directors really do believe in an overwhelming *moral* right to the companies they have hitherto managed.[47]

Without doubt, the biggest and most important institutional articulator of industrial directors' interests is the aforementioned Russian Union of Industrialists and Entrepreneurs (RUIE) under the chairmanship of Arkadii Vol'skii. As the successor organization of the Scientific Industrial Union of the USSR, it has been estimated that the members of RUIE employ more than one-third of Russia's entire labour force, with nearly a quarter of the members coming exclusively from the defence sector.[48] RUIE is frequently stigmatized (by the advocates of Westernization) as nothing more than an organizational home for the class of 'Red Directors'; nevertheless, this intended slur on its image belies a very complex, if not contradictory, internal make-up; albeit one, in reality, which is fully in keeping with centrism's overall approach to the kind of transition needed in Russia.

For the leadership of RUIE the *raison d'être* of their organization is to prevent the thoroughgoing de-industrialization of Russia. From their perspective, then, the question of ownership, though vital, is certainly not as important as the fact that the state must continue to play a leading role in the preservation of the country's manufacturing base. On this basis, therefore, it has consciously attempted to amalgamate the interests of Russia's manufacturing base, irrespective of its ownership status. Enterprises still firmly within the state sector should continue to receive the necessary subsidies to avoid bankruptcy and the consequences of mass unemployment. Enterprises within the emerging non-state sector, however, are equally reliant on state protectionist measures.

Certainly, in the long term the balance struck by RUIE is a precarious one; but in the short term it is convinced that the nature of the transition in Russia supplies its own strong rationale for just such an approach. And as Eric Lohr has argued, a list of RUIE's founders and sponsors (from across the state and non-state domain) would appear to bear out this rationale to a considerable extent.[49]

Apart from RUIE, the other main articulator of industrial directors' interests is the Congress of Russian Business Circles. A considerably smaller organization than RUIE, it too has nevertheless attempted to recruit members from both old and new structures, appealing in particular to commercial banks and investment companies. Although the Congress has had somewhat greater, or at least *earlier*, access to the prime levers of power than RUIE – its leading members having served on an official government advisory agency from the early spring of 1992 – it should not be considered in any sense a competitor of RUIE: aptly demonstrated by the fact that its leader, Aleksandr Vladislavlev, is also First Vice-Chairman to Vol'skii in the leadership of RUIE.[50]

When it comes to the other perceived main social pillar of the centrist orientation, the industrial workers, their sense of 'loss' from the process of transition enacted in Russia is equally easy to discern. With industrial managers often unable to pay wages for the simple reason that they have no funds available to them; with such high levels of the population, in any case, estimated to be on wage levels below 'starvation point'; and with the constant threat of unemployment looming over them, it is small wonder that the centrist advocacy of greater welfare protection, as well as greater access to ownership rights within the enterprise, is an orientation that many workers feel is a *positive* alternative to the Westerners' advocacy of harsh free-market realism, or the apparent negative Russophile advocacy of a return to the past.

Institutionally, the main base of industrial workers in Russia today is the Federation of Independent Trade Unions (FITUR), the main successor organization to the Soviet-era Trade Union movement. An affiliation of more than 40 branch unions, FITUR professes to have a membership of approximately 60 million members (out of a total workforce of 72.5 million). Although more than 40 independent unions have been created, for the most part in direct opposition to the policy orientation pursued by FITUR (in such sectors as coal mining and airline pilots), the mere fact that very few of them have achieved a membership base of more than a few thousand clearly leaves FITUR in a dominant position. The extent to which it has been able to use this dominance, however, is another matter entirely.

Recognizing that both these social groups have clearly been most threatened by the post-Soviet transition process so far is clearly only part of the task at hand. An equally important task is to understand the way in which these groups have been thrown together in a *shared* link with the centrist orientation. Undoubtedly, a good part of the answer here lies in an appreciation of the internal structure and the internal operational mechanisms of the old Soviet-era enterprise, subject as it was to the norms of command-administrative principles. The most common description of the relationship between management and workforce (as represented by the enterprise trade union) was one of *collusion*; and there were clearly sound reasons for the utilization of this term.

The real irony of the situation, however, is that far from breaking the old collusive bonds between managers and workers, post-communist privatization, in its initial phases at least, has in many ways only *strengthened* those bonds – especially in the format of the so-called *second variant* of privatization, which has been by far the most popular option chosen up until now. In very general terms (as Figure 5.1 demonstrates), this second variant of privatization gave provision for employees to acquire 51 per cent of voting shares at a nominal price fixed at 1.7 times the book value of the company at the time of sale. The remaining shares were then available – primarily at auction, where individual vouchers could also be used.[51] Massively supported by the leadership of both RUIE and FITUR (who saw it as a primary means of securing greater degrees of job security for the ordinary worker), it was an option that was clearly forced on a reluctant Gaidar-led government, which in no uncertain terms stressed its own preference for the first variant, which envisaged much stronger degrees of outsider investment and control.[52]

Summing up the *raison d'être* for the strength of support for the second variant, Evgenii Yasin, head of RUIE's Expert Institute (who also acted at this time as the government's representative in the Supreme Soviet), was nevertheless adamant that 'the buying out of the means of production by

Figure 5.1   Variants of Privatization

[As stipulated in the Programme for the Deepening of the Economic Reforms, June 1992]

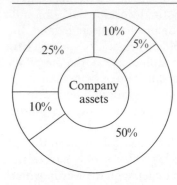

Option 1

25% of non-voting shares to be distributed free of charge amongst the employees.

10% to be made available to the workforce at a 30% discount.

5% to be reserved for management at a nominal price.

10% to be auctioned to the general public.

50% to be sold at auction or through a tender to an investor or consortium in a single block.

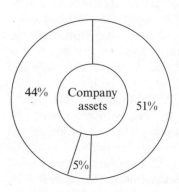

Option 2

51% to be made available to the workforce for cash and/or vouchers and/or the retained earnings of the enterprise for a price fixed at 1.7 times the book value of the enterprise.

44% to be sold at auction.

5% to be made available to the workforce at a discount price through an employee share-owning programme.

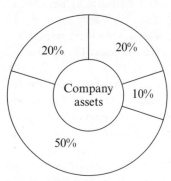

Option 3

20% to be offered to the workforce at a 30% discount.

20% to be offered to the workforce at the full selling price.

10% available through the employee share-owning programme.

50% available at auction.

Source: *Programma uglubleniya ekonomicheskikh reform* (Moscow, 1992)

labour collectives is a very promising approach, since it promotes the harmonisation of the interests of various social groups at the same time as it ensures a rather high degree of economic effectiveness'. In contrast, he went on, the form of privatization as envisaged in the first variant was far too 'fraught with the possibility of social explosion'.[53]

Within the rubric of this self-professed concern for the maintenance of social harmony within the enterprise, of course, it is not too hard to discern other motivations at work, especially when it comes to the motivations of the enterprise directors themselves. As a number of detailed studies have shown, they know full well that by keeping the privatization process firmly 'in house', they stand to gain a great deal. First, they have every confidence that after most of the shares have been given to the labour collective, they will nearly always retain their job as enterprise director.[54] Secondly, they also know that once shares have been given to workers, it will not be too difficult to find ways of 'encouraging' these workers to part with their shares, thereby providing management, sooner or later, with the main concentration of share ownership.[55] And thirdly, as the main representative of the labour collective, they also have other mechanisms to ensure that their overall degree of control is just as effective as it was in the past. In particular, by maintaining many of the old social provisions that were such an intrinsic part of the Soviet enterprise (not least, for example, the distribution of consumer goods through the workplace), they can be reasonably sure that they can effectively 'buy' the continued loyalty and support of the workforce. It is thus small wonder that one expert has defined the second variant of privatization as nothing more than 'an attempt to reconstitute the Soviet system from below, on the basis of the existing social relations of production'.[56]

The essence of the co-operation/collusion that has taken place *inside* the enterprise is likewise mirrored in a range of other, external institutionalized forms. In May 1992, for example, it was announced that the then leader of FITUR, Igor' Klochkov, had reached an agreement with Arkadii Vol'skii of RUIE to co-publish the daily newspaper *Rabochaya tribuna* as a new publication officially promoting the goal of 'social partnership and social defence'.[57] And although this represented the first *public* expression of their co-operation, it is widely recognized that on an individual level at least, Klochkov's and Vol'skii's partnership had originated as far back as autumn 1991.

By far the strongest institutionalization of post-Soviet worker–manager collaboration, however, is the Russian Assembly of Social Partnership, set up in July 1992. This organization emerged out of the initial attempt (at the end of 1991) to operate a *government-sponsored* form of social partnership in the guise of the Tripartite Commission on the Regulation of Social and Labour Relations, a consultation body linking government, trade unions and employers which was meant to discuss all important matters of social policy with a view to facilitating the defusion of potential conflicts. When this body ran into difficulties – first on the issue of who precisely was going to be represented, and secondly following accusations of a lack of any genuine government interest in the social partnership mechanism – Klochkov and Vol'skii, as leaders of the employers and union side, decided to create what they termed a 'real' alternative to the Tripartite Commission.

An indication that a breakaway alliance was in the making had been hinted at sometime earlier by Gennadii Semigin, an employers' representative on the Tripartite Commission from the Congress of Russian Business Circles. Writing in the Trade Union newspaper *Trud* in April 1992, he made it plain that the government's main intention of establishing the Commission had merely been to play the new unions off against the old, while at the same time playing the employers off against the unions. This, however, had singularly failed to work. What in effect had happened was that employers and workers had often sided with each other in direct opposition to the government.[58] Semigin's criticism of the government line was also taken up by Aleksandr Vladislavlev; and to nobody's surprise, the Congress of Russian Business Circles was also a key participant in the creation of the new social partnership assembly.[59]

Although the assembly wields little genuine power, its creation was nevertheless a significant development, representing as it did a definitive sign that the main post-Soviet Trade Union organization clearly had no intention whatsoever at this stage in articulating an exclusive working-class set of interests in opposition to their employers. Indeed, as Clarke has argued, 'while enterprise Directors have been celebrating their independence at the expense of their common interests as a class, it has been the trade unions who have played the most active role in forging the class unity of the industrialists and entrepreneurs'. For the most part, he went on, trade-union leaders have, ironically, been far more enthusiastic about 'Vol'skii's organization' (the Assembly of Social Partnership) than the enterprise directors he supposedly represents.[60]

Forging the Political Base of the Historical Bloc

On the political front, the fortunes of Russian centrism have been – uncharacteristically from the logic of its own self-definition, but all too characteristically from a broader understanding of post-Soviet political experience – highly erratic, spanning the ever-volatile extremes of success and failure with unnerving frequency and even more unnerving rapidity.

As Aleksandr Rubstov has noted, if everything in Russian political life began with an all too simplistic understanding of 'democrats versus communists', it did not take too long for a centrist spoke to upset this reductionist applecart. 'All of a sudden, centrism appeared to be the most comfortable and victorious platform.'[61] To its own cost, however, it quickly became apparent that sustaining that political momentum was no easy task. The suddenness of its apparent 'victory' was all too easily transformed into the suddenness of its apparent political demise. The organizational embodiment of this political capriciousness has been Civic Union, an amalgamation of a variety of centrist forces which was formally created in June 1992. Before analysing the organization as a whole, it is certainly worth looking more closely at the individual components.

At its height, Civic Union consisted of three of the strongest recognizable political parties to have emerged out of the post-Soviet transition (the People's Party of Free Russia, the Democratic Party of Russia and the All-Russian Union 'Renewal'), one youth movement (The Russian Youth Union), one 'association' (The Russian Social Democratic Centre) and one parliamentary faction in the Supreme Soviet (*Smena*, or Change and New Policy). It could also rely on the support of six other parliamentary factions (Industrial Union, Free Russia, Left Centre, Sovereignty and Equality, the Workers Union and Nonparty Deputies). Finally, although it was not officially a constituent member because of legal rules prohibiting its explicit political affiliation, the highest consultative council of Civic Union also included Igor' Klochkov, the leader of FITUR.

Turning first of all to the People's Party of Free Russia (PPFR), this was established at the end of October 1991 under the leadership of the then Vice-President Aleksandr Rutskoi and Vasilii Lipitskii. A direct successor of the short-lived Democratic Party of Russian Communists, it was largely made up of three elements: the Soviet-era Russian parliamentary faction Communists for Democracy, the Democratic Movement of Communists, and part of the Democratic Platform of the former CPSU. Right from the outset – especially given its personal association with Rutskoi – one of the main issues of concern for the party was the nature of its relationship with President Yeltsin. At its founding congress in October 1991, the attitude among most delegates was one of ambivalence. Although there was some support for the basic orientation associated with Yeltsin, there were nevertheless repeated warnings that the party should never be allowed to turn into a simple 'pocket organization' of the President. It was not too long, however, before this ambivalence was irremediably clarified. During a tour of Siberia in winter 1991 – which took in a number of visits to enterprises which were part of the military–industrial complex – Rutskoi encountered nothing but 'grievances, bewilderment and indignation prevailing everywhere'.[62] Determined to give some political embodiment to these outpourings of hostility, he now firmly identified himself as a

vigorous opponent of the pro-Western orientation that had been adopted
by those in government, referring to the likes of Gaidar and company as
nothing more than 'young boys in pink shorts, red shirts and yellow boots',
whose actions were destroying Russian statehood – comments that led
one journalist to portray Rutskoi, even at this early stage, as both a potential leader of *all* anti-Westernization forces and, more intuitively, a
potential leader of a second putsch.[63]

Of all the issues to have caused an irreparable gulf between Rutskoi and
Yeltsin, however, it was the latter's support for the disintegration of the
unified state formation of the USSR that was paramount. Claiming later
that he was never informed of Yeltsin's 'surprise initiative' at the Minsk
Summit with Ukraine's Leonid Kravchuk and Belorussia's Stanislav
Shushkevich,[64] Rutskoi was regularly to be heard criticizing the agreement
as a 'fouling up' of the Soviet Union, carried out 'from behind a corner in
some thievish, secretive way'.[65]

Above all, it was a series of four articles in major national newspapers
in the space of two weeks (between the end of January and the middle of
February 1992) that did most to establish Rutskoi's political creed. In the
first of these – a *Pravda* article entitled 'In Defence of Russia' – Rutskoi
unequivocally equated the reforms with a 'national humiliation' of tragic
proportions.[66] Indeed, nothing less than Russia's existence was now at risk.
Because of the actions of those who had come to power 'on the crest of a
wave of national-careerism', Russia had been forced to cede territory that
had helped to shape and define its thousand-year history.

As for the second of his articles – a piece in *Izvestiya* which carried the
title 'Holy Communion at McDonalds: Reflections on What Will Happen
to Us on Judgement Day' – Rutskoi's lyricism and evident loathing for the
pro-Western orientation now touched ever grander heights.[67] Not wanting
to believe that the average Russian in the street had suddenly succumbed to
Philistine traits, Rutskoi was nevertheless despondent at all those people
who had slavishly submitted themselves to the temptation of enjoying 'a
fleeting communion with the Western way of life after decades of living
locked up in a totalitarian utopia'. The daily pilgrimage to McDonalds, of
course, was only a small symbol of Russia's growing cultural decline. The
continuing emigration of its cultural elite to the West; the bankruptcy of
brilliant minds ravished by the desire to plunder money through 'postbox
enterprises'; the ready availability of the cheapest of Western 'kitsch' on its
bookshelves and the 'tawdry offerings' on its television screens, all signified
a demeaning surrender at the hands of its cultural victor, which was close
to producing a universal cynicism.[68]

In the third of his articles – another piece in *Pravda* entitled 'Is There a
Way Out of the Crisis?' – Rutskoi once again concentrated his attack on
(what elsewhere he had termed) the 'barricade radicalism' of the Westerners,

which had resulted in the socioeconomic degradation of the country and the emergence of a mafia-controlled economy presiding over a mass underclass of poor, lumpenized citizens.[69] And finally, offering his services this time to *Nezavisimaya gazeta* in an article entitled 'The Alternative: A Strong Authority for Democracy', Rutskoi returned full circle to his pet theme of the degradation of the Russian state, once again conjuring up images of a great and powerful country that was 'turning before our eyes into something vague, with no clear borders, statehood or even properly recognized name'.[70]

Within his own party, it has to be said, Rutskoi's ideas were not always unanimously accepted; and one member of the party's governing 'board of directors', Professor Grigorii Vodolazov, was a frequent critic, who went on to lead an internal faction aimed at preserving a more genuine 'leftist' image for the PPFR. Nevertheless, for the most part, Rutskoi's leadership nearly always went unchallenged, and the synonymity of the PPFR with the label 'Rutskoi's Party' was a good indication of the personal level of control and influence he wielded.

The PPFR's relationship with other self-styled centrist organizations originated in March 1992 at a conference of public forces committed to 'reviving Russian statehood'. At the conference, a formal agreement was signed with the Democratic Party of Russia (DPR) which in broader terms paved the way for the formation of the Civic Union in June that year, and in narrow terms even envisaged a possible unification of the two parties within the space of a year or two.[71] Another party to have emerged out of the Democratic Platform of the former CPSU, the DPR was formally established in May 1990. Classifying itself as the first genuine alternative political party to the CPSU, it has been most closely associated with Nikolai Travkin, a former student of the CPSU's Moscow Higher School for Party functionaries who, by all accounts, converted away from his communist beliefs 'on the road to Stockholm' in 1989.

Arguably the most remarkable and distinctive feature of the DPR has been its capacity for survival, notwithstanding the fact that at virtually every party conference and congress it has witnessed some kind of split or division within its ranks. The fact that it has survived at all in the face of all these internal upheavals is due in no small part to Travkin himself, whose personal influence over the years has been second to none in the world of party construction. Although he has often been the cause of such splits, there can be no denying that he has established one of the best-organized political parties in post-Soviet Russia. It is also one of the few parties with branches in all regional centres of the Federation, as well as many districts and villages; and again, much of the credit here must go to Travkin personally and his commitment to establishing a genuine multi-party system in Russia.[72] As he himself once told an interviewer, building up a network of party organizations throughout the country is extremely hard work: 'It doesn't mean going to Paris. It means going to Ryazan. And not only that. You go there, you establish new structures, and then, within a month, they fall out and you have to go back and start all over again. And then they complain because you haven't been running the party and getting ready for the congress. . . .'[73]

Consistent with those of most other political parties, the DPR's policies have often tended to blow with the prevailing wind. Two issues, however, have remained a fixed posture in all its programmes, and have largely defined the basic orientation of the party. It is a firm believer in a strong and indivisible form of Russian statehood; it has continued vehemently to condemn the break-up of the USSR, and remains committed to the establishment of a reintegrated union on the old territory of the Soviet Union (the three Baltic states excluded if they do not voluntarily wish to rejoin).

The third party to join up with the PPFR and DPR as a constituent member of Civic Union was the All-Russian Union 'Renewal' [*Obnovlenie*], which was established at the end of May 1992, primarily as the political wing of the Russian Union of Industrialists and Entrepreneurs. Most closely associated – not surprisingly – with Arkadii Vol'skii and Aleksandr Vladislavlev, the other main leaders of the party were Igor' Smirnov (who was the official chairman of the party's Executive Committee), Iosif Diskin and Anatolii Dolgolaptev.[74]

Defining itself as a 'manager in politics and politicians in industry' party, Renewal certainly lived up to its name in terms of the numbers of former CPSU functionaries for whom it was able to provide a new political home. No fewer than ten former heads of Central Committee departments in the old CPSU attended its founding conference, not to mention 'almost the entire membership of the Industrial Department'.[75] The party was also successful in attracting the support of many local government officials. At its first full congress at the end of February 1993, it was announced that the administration heads from 36 territories and regions were active members of the party, the most prominent being the then Chairman of the Moscow City Council, Nikolai Gonchar. The other most notable supporter of the party was Vladimir Shumeiko, who had recently become a deputy Prime Minister in Gaidar's Cabinet and acted as a co-President of the inaugural conference.

Recognized by many at the time to be the real adhesive of the Civic Union alliance, the Renewal Party was highly successful in establishing an 'international' support base for its centrist ambitions across the territory of the former Soviet Union.[76]

Turning to the main constituent parliamentary faction, most commentators are agreed that in *Smena*, Civic Union had the support of one of the most professional and efficient factions in the old Supreme Soviet.

Established at the first, Soviet-era session of the Russian Congress of People's Deputies, it had originally affiliated itself to the Democratic Russia movement, until its change of direction following the emergence of shock-therapy reforms.[77]

Of the remaining parliamentary 'supporters', undoubtedly the most prominent was the Industrial Union [*Promyshlennyi Soyuz*], established in 1991. It was led by Yurii Gekht, a director of a paper mill in the Moscow province of Serpukhov, and all the members of the faction were closely associated with large state enterprises, primarily in the military–industrial sphere, which relied almost exclusively on the continuation of state subsidies. Outside the parliamentary realm, they were also closely associated with a recognizably more conservative section of Vol'skii's RUIE.[78]

The final constituent member of Civic Union that deserves attention is the Russian Social Democratic Centre. Originally a faction within the Social Democratic Party of Russia, the Centre declared its autonomy in May 1992 and then went on to organize a founding conference of the new association in December 1992. The leaders were Oleg Rumyantsev (who at that time was the Executive Secretary of the parliament's Constitutional Commission), V.M. Nyrko (chief editor of the Social Democratic newspaper *Alternativy*) and Sergei Khramov (Chairman of the independent trade union Sotsprof), and the main basis of the divorce from the rest of the party was the more explicit statist and nationalist orientation of the members of the Centre. In January 1993 the Centre created a formal alliance with Rutskoi's PPFR, and a month later it formally joined Civic Union.[79]

In assessing the fortunes of Civic Union in the weeks and months following its creation in summer 1992, it is clearly tempting simply to follow the dictates of hindsight. If we allow foresight to take precedence for a moment, however, we can at least understand how it was that a number of features undeniably prompted many analysts to view this political alliance with a great deal of seriousness.

One feature in its favour appeared to be the apparent sense of complementarity between the three main constituent parties and their respective leaders. Outside their party positions, for example, each leader held a position of authority that could clearly assist the alliance's overall ambitions – with Rutskoi occupying the vice-presidency, Vol'skii in charge of the country's main employer association and Travkin gaining valuable experience as the head of the local administration in the Shakhovskoi district of Moscow province (a post he held from December 1991). In addition, since they enjoyed such high status in the former CPSU, one group of analysts even went so far as to talk of their common 'genetic' connections – which, if nothing else, appeared to provide each leader with a political survival instinct second to none.[80]

In broader party terms, an excellent functional division of labour existed between the three groups, with the Renewal organization concentrating on economic issues and the PPFR and DPR concentrating primarily on fundamental issues of Russian statehood, both from an internal and an external perspective. Collectively, meanwhile, unlike some of its counterparts, the Civic Union had a coherent and very well-directed programme of aims and ambitions, in both domestic *and* foreign policy.[81] It had a good research–technical support base and, in the Gorbachev Foundation in particular, access to resources that few of its opponents could match. Its highest co-ordinating organ, the Political Consultative Council, was generally acknowledged to be run on very effective lines, and in the person of Vasilii Lipitskii, who chaired the executive committee of the alliance, the Civic Union secured its real 'propellent'. In the guise of the weekly newspaper *Rossiiskoe vremya* (which took over the publication of the DPR's *Demokraticheskaya gazeta*) and, of course, in *Rabochaya tribuna*, it had a reliable information and propaganda outlet; and again, unlike some of its opponents, it had no shortage of funds, even to the point of being able to hire the services of an American lobby organization.[82]

Perhaps more than anything, however (and notwithstanding its 'opposition' identity), it had extremely good access to the legislative and executive decision-making structures. Indeed, from its creation in the summer of 1992 to the spring of 1993 in particular, the Civic Union's influence on decision-making was paramount. Nowhere was this more noticeable than in the sphere of personnel appointments. By the end of 1992, self-professed centrists were in charge of the Security Council (in the person of Yurii Skokov), the Central Bank (Viktor Gerashchenko) and, most significantly of all, of course, the government itself (following Chernomyrdin's replacement of Gaidar).[83] Since this came on top of other ministerial appointments in their favour, it was hardly surprising that some commentators were now openly beginning to consider centrism as the new official political orthodoxy.

And just to add credence to this belief, President Yeltsin himself now started to take a far greater interest in the affairs of Civic Union than ever he had done previously. In late February 1993, for example, he attended a key Civic Union forum *instead* of a Democratic Russia forum held at the same time in Nizhny Novgorod.[84] This was followed in April by his attendance at the fourth congress of RUIE, where he confirmed that from now on his consultations with representatives of Civic Union and its component organizations would be held on a regular basis, and that having familiarized himself with the centrists' core political and economic proposals, he was sure that there were no real insurmountable differences between himself and Civic Union.[85]

Writing in the aftermath of this undoubted high point of success – which also included the incorporation of some key centrist economic recommendations on issues of price control, privileged loans for defence conversion and state orders into an official new reform programme – Aleksandr Vladislavlev was now very upbeat about the possibilities of widening the political support base of Civic Union.[86] Widening, however, did not mean mystifying the essential basis of centrism. The nucleus of the social base of Civic Union would have to remain extremely cohesive, and a clear-cut programme of viable aims would have to be adhered to. Likewise, as was being made clear in a number of centrist circles, an undisputed leader of the movement would have to be selected sooner rather than later on the basis of his capacity to embody and to articulate the basic concerns of the people with whom the orientation identified. And indeed, for a time this desire to widen Civic Union's depth of support looked as though it was going to meet with considerable success. In early spring 1993, for example, negotiations were concluded with Dmitrii Rogozin's Union of Russia's Renaissance, which had been formally established in January 1993 largely as an amalgamation of breakaway factions from the Russian Christian Democratic Movement and the Constitutional Democratic Party, did not want to be explicitly associated with the National Salvation Front.[87] This was then followed by a series of negotiations with two democratic left organizations, Roi Medvedev's Socialist Party of Workers and the Party of Labour, most closely identified with Boris Kagarlitsky and Aleksandr Buzgalin. Indeed, at a round table organized by Civic Union in May 1993, representatives from thirty different associations and organizations were discussing the possibility of establishing a common alliance; and by early June that number had reached thirty-six.[88]

Once again, however, what appeared to be a movement's high point in Russian political life quickly transformed itself into the start of its rapid descent. Consequently, with the benefit of hindsight a very different gloss can be put on the situation that had been developing throughout the course of early spring and summer 1993. At exactly the point when talks were taking place to strengthen the centrist coalition around Civic Union, so the original basis of that coalition was slowly but surely starting to unravel.

In the view of a number of commentators, the process that was to result in the eventual break-up of Civic Union was one that was in no small part carefully *engineered* by no less a person than President Yeltsin himself, who, it is argued, surreptitiously enticed the 'centrist moderates' away from the 'centrist radicals' with the increasing lure of patronage inducements traded off for personal loyalty to the presidential office.[89] While this is not entirely off the mark, my own emphasis, as before, is much more orientated to the intrinsic contradictions and antagonisms within Civic Union which encouraged the disaggregating tendencies to reach their logical conclusion.

Some of the most pertinent issues here will be dealt with in the analysis below on the overall hegemonic potential of centrism. Suffice it to say for now that the appearance of any kind of cohesiveness in and around Civic Union was always extremely deceptive. While the aforementioned complementarity between the likes of Travkin, Vol'skii and Rutskoi had some genuine credence to it, there was never really any doubt that an awful lot of things divided them. This was certainly the case when it came to key specific matters of policy, where nearly all co-ordinated Civic Union programmes would be concluded with an addendum making it clear that the respective authors were not in absolute agreement with all aspects of the final text, and would not, therefore, take individual responsibility for it.[90] It was likewise very much the case in terms of their own individual relationship with each other – what one commentator called 'problems in interpersonal communications'.[91]

Gordon Hahn was thus perfectly correct to describe Civic Union as essentially 'an alliance of convenience, serving ambition rather than [strict] ideological affinity or policy preferences'.[92] Though perhaps the best analogy that was used to interpret the essence of this alliance between Vol'skii, Rutskoi and Travkin was the frequent journalistic reference to Ivan Krylov's famous fable of the swan, the pike and the crab, with each pulling a truck in different directions and inevitably getting nowhere.

When a number of key centrist figures began to indicate that the alliance needed an undisputed leader, they were absolutely correct. What all of them seemingly failed to appreciate, however, was that while this would undoubtedly add to its potential, it would also be the inevitable cause of its downfall, given the nature of things as they then stood. In short, the head of each political party was absolutely adamant that he should be the nucleus around which the rest of the alliance should be framed. Sooner or later, therefore, it was only natural that the internal struggle for hegemony *within* Civic Union would begin to outweigh the external struggle with its main political opponents. Moreover, given the self-recognized amorphousness of centrist ideology (or at least its lack of self-assuredness), the scope for movement *between* political organizations on either side of it was always going to be a strong possibility.

The first real indication of substantial differences came at the time of the April 1993 referendum campaign. To put the matter bluntly, there was *no* campaign, at least from a co-ordinated Civic Union perspective, with each of the component groups invariably contradicting each other from one day to the next.[93] As the primary co-ordinator of the alliance, Vasilii Lipitskii seemed to spend more time in attempting to rebut allegations of divisions than he did in genuinely setting out a Civic Union stance on the four questions that were asked.[94]

What remained partially hidden at the time of the referendum, however,

did not take too long to burst asunder afterwards, as one by one individual components of Civic Union either voiced their tired disillusion with the
alliance or simply broke away from it altogether in order to seek out new
allies.

First to go was the Industrial Union; though perhaps of all the splits
and divisions this was the least unexpected. For a long time relations
between Gekht and Vol'skii had been somewhat tense, to say the least, as
the former increasingly tried to steer the latter in a more radical
statist/nationalist direction and, in the process, challenged Vol'skii's leadership of the overall 'industrial lobby'.[95] The next group to express its
outright dissatisfaction with the Union was the *Smena* parliamentary faction. During the proceedings of the ninth (extraordinary) Congress of
People's Deputies in March 1993 (called in response to Yeltsin's televised
threat to declare a period of 'special rule'), they became disillusioned with
the overall lack of abilities of the extra-parliamentary leaders to provide
any kind of strong, concerted and unified leadership. In short, they too
realized that in the climate then prevailing, the space for any centrist kind
of compromise was fast disappearing.

Next on the departure list, in summer 1993, was Travkin's DPR. Since
they had already joined and left two earlier political alliances prior to
Civic Union, at least one could not accuse the DPR of inconsistency here.[96]
Several reasons, meanwhile, figured prominently in their decision to leave.
On issues of policy, for example, it had always been apparent that the
party was a much stronger supporter of a Western-style free market, based
on strict private ownership rights, than the other members of Civic
Union – something that was clear not only from their party programmes
but from Travkin's actual experience of introducing reforms in his native
Shakhovskoi district.[97] On the personality front, there was little mutual
trust between Travkin and Rutskoi in particular, and when the latter
started giving the impression that Civic Union was nothing more than a
vehicle for his own presidential aspirations, it was clear that Travkin's position would no longer be tenable, reluctant as he was ever to play second
fiddle to anyone else's interests. Nor did Travkin appreciate Rutskoi's ever-
closer *rapprochement* with the Russophiles, and when the leaders of the
DPR branch in Smolensk described a speech given by Rutskoi in their city
in August 1993 as nothing more than an 'unrestrained populism in the
spirit of the National Salvation Front which discredits the very idea of
political centrism', this was the final straw that broke the camel's back.[98]

The DPR, likewise, was firmly against the broadening of the existing
Civic Union alliance. For one thing, they fundamentally objected to the
incorporation of parties with an explicit socialist orientation, and refused
outright to attend the round-table negotiations then taking place. For
another thing, they never camouflaged the fact that the party entered a

broader alliance not to subsume their interests to that alliance, but to help broaden the base of the party itself. It was significant, for example, that when Travkin addressed his party's fourth congress in December 1992 he made it perfectly clear that while the DPR's membership of Civic Union had in general terms been quite a positive factor throughout the second half of 1992, and had done much to give it a more prominent public profile, the party had nevertheless 'incurred certain political losses' in the sense that it had too often worked for the overall benefit of Civic Union at the expense of building up its own political identity and base.[99] When in his own words, then, he had recognized a condition of exhaustion setting in in Civic Union, Travkin had no compunction about being the first of the major constituent parties to break away.[100]

Never one to be associated with a sinking ship, Arkadii Vol'skii was likewise spending the summer of 1993 slowly but surely distancing himself from Civic Union, while simultaneously toying with the idea of transforming Renewal into a brand-new Industrial Party. Somewhat like Travkin, Vol'skii had always astutely refrained from defining Civic Union as an explicit opposition movement to President Yeltsin. He too, therefore, became increasingly aggrieved at the antics of Aleksandr Rutskoi and his attempts to monopolize the organization for his own personal ambitions. Indeed, at one point Vol'skii even announced that his departure from Civic Union was not at issue, for the simple reason that he had never actually been a member of the organization.[101]

As for the major cause of both Vol'skii's and Travkin's disillusion with Civic Union, Aleksandr Rutskoi, he – not surprisingly – was offering a very different slant to the criticisms voiced by his erstwhile allies, accusing them in turn of being 'spineless' political figures with their own hidden motives and personal ambitions.

In an essay on the characteristic features of 'Rutskoism', Lev Ovrutsky had once argued that one of the unique features of the Vice-President was his endeavour to be all of Dostoevsky's Karamazov brothers in one person – 'to equal Alyosha in piety, to be as philosophical as Ivan, and to exceed Mitya in recklessness'.[102] Few could doubt that by the summer of 1993 it was 'Mitya Rutskoi' that was gaining the upper hand. To be fair to Rutskoi, however, his allies could hardly complain of being ignorant of his more radical (or 'reactionary') interpretation of the centrist orientation. They knew only too well of his background in the patriotic-cum-chauvinistic organization *Otechestvo* (Fatherland); they could clearly judge the continuing strength of his nationalist feelings in his *Pravda* article 'In Defence of Russia' and many others besides;[103] they saw for themselves his participation in the Congress of Civil and Patriotic Forces in February 1992, and heard his repeated demand for a 'united Great Rus';[104] and while they were promoting the centrist legacy of people like Stolypin, Rutskoi was constantly making known his greater affinity to thinkers like Il'in, Rozanov and Fedotov.[105]

Tracing the beginnings of Rutskoi's definitive shift away from the moderate stance usually associated with Civic Union, it is clear that the first indications were there for all to see in his *Pravda* interview with Boris Slavin in May 1993, where, among many other things, he now openly accused the CIA of being behind the collapse of the Russian economy.[106] This was followed in July by a meeting with many members of the Russophile intellectual elite (attended also by Ruslan Khasbulatov). In the presence of Aleksandr Prokhanov, Yurii Bondarev, Petr Proskurin and many others, Rutskoi praised *them* for their afforts in combating the scourge of 'cosmopolitanism' that was afflicting the country's traditional cultural heritage, while *they* praised *him* for his ever closer association with the National Salvation Front.[107] And in August there was his explicit call for the restoration of the Soviet Union, accompanied by constant paeans to the 'great and mighty Soviet people';[108] as well as his explicit support (in a separate speech the same month) for the old 'socialist methods of production and development of the economy'.[109]

Notwithstanding several warnings from high-ranking members of his own party,[110] Rutskoi's strategic switch of orientation continued unabated, reaching its climax, as we saw in Chapter 4, with his total denunciation of centrist ideology, centrist pragmatism and centrist politicians. His eventual imprisonment for his part in the October 1993 parliamentary rebellion was by this stage, then, nothing more than the final nail in the coffin.

By the time it came to the December 1993 parliamentary elections, Civic Union was clearly nothing more than a relic of its former self. In an attempt to gloss over its past association with Rutskoi, the organization was officially renamed Civic Union for Stability, Justice and Progress, and Vol'skii and Vladislavlev (after first of all realizing that there was no political mileage yet for a new Industrial Party) now took over the definitive reins of the leadership. Needless to say, repeated claims that only the old centrist ideals and not the old centrist methods had been inherited from 'Civic Union Mark 1' carried little weight with the electorate or with much of the media, which unanimously dismissed such pronouncements as the defying of any kind of logic or common sense.[111]

Although joined on their party list by prominent figures like Oleg Rumyantsev, Aleksandr Tsipko, Pavel Voshchanov (the former presidential press secretary) and Nikolai Bek (chairman of the huge KAMAZ enterprise), they themselves frequently admitted to running a campaign that only served to highlight their lack of unity, their confusion over what they stood for, and their tactical incompetence.[112] Relying in the end on picking up the support of the hitherto 'silent majority' in the country, they soon found that the operative word here was 'silent' rather than 'majority'. In a humiliating poll they picked up a mere 1.93 per cent of the proportional vote (well short of the 5 per cent threshold for seats), which was only partially offset by the election of a handful of Civic Union members and 'supporters' in the single-seat constituencies for the State Duma and in seats for the Federation Council.

The DPR, meanwhile, after briefly flirting with the idea of teaming up with Yurii Skokov's new movement Concord for the Fatherland, decided in the end to do what they were most suited to do: stand on their own. Supported by several prominent newcomers – including Nikolai Fedorov (the former Justice Minister), Stanislav Govorukhin (the film director), Sergei Glaz'ev (the former Foreign Trade Minister) and Oleg Bogomolov (director of the Institute of International and Political Studies) – they ended up with at least a more respectable 5.52 per cent of the vote (14 seats). Of most disappointment, however, was the victory of Zhirinovsky's Liberal Democratic Party in Travkin's 'sacred' Shakhovskoi district.

Other self-styled 'centrist' organizations, meanwhile, like the New Russia bloc (led by Tel'man Gdlyan and consisting of his own Russian People's Party, the Russian Social-Liberal Party, the Christian Democratic Union and the Bourgeois Democratic Party) either failed even to acquire the necessary 100,000 signatures of support to participate in the election proper, or joined Civic Union in failing to cross the 5 per cent threshold; the latter, for example, applying to the Future of Russia–New Names bloc led by Oleg Sokolov, which also included several members of Rutskoi's PPFR.

Hegemonic Potential

A question frequently posed by many intellectuals over the past few years has been: Is Russian political culture intrinsically anti-centrist? Not surprisingly, the replies have been varied. For some the response can only be in the affirmative, manifested by the assertion that until stability takes hold in Russia – and, more importantly, until a definitive middle class is established – centrism remains a notion ahead of its time.[113] Others, meanwhile, have firmly negated the question in its entirety, but all too often with a substantiation that amounts to nothing more than a simple truism: centrism has existed and will exist for ever, simply because there is not a country in the world where there is only a Left or a Right.[114]

One analyst who has adopted a much more thorough and balanced approach to the question is Vladimir Mironov. In a wide-ranging article in June 1993 he made it clear that if centrism was finally to make its mark on Russian political life, then the real task it had to accomplish was a genuine degree of political autonomy. This, in turn, depended on two factors. First, the consolidation of the centrists' own nucleus; second, they had to be prepared to engage seriously in an attempt to 'conquer hegemony within the realm of social consciousness'. For the latter to happen they would have further to successfully resolve a number of concrete problems that stood in their way.[115] By following Mironov through a perusal of these tasks, we should be able to end up with a clearer understanding both of centrism's hegemonic potential in present-day Russia and of its overall compatibility with its own indigenous political culture.

For Mironov, the first issue of substance was a recognition that political experience over the last few years has shed a considerable degree of light on a unique Russian phenomenon: the ever-increasing multiplication of 'professional patriots' who are nevertheless incapable of loving Russia – not Russia in general but, more specifically, their town, their village and their region, where real, tangible people live out their lives. This patriotism, he asserted, is dependent on a series of neuroses and phantasies of 'our national unconscious', a way of compensating for the myth of Russia's great-power [*derzhava*] complex and of each individual's own personal inferiority, which is all too demonstratively borne out on every street corner.

The task facing centrism, then, was not to parade or to exhibit its feelings with respect to this complicated problem. It should not give in to right or left radicals, and it should not succumb to all the emotional facets that stand behind the identification 'Russia'. Instead, centrists should attempt to find a synthesis between patriotism and democracy. They should concretely define and articulate the national interests of Russia, and they must rationally address the problem of developing normal and healthy feelings of animosity towards other nations, if and where necessary. Above all, the most dangerous temptation for the centrists would be alignment with the Russophiles and the national patriots for the sake of power considerations.

It is not entirely clear whether or not Mironov had Rutskoi specifically in mind when he wrote his article. If he did – and, more importantly, if one accepts Rutskoi as the main political embodiment of centrism at this time – then of course one is left with an overpowering sense of centrism's failure here. Precisely for the sake of power considerations, Rutskoi's understanding of centrism did indeed become totally indistinguishable from mainstream Russophilia. If, however, one is prepared to see a political and an ideological form of centrism distinct from the embodiment with which Rutskoi came to endow it, then clearly this cannot help but change our perception. Thanks to the efforts of the centrist 'integrationists' – original advocates and converts (like Karaganov) included – the intellectual debate on Russia's primary national interests has for the most part been decisively won; and this intellectual triumph has started to have an undeniable influence in the policy-making domain – nowhere more so than in terms of Russia's developing relationship with the so-called 'near abroad'. The much-trumpeted notion of a Russian *Monroe Doctrine* is now effectively in force, and some commentators have even begun to equate this with a clear-cut *Kozyrev Doctrine*.[116] A commitment to ever-stronger degrees of integration (particularly in the economic, social, cultural and military spheres) is now the order of the day, and (apart from the most rabid of the Westerners) few in Russia, at least, deny the logic of its right to be considered *primus inter pares* in the new relationship.[117] Moreover, where Russophiles are treated as outdated 'imperialists', the centrists have proffered a foreign policy understanding of 'hegemony' in this domain that clearly finds a degree of resonance, if not outright sympathy, in many Western corridors of power as well.

Of course, this is not to say that there are no prescribed limits to the centrists' success. A formal proposal, sponsored by President Nursultan Nazarbaev of Kazakhstan in March 1994, to establish a brand-new, definitive *Eurasian Union* very much akin to the present-day, post-Maastricht European Union – a project that received considerable support from all Russian centrists – was quickly withdrawn for being 'too premature'.[118] Nevertheless, the momentum for such a Union clearly exists (in January 1995, for example, Kazakhstan and Russia agreed formally to unite their armed forces) and most would accept that it is only a matter of when, not if, such a co-ordinated entity is finally created.

The second task in Mironov's hegemonic framework related to the economic preconditions for centrism's success. The concept of the market, as signified by the flowering of individualism and isolation [*obosoblenie*], he asserted, has historically been the main enemy of the Russian idea of conciliarism [*sobornost'*]. For the centrists, therefore, the main task is to develop a concept of the market that is clearly endowed with Russian specificities. That is to say, it must develop a form that can conspicuously be differentiated from its Western counterpart. Russian centrism, he continued, will always be connected with the idea of the state. Centrists, therefore, must maintain a strong role for the state in the life and affairs of a market-based economy, especially in the sphere of social welfare, though in so doing it must avoid a second temptation: moving too close to the position of orthodox communist forces.

On this issue as well, then, the overall judgement of centrism's hegemonic potential would *appear* to be quite favourable, subject once again to a number of significant limitations.

In the aftermath of Viktor Chernomyrdin's replacement of Yegor Gaidar as Prime Minister in December 1992, and even more noticeably in the aftermath of the December 1993 election results, there can be few doubts that some of the main tenets of market radicalism, so closely identified with the Westerners, have been replaced by a form of market gradualism, clearly embodying some of the key themes of the centrist orientation. Indeed, if at the end of 1992 the main debate among economic theoreticians appeared to revolve around a discussion of the niceties of the Anglo-Saxon versus German model of capitalism, by the end of 1993 this had now been replaced by a very different kind of discussion altogether: is the Russian economy going more closely to resemble a *state capitalist* or a *state socialist* model of development?

This change of perception, it has to be said, was in no small part due to the growing influence of Chernomyrdin himself. Although he was never an actual member of any centrist organization, he has never bothered to hide his affiliations, repeatedly asserting his allegiance to centrism, as opposed to the extremes of Left and Right.[119] And of course, his whole background in the Soviet-era establishment undeniably shaped his conscious attachment to such an orientation: he had risen through the ranks to become Gorbachev's Minister of the Gas Industry in 1985, and later Chairman of *Gazprom*. The real irony of Chernomyrdin's position following the December 1993 elections, of course, was not lost on anybody. Not himself a candidate for a parliamentary seat, he nevertheless emerged the undoubted victor in terms of enhanced power, stature and authority. Likewise, as Pavel Bunich has aptly expressed it, this also meant that while the centrists (in the guise of Civic Union) undoubtedly *lost* the elections, they nevertheless *won* the government, with virtually all the post-election appointees to the Cabinet possessing similarly strong centrist credentials to their leader.[120]

Given the contradiction between the actual results of the 1993 election and the enhancement of the centrist orientation, one might almost be tempted to argue that centrism's whole future rests very much on the shoulders of an individual, rather than a movement of one kind or another. *If* that was the case (and it is only an 'if'), one would have to recognize the obvious precariousness of such a situation. This is not simply because an individual can never be a proper substitute for an orientation desirous of achieving a genuine hegemonic victory. It is also because in Chernomyrdin, notwithstanding everything that has been said about him, there are at least *some* doubts as to how strong his commitment to a centrist orientation really is in practice.

A common refrain of the Westerners in the early weeks and months of 1994 was that the new centrist government would be given just enough decision-making 'rope' effectively to hang themselves. That is to say, there was a confident expectation that the implementation of their key ideas would so discredit them that the terrain of struggle would once again be left to the Westerners and the Russophiles to 'slog' it out. Hyperinflation, an end to serious privatization, an ever-spiralling budget deficit – in short, a thoroughgoing 'Ukrainization' of the Russian economy – were all projected on the short-term horizon. In the event, none of these things happened; and the fact that they did not happen can be explained in one of two ways. Either the key centrist policies with which Chernomyrdin regularly identified himself were an undisputed success in practice, or those policies were for the most part never in fact implemented.

The evidence here is not conclusive either way, but there are at least a number of features that support the second assertion, rather than the first. For example, rather than adding to the state bureaucracy, which a significantly enhanced role for the state would have implied, the bureaucracy was significantly reduced in the first six months of 1994. Privatization was not slowed down but increased, and was scheduled in the 'post-voucherization' phase to make further inroads into the old state enterprise fiefdoms. And most significantly of all, Chernomyrdin did not use his close association with the Chairman of the Central Bank, Viktor Gerashchenko (nor with his replacement after October 1994, Tatyana Paramonova), to increase the money supply in the form of state handouts to industry; instead he significantly *stemmed* the flow of support. Small wonder, then, that unemployment likewise noticeably increased throughout 1994, and many enterprise directors began openly to wonder 'whose side Chernomyrdin was really on'. As for the most probable cause of this turnaround, or at the very least *temporizing* attitude, this also has been the subject of much rumour and conjecture. Arguably the most rational explanation has highlighted the fact that after the elections Chernomyrdin was suddenly left in a situation where he *alone* would now have to face the responsibility for the economic programme (as distinct from the previous situation, where the Westerners in the Cabinet still held significant sway). It was this basic fear of ultimate responsibility (an all too common trait in the centrist character, so critics would say) that thus made him resist any major new (centrist) innovations wherever possible, let alone a full-scale 'counter-revolution'.[121]

The third task outlined by Mironov came in the form of a question: Have the centrists obtained sufficient wisdom to counter the tendency of the centralization of power? In today's Russia, he went on, the regions possess powerful reservoirs of democratization. For that reason it is important to find a new balance between the periphery and Moscow. Similarly, the 'de-provincialization' of Russia's provinces is another important task. Any distortion in the outcome – either in the direction of buttressing the dictate of Moscow or in fostering some kind of 'watery' confederation – would both be equally ruinous for Russian statehood. The main orientation, nevertheless, should be the de-concentration of power in the capital.

Fortunes here have also been mixed. On the plus side, for much of 1994 there were a number of indications that the centre–periphery relationship had started to show signs of improvement, if not outright harmony. The power-sharing treaty signed between Moscow and Tatarstan in February

1994, for example, helped to alleviate some of the tensions – not only in Kazan', but in other recalcitrant republics as well (such as neighbouring Bashkortostan). To add to this, at the end of April 1994 nearly all of the regional and republican leaders of the Federation (with the exception of the Republic of Chechnya and the legislative representatives of the *oblasti* of Vladimir and Kemerovo) put their signatures to the Civic Accord Treaty promoted by Yeltsin and Chernomyrdin as a means of bringing a new sense of stability to the country.[122] And although the treaty failed to include a provision which would have prohibited efforts to change the constitutional status of regions and republics, it did nevertheless include a strong pledge of loyalty to the unity of the Federation, as well as a commitment from participants to abide by a new tax regime designed to ensure that the centre receives its full proportional share of revenue from the different constituent members. Similarly, most commentators were agreed that a new sense of harmony also prevailed in the Council of the Federation – the parliamentary upper chamber which is made up of an equal number of representatives from each of the constituent members of the Federation.

Of course, whether the centrists themselves had a direct influence on this new, more balanced set of relationships is not all that clear. Certainly, if Anatolii Dolgolaptev is to be believed, the *'new* centrist orientation' that emerged in the aftermath of the October 1993 rebellion was much more focused on the regions, if not entirely succumbing to the devolutionist ambitions behind the notion of regionalism.[123] And indeed, in the parliamentary arena one of the most prominent self-professed centrist forces throughout 1994 was the grouping 'New Regional Politics' which was specifically set up on the basis of promoting regional political and socio-economic concerns. Again, however, just how convincing this supposed transfiguration really is is not entirely apparent. Certainly there are many things here that do not sit nicely with the much stronger statist and centralist heritage of the orientation's ideological foundations.

Meanwhile, on the negative side, no amount of centrist influence could prevent the eruption of full-scale military conflict in Chechnya in December 1994.

If the centrists have up until now fared *reasonably* well with the hegemonic tasks outlined by Mironov, we now reach a point at which they come up against a number of deep-seated problems, the likes of which have in the past mitigated much of their potential, and probably will continue to do so in the foreseeable future.

Writing at a time when the confrontation between the political extremes was reaching 'fever pitch', Mironov was adamant that one of the key, pivotal tasks of the centrists had to reside in their self-professed ability to be able both to *transcend* and to *subdue* such a confrontational paradigm. As we now know, not only were they completely unable to do this; what was even more remarkable was to note the *speed* at which the centre was absolutely dissipated by the onslaught it faced. Signs of their weakness had certainly been there for all to see, but the reality of the extent of their brittleness did come as a genuine shock; and no amount of centrist-sponsored catechism has yet been able to dispel that shock. To be fair, of course, the real danger that existed after the December 1993 elections – of the centrists being devoured once and for all by the extremes – has not materialized. In fact, if anything, the opposite is more in evidence. The extremes have merged towards the centre in an apparent triumph of rational pragmatism and compromise, as witnessed, for example, by the signing of the Civic Accord Treaty at the end of April 1994.[124]

Notwithstanding the apparent success of the Accord, however, nor even the much-publicized claim that centrism is at last promoting itself as the political culture of the future in Russia,[125] one cannot help feeling that this is nothing more than a form of posturing so as to allow the extremes to regroup: another lull before the storm which will see the centrists once again washed away in a tidal onslaught. Just as significantly, it should also be noted that this merge towards the centre has come at a considerable price. With every participant wanting to play the pragmatist; and indeed, with everybody wanting to claim the new middle ground and the new centrist label – from Shakhrai's Party of Russian Unity and Accord and Popov's Movement for Democratic Reforms to the Women of Russia movement, the Agrarians and even Zyuganov's Communist Party – it has left the basic understanding of the values of 'centrism' in a state of utter confusion and outright contradiction. The common refrain that 'we are all centrists now' has in the process virtually destroyed centr*ism,* making it once again a form of pragmatism that is entirely rootless and amorphous.[126]

This increasing incoherency and indeterminacy is also not unconnected with the final hegemonic task outlined by Mironov back in June 1993. Any vision that centrism might possess would be of significance only for as long as it was articulated by a strong, cohesive, organized force. Referring to the main priority here, Mironov went on to assert that they had to learn how to conquer and democratize the masses. They had to learn how to isolate their extremist opponents, while at the same time being prepared to work with those sections of the population who nevertheless demonstrated support for one of the extremes. They had to learn how to organize resistance, but not let that resistance get out of control. They had to learn how to repudiate the explosive incursions on the political masses so favoured by the extremists and the 'ultras', while simultaneously learning the democratic ways of mobilizing the masses. Above all – and here was the real crux of Mironov's analysis – the centrists could save themselves and democracy in Russia only if they were able to surmount their 'apparat-syndrome' and appeal to a wider audience. If they could not fulfil this task, then they ran the risk of once again disappearing from the Russian political scene for many years to come.

If anything best epitomized the failure of the centrists in post-Soviet Russia, it was almost certainly this. Mironov's identification of their propensity to rely on key sections of the old established apparat and the operational mechanisms that accompanied this could not have been more precise. And as for their abilities to mobilize the masses, it did not take the December 1993 election fiasco to demonstrate what had long since been apparent: these abilities were minimal, to say the least.

In a reply to Mironov's article, Vladislav Inozemtsev supplied his own reasons for the centrists' failure here.[127] In contrast to the more sympathetic tone of Mironov's analysis, Inozemtsev was by no means certain that one could intuitively characterize centrism's mere existence as a positive political phenomenon. It clearly did not arise, he asserted, in possession of a balanced programme and capable words about how to construct civil peace in the country. Instead, it was established on nothing more than the basis of disagreement against politicians who may well have possessed 'extremist ideas' but who, for all that, did nevertheless possess concrete programmes of action.

The centrists' programme was in essence an impossible synthesis of the pro-Western liberals and the radical Russophiles. Obtaining a synthesis of the two extremes was always seen as more important than constructing a programme that was genuinely orientated towards the objective crisis the country was facing. Its lack of a mobilizationary capacity, therefore, was self-evident. It could outline for itself the different mechanisms involved as regards conflicts of power within the realm of the elite, but it always lacked a whole range of other *qualitative* factors to build upon this. Above all, its most symptomatic failure, from an organizational point of view, was that it was never really enriched from below with new, young, emerging leaders. Instead, its ranks were always strengthened from above with people who often associated with the centrists for the worst kind of reasons, not least out of 'a primitive, professional unfitness'. This last point, of course, was a scarcely hidden attack on Civic Union, and it was an attack that was certainly not lacking in substance. If Civic Union resembled anything, it was a corporate interest or lobby group. As a 'backroom' operator in the corridors of power it was quite effective, but this was the ultimate limit of its success, and while this kind of organizational activity may have had its successes in the Gorbachev era, it was ultimately a recipe for electoral disaster.

Where, then, is a new centrist political movement with strong popular support going to come from? Any positive answer to this is hard to come up with. The DPR, true to form, continues to be preoccupied by its own internal divisions, which were not made any easier by Travkin's resignation from the party leadership in December 1994 and his replacement by Sergei Glaz'ev.[128] The Civic Union's decline has continued unabated, and periodic efforts to establish new coalition blocs have largely faltered long before they got off the ground. Moreover, while it is true that former Soviet President Mikhail Gorbachev appears to be willing to place himself at the political disposal of any possible new centrist organization, his periodic offers nearly always seem to go unanswered. Rightly or wrongly, his unpopularity among the Russian population appears not to diminish as time goes by, and while his efforts to provide organizational and financial support (through the Moscow-based Foundation) are much appreciated, there can be no doubt that his much-touted 'comeback' is something of a millstone around the centrists' neck.[129]

This apparent inability to *mobilize* its potential supporters has, not surprisingly, also thrown into doubt the full extent to which the centrist orientation *has* potential supporters to mobilize in the first place. That is to say, questions have been raised as to whether the real centrist problem is a political one or a *social* one. If it is the latter, then of course the capacity for any centrist hegemony will almost certainly be terminally weakened, and history will show it to have been nothing more than a peculiar phenomenon in the transition from the old order to the new. At the heart of the matter here is a threefold dilemma for the centrists. First, as the privatization process continues, what kind of ongoing effect will this have on the directors? As they adapt themselves to their new role as shareholders and entrepreneurs, how will the perception of their fundamental interests change over the course of time? Secondly, what is the likelihood of some kind of social pact being sustained between enterprise directors and the workforce? And thirdly, who will be the main beneficiary of that pact if it is sustained, and who will benefit if it is not?

As regards the first of these issues, there can be no doubt that the so-called 'directors' corps' has for some time now been seriously fragmenting, and any supposition that *one* orientation (let alone *one* organization) will be able to articulate the concerns of this social group is certainly no longer feasible (if it ever was). The real pivotal issue, it seems, concerns the question of the internal workplace relationship between the directors and the workers. If the old form of paternalism can be maintained in a new guise, then the chances are that the centrist project will retain both viability and a strong potential, subject to it finding a credible *political* articulatory form. The maintenance of this paternalist corporatism will also mean that centrism's main opponent as regards the desire to articulate and embody the fundamental interests of these forces will be those elements of the Russophiles who themselves clearly share a disposition for the old social relations of production. If, on the other hand, the enterprise paternalism begins to break down, then this would almost certainly leave the centrists socially marginalized. It would also create totally new patterns of social conflict from which the Westerners would certainly strive to gain advantage; as, too, would the Russophiles from a more negative, reactive point of view.

As mentioned on a number of previous occasions, most of the evidence would seem to suggest that the old-style social productive relations are, for the most part, being reproduced in the transition process. As Simon Clarke has ventured to suggest, however (albeit tentatively), no one should be in any doubt that as the transition progresses the *potential* for a fundamental change of relationship patterns within the workplace does at least exist. If nothing else, the reforms implemented so far have provided 'a framework in which a struggle for control is put on the agenda, and through which it can develop'.[130] The fact that that struggle has so far been restricted does not detract from the fact that the possibility of development is there.

Of course, it is not only the Westerners and the Russophiles who would seek to exploit the new set of circumstances that would be created by a breakdown in the old enterprise social structure. This is also the one factor that *might* just pave the way for the emergence of a much stronger counter-hegemonic challenge from the forces encompassing the new Left in Russia today. For this to happen, brand-new, independent working-class organizations would have to be created, firmly orientated to the task of destroying the old passive conformism of the workers and substituting for this a new concerted understanding of a specific working-class consciousness framed around a new class struggle.

Without doubt, of course, to achieve this would be a phenomenal occurrence, given the history of the past seventy years. It is this challenge, then, that will now be assessed in the final chapter.

6

Possibilities for a Future
Socialist Hegemony

No one, it seems to me, can contest the fact that a dogmatics is attempting to install its worldwide hegemony in paradoxical and suspect conditions. . . . To the rhythm of a cadenced march, it proclaims: Marx is dead, communism is dead, very dead, and along with it its hopes, its discourse, its theories, and its practices. It says: long live capitalism, long live the market, here's to the survival of economic and political liberalism!

Jacques Derrida, *Specters of Marx*

Let us be clear about one thing right from the outset, so as to avoid any kind of misunderstanding or even deception. The inclusion of a chapter on the democratic socialist or democratic Left movement in Russia today does not in any way imply that they should be considered an *equal* contender in the current hegemonic struggle. To draw such an inference would be naivety of the first order, and would be promoting a form of wishful thinking above and beyond the requirements of objective analysis. Indeed, even to talk of a socialist or Left movement in Russia today may in itself be erroneous.

Why, then, include a chapter devoted to this political-ideological tendency? Not to do so would belittle the efforts of those who, over the past few years, have fought long and hard for the creation of such a movement. It would also imply that the parameters of a hegemonic struggle in Russia are in some way fixed around the aforementioned orientations, which is far from being the case. Constant flux and changeability are the real leitmotivs of the current situation in Russia, and this intrinsically provides a lot of scope for many alignments that might at present appear to be marginalized.

Given also the fact that the largest social force in Russia today – the working class – might not remain for ever in its hitherto condition of anaemic, atomized lethargy, it is therefore imperative that we consider the longer-term potential of those forces that regard it as their main task both to mobilize this class into some form of sustained, conscious activity and to articulate what it hopes will be the main desires and ambitions of such mobilized activity.

The underlying reasons for the current marginalization of a democratic socialist orientation are varied and complex, but for the sake of some degree of clarity it is possible to analyse those reasons from two main perspectives.

Post-CPSU Trends

The first perspective concerns the extent to which the vast majority of the parties and groups emerging out of the CPSU (i.e. those with a real potential social base already established) did not align themselves, or even *wish* to align themselves, to the basic cause of democratic socialism.

Writing at the end of 1991, the Swedish writer and sociologist Göran Therborn was convinced that the collapse of the communist tradition would come to signify 'the end of the future', at least 'as a new place which might be visited'. 'When the frustrations of a marketised present start mounting', he argued, one should not be surprised that the dominant tendency will be to resurrect the *past* glories of one's nation.[1]

In the Russian communists' case, one did not have to wait too long for the banner proclaiming the slogan 'Forward to the Past' to be hoisted. Under the circumstances, the immediacy of their call was more than foreseeable. What was certainly less foreseeable, at least in some cases, was the rather bizarre way the actual image of the past could be conjured up and be made to work in their favour. One of the main trendsetters here was the Russian Communist Workers Party (RCWP), which was officially founded in November 1991 on the basis of two earlier organizations: the workers' soviets of the United Working People's Front and the Communist Initiative Movement.

Led by Viktor Anpilov and Viktor Tyul'kin, among others, the party is unashamedly 'national-Bolshevik' in orientation, and has continually maintained close links with a range of neo-fascist organizations, most prominently with Aleksandr Barkashov's Russian National Unity Movement. Many articles in the party's newspaper *Molniya* (Lightning) are distinctly anti-Semitic, and all its publications regularly feature glowing tributes to Stalin under prominent portraits of the former Soviet leader in full military regalia.

A self-styled 'vanguard' party firmly adhering to the organizational principles of a dogmatic form of democratic centralism, the party has been in the forefront of organizing anti-government demonstrations and provocations, usually in conjunction with the Working Russia Movement, which is led by Anpilov and is therefore closely associated with the

RCWP executive. Many of its most senior members (among them General Albert Makashov) were prominent supporters of the August 1991 coup attempt and were also in the forefront, not surprisingly, of the opposition forces at the time of the October 1993 confrontation with the incumbent regime.

None of this, however, has dampened the enthusiasm of its members, nor has it affected the party's capacity to recruit new members. From an estimated membership base of 10,000 at the time of its foundation, it has since grown almost tenfold, making it one of the largest parties in the whole country. What is even more remarkable is that this success has come about despite periodic reports of serious internal power struggles between Anpilov (leader of the Moscow branch) and Tyul'kin (leader in St Petersburg). There have also been a number of acrimonious splits and breakaway factions, particularly involving the former ideological secretary of the party, Mikhail Popov, who eventually went on to establish his own Workers and Peasants Russian Party.[2]

As for its main social support base, judging from its own documents as well as from the protest actions it has organized, the party is strongly supported by some of the most deprived sectors of society, and it relies heavily on the allegiance of functionaries at the lower level of the former CPSU party organization. Its influence in industrial centres outside Moscow and St Petersburg – in cities such as Chelyabinsk, Sverdlovsk, Khabarovsk, Rostov on the Don and Nizhny Novgorod – is said to be especially large. What the party has singularly failed to do, however, is to make any real kind of impact on the skilled workforce and the intellectual class. This, and the ideological orientation it has adopted for itself, has – not surprisingly – left it isolated from many other left-wing trends in Russia today, as well as from the trade-union movement, both of which would claim that the activities of the RCWP do more to *discourage* working-class activity than promote it. For this reason, its closest ally is that other orthodox, fundamentalist Stalinist party, the all-Union Communist Party of Bolsheviks, led by the anti-*perestroika* heroine Nina Andreeva.

If few expected the likes of Anpilov, Tyul'kin, Makashov and Andreeva to forgo the habits of a lifetime and suddenly adopt the mantle of democratic socialism in the aftermath of the demise of the old Soviet order, the expectations were slightly higher, if not exaggeratedly so, that a revived *official* successor to the old CPSU on Russian soil might have drawn some appropriate lessons from the past.

In an interview shortly before the re-foundation congress of the Communist Party of the Russian Federation (CPRF) in February 1993, the former leader of the Marxist Platform inside the CPSU, Aleksandr Buzgalin, summarized his expectations as follows.[3] The revival of an official Russian heir to the CPSU was a positive phenomenon that needed to be supported, for even if the party did not satisfy the optimal hope of transforming itself, phoenix-like, into a truly progressive democratic socialist organization, there were a number of minimal hopes that might nevertheless be satisfied. First, even if it relied inordinately on old slogans and propagandistic appeals, it would nevertheless be a mass movement through which those on the independent Left could seek to channel their ideas and try to influence it by means of a genuine dialogue and debate. Secondly, the independent Left hoped that at the very least they would have the chance of forming an eventual electoral bloc with the CPRF, which would then give them an opportunity of getting their own representatives elected into the parliamentary arena on the coattails of the still highly efficient Communist Party structure. What was envisaged, in other words, was an anti-capitalist Popular or United Front that could act as a strong magnet to all those disparate forces vehemently opposed to the then prevailing creed of shock-therapy neo-liberalism. And thirdly, there was also an assumption that the new Communist Party organization would itself feel a *reciprocal* need for an alliance with the independent Left, based on a desire to broaden their 'communist' appeal by an alliance with a new generation of young intellectuals and theorists largely untainted by a past association with the worst tragedies and mistakes committed by the CPSU.

As events turned out, of course, even these minimal expectations were completely destroyed by the actual proceedings of the re-foundation congress, and in particular by the near-unanimous election of Gennadii Zyuganov as Chairman of the Presidium of the new party's Central Executive Committee.

At one level, Zyuganov's ascendancy was in perfect keeping with the political climate prevailing in Russia. In virtually all quarters of political opinion there was (as there still is) a popular perception that what Russia needs more than anything else is a 'strong leader': a good and kind Tsar. Zyuganov, therefore, fitted the bill for the CPRF. In the run-up to the congress he consciously and persistently portrayed himself as a viable alternative to the others who would similarly like to think of themselves in this particular way – namely Yeltsin and Zhirinovsky. And above all, he has been able to convince his followers that this kind of strong, authoritarian, yet at the same time paternalistic type of leadership is in perfect conformity with Russian political traditions. At another level, however, Zyuganov's ascendancy at the top of the country's foremost communist organization was a complete and utter contradiction in terms, and nothing has demonstrated this contradiction more than the articles and writings he has put his name to in the period since his recent leadership victory.[4]

Openly acknowledging that he had always previously camouflaged many of his true ideas (and this from a man who had been a former Central Committee Secretary in charge of ideology in the Soviet-era Communist Party of the RSFSR), and that only now was he free to espouse them publicly, Zyuganov has taken as the watchwords of his 'new' orientation the familiar triad of Orthodoxy [*Pravoslavie*], Autocracy [*Samoderzhavie*] and a form of folk nationalism that is not easy to give an exact equivalent of in the English language, but which in Russian is known by the concept of *Narodnost'*.

Strongly influenced by a historical affinity to the millennium-long form of Russian statehood, as well as to the correlation that links Moscow with a 'Third Rome', Zyuganov has interpreted the notion of Orthodoxy as the embodiment of moral substance and altruism which has the unequalled capacity of acting as a force of moral-political unity in society. As for Autocracy, this he sees as the only true foundation of state sovereignty in Russia (compatible, it should be said, with the former 'leading role of the CPSU'); it too is the embodiment of a moral ideal of statehood that needs to be reanimated in the form of conscience, honour and patriotism. *Narodnost'*, meanwhile, is the concept of a national-based unity; of a people ultimately striving for a new historical community and opposed to all forms of social disaggregation. And just for good measure, these concepts are regularly accompanied in his articles by a none-too-implicit allegiance to anti-Semitism and to repeated references to 'cosmopolitan Russophobes' perpetually intent on destroying the great traditions of Russia.

Such nostalgia for a long-distant past is likewise intermeshed with a thoroughgoing re-evaluation of the Marxist and communist legacy. Gone, for example, is the whole notion of the class approach to social existence. Social classes, he affirms, do exist, but the contradictions between them can be marginalized by an adherence to higher principles such as the old Orthodox form of *sobornost'* (conciliarity). Indeed, the real social division, in Zyuganov's view, is essentially represented in the dichotomy between those who give an allegiance to 'my country' (by which he means workers, peasants, the military, the patriotic intelligentsia and national capitalists) and those who have a conception of 'this country' (particularly the Westernized intelligentsia and the comprador capitalists). It is on this basis as well that the 'long-hoped-for' unification of the 'reds' and the 'whites', whose division dates back to the time of the Civil War, can finally be achieved.

Gone, too, is any conception of internationalism as traditionally under-stood by Marxists. For Zyuganov, an attachment to this idea (particularly in the understanding of a working class possessing no Fatherland) was at best antiquated, and at worst synonymous with 'cosmopolitanism', a term possessing exclusively negative connotations for the CPRF leader. The one and only criterion for the state, he maintains, should always be the pursuit of its own national interests. And last, but not least, Zyuganov is adamant that communists should renounce their militant atheism and adopt instead what he terms a 'healthy' and positive attitude towards Orthodox religion, the one and only true ideology that can genuinely save the country from the Western ideological offensive.

All of this, then, is clearly not the language of Marx or Lenin, or of any variant of Marxism, Leninism or communism. One cannot even credit it with being a form of Marxist 'revisionism'. This is the pure language of nineteenth-century anti-Enlightenment Russian mysticism, borrowed direct from such thinkers as Count Sergius Uvarov (Tsarist Minister of Education from 1833 to 1849, and the first publicly to promote the trilogy of Orthodoxy, Autocracy and Nationality), with a smattering of George Florovsky and Ivan Il'in thrown in for good measure.

Nor is it a peculiarly crude variant of a specifically Russian socialist tradition – unless, that is, one stretches the imagination and credulity so far to include such figures as Konstantin Leont'ev in that tradition (another figure that Zyuganov is fond of citing). Described by Berdyaev as the 'Russian Nietzsche',[5] Leont'ev was a strong believer in the notion that any doctrine worth its name had to be one that sanctioned 'suffering, wrongs, and the injustices of life on earth'.[6] Towards the end of his life (in the early 1890s) he reached the conclusion that the future of Russia did indeed belong to socialism. For Leont'ev, however, Russian socialism could not be separated from a deep-rooted tradition of mysticism in the country's cultural legacy, nor from a deep-rooted form of conservatism. Prophesying that the Tsar himself might one day lead the socialist movement in Russia, he was convinced that the socialists would need to make use of the tradition of terror, discipline, humility and the habit of obedience. 'Nations who (let us suppose) have managed successfully to reconstruct their economic life, but have nevertheless failed to find satisfaction in life on earth,' he went on, 'will blaze up with renewed enthusiasm for mystical doctrines.'[7] Given that Zyuganov has often been in attendance at monarchist, revivalist assemblies, this prediction of a Tsar leading the socialist [sic] movement might not appear quite so fanciful after all.

At the time of writing, the security of Zyuganov's tenure of the party leadership looks reasonably strong. This is not to say, however, that there is no internal dissension from the kind of orientation he has adopted. During the third party congress in January 1995, for example, some open criticism could be heard, either in the congress forum itself or in newspaper articles by Communist Party members.[8] More significantly, perhaps, a variety of opposition factions exist within the top echelons of the CPRF, led by such prominent figures as Anatolii Lukyanov, Richard Kosolapov and Boris Kurashvili.

Of all Zyuganov's internal critics, however, no one has voiced a more vehement and concerted attack on his populist, spiritualist demagogy than Boris Slavin, a deputy editor of *Pravda* and a leading member of the party's Central Executive Committee. In an open letter addressed to Zyuganov and published in a number of communist newspapers in May 1994 under the title 'The Repudiation of Marxism Will Destroy the Communist Party', Slavin launched a vigorous attack on Zyuganov's renunciation of the centrality of the class struggle, militant atheism and proletarian internationalism and their replacement with religious and nationalist values, all of which represented a nihilistic return to the Middle Ages.[9]

On the issue of class struggle, Slavin demanded to know from his party leader how this concept could be jettisoned at precisely the moment when virtually everyone else acknowledged that the class struggle was reaching its height in Russia. On the issue of the state, he reminded Zyuganov that for a communist this institution was at best a necessary evil, one whose powers must be progressively passed down into society, not strengthened in an autocratic manner and as something that comes to personify the whole nation in a monist, totalitarian form. On the issue of state patriotism, he accused Zyuganov of placing an affinity towards the state over and above that of the people. Zyuganov, he asserted, refused to acknowledge the true nature of the current social heterogeneity of the 'people' and the need to struggle for the primary needs of social justice. Worse still, Zyuganov appeased the authoritarian tendencies evoked by Yeltsin's policies, and justified this on the basis that the state needed strengthening *at all costs.* This was also the basis, continued Slavin, for Zyuganov's prioritization of Russia's national interests over and above a genuine internationalist outlook. Zyuganov's affinity towards some kind of new 'Eurasian' Union was based on nothing more than an old-fashioned Russian domination of this geopolitical space; a domination, in Slavin's view, that was established on quasi-racist principles.

As for Zyuganov's affinity towards Russia's supposedly unique spiritual legacy of Orthodoxy, this was nothing more than an espousal of a form of militant clericalism, based on the most naive, irrational principles. It relied on a form of passive conformism of the people, rather than advocating ways in which they could take active control over their own affairs and the affairs of society as a whole. All in all, concluded Slavin, Zyuganov's espousal of such principles represented the worst possible kind of 'trivial opportunism'. This was also the judgement of another open letter that Slavin (along with Aleksandr Buzgalin, Andrei Kolganov and Sergei Novikov, a member of the Political Council of the Russian Party of Communists) addressed to the whole communist and socialist movement at the beginning of 1994. Concentrating in particular this time on the 'disease of nationalism afflicting the Left', the authors made it implicitly clear that there was virtually no distinction between Zyuganov and Zhirinovsky, and that if this association between narrow-minded national chauvinism and communism was not defeated quickly, there was every likelihood that a left alternative in Russia would be permanently discredited.[10] And as a direct response to the apparent strengthening of nationalist tendencies across the whole spectrum of the Left, a conference was organized in spring 1994, one outcome of which saw the creation of a new inter-party movement known as the Union of Internationalists (led by, among others, Buzgalin).

Notwithstanding the strength and conviction of this powerful reaction among many different circles of the Russian Left, it is nevertheless glaringly apparent that the hurdles that need to be surmounted, particularly on the issue of nationalism, are nothing short of daunting. As the vast majority of analysts would testify, no political party in Russia today, seriously wanting to make an impact on the political scene, can afford to ignore the popular impression that the issue of nationalism has made in the public consciousness. Virtually every party in existence at the moment has provided some ideological or programmatic affirmation concerning the needs and requirements of Russia's national resurgence, and provided some justification for this on the basis of its great-power traditions. Nearly all of them have likewise promoted some degree of adherence to the idea of special characteristics in the Russian ethnic/national composition that has always underpinned the country's claim to a great-power status. The need for the democratic socialists to work out their own principled stance on this issue, then, is more than perfectly clear, yet everyone recognizes the tremendous complexity of having to fight on this particular terrain.

For the committed internationalist, Isaac Deutscher's eloquent proposition remains one to which they are committed:

> Socialists must be internationalists even if their working classes are not; socialists must also understand the nationalism of the masses, but only in the way in which a doctor understands the weakness or the illness of his patient. Socialists should be aware of that nationalism, but like nurses, they should wash their hands twenty times over whenever they approach an area of the labour movement infected by it.[11]

At the same time they must avoid permanently marginalizing themselves because of this stance.

One tentative solution, suggested by Slavin and others, is to focus attention on the concept of patriotism rather than nationalism, since this, it is argued, is intrinsically closer to a traditional socialist understanding of internationalism. In its socialist variant it can be used to highlight both national and social forms of oppression not only against one's own people but also against the enslavement of other peoples, producing in turn a sense of class solidarity with workers of all nations in a common struggle against national *and* international capital.[12]

Whether this is sufficient to overcome the dilemma that they face in the present Russian context, however, remains doubtful. As a round table devoted to this issue in the pages of the journal *Alternativy* demonstrated all too clearly, the democratic Left remains a long way from achieving any kind of consensus on this question.[13]

Not all the parties emerging out of the former CPSU, it has to be said, were defined by their adherence to the backward-looking Stalinist or nationalist, mystic faith. The one major exception here was the Socialist Party of Workers (SPW). Established in October 1991, primarily with the support of middle-level *apparatchiks* of the former CPSU, the party essentially aspired to replicate the Eastern European experience of creating a new type of reformist party on the basis of the old dominant party structure. A highly ambitious – not to mention contradictory – project in the Russian context (especially in the light of the Gorbachev experience), the new party nevertheless seemed to get off to a promising start.

Led initially on a collective basis by such prominent figures as Anatolii Denisov, Vitalii Sevast'yanov, Ivan Rybkin, Mikhail Lapshin, Gennadii Sklyar, Aleksandr Mal'tsev and Ludmilla Vartazarova, the party was nevertheless most closely identified in its early phase of development with the former dissident Marxist historian Roi Medvedev, an association which undoubtedly lent the party an aura of popular respectability, as well as a degree of 'moral supremacy' that few, if any, of the other post-CPSU organizations could match. For Medvedev, the ultimate goal was to try and create a party of the democratic Left closely resembling the traditions of the Italian Communist Party. It had to be a party open to free discussion, a party in which dissension could be tolerated and different factions could be free to organize. It also had to be a party committed to overcoming all forms of dogmatism and orthodoxies, and one in which the self-adopted socialist orientation could become genuinely associated with a fundamental renewal of society as a whole, rather than the revival of discredited, outdated structures.[14]

At its constituent congress in December 1991 the party attempted to give credence to these ambitions by adopting as its official programme the final Gorbachevian draft of the last CPSU programme which had been ratified just before its demise, a programme Medvedev was convinced was a platform for democratic socialism, rather than an old-style communist programme. In the aftermath of the December congress the party's membership base climbed to a high point of 80,000. It also built up a stronger degree of representation in the parliamentary arena than most other 'parties' at this time, and also achieved a relatively strong organizational base in many of the regions of the Federation. To add to its importance, the association with Medvedev also started paying dividends in one other key respect as well, in that it gave the party considerable access to international contacts (especially in Germany and Italy) that were again well beyond the scope of any other party on the Russian Left.[15]

Given its self-definition as a democratic socialist party intent on building on what was best in the Russian communist tradition, it is also important to note that the party acquired for itself a vital *strategic* role in Russian left politics at this time, often acting as a link between the traditional communist and the emerging non-communist Left in the country. What appeared to many as a potentially strong emerging force, however, quickly faded during the first few months of 1993, when many of the contradictions in its ambitions started to show. The real turning point in its fortunes came at the time of the re-foundation congress of the CPRF. Having strongly supported the initiative of a greater degree of communist unification, a number of top party officials simply could not accept the outcome of the congress, which had witnessed the supremacy of the Zyuganov line. Plans to pursue a more integrationist policy were therefore shelved in favour of the continuation of an autonomous SPW identity.

What was even worse, however, was the degree to which the SPW leadership had become totally divorced from its own membership base in the period since its foundation. To its consternation, it soon discovered that the vast bulk of its members were in fact desirous of a form of unification with other sectors of the communist past *at any cost*. Indeed, such was the extent of this desire that by the time of the second congress of the SPW in June 1993 more than 80 per cent of its membership had effectively 'defected' to the CPRF. Not surprisingly, the party has never really been able to recover from this setback. To make matters worse, however, it has spent the intervening period 'experimenting' with one political and ideological orientation after another.

In the aftermath of the second congress – which had also witnessed the election of Ludmilla Vartazarova to the position of sole leader of the party – the SPW decisively threw its remaining weight behind the attempts to establish a genuine democratic socialist alternative to the CPRF. Regular contacts were made with a number of independent left groups, and at one point in the summer of 1993 there was even a suggestion that the SPW and the Party of Labour (the major representative of the independent Left) would formally merge and establish a unified party organization.

With the announcement in September 1993 that parliamentary elections were to be held at the end of the year, the leadership of the SPW appeared to give its full backing to the intention to create an independent left democratic electoral bloc (to be known as the Russian Union of

Labour), which would be made up of the SPW, the Party of Labour and the left faction from the Social Democratic Party (the United Social Democrats), together with a number of other small left-wing parties and organizations. During the party's third congress in mid October, however, this proposal was effectively nullified. In her address to the assembled delegates Vartazarova announced that a majority of the SPW leadership were of the opinion that the proposed electoral bloc would now have to consist of a much broader range of forces. An exclusive democratic socialist alliance would clearly not stand much chance of doing very well, and to this end she announced that the leadership had already made contact with a number of 'liberal' nationalist forces, most notably with the Union of Russia's Renaissance (led by Dmitrii Rogozin), the Union of Cossacks, and the Union of Oil Producers. In a further justification of this volte-face, Anatolii Denisov announced that, at heart, there was no real fundamental contradiction in the party's initiative to campaign for a form of socialism that went via a patriotic or even, if necessary, a monarchist road.[16]

With the eventual failure of this SPW-led national-patriotic 'Fatherland' alliance even to secure the required number of signatures actually to participate in the December parliamentary campaign, the party once again executed a change of direction. In early January 1994 it entered into negotiations with a number of centrist organizations, including the remnants of Aleksandr Rutskoi's People's Party of Free Russia and the so-called Humanitarian Party. Links with Dmitrii Rogozin's Union of Russia's Renaissance were maintained, and closer contacts were also forged with Arkadii Vol'skii's RUIE and what remained of Civic Union. Finally, at the party's fourth congress in February 1994, the adoption of a new party programme now committed the SPW to an essentially social democratic orientation with Russian specifics, all of which was to be underpinned by a concept to be known as 'new society'. Dismissing the former Soviet era as a period of 'state socialism', the concept of a 'new society' supported a mixed economy, hired labour, private forms of property and a Western-style (i.e. 'civilized') market.

Speaking to the assembled delegates, the Chairman of the Programme Commission, Vladimir Kalashnikov, made it clear that despite some objections that the new programme was not sufficiently socialist in outlook and reneged on earlier party commitments to support principles of workers' self-management, such objections had not been taken on board. Not only were such demands perceived as 'unrealistic', they would also alienate the masses, who would look upon the party as a party of romantics. More significantly, perhaps, Kalashnikov was not afraid to admit that such calls would also effectively alienate many elements of the emerging private sector to which the party was keen to appeal.[17]

With the perceived 'defection' of the SPW to the centrist camp, this has effectively left just one post-CPSU organization committed in some form or another, however loosely, to a basic democratic socialist orientation, willing to enter into an alliance with other non-CPSU connected left forces; and that organization is the Russian Party of Communists (RPC).

Established in December 1991, this particular party essentially grew out of the 'centrist' current of the Marxist Platform of the CPSU in alliance with the *Vozrozhdenie* (Revival) initiative group and the Committee for the Unity of Communists. Led by Anatolii Kryuchkov, the RPC has been a vociferous opponent of Zyuganov's leadership of the CPRF and his total marginalization, if not absolute negation, of traditional socialist criteria such as the pivotal position of class. Although it is strongly committed to the teachings of Marx and Lenin, it has nevertheless adopted an undogmatic, flexible approach to questions of ideology, and its programme statements are strongly imbued with a sense of realism, based on the practical conditions existing in today's Russia. A good example of its flexibility can also be seen in its own internal organizational structure. Although the party espouses a commitment to democratic centralism, it is nevertheless extremely tolerant of a whole range of different factions (a minority of which, it has to be said, perhaps have a greater affinity with national-patriotic ideas than the majority of the party would prefer).

Notwithstanding the overall allegiance of the RPC to the democratic socialist cause, one should nevertheless note its clear weakness in the overall spectrum of post-CPSU forces. A membership base of approximately 6,000 (compared with nearly 600,000 for the CPRF), and just a few hundred local organizations (compared with more than 20,000 for the CPRF), gives a good impression of just how badly the democratic socialist orientation fared in the post-CPSU process of realignment. Moreover, while stressing its desire to represent the interests of hired labour and collective farmers, the RPC, not alone in the current party political spectrum, nevertheless tends to be largely made up of intellectuals, scientific workers and social scientists.

In addition to a number of independent left groups, the main ally of the RPC within the existing 'communist' spectrum in Russia is the Union of Communists, which is essentially the successor of another ('left') faction of the Marxist Platform, under the leadership of Aleksei Prigarin. A much more 'traditionalist' organization than the RPC, the Union has primarily sought to maintain a sense of positive continuity with the communist system of the past (especially in such spheres as proletarian internationalism and social justice) and has likewise been in the forefront of attempts to re-create a unified Communist Party structure covering all the former republics of the USSR. Since the collapse of the old order it has often distinguished itself by the real vehemence of its opposition to privatization in all its variants.

The Non-Communist Left

If one of the main reasons for the weakness of the democratic socialist orientation has been the incapacity and unwillingness of the old CPSU effectively to renew itself in a progressive direction, the second main reason is not far behind in importance. Indeed, if one is looking at the longer-term potential of this orientation, it is this second reason that carries by far the greater significance. To add to the failure *inside* the old CPSU, the new independent forces of the Left *outside* the old party structure have simply not been able to organize themselves into any kind of strong, cohesive form.

The failure here has perhaps been all the harder to take when one remembers the kind of comments that were being written just a few years ago. In the early, heady days of *perestroika*'s official sanctioning of the notion of 'pluralism' and 'civil society', it really did appear to many that socialist ideas had gained quite a hegemonic stronghold within the ranks of the *neformaly* movements, thus providing a good many left-orientated commentators and sympathizers with a great deal of optimism for the future course of development. Notions of a 'new Soviet Left' in the making were regularly trumpeted and a good many of the political battle lines were described in bi-polar terms, pitting the new Left against the old, encrusted, bureaucratic, authoritarian CPSU.

Such optimism may have been sweet at the time, but it was also short-lived, and for many good reasons. Apart from the inevitable factors external to these movements' development, which were fast destroying this myth of a socialist-led renewal of the USSR, there were also many internal factors that made all talk of the emergence of a mass, popular socialist regeneration excessively, even ridiculously, premature. Sectarianism; marginalization; lack of any real effective social base; lack of any real administrative or organizational structure, especially outside Moscow and Leningrad; lack of finance; the lack of any ideological clarity; divisions over how to interpret the legacy of the past; little or no media access . . . the list of their deficiencies could go on and on.

A good many of these deficiencies, it goes without saying, were conditioned by the very climate that these groups were attempting to operate in in their *neformaly* phase of development, and were hence far beyond their control. Others, however, were self-inflicted failures to which many of the participants would themselves be the first to admit today. The degree of sectarianism within the Socialist Party, for example, which existed for two years before its official disbandment in spring 1992, was almost legendary for a party that had no more than a few hundred members. And exactly the same could be said of all the other broadly 'left' forces at this time, such as the radical Green Party, the Confederation of Anarcho-Syndicalists or the Marxist Workers Party.

If there has been one organization in the post-Soviet period that has come anywhere near to tackling some of the previous deficiencies of the *neformaly* independent Left, it has been the Party of Labour. At the time of writing, however, one would still have to recognize that this organization is likewise finding the new political terrain difficult to negotiate, and serious doubts remain as to its short-term, let alone its long-term viability. To its credit, however, it has renewed a small amount of that optimism that once pervaded left-wing sympathizers at the beginning of the Soviet reform era.

The origins of the Party of Labour date back to summer 1991. In July of that year a number of meetings were organized by representatives of the Socialist Party (led by Boris Kagarlitsky), the Confederation of Anarcho-Syndicalists (led by Andrei Isaev) and the Moscow Federation of Trade Unions (led by Mikhail Shmakov) to discuss the possibility of establishing a unified political organization 'of a labour type' modelled on the pattern, first and foremost, of the Brazilian Workers Party. In late August 1991 these meetings were followed by the creation of a formal initiative group which addressed the public with an appeal to establish a new Party of Labour that would be orientated around socialist values and the protection of workers' interests.

Carrying the signatures of Kagarlitsky, Isaev, Vladimir Kondrat'ev (a Socialist Party member and deputy of Moscow City Council), Mikhail Nagaitsev (Shmakov's deputy at the Moscow Federation of Trade Unions), Anatolii Buranov, Aleksandr Popov (the latter two being journalists) and Nikolai Gonchar (President of Moscow City Council), the appeal formally acknowledged that socialist values and ideas concerning the emancipation of labour had been extremely discredited by the past decades of totalitarian communism. Nevertheless, the appeal went on, the signatories were convinced that such values 'did not arise from the armchairs of intellectuals', but instead sprang from the very real need for a political defence of the workers. Consequently, they were convinced that the 'defeat of the CPSU' finally opened up the possibility of creating an authentic left-wing movement that could give expression to this need.

Vehemently rejecting the notion of a vanguard party, the signatories were categorical that the new party had to be founded on the initiative of its perceived rank and file, and that it had to be a party integrally attached to the trade unions' and workers' movement. Above all, the proposed party saw its main task in the sphere of defending the right to work; reforming the old-style system of social welfare; promoting the goal of economic democracy by encouraging workers' participation in the enterprises and giving them controlling influence over decisions affecting their material situation and basic conditions of work; securing the independence of the rights of trade-union organizations in the workplace;

promoting the development of collective and municipal forms of property, along with the transformation of the state sector of the economy into a decentralized modern social sector; bringing an end to the unregulated process of *nomenklatura* privatization and the transformation of state monopolies into private monopolies; defending the rights of the consumer and of independent domestic entrepreneurs; introducing democratic ways of regulating the economy; combating all forms of gender inequality and promoting the rights of women to participate fully in the life of society; and defending the rights of national, cultural and religious minorities.

Following the publication of the appeal, the initiative group was transformed into an organizing committee to prepare for the constituent conference of the party (which was due to take place in 1992). The committee was immediately joined by Aleksandr Buzgalin, who, as already mentioned, had previously been the leader of the Marxism of the Twenty-first Century faction of the CPSU Marxist Platform. The left-wing faction of the Social Democratic Party also agreed to be an active partner of the new party; as too did a number of representatives from the General Confederation of Trade Unions (which, at this stage, was the main successor organization to the Soviet-era Trade Union movement). And although splits occurred in both the Socialist Party and the Confederation of Anarcho-Syndicalists over the plans for the new party, a majority in both organizations did eventually back their respective leaders' position.

That the party had made some impact on the political scene in Russia, even at this early stage, was made clear in an editorial comment in the pro-liberal newspaper *Moskovskie novosti*. Fundamentally opposing the party's socialist ideology and its desire to arouse the radical consciousness of the Russian workforce, it nevertheless defined the Party of Labour as 'a very real and tough opposition to the democrats and a natural component of the political spectrum'.[18] Moreover, it even gave the party's leaders some access to the pages of the newspaper.

One immediate advantage of the party, then, was the undoubted fact that it represented a much more coherent alliance of compatible forces – not totally compatible, to be sure, but much more than previous attempts at some form of socialist-based unification. Another undoubted advantage was the fact that it managed to gain some parliamentary representation at the *national* level rather than just at the local or city level, which had previously been the limit of socialist penetration. This was largely thanks to the allegiance of Oleg Smolin, who had earlier been elected to the Congress of People's Deputies in 1990 and has since gone on to be an elected deputy in the new parliamentary upper chamber, the Council of the Federation. Indeed, because of Smolin's seniority here, he was formally elected as chairman of the party's council, hence its *de facto* leader. Apart from Smolin, the party also received a good degree of unofficial backing from the old parliamentary faction 'Workers Union – Reforms without Shock'.

From a programmatic perspective, the initial appeal that was published in August 1991 was eventually turned into a much broader and much more well-defined official programme of aims and ambitions. Politically, the main emphasis of the programme was on the promotion of principles of grass-roots democracy in all areas of social and political life, under-pinned by the slogan 'the state for its citizens, not citizens for the state'. There was a full acceptance of all the essential United Nations-recognized human rights, and a particular stress on the need to establish equality in all areas of life, especially between the sexes; with the desire to mobilize the support of emerging feminist groups in Russia a key strategy here. Likewise, all the programmatic statements of the party have given con-siderable priority to a number of key ecological ambitions, both as recognition of the valuable input that many green activists have already given to the party and in the hope that this would be another source of hitherto untapped popular support.

From the economic point of view, meanwhile, the party has been in the forefront of instigating a thoroughgoing 'Anti-Crisis Programme of the Democratic Left', which has been widely circulated and even quite well received in the corridors of parliament.[19] Drawn up principally by Aleksandr Buzgalin, Andrei Kolganov and Galina Rakitskaya (the leader of the left faction of the Russian Social Democrats), with the additional collaboration of the English economist John Ross, the American professor David Kotz, and a group of specialists from the Moscow-based Institute for Economic Prognoses (attached to the Russian Academy of Sciences), the programme essentially highlighted two main differences from all other economic variants. First, it focused on a different set of *strategic* interests; and secondly, it focused on the potential democratic character of state regulation in conjunction with non-governmental, social forms of economic regulation.

As for the monetarist variant of reform, the authors considered this to be totally ill-suited to the real existing economic conditions in post-Soviet Russia. The monetarists of the shock-therapy approach had not only made serious tactical mistakes – for example, in their efforts to control inflation and limit the extent of the budget deficit, etc. – but their whole basic strat-egy was a misguided one, conditioned almost exclusively as it was by the interests of the International Monetary Fund. Instead, the overall strategy, it was argued, had to be based on the reality of Russia's past economic development, and above all it had to be guided by the *social* priorities facing the country. This encompassed three main factors.

First, and perhaps most crucially, there had to be a fundamental 'humanization' of the economy. A stable and effective form of development could only ever be realized if it was genuinely geared towards satisfying the interests and aspirations of many different groups in society. For as long as the transition process focused exclusively on the narrow interests of a narrow socioeconomic elite, the economic crisis would continue. In short, economic stability must intrinsically be connected to a satisfaction of widespread social needs. Secondly, and connected with this, there was an emphasis in the programme on the priority of 'human capital' as the main resource of the economy. Maximizing the potential of this human capital was far more important than squandering efforts on the primitive accumulation of more traditional forms of capital as understood by Western capitalists. And thirdly, this emphasis on human capital provided the key to overcoming a number of 'structural' problems facing the country in its post-communist crisis. Ordinary workers had to be provided with a sense of motivation as well as of responsibility for their actions, and this could be achieved only by giving them a genuine stake in the activities of their workplace; that is to say, by giving the workers' collectives already established in the enterprises a genuine sense of empowerment and control over management. It also encompassed a new approach to the question of ownership, which could not be resolved without recourse to basic democratic principles. A radical restructuring of the state bodies which decide how state property is to be privatized was the key recommendation here, along with an emphasis on the need to decentralize ownership by transferring state property, for example, to local councils and bodies of local self-management. Small-scale private entrepreneurs, meanwhile, would also be supported, though only on condition that their businesses were developed through their own efforts, and not through machinations with state bodies or criminal entities.

In terms of any need for labour 'rationalization' in certain industrial sectors, the main commitment in the programme was to schemes of job-sharing and a reduced working week, which (implicitly following the ideas of André Gorz) would likewise promote a sense of freedom in the amount of free time that would be left at the disposal of workers.

Not surprisingly, a large part of the programme was committed to the maintenance of social welfare schemes, though this was accompanied by a strong commitment to moving away from the idea that these should be considered 'privileges for social parasites'. First and foremost, there needed to be a full indexation of guaranteed minimum wages, pensions and student grants (at a coefficient of no less than 0.9 times the rise of consumer prices). Free medical care and other social welfare provisions would be guaranteed, as too would the continuation of state subsidies for cultural activities, museums and libraries, and so on.

In order to control inflation tendencies, a recommendation was given to resort to periodic price freezes on the most important resources of industrial raw materials, transportation services and, if necessary, rationing on the most essential consumer products. Prices elsewhere, it was argued, could be stabilized on the basis of agreements reached between newly created producer and consumer associations, which would also take on the effective task of economic regulation. In addition to this, indirect taxes (on added costs) should be decreased; taxes on profits should be raised, although at the same time incentives should be provided to finance capital investments.

Indeed, on the issue of extracting the economy from its 'investment hole', it was recommended that the existing level of state capital investments should be preserved, mainly at the expense of the indexation of the amortization funds of enterprises. Likewise, there needed to be a stimulation of economic growth in those key sectors of the economy which produce consumer goods, with investment here being the major priority. Rigid monetary reform and the introduction of credit as a means of stimulating the economy were also proposed.

Finally, in the field of foreign economic policy, it was argued that special rates of exchange should apply to manufactured products which stimulated export, and on areas which facilitated the import of materials necessary for import-dependent industries. A policy of refusing to accept the speculative determination of the exchange rate of the rouble should be adopted, in conjunction with certain restrictions on the export of capital. Last, but not least, it was also proposed that priority should be given to the production of hi-tech consumer goods and the development of hi-tech industries in order ultimately to reduce the degree of import dependence.

Concluding the programme, the authors were perfectly clear in their recognition that the realization of such measures could be achieved only 'through the active efforts of an interested majority of the population. Without such support from below, there is no use in even thinking about its realisation.' Here, of course, to some extent, was the main *potential* advantage of the Party of Labour, as distinct from previous independent left organizations. Right from its inception the party knew precisely what its key strategy for the future should be. It aimed to be a political organization orientated towards the defence of the interests of ordinary workers, based on a close partnership and alliance with democratic labour movements, and first and foremost with the trade-union movement: a united workers' front with the Party of Labour as its main political representative. It was here, then, in its relationship with the trade-union movement, that the party would either make a significant impact or fade away into some future oblivion. The record of its achievement is not yet conclusive or definitive, though one would have to recognize that up until now its successes are markedly fewer than its failures and disappointments.

The first major dilemma facing the party concerned the question of whom it should give tactical priority to: the old established unions or the new emerging, independent unions. Having striven at first to make little distinction between them, the organizers of the party quickly realized that a definitive choice did indeed have to be made.

For Andrei Isaev, the decision was clear-cut. From the very outset he had always firmly believed that a strong labour movement could develop in Russia only through the renewal and the revival of the *old* trade-union organizations. And it was Isaev's view that carried the day – not only for obvious logistical reasons concerning the overwhelming predominance of the old unions in terms of size, membership and organizational capacity, but also for reasons concerning the manner in which new trade unions had actually evolved since their emergence in the late 1980s.

To put it bluntly, there was a general recognition that the vast majority of the new unions had not only come to perceive themselves as the representatives of a new narrowly based working-class 'elite'; more importantly (not unlike the post-communist experience in Poland), they had also become key supporters of the whole capitalist transition process taking place under Yeltsin's leadership. Certainly a common occurrence in the aftermath of the August 1991 coup attempt was many leaders of the old independent strike committees either engaging themselves in commercial activities, or accepting high-powered jobs in the new Russian administration.

From being closely affiliated with the Socialist Party, for example, the Sotsprof trade union was eventually taken over by the supporters of Democratic Russia, and in the process Sergei Khramov, its leader, was co-opted into the administration as an adviser to a commission of the Supreme Soviet. More surprising still were the changes afoot within the miners' movement. Two of the most prominent leaders in the Kuzbass strike committee, Mikhail Kislyuk and Anatolii Malykhin, were now appointed head of the regional administration and the personal representative of the President respectively. Meanwhile, Vyacheslav Golikov, who had previously been the co-chairman of the Council of Workers' Committees, was likewise co-opted into the administration as a member of Yeltsin's Presidential Council – a position he used to promote the idea of establishing a free economic zone in the Kuzbass.[20]

As for the perceptions of their new 'elite' status, this was clearly demonstrated in the exclusive relationship many of the new union leaderships built up with Yeltsin after August 1991, which thus allowed them to receive benefits unheard of in the old union sector. Likewise, it could also be seen in their repeated condemnation of other unions – most notably in the health and education sector – which ultimately resorted to strike action to assist their members, the vast majority of whom were well known to be among the poorest groups in Russian society.[21] Add to this the degree to which many of the new unions have established lucrative ties with a number of American organizations (not least the main trade-union organization, the American Federation of Labor–Congress of Industrial Organizations) in return for their promotion of the liberal ideology of the Yeltsin regime, and one can perfectly understand why it is that the Party of Labour ultimately came to rely on its links with key sections of the old trade-union organization.[22]

Once it had opted for this course, the next hurdle facing the Party of Labour concerned the depth of support 'progressive' forces actually enjoyed in the trade-union movement. As has previously been mentioned, a positive start had already been made to the extent that the Moscow Federation of Trade Unions (MFTU) had tentatively been won over to the cause espoused by the party. This clearly gave the new party a number of important benefits. For one thing, an invaluable source of financial backing; for another, a vital media outlet in the form of the Moscow Federation's newspaper *Solidarnost'*, which is edited by Isaev and has officially promoted the party's political aspirations. And although the newspaper's readership is largely confined to the capital, it was nevertheless one of the few newspapers that was able to increase its circulation in the post-Soviet period, rising from a starting point of 5,000 in August 1991 to almost 40,000 by the middle of 1993.[23]

Capturing the support of the Moscow leadership, however, was still only a small victory. Above and beyond this there was the question of how much influence the leadership of the MFTU possessed over its own rank-and-file members, and whether it could really mobilize these ordinary members to support the Party of Labour. Similarly, there was also the question of whether the support given by Moscow could be reciprocated at other regional levels and within the national leadership of the umbrella organization, FITUR. It is on these issues that the balance sheet is not in the Party of Labour's favour.

On the *positive* side, the party has attracted some degree of regional trade-union support outside Moscow, most notably in St Petersburg, Perm, Omsk and Irkutsk. Apart from the access this gives it to direct agitation among the workers, it has also helped it to establish up to fifteen major regional branches, and to get a number of party representatives elected on to regional and city councils. On the national level, meanwhile, it was able to enter into a series of open-ended discussions with the FITUR leadership throughout the summer of 1993, at a time when the union's opposition to the government was becoming increasingly hostile. No formal outcome resulted from these talks, however, largely because of their interruption by the events in September and October of that year.

The list of *negative* factors, however, is both longer and far more substantial in terms of effect.

On the question of the depth of support given to the party by the MFTU leadership, it is important first of all briefly to clarify the basic structure of this organization. As a Federation in its own right the MFTU has no fewer than 39 affiliated unions attached to it, representing the interests of nearly 6 million workers in both the city and the outlying districts of the Moscow *oblast'*. The main affiliated unions are those in the sphere of construction, science and education, health, engineering and railways, with the average membership of these major sectors being somewhere in the region of 400,000–600,000 workers.

One of the first things to note concerning this structure is the extent to which each affiliated union within the Federation is almost completely autonomous from the centre, including in the vital sphere of finance. This in itself, therefore, intrinsically prevented any genuine form of co-ordination, let alone solidarity, from emerging, and has certainly prevented any kind of effective mobilization of resources necessary to create a brand-new kind of apparatus, which the Party of Labour organizers feel is an important prerequisite to their ambitions. This, likewise, has limited the organizational abilities of the central MFTU leadership, and given them little incentive really to activate rank-and-file opinions.

Another consequence of the structure of the Moscow Federation, which has been exacerbated by the crisis conditions in which they are having to operate, is the degree to which every industrial branch, every category of the working class, every enterprise, every town and every district has effectively been reduced to concentrating exclusively on its own *parochial* concerns. In other words, the relationship within the Federation is defined more by competition and hostility than in seeking a mutual alliance. This pattern, needless to say, is repeated across the whole country, and in itself is often seen as one of the main contributory factors to right-wing political groups being able to capitalize far more on workers' discontent than left-wing forces can.

This last point partly explains another major deficiency in the effectiveness of the MFTU leadership in mobilizing its rank and file throughout the post-Soviet period. On the one hand, they have clearly had little effective capacity to wage a struggle with the incumbent political authorities, since virtually all the cards were stacked in the latter's favour. On the other, they themselves have acknowledged an extreme reluctance to lead the workers out on to the street for fear of losing control over them.

Last, but not least, notwithstanding the more progressive and supportive line adopted by Shmakov to the overall ambitions of the Party of Labour during his time as leader of the MFTU, a number of party members did express strong doubts as to where the limits of his commitment lay. And just as significantly, it is also important to recognize that he by no means carried a majority of the executive apparatus with him, and certainly much of the second-tier leadership structure continued to be dominated by old-style *apparatchiks*.

Outside the Moscow organization, the situation *vis-à-vis* the Party of Labour's attempts to forge a new relationship with the trade-union movement looks, if anything, even bleaker.

Officially, the union leadership, particularly at national level, have consistently expressed an unwillingness to assimilate themselves too closely with *any* political organization, which is hardly surprising given their relationship with the old CPSU. *Unofficially*, when they have engaged in politics, as we saw in Chapter 5, they have overwhelmingly seen the centrists as their main political partner in the current circumstances now prevailing, sticking rigidly to their faith that some kind of benevolent paternalism is the answer to all their problems. Similarly, within the enterprise – again as was argued in Chapter 5 – the old unions have rarely been able or willing to overcome their traditional operational mechanisms; nor have they transcended their old *raison d'être* as organizations firmly allied to management structures. What is even more debilitating is the fact that more active unionists who have sought to combat the old-style collusion with management have often been victimized and/or dismissed.

In terms of overall union lethargy over recent years, one should also not downplay successful government attempts to 'divide and rule' the workers' movements and the powerful levers of control they can exercise over the unions. More generally, as many Party of Labour activists are reluctantly willing to admit, they have too often hitherto encountered a Russian workforce too content with their condition as *passive* recipients of handouts of one kind or another from above, rather than being *active* organizers and shapers of their own conditions, particularly in areas that far transcend the level of welfare. Changing this entrenched mentality, in other words, is going to be neither easy nor quick. And if anything, recent experience would suggest that the constant *threat* of unemployment has tended to make the vast majority of workers more, rather than less, passive. Add to this a general climate of working-class atomization – in which people are looking to survive individually rather than collectively – and a general sense of demoralization at the whole situation that has developed, and one can understand the huge difficulties confronting a small-scale organization like the Party of Labour.

Apart from its own individual attempts to build up its social base of support, the Party of Labour has also played a significant role since its foundation in trying to organize a much broader form of democratic left unity in the shape of an alliance or bloc of forces capable of competing more equally with the respective blocs of the other hegemonic combatants. The most significant initiative here came at the end of November 1992 with the convening of a Congress of Democratic Left Forces. Attended by more than one thousand delegates from across the length and breadth of the Russian Federation, the congress brought together activists from the Party of Labour, the Socialist Party of Workers, the Russian Party of Communists, the left-wing factions of the Social Democrats and the People's Party of Free Russia (Grigorii Vodolazov), as well as more than a dozen non-party organizations representing such interests as labour collectives, women's organizations and radical green movements.

United by a desire to oppose the increasing signs of authoritarianism then being espoused by the ruling regime and by the forces of the 'irreconcilable opposition', together with a need to try to give a much stronger form of representation to a much broader range of social groups which were clearly showing signs of increasing antagonism to the 'new order', the congress did at least result in the signing of a common declaration of principles for future co-operation and the establishment of a standing consultative council, which was to be co-ordinated by Aleksandr Buzgalin.[24] The ultimate ambition of establishing a genuinely cohesive and permanent bloc or alliance, however, was not achieved, and as on many other occasions, the divisive power of sectarianism often proved to be a stronger left-wing phenomenon than the rallying call for unity.

One of the main sticking points, it later emerged, was the repeated attempt by the leadership of the Socialist Party of Workers to advance its claim to be the one real backbone of the entire democratic left movement, a nucleus to which other forces would have to submit. As this was clearly not acceptable to a vast majority of the forces represented at the congress, it reduced its ultimate impact. What is also clear is that this undoubtedly paved the way for the SPW's later shift away from the main ranks of the democratic left movement.

For the Party of Labour, then, the period since autumn 1993 has perhaps been the most difficult in all its short history. With the decision of the SPW to renege on its earlier commitment to establish an autonomous democratic left electoral pact, it left senior party members not only 'stunned' and 'bewildered', but also out in the cold in terms of their capacity to participate in the elections. Other events at this time, of course, did leave them free to make a virtue out of necessity in terms of their ability very effectively to portray the whole electoral process in December 1993 as a 'rigged sham', stained with the blood of Russian citizens killed on the orders of an increasingly brutal autocrat. How much of a real compensation this was, however, is hard to say.

To make matters worse, the change of leadership of FITUR after the October 1993 crisis, which saw Shmakov replace Igor' Klochkov, did not produce any fundamental dividends for the party. The old persistent doubts about Shmakov's real commitment to the project of a Brazilian- or even a British-style Labour Party in a close partnership with the trade unions were, it seems, very well founded. In effect, Shmakov appears to have reached the conclusion that the unions essentially do not need a political party (or at least a close, *integral* alliance with a political party) to represent their interests, since they are better off trying to take care of themselves through their own established structures. His defence also appears to be that in the aftermath of the September and October 1993 political crisis – which saw the government 'expropriate' some of the previously entrenched powers of the unions to control the adminstration of social security provisions – it is in the unions' primary interest not to antagonize the incumbent political authorities any more than they have to.

The ultimate validity of this defence, of course, is at the moment a moot point. The primary effect has been a distinct cooling of relations between Shmakov and leaders of the Party of Labour, and an increasing recognition that their previous strategy of trying to work with and through the old trade-union structure has simply not worked. Last, but not least, this has inevitably led to tensions inside the party, particularly concerning Andrei Isaev's position. According to Boris Kagarlitsky, for example, Isaev's own commitment to the labourist project is likewise very much in doubt, and he openly accuses Isaev of lately turning *Solidarnost'* into a newspaper for trade-union bureaucrats, epitomized (so Kagarlitsky would claim) by the recent loss of half of its readership.[25]

In an attempt to recapture any initiative that the party may once have had, endeavours have been made throughout 1994 to try to advance the cause of a new, fully unified political organization composed of three distinct, though mutually compatible, tendencies. At the core of the new organization would be the existing forces of the Party of Labour still committed to their labourist project; to the right of them would be a recognized social democratic tendency, and to the left a recognized communist tendency made up of those disaffected forces within the current Zyuganov-led CPRF, as well as from other communist forces. The evidence suggests, however, that once again these attempts have borne little or no fruit.

Signs of Optimism?

What encouraging signs are there then, if any, for the democratic socialist orientation in the ongoing struggle for hegemony in Russia?

One thing that can be said here is that there is undoubtedly a fair degree of intellectual vitality concerning the need to reinvigorate the socialist cause in a Russian setting. This can be seen in a number of different contexts. It can be seen, for example, in the variety of associations and organizations that have emerged in recent years committed to engaging in a widespread, usually international, debate on the fundamental nature of socialism, both in its retrospective environment and as regards its future perspective. Groups such as 'Economy and Democracy' and the Moscow-based International Association 'Scholars for Democracy and Socialism' are by now well-established forums, and their annual conferences are lively, intellectually engaging affairs, which often attract a good deal of media interest. Similarly, albeit on a smaller, intimate scale, associations like 'Open Marxism', the 'Left Club of the Russian Academy of Sciences' and the seminar group 'Lenin's Readings' are also forums devoted to revitalizing the socialist tradition across the intellectual milieux.

Such vitality can also be seen in the scope of recent publications, ranging from T.G. Zuraev's 'Path to Socialism' [*Put' k sotsializmu*] and P.L. Kruchinin's 'Renaissance of Marxism' [*Vozrozhdenie marksizma*] to Boris Kurashvili's latest work, 'Where is Russia Going?' [*Kuda idet Rossiya*?], which includes his much-discussed Manifesto of New Socialism.[26]

As one of the few representatives of the older generation of Communist Party intellectuals to have genuinely clung on to radical democratic socialist convictions – he was born in 1925 and, having served in a consultancy capacity to the KGB, went on to become head of the Institute of State and Law for nearly twenty years – Kurashvili's Manifesto is undoubtedly a document of some considerable weight and importance. Apart from his positive espousal of principles of personal liberty in conjunction with social equality, and his recommendation for a full development of political pluralism, separation of powers, a law-based state and mechanisms genuinely to enhance forms of popular sovereignty, Kurashvili has also done much to define the precise parameters of a future socialist renovation based on a willingness to learn, and subsequently apply, the lessons of past mistakes. This is particularly noticeable, for example, in his writings on the nature of bureaucracy; in his conviction that Russian Marxists need to broaden their traditional understanding of the phenomenon of class interests considerably not only to incorporate socioeconomic issues, but also to examine the *social-psychological* structure of class relations; and in his emphasis on the need to formulate a comprehensive approach to the concept of a socialist form of civil society as the primary means of overcoming the ingrained tendency in all social structures for an overconcentration of power in one person's or one institution's hands.

To be sure, there is undoubtedly a lot of disagreement here, both as regards Kurashvili's and all the other recommendations to which socialist intellectuals have been giving vent, but this in itself should clearly not detract from the innovative thinking that is generally taking place. As a doctrine, it is at least possible to see that socialism is far from being 'a dead creature' or an 'empty gesture', and it is certainly no longer an 'official ritual' in many intellectual quarters.[27] Just as significantly, the very notion of 'socialism' is also no longer the subject of *popular* derision as it perhaps was two or three years ago. Burawoy (along with many others) has thus been proved correct in his prediction that the inevitable chasm that would be generated between capitalist ideology and reality, promise and actuality, would inevitably provide fresh scope for the socialist imagination.[28]

Amid the optimism of this latter point, however, one should certainly not lose sight of one very important – indeed, crucial – proviso. If the popular socialist imagination has indeed been refertilized, it has been done in a backward-looking rather than forward-looking way. And this remembrance of things past is predominantly a nostalgia for the kind of paternalistic ritualism that was the embodiment of Brezhnev-type socialism. In other words, it does not really have a great deal to do with the kind of democratic socialism that is being offered to the Russian public by the likes of Buzgalin, Kagarlitsky, and other activists of the democratic Left. Indeed, having been the butt of jokes and satires in the Gorbachev era, Brezhnev has lately achieved a veritable new reverence. It is certainly interesting to note, for example, that virtually no member of the incumbent regime now dares to make any kind of criticism of the Brezhnev years for fear of conjuring up images of stable, good times for the vast majority of people. And as one contemporary joke puts it: why did Brezhnev request on his deathbed that he be buried face down? Because he knew that for the first few years after his death everybody would want to spit in his face. After this period, however, everything was bound to change, and he therefore wanted to be face down so that everybody could kiss his arse.

In short, there is still a general preference for clinging to past certainties rather than future uncertainties. And because of this *status quo ante* orientation in key areas, other political forces (like the Zyuganov-led CPRF, as well as Zhirinovsky's Liberal Democrats) are likely to continue to accrue greater political profit than forces like the Party of Labour.

It could be argued, then, that the democratic Left is faced with a threefold intellectual dilemma. First, it has little choice but to differentiate itself from the past version of socialism. If it oversteps the mark and is seen as an apologist for the past, then it will totally lose its primary *raison d'être*. At the same time, given the current climate in Russia today, it has to try to demonstrate that it is an orientation rooted in the Russian tradition. This was certainly the essential gist of Boris Kagarlitsky's earlier-cited assertion that the neo-liberals had lost an enormous degree of popularity and credibility because of their association with an *alien*, Western tradition that often made them appear totally isolated from society, and therefore profoundly hostile to the people's own conscious perception of what their traditions, their culture and their history amounted to.

Many activists are slowly, but surely, beginning to realize and to appreciate that there is a rich legacy in the distinctively Russian socialist tradition that has not been sufficiently tapped. The aforementioned ideas of Leont'ev, for example, could be opposed by a counter-propagation of the ideas of someone like Nikolai Chernyshevsky and the popular tradition he and others represent. The great cultural movement that emerged in the first quarter of the twentieth century could be advantageously utilized by the present-day socialists, particularly poets like Mayakovsky. And last, but not least, there is Lenin. The first Soviet leader's popularity in the public consciousness remains remarkably high given the backdrop of the post-communist transition, and few can doubt that the democratic socialists could make more capital of this than they do at present (in a discerning way, of course).

There remains, however, a third dilemma for the Left. Apart from differentiating itself from the past while simultaneously locating its roots in its *national* tradition, it cannot afford to fall into the trap of promoting a form of *national socialism*. As was made clear earlier, and as was consistently made clear in a round table of left-wing activists conducted in Moscow by the present author in June 1994, the democratic Left must retain a firm adherence to the principle of internationalism.[29]

A second *possible* manifestation of optimism for the democratic Left represents, perhaps, a natural progression from the first point, and leads us further into that ever-complicated realm of culture. In his recent – almost by now *infamous* – lecture on the Spectres of Marx (delivered on his tour of the United States in 1993), Jacques Derrida was convinced that no matter how anti-Marxist or anti-communist an individual was, few could seriously deny the obvious fact that '[we] all live in a world, some would say a culture, that still bears, at an incalculable depth, the mark of this inheritance, whether in a directly visible fashion or not'.[30] If this is true of Western civilization and culture, what about Russia, which not only experienced seventy-four years of official state-sponsored communist cultural iconolatry, but has pre-revolutionary cultural norms and affinities often popularly portrayed as having been closer in spirit to communist and socialist values than its Western counterpart has ever been? Is there really, for example, a deeply ingrained sense of *collectivism* and a desire for *social justice* in the Russian culture that is more than the stuff of romantic idealization? Is the communal 'we' rather than the Anglo-Saxon 'I' really that organically innate?

Supposing, for the sake of argument, that we do accept these assertions at face value, does it necessarily follow that the cultural context is ultimately quite favourable for the Left in Russia, which, after all, undoubtedly seeks to articulate these values in all its key aspirations?

The short answer to this is: there is no obvious intrinsic benefit to the Left, unless two other points can be demonstrated. First, there is a need to demonstrate that this sense of collectivism and social justice is successfully holding off the challenge currently being exerted by the new state-sanctioned allegiance to the icons and dogmas of possessive individualism. And secondly, and just as crucially, there is likewise a need to demonstrate that the democratic Left's attachment to a *rationalized* understanding of such phenomena can ultimately win the day in the parallel struggle with the Russophiles and their own attempt to capitalize on an allegiance to a more *irrational, emotional* understanding of these notions.

According to Ludmilla Bulavka, one of the Left's leading intellectual doyennes on all matters of culture, when the argument comes down to these two very specific issues, what might have been perceived as signs of optimism for the Left at a general cultural level now begin to look far less promising.[31]

On the issue of the impact of the cultural norms of Western capitalism and its espousal of the centrality of possessive individualism, Bulavka is of the opinion that while no definitive outcome of this *Kulturkampf* will be witnessed for a considerable period of time, nevertheless the Westerners have started to make some considerable inroads. The fundamental essence of post-Soviet culture, she has argued, is its differentiation from both its Soviet and its pre-revolutionary Russian forebears. The main bond between the earlier Russian and Soviet culture was indeed its common search for a form of social harmony and social collectivity between its people. In Russian times the democratic ideal was the main goal, whereas in Soviet times it was the socialist ideal. Nevertheless, in both situations the creative arts played a major role in trying to establish a common set of social bonds between people. Classical literature was the main bonding mechanism in the nineteenth century, whereas throughout the early period of Soviet rule it was the cinema that largely performed this role; but whatever it was, at all times people related to each other through cultural mechanisms – the books they had read, the music they had heard and the plays they had seen.

The real point, then, is that in both these earlier formations, culture played a role of *social communication* between the people, this being the main democratic mechanism at their disposal. It is precisely this culturally engendered sense of social community, however, that the new regime has set out to destroy, and its success rate is increasing all the time. On the one hand, it has successfully reduced both the quantitative degree of access to different forms of cultural activity and the qualitative nature of that cultural activity, based as it is now on the new credo of consumerism and marketization. On the other, culture today is no longer the collective phenomenon it was in the past; like everything else, it is slowly but surely becoming 'privatized' to the extent that it is more and more a private, individual activity. Indeed, given these tendencies, Bulavka's ultimate worry is that Marxism and socialism alike might also become a private affair and not things that induce or stimulate collective activities of one kind or another.

As for the democratic Left's struggle with the Russophiles to preserve and articulate the best traditions of Russian collectivism and social justice, Bulavka is equally concerned that the Left is not the dominant force here. Very reluctantly, she is forced to admit that the most effective form of discourse with the masses in Russia today can be only an irrational, emotional one.[32]

Underpinning both these features, meanwhile, is the overall *demise* of culture in Russia, a phenomenon closely interrelated with the causal nature of the old order's crisis and ultimate collapse. For Bulavka, the real essence of any 'culture' is its understanding as a critical, creative force in opposition to any type of conformist (or consumerist) trend. It was this ideal of culture that Soviet artists, at least after the late 1920s, were never able to live up to. Having lost the basis from which they could engage in a genuine form of social creativity, they not only defied the logic of culture, they negated it entirely. By becoming conformist tools of the bureaucratic system, servants of nothing more than an artificial, lifeless ideology, they did not perform a non-cultural so much as an *anti*-cultural role.

This, then, was the realization of the artificial world of the artist alienated from the process of social creativity. And what we find today, argues Bulavka, is a continuation of this phenomenon. Having served the old conformism of Soviet-style socialism, many of these pseudo-intellectuals have no qualms about serving the conformism embodied in the new ideology. What we have, in other words, is a cultural continuity in the nature of the interrelationship between ideology, power and alienation. Only its superficial appearance has changed, so that nowadays it is things like advertising and beauty competitions that personify the new cultural norms.

The final area that might inspire at least a small degree of optimism hinges on the belief, or the hope, that there is no ingrained permanence in the lack of any real or consistent working-class backlash against the kind of transition that has been put into effect over the past few years. In other words, given the current extent of the crisis, as well as its expected longevity, new conditions may well emerge in the near future. It is perfectly true, of course, that this has been a long-held expectation in many different quarters that has simply not come to fruition so far. And the present study, drawing on the earlier research findings of specialists like Simon Clarke and Micheal Burawoy *et al.*, has tried to indicate why those expectations have so far not materialized.

Nevertheless, 1994 has witnessed a significant increase in strike action over the previous two years,[33] and as Igor' Gotlib has indicated, there is now every reason to expect a considerable rise in the number of spontaneous protest actions as the real consequences of the transition process – particularly the transformation of the threat of unemployment into real unemployment – start to hit home.[34]

The operative word here is *spontaneous*. Many of these strikes are not comprehensively prepared or organized, nor for the most part are they officially sanctioned by the trade unions. Should Gotlib (and others) be proved correct, then an increase in such spontaneous protest is going to pose a number of serious challenges. First, they are clearly going to add to the pressure on the trade-union organization to move definitively away from the notions of social partnership with government, and especially collusion with management. In Andrei Kolganov's view, for example, the signs that this collusion is indeed beginning to weaken are more and more apparent by the day, as the enterprise trade unions gradually shed their illusions of the perceived benefits of this relationship. Nevertheless, no one doubts the depth of dependency that needs to be overcome, and considerably more pressure from the rank and file needs to be put on the union leadership.[35] Secondly, and perhaps even more significantly, the spontaneity of such protests is going to bring to the forefront the age-old dilemma of such types of action: what is the real potential of this spontaneity? Can it be turned into a conscious, *creative* force of change, or will it be more the embodiment of an unconscious, *destructive* force? For many of the Russophile forces of opposition, of course, the latter option is often the preferred one.[36] For the forces of the democratic socialist orientation, the desired preference is undoubtedly the former.

The pivotal strategy for the democratic Left in their endeavour to fashion a creative force for change in the persona of the working class has always been their reliance on the propagation of schemes for *self-management*. Aleksandr Buzgalin and Andrei Kolganov, in particular, have for many years worked on the theoretical considerations of this principle and, to their considerable credit, have developed extremely comprehensive models and ideas. They are convinced, for example, that in *all* existing economic systems there is an objective logic at work stimulating the development of such processes, and they are even more convinced that the present Russian conjuncture offers some advantages, at least in so far as the capitalist requirements of the market and of ownership have not yet become truly mystified in ordinary people's consciousness.[37]

Nor are they alone in this endeavour. The notion of workers' self-management is the pivotal aspect of Boris Kurashvili's 'New Socialism', and Kurashvili, along with Aleksei Prigarin and eleven other economic specialists, was responsible for the formulation of a comprehensive Draft Law on the Self-Governing of People's Enterprises in spring 1992.[38]

Moreover, even many *non*-socialist activists and intellectuals have likewise made the principle of self-management the central aspect of their alternative economic programmes, with perhaps the best example here being that of Vadim Belotserkovskii, a committed advocate of convergence theories, continuing the Russian legacy of intellectuals such as Cheryanev, Mindeleev and Andrei Sakharov.

Others, however, at one time equally committed to the centrality of self-management models, have started to express serious doubts as to the real effectiveness of this strategic orientation, and would point in particular to the recent failed experiences of the Gorbachev-era Labour Collective Councils (STKs) to back up their hesitations.[39] Likewise, many would point to the fact that the fundamental notion of 'self-management' can often mean very different things; this not only adds to the already high levels of sectarianism within the Left, it also ends up increasing the existing depths of confusion and contradiction that pervade the consciousness of rank-and-file workers.[40]

This issue, then, is clearly going to be at the heart of the internal debate within the democratic Left for quite some time. Whatever the outcome of the debate, however, there is nevertheless a unanimous recognition of the importance of the main task: ultimately to insert some kind of creative consciousness into the spontaneous actions of the disaffected workers. If the focus of strike activity remains at the level of desiring short-term parochial goals, such as the receipt of non-paid wages, then this is not going to be of much help to the overall cause of the Left. Transforming social protest away from such parochialism towards a more elaborated, constructive form of opposition activity, however, remains a formidable hurdle to overcome. What this latter issue also highlights is the extent to which the main debates and fault lines inside the Left at the moment are as much to do with strategies as they are with ideological principles. This is even more noticeable when the difficult question of the current viability of the Left's *independence* is raised in the context of realistic political options open to it over the next few years.

For Oleg Smolin, arguing from the perspective of his parliamentary experience, the Left has little choice but to affiliate (and hence subordinate) itself to other anti-capitalist opposition tendencies. This does not mean to say that no autonomous agenda of its own cannot be preserved. It is, however, a recognition of the fear that without incorporation into the larger political scene, the Left risks permanent isolation and marginalization.[41] A somewhat related argument has also been put forward by Aleksandr Buzgalin. Speaking in the aftermath of the military assault on the old Russian parliament, he was adamant that the Left had to engage itself actively in a broad anti-authoritarian opposition movement, within which ideological sectarianism would come a distant second to a common promotion of basic principles of human rights and democratic norms. Concerned at the ever-growing strength of neo-fascist, populist, authoritarian forces in the country, Buzgalin was by now convinced that no matter how loosely the notion of the 'Left' was interpreted, it simply was not strong enough either to lead or to carry the fight on its own. And as he himself was only too keen to stress, there were simply too many forces and too many social elements traditionally associated with the Left that had either been co-opted into the anti-democratic camp or were willing to play very dangerous games with such forces. 'We must once and for all recognize', he asserted, 'that the time for playing games with these kind of people is over.'[42]

For many others, however, the preservation and prioritization of the Left's independent agenda for radical change is absolutely sacrosanct. Either the Left preserves its full political and ideological purity and bides its time for a future opportunity, or it 'sells its soul' and loses that opportunity for good. What we have here, then, to some extent, is a replay of many of the arguments that were predominant in the long build-up to the October Revolution of 1917. Indeed, in terms of the debate about hegemony and the original Russian context of that debate, we may even have come full circle and arrived back at an updated version of its Plekhanovite starting point. Does the Left strive for a maturation of a (bourgeois) demo cratic revolution, and only then seek to engage in the 'real' struggle for a genuine radical socialist transformation of society, or does it hope to get its way more immediately by other means available to it?

In Lieu of a Conclusion

Something has been clarified there, but something still remains obscure.

Vladimir Voinovich[1]

The emphasis of the present study throughout has been on a twofold understanding of a hegemonic struggle in post-communist Russia. First, it has focused on the struggle for the conditions to emerge whereby different competing visions of a new hegemony based on consent, not force or authoritarian domination, can actually materialize. Secondly, it has focused on the actual struggle among the major hegemonic combatants themselves. What can one say about the different aspects of those struggles at the end of 1994/early months of 1995?

As regards the contextual situation, no one can doubt that the struggle is proving long and arduous in conditions which are far from optimal. State power continues to be institutionally underdeveloped, and is essentially utilized according to discretionary criteria. Clientelism is rife, and few of the political parties and interest groups provide a genuine articulatory forum for different social interests. Many of these factors are exacerbated by the predominance of irredentist ethnic considerations; there is tremendous dislocation and uncertainty in the economic realm; and the lack of any democratic tradition to fall back on is severely felt. It is thus small wonder that successive opinion polls highlight the ordinary citizens' despondency at the future political prospects for the country; nor should one be surprised at the frequent allegations of classic *oligarchical* tendencies afflicting the ruling bodies.[2] Summing up the situation, Irina Khakamada has written:

Today's political marketplace – which should be a meeting place for leaders and citizens – is beginning all the more to resemble that which has established itself in the economic realm. It is a market for sellers, not for consumers. It is narrowly shaped and monopolized, and it is for the most part highly regulated, of *apparatchik* descent, closed and self-sufficient.[3]

And certainly a number of developments in late spring 1995 gave considerable weight to these misgivings, not least attempts by Duma Speaker Ivan Rybkin and Prime Minister Viktor Chernomyrdin to establish new electoral groupings based on nothing more than a common aspiration of those in positions of legislative and executive power to preserve their positions irrespective of differing ideological beliefs. Of the two it was the Chernomyrdin bloc in particular (called Our Home is Russia) that widely merited the label 'the Party of the *Nomenklatura*' and supported as it was by many regional administrative heads and corporate giants (such as the state-owned Gazprom gas company), the oligarchical nature of the new grouping could hardly be disputed.[4]

If anything best describes the hegemonic context in Russia at this time, however, it is the notion that there is a striking surreal-like quality that pervades the country's political life. Not for the first time in Russian political history – and certainly not for the last, I am sure – there is a sense in which what is presented to the observer is comprised of such a bizarre kind of logic that the difference between what is real and what is unreal becomes totally confused.

Take the case, for example, of the MMM share-issue scandal, which was briefly alluded to in Chapter 3. Virtually nothing about this case bore any resemblance whatsoever to any kind of reality – at least one that a logical, rational mind could easily comprehend. Right from the outset the nature of the company's activities were unreal, or at least surreal, in trying to operate a 'pyramid' ruse. The massive advertising campaign that constantly promoted the company was simplistic beyond any rational belief – aptly described by one journalist as at least proving the premiss that 'naive, gullible people could be persuaded to buy shares by TV advertisements showing a naive, gullible man buying shares'.[5]

When the company eventually collapsed, causing thousands of ordinary citizens to lose all their financial income, it was not the company's president, Sergei Mavrodi, who was universally blamed, but all manner of other institutions, most notably the government. Indeed, following Mavrodi's arrest on charges of tax evasion, thousands of impoverished MMM investors took to the streets to voice their loyalty and support for their 'hero'. Following his eventual release from jail (on conditions of bail) in October 1994, Mavrodi then stood in a parliamentary by-election for the State Duma in the suburbs of Moscow, a seat which had become available only due to the *assassination* of the previous deputy (one of several to have been murdered within the space of a few months). Campaigning on a platform of 'popular capitalism', Mavrodi was openly supported by members of the Communist Party of the Russian Federation. And following his victory over eleven other candidates, he was thus able to gain legal immunity from any further proceedings against him. Just to complete the 'story',

Mavrodi has since gone on to try to establish a parliamentary faction of his own, known as 'People's Capital'. Moreover, this pseudo-businessman, who owns a pseudo-investment company, has openly allied himself with that most prominent of all pseudo-liberal democrats, Vladimir Zhirinovsky.

Turning to the actual hegemonic combatants themselves, the first thing that must be re-emphasized is the fact that all of them have barely begun the process of suturing together the needs of their socioeconomic base with a recognized political-cultural vision of a future Russia – the main hallmark of a 'historical bloc'. As for Leszek Kolakowski's established maxim that 'an ideology is always weaker than the social forces which happen to be its vehicle [and carrier] of its values',[6] this too has been proved correct in contemporary Russia – subject to the proviso, of course, that the recognized social forces are themselves quite weak and ill-defined at the present moment.

Another widespread view that one could encounter at the end of 1994 was the belief that there was a growing *rapprochement* between the different combatants and the orientations they adhered to. This *rapprochement* or convergence, it was argued, was focused primarily on the authoritarian statist axis, with the predominant need for 'order' replacing earlier aspects of the political/ideological dividing line. To some extent, such an argument was a perfectly valid one. There was certainly a sense in which by the end of this period many people had begun to view the political situation as one representing a fundamental choice: *either* democracy *or* stabilization. What was excluded was the belief that both these phenomena could be achieved at the same time. The Chechen conflict, not surprisingly, did much to exacerbate perceptions of this kind, but it was not the sole factor. The ever-increasing levels of organized crime, and in particular, the number of murders carried out on the streets of Moscow and other major cities, were equally powerful factors in the desire for 'order at all costs'.[7]

Notwithstanding the validity of this argument, however, one should nevertheless not overlook the genuine differences between the Westernist, centrist and Russophile orientation; nor should one overlook the emphatic sense in which they have been genuine rivals in the past, and will certainly remain rivals in the foreseeable future.

Arguably the main feature to note as regards the hegemonic struggle thus far is in fact the degree to which it has not been the conflict *between* the major combatants that has shaped Russian political life so much as the conflict *inside* each respective aspiring hegemonic bloc; the struggle, in other words, for primacy and supremacy among different constituent groups which essentially adhere to the same overall set of values, but nevertheless have different perspectives on how those values should be developed in a concrete sense. By autumn 1994, new defining features were beginning to reshape the nature of this internal conflict. Within the camp of the Westerners, for example, one of the main dividing lines was between the 'liberal-conservatives' (supporters of Gaidar's Russia's Choice Party) and 'radical-liberals' (Ponomarev's Democratic Russia Party), the notion of conservatism here being closely equated with its English (Thatcherite) form.[8]

Within the centrist camp, the main internal conflict was between the 'industrial corporatists' (the directors' lobby) and the self-styled 'social democrats' who had begun to reconfigure, partly around the *perestroika*-era notion of centrism and partly around those who adhered to a distinctive Russian version of social democracy.[9] This had subsequently given rise to two new political organizations. On the one hand, there was the Party of Social Democracy which reunited senior figures from the Gorbachev era such as Aleksandr Yakovlev, Yevgenii Shaposhnikov, Stanislav Shatalin and Fedor Burlatskii. On the other hand, and perhaps far more significantly, there was also the new movement that went by the name of the Russian Social Democratic Union. Led by Vasilii Lipitskii, Oleg Rumyantsev and Aleksandr Obolenskii, with some support from the leader of FITUR, Mikhail Shmakov, and from a breakaway section of the Party of Labour (most notably Andrei Isaev), the movement's *raison d'être* was its emphasis on the parallel requirements of patriotic and national interests in conjunction with a prioritizing of the *social* aspects of any process of economic transition.

As for the internal struggle within the Russophile camp, one of the main battle lines here at this time was drawn between the 'moderates' and the 'extremists'; and what lent this particular internal conflict such renewed interest and vigour was the return of Aleksandr Solzhenitsyn to his beloved Russian homeland in May 1994. To put it quite simply, hopes were now raised (among many different forces on the political battlefield in Russia) that Solzhenitsyn's presence would at last provide a much-needed impetus to the hitherto weakened and depleted forces of moderate Russophilia. Two questions, however, clearly need to be asked with respect to such hopes. Has Solzhenitsyn the capacity and the continued authority to provide that impetus? And, perhaps more significantly, should he even be classed in the first place as an advocate of a moderate form of Russophilia?

As for the first question, the published debate among the Russian intelligentsia since his homecoming has been evenly split on this issue, although virtually everyone recognizes that given his age (seventy-five), no one is envisaging an explicit political career for him. As for the second, this is clearly not the place to rake over all the old ground of a debate that has gone on continuously now for over three decades, spanning the years both before and after his forced exile from Russia. Nor is it even the place to reopen the debate that was sparked off by his much-publicized exegesis on

'How we should structure Russia', which appeared, amid considerable controversy, in the Soviet press in 1990.[10]

What can be said, however, is that since his return to Russia in May 1994, most of his public comments and speeches have not demonstrated many real signs of moderation. Indeed, by choosing in particular to focus constantly on the plight of the Russian diaspora in what he calls the 'provinces' of Russia (i.e. the new independent countries of the former USSR), he has, wittingly or unwittingly, given considerable extra succour to the extremists. An ally of Zhirinovsky and Rutskoi he will never be, but few can be surprised if ordinary citizens perhaps draw the conclusion that the only fundamental difference at heart is that Solzhenitsyn speaks with an untouchable moral authority because of his past sufferings. One thing is for sure, however. His return home has not been, and will not be, good news for the Westerners; and in a perfect piece of theatrical symbolism he made sure that when he did return to Russia, he entered the country from the East, not from the West.[11]

If this was the 'state of play' in late autumn 1994, by the beginning of 1995 the outbreak of hostilities between Russia and Chechnya had not only created a brand-new set of parameters to the political struggle, it had also seriously affected the whole balance of power in the Russian political domain. Whether this change of balance proves to be permanent or temporary is thus the major question on everybody's lips at the moment.

In terms of political winners and losers, no one can doubt that the Chechen conflict has had the most adverse effects on the political fortunes of the Westerners. While some groups (Russia's Choice, Democratic Russia and YABLoko) have vehemently opposed the war, others (such as Boris Fedorov's Liberal Democratic Union) have been far more ambivalent. And while none of these groups has come out in support of Chechnya's bid for independence, this has been the firm stance taken by Konstantin Borovoi's Party of Economic Freedom. In their act of opposition to the war, some groups, meanwhile, have suffered serious internal splits and divisions. In the case of Russia's Choice, for example, the adopted line has subsequently led to the resignation of such prominent figures as Valentin Lednev, Vladimir Bauer and Oleg Boiko. And most damning of all was the hostile line taken by Foreign Minister Andrei Kozyrev, who openly accused his erstwhile allies of pursuing a frenzied form of 'extremism' which failed to understand the correlation between Russian democracy and the integrity and the authority of the state.

While the act of opposition to the war from the aforementioned political forces has been generally in line with Russian public opinion, much of the public, not to mention their political opponents, have perceived and portrayed the Westerners' opposition in the most hypocritical terms. It was, after all, Russia's Choice and Democratic Russia who were the strongest supporters of the creation of a powerful, almost absolute, form of presidential executive authority, and also supported the use of military action on the streets of Moscow in October 1993 which thus paved the way for the new constitutional arrangements. In this sense, then, they are clearly vulnerable to being tarnished with the brush of responsibility. Finally, and more specifically, Yegor Gaidar in particular has also found it hard to escape responsibility for his policies towards Chechnya while holding the post of acting Prime Minister – policies, for example, which witnessed a number of payments to the Chechen President, Dzhokhar Dudaev, which were subsequently used to purchase military hardware.

Arguably the only group from the Westerners' camp to have emerged from the conflict in an enhanced political position is the YABLoko organization under the leadership of Grigorii Yavlinskii.

The real underlying problem for all the Westerners in the aftermath of the Chechen conflict, however, is the extent to which the central focus of Russian political life has switched to the crucial issues of statehood, statism and patriotism. It is this that will ultimately cause the Westerners some degree of potential *long-term* harm, because it is a terrain that is clearly not suited to them and the overall objectives that they have traditionally sought to pursue. The association of their Western, 'alien' values with some kind of Russophobia is going to be very hard to uncouple, and this is certainly underpinned by an opinion poll at the end of December 1994 which indicated that only 13 per cent of Russian citizens now positively identified themselves with western, liberal values in contrast to 16 per cent who orientated themselves towards 'Soviet' values, and no less than 60 per cent whose affinity was with 'traditional Russian values'. And of the latter, the majority took this to mean *ethnic* Russian values over and above those of other ethnic groups who bore the status of Russian citizens.[12]

Perhaps the one and only (small) comfort that the Westerners could take from the Chechen conflict and its political impact was the knowledge that their opponents have likewise been split by their different attitudes to the war. Within the ranks of the 'communist movement', for example, Zyuganov's CPRF has been able to make a great deal of popular capital out of its opposition to the use of military force and its repeated claim that the actions of the executive authorities in Moscow might ultimately destroy the integrity of the Federation, rather than preserving it. The party's stance, however, has not done anything to endear it to other elements of the movement. For the likes of Viktor Anpilov's Russian Communist Workers' Party and a number of other communist organizations, for example, the Chechen secessionists should be openly supported in the war against Moscow as a means of inflicting a humiliating and potentially decisive defeat on the representatives of the 'bourgeois state authorities'.

As for the broad ranks of the Russophile camp, they too have found it impossible to agree on a common line. Leading the ranks of those who vehemently supported the actions of President Yeltsin and the military has been Vladimir Zhirinovsky's Liberal Democratic Party – a new-found support for Yeltsin that also included other policy initiatives in the realm of budgetary issues and the new proposed crackdown on organized crime in the country. Other prominent Russophile supporters, meanwhile, included Eduard Limonov, Aleksandr Nevzorov and Aleksandr Barkashov's neo-fascist Russian National Unity Movement. In the ranks of opponents of the war, however, were the equally prominent figures of Aleksandr Prokhanov and Sergei Baburin,[13] both of whom feared that the manner in which the Chechen problem was dealt with would ultimately harm the much broader aspirations of the Russophiles; in particular, their desire to see the reintegration of the republics of the former USSR under some kind of Russian control.[14]

Given the extent of the impact of the Chechen conflict following its outbreak in December 1994, one can certainly understand those commentators who argue that it may well be the most decisive event in Russian political life for many months, perhaps even years, to come. Certainly in terms of the immediate, foreseeable future there can be no doubt whatsoever that it will play a pivotal role (one way or another) in the parliamentary and presidential elections scheduled for the end of 1995 and the summer of 1996 respectively. If – as some leading political figures wish and others predict – these elections do not take place, then this, of course, will tell us a great deal about the contextual conditions of the hegemonic struggle and the potential destination of post-communist Russia (in a negative sense). If they do take place, then they should clarify a great deal about which of the orientations, and which of the combatants, are truly beginning to come out on top.

The elections should also confirm, one way or another, whether the country has reached the end of the Yeltsin era. Writing from the perspective of the beginning of 1995, it is clear that virtually all the major combatants would like to see this era come to a decisive end. Among most of the Westerners there is now an almost unanimous opinion that Yeltsin, just like Gorbachev before him, has become far more of a hindrance and a liability than an asset to their prospects.[15] As for the other major combatants, while there is undoubtedly some satisfaction that Yeltsin is more and more beginning to speak their political language, there is certainly no great willingness to embrace him openly. Yeltsin, then, is thus increasingly left to steer a course between a Scylla and a Charybdis of his own making. While he is being left 'a stranger amongst his own people', he must ponder the extent to which he can genuinely remain 'his own man among strangers'.[16] His comments to the French newspaper Le Figaro, that he regards *any* future President of Russia as the greatest danger for the country certainly does not bode well for the future.[17] Nor, for that matter, does his ever-increasing reliance on a personal security apparatus (led by Aleksandr Korzhakov) whose tentacles in the realm of policymaking are becoming greater by the day.

Can a definitive conclusion, then, be drawn at this stage in Russia's post-communist transition? I think not. It is one thing for the likes of Daniel Yergin and Thane Gustafson to paint images of Russia in 2010 and state categorically that they are convinced that a capitalist miracle [*chudo*] is inevitable, but I would suggest that this is nothing more than a flight of fancy on their part.[18] It is also about as likely as the image of Russia in 2042 as depicted several years ago by Vladimir Voinovich;[19] and at least the latter has the advantage of being meant as explicit satire. Indeed, given the track record of predictions by Sovietologists and Kremlinologists, it is somewhat surprising that Western observers are still willing to play this futuristic game. I can only suggest that with Russia's present and past appearing so unfathomable, there is some solace or compensation in claiming such a degree of certainty about the country's future.

In essence, then, what one can say from the current perspective is that Russia has barely begun to travel down that road that leads away from the old order. What I have attempted to do in this study has been to provide the reader with a general map of the different possible destinations on offer in this first phase of the country's journey. What the final destination will be remains an unanswered question. One can say for sure only that the road will be long, and there will be many twists and turns and not a few diversions, roadworks and maybe even dead ends as the journey progresses.

All in all, Vladimir Voinovich, in the words used as the epigraph to this chapter, has probably got it spot on. Something has been clarified in Russia, but a lot remains to be sorted out.[20] The struggle, in all its different meanings, continues.

Appendices

Appendix 1

Summary of Results of the December 1993 Elections to the State Duma

Party/Bloc	% of Party List Vote	No. of Seats on Party List	Single-party Constituencies
Russia's Choice	15.51	40	30
Liberal Dem. Party	22.92	59	5
Communist Party	12.40	32	16
Agrarian Party	7.99	21	12
YABLoko	7.86	20	3
Women of Russia	8.13	21	2
PRUA	6.73	18	1
DPR	5.52	14	1
RMDR	4.08	–	4
Civic Union	1.93	–	1
New Names	1.25	–	1
Constructive Ecology	0.76	–	–
Dignity & Charity	0.70	–	2
Against All	4.36	–	–
Spoiled Ballots	3.10	–	–
Independents	–	–	141
Postponed	–	–	6[*]
TOTAL	–	225	225

Source: Byulleten' Tsentral'noi izbiratel'noi kommissii Rossiiskoi Federatsii, no. 12, 1994, p. 67

N.B. The figures in column 1 exceed 100 due to the reconfiguration of the results of those parties and blocs which exceeded the 5 per cent threshold

[*] Only 444 seats (instead of 450) were contested in December. No elections took place in Chechnya, and the contests in 5 seats in Tatarstan were either invalidated or postponed.

Appendix 2

Candidates Elected to the State Duma in December 1993 in Single-member Constituencies

Electoral District	Constituency	No. of Candidates	Deputy Elected	Party Membership
001	Adygeiskii – Republic of Adygeya	6	Valentin Lednev	None
002	Baimakskii – Republic of Bashkortostan	5	Akhmetgali Galiev	None
003	Birskii – Republic of Bashkortostan	7	Ramil' Mirsaev	None
004	Kalininskii – Republic of Bashkortostan	4	Aleksandr Airnin	Party of Russian Unity and Accord
005	Kirovskii – Republic of Bashkortostan	7	Rais Asaev	Agrarian Party
006	Sterlitamakskii – Republic of Bashkortostan	10	Yurii Utkin	None
007	Tyumazinskii – Republic of Bashkortostan	6	Zifkat Saetgaliev	None
008	Buryatskii – Republic of Buryatiya	5	Nikolai Kondakeev	Social Justice Bloc of the Buryat Republic
009	Gorno-Altaiskii – Altai Republic	4	Mikhail Gnezdilov	None
010	Buinakskii – Republic of Dagestan	10	Gamid Gamidov	None
011	Makhachkalinskii – Republic of Dagestan	15	Magomed Tolboev	None

Electoral District	Constituency	No. of Candidates	Deputy Elected	Party Membership
012	Ingushskii – Republic of Ingushetiya	14	Aleksandra Momdzhyan	None
013	Kabardino-Balkarskii – Republic of Kabardino-Balkariya	9	Khachim Karmokov	None
014	Kalmytskii – Republic of Kalmykiya Khal'mg Tangch	8	Bembya Khulkhachiev	None
015	Karachaevo-Cherkeskii – Karachai-Cherkess Republic	6	Azret Akbaev	None
016	Karel'skii – Republic of Kareliya	3	Ivan Chukhin	Russia's Choice
017	Pechorskii – Komi Republic	3	Valerii Maksimov	None
018	Syktyvkarskii – Komi Republic	7	Nikolai Gen	Future of Russia – New Names
019	Mariiskii – Republic of Marii El	4	Anatolii Pozhev	Democratic Movement of 'Marii Ushem'
020	Mordovskii – Republic of Mordoviya	7	Vladimir Kartashov	Communist Party of the Russian Federation
021	Yakutskii – Republic of Sakha (Yakutiya)	6	Egor Zhirkov	None
022	Severo-Osetinskii – Republic of North Osetiya	14	Aleksandr Dzasokhov	None
023	Al'met'evskii – Republic of Tatarstan	2	Void	Void
024	Moskovskii – Republic of Tatarstan	4	Void	Void
025	Naberezhno-Chelninskii – Republic of Tatarstan	1	Void	Void
026	Nizhnekamskii – Republic of Tatarstan	2	Void	Void
027	Privolzhskii – Republic of Tatarstan	7	Void	Void
028	Tuvinskii – Republic of Tyva	4	Kara-Kys Arakchaa	None
029	Izhevskii – Republic of Udmurtiya	3	Aleksei Krasnykh	Party of Russian Unity and Accord
030	Udmurtskii – Republic of Udmurtiya	3	Mikhail Vasil'ev	None
031	Khakasskii – Republic of Khakasiya	2	Mikhail Mityukov	Russia's Choice
032	Republic of Chechnya	Void	Void	Void
033	Kanashskii – Republic of Chuvashiya	7	Valentin Agafonov	None

Electoral District	Constituency	No. of Candidates	Deputy Elected	Party Membership
034	Cheboksarskii – Republic of Chuvashiya	12	Nadezhda Bikalova	None
035	Barnaul'skii – Altai krai	5	Aleksei Sarychev	Russian Movement for Democratic Reforms
036	Biiskii – Altai krai	2	Pavel Efremov	Russia's Choice
037	Rubtsovskii – Altai krai	4	Vladimir Bessarabov	None
038	Slavgorodskii – Altai krai	2	Sergei Openyshev	Agrarian Party
039	Armavirskii – Krasnodar krai	10	Anatolii Dolgopolov	None
040	Kanevskii – Krasnodar krai	4	Anatolii Kochegura	None
041	Krasnodarskii – Krasnodar krai	12	Sergei Glotov	None
042	Novorossiiskii – Krasnodar krai	6	Nina Zatsepina	None
043	Prikubanskii – Krasnodar krai	7	Petr Kirii	Agrarian Party
044	Tikhoretskii – Krasnodar krai	8	Nadezhda Verveiko	None
045	Tuapsinskii – Krasnodar krai	7	Vadim Boiko	Democratic Party of Russia
046	Achinskii – Krasnoyarsk krai	3	Vasilii Zhurko	Liberal Democratic Party of Russia
047	Eniseiskii – Krasnoyarsk krai	7	Valerii Kolmakov	None
048	Kanskii – Krasnoyarsk krai	4	Anatolii Yaroshenko	Agrarian Party
049	Krasnoyarskii – Krasnoyarsk krai	6	Vladimir Tikhonov	None
050	Arsen'evskii – Primorskii krai	5	Valerii Nesterenko	None
051	Vladivostokskii – Primorskii krai	6	Mikhail Glubokovskii	YABLoko
052	Ussriiskii – Primorskii krai	5	Igor' Ustinov	None
053	Georgievskii – Stavropol' krai	6	Viktor Borodin	None
054	Kavminvodskii – Stavropol' krai	8	Vladimir Katrenko	None
055	Petrovskii – Stavropol' krai	3	Vasilii Moroz	Agrarian Party
056	Stavropol'skii – Stavropol' krai	7	Aleksandr Traspov	None
057	Komsomol'ski-na-Amure – Khabarovsk krai	4	Vladimir Baryshev	Russia's Choice
058	Khabarovskii – Khabarovsk krai	5	Valerii Podmasko	None
059	Blagoveshchenskii – Amur oblast'	3	Andrei Zakharov	None

Electoral District	Constituency	No. of Candidates	Deputy Elected	Party Membership
060	Arkhangel'skii – Arkhangel'sk oblast'	3	Sergei Shul'gin	Civic Union for Stability, Justice and Progress
061	Kotlasskii – Arkhangel'sk oblast'	2	Aleksandr Piskunov	None
062	Astrakhanskii – Astrakhan oblast'	10	Vladislav Vinogradov	None
063	Belgorodskii – Belgorod oblast'	8	Viktor Berestovoi	None
064	Novooskol'skii – Belgorod oblast'	7	Boris Zamai	None
065	Bryanskii – Bryansk oblast'	5	Anatolii Vorontsov	Agrarian Party
066	Pochepskii – Bryansk oblast'	7	Oleg Shenkarev	Communist Party of the Russian Federation
067	Vladimirskii – Vladimir oblast'	6	Gennadii Churkin	Agrarian Party
068	Sudogodskii – Vladimir oblast'	4	Evgenii Buchenkov	Communist Party of the Russian Federation
069	Volzhskii – Volgograd oblast'	11	Valerii Nikitin	None
070	Krasnoarmeiskii – Volgograd oblast'	6	Vladimir Kosykh	None
071	Mikhailovskii – Volgograd oblast'	3	Vladimir Plotnikov	None
072	Tsentral'nyi – Volgograd oblast'	11	Igor' Lukashov	Social Democratic Party of the Russian Federation
073	Vologodskii – Vologda oblast'	8	Tamara Leta	Agrarian Party
074	Cherepovetskii – Vologda oblast'	4	Vasilii Kovalev	None
075	Anninskii – Voronezh oblast'	11	Nikolai Parinov	None
076	Levoberezhnyi – Voronezh oblast'	9	Viktor Davydkin	Russia's Choice
077	Pavlovskii – Voronezh oblast'	4	Petr Matyashev	None
078	Pravoberezhnyi – Voronezh oblast'	11	Igor' Murav'ev	All-Russian Union 'Renewal'
079	Ivanovskii – Ivanovo oblast'	5	Viktor Ze enkin	Russia's Choice
080	Kineshemskii – Ivanovo oblast'	4	Sergei Zenkin	None
081	Angarskii – Irkutsk oblast'	3	Viktor Mashinskii	None
082	Bratskii – Irkutsk oblast'	5	Vitalii Shuba	None

Electoral District	Constituency	No. of Candidates	Deputy Elected	Party Membership
083	Irkutskii – Irkutsk oblast'	6	Yurii Ten	Civic Union for Stability, Justice and Progress
084	Tulunskii – Irkutsk oblast'	4	Anatolii Turusin	Agrarian Party
085	Kaliningradskii – Kaliningrad oblast'	6	Yurii Voevoda	Russian Movement for Democratic Reforms
086	Dzerzhinskii – Kaluga oblast'	11	Pavel Burdukov	Agrarian Party
087	Kaluzhskii – Kaluga oblast'	14	Ella Pamfilova	Russia's Choice
088	Kamchatskii – Kamchatka oblast'	6	Aivars Lezdin'sh	None
089	Anzhero-Sudzhenskii – Kemerovo oblast'	3	Galina Parshentseva	None
090	Kemerovskii – Kemerovo oblast'	7	Sergei Burkov	None
091	Novokuznetskii – Kemerovo oblast'	6	Viktor Medikov	None
092	Prokop'evskii – Kemerovo oblast'	6	Nina Volkova	None
093	Kirovskii – Kirov oblast'	5	Mikhail Vakulenko	Liberal Democratic Party of Russia
094	Sovetskii – Kirov oblast'	5	Egor Agafonov	None
095	Kostromskoi – Kostroma oblast'	5	Andrian Puzanovskii	Dignity and Charity Movement
096	Vostochnyi – Kurgan oblast'	6	Nikolai Bezborodov	None
097	Zapadnyi – Kurgan oblast'	5	Gennadii Kalistratov	None
098	Kurskii – Kursk oblast'	12	Aleksandr Mikhailov	Communist Party of the Russian Federation
099	L'govskii – Kursk oblast'	8	Aleksandr Potapenko	Communist Party of the Russian Federation
100	Volkhovskii – Leningrad oblast'	4	Yurii Sokolov	None
101	Vsevolozhskii – Leningrad oblast'	6	Evgenii Fedorov	Russian Movement for Democratic Reforms
102	Eletskii – Lipetsk oblast'	12	Viktor Repkin	None
103	Lipetskii – Lipetsk oblast'	9	Tamara Chepasova	Women of Russia
104	Magadanskii – Magadan oblast'	6	Evgenii Kokorev	None

Electoral District	Constituency	No. of Candidates	Deputy Elected	Party Membership
105	Dmitrovskii – Moscow oblast'	14	Artur Murav'ev	None
106	Istrinskii – Moscow oblast'	5	Vladimir Gaboev	Democratic Russia
107	Kolomenskii – Moscow oblast'	9	Sergei Skorochkin	None
108	Lyuberetskii – Moscow oblast'	9	Anatolii Gus'kov	Russian Party of Free Labour
109	Mytishchinskii – Moscow oblast'	17	Andrei Azderdzis	None
110	Noginskii – Moscow oblast'	12	Nikolai Stolyarov	None
111	Odintsovskii – Moscow oblast'	9	Vladimir Lukin	YABLoko
112	Orekhovo-Zuevskii – Moscow oblast'	10	Vladimir Kvasov	None
113	Podol'skii – Moscow oblast'	10	Grigorii Bondarev	Republican Party of the Russian Federation
114	Shchelkovskii – Moscow oblast'	7	Vladimir Zhirinovsky	Liberal Democratic Party of Russia
115	Monchegorskii – Murmarsk oblast'	6	Vladimir Manannikov	Russia's Choice
116	Murmanskii – Murmansk oblast'	10	Andrei Kozyrev	Russia's Choice
117	Avtozavodskii – Nizhny Novgorod oblast'	13	Aleksandr Tsapin	None
118	Arzamasskii – Nizhny Novgorod oblast'	9	Sergei Voronov	None
119	Dzerzhinskii – Nizhny Novgorod oblast'	8	Mikhail Seslavinskii	None
120	Kanavinskii – Nizhny Novgorod oblast'	10	Vedim Bulavinov	None
121	Semenovskii – Nizhny Novgorod oblast'	6	Tat'yena Chertoritskaya	None
122	Sergachskii – Nizhny Novgorod oblast'	5	Evgenii Bushmin	None
123	Novgorodskii – Novgorod oblast'	4	Oleg Ochin	Party of Russian Unity and Accord
124	Barabinskii – Novosibirsk oblast'	3	Nikolai Kharitonov	Agrarian Party
125	Zavodskoi – Novosibirsk oblast'	9	Ivan Anichkin	Dignity and Charity Movement
126	Zael'tsovskii – Novosibirsk oblast'	10	Vasilii Lipitskii	People's Party of Free Russia
127	Iskitimskii – Novosibirsk oblast'	9	Ivan Starikov	Russia's Choice
128	Bol'sherechenskii – Omsk oblast'	7	Oleg Zharov	None
129	Omskii – Omsk oblast'	3	Viktor Lotkov	None
130	Tsentral'nyi – Omsk oblast'	7	Sergei Baburin	Russian All-Peoples Union

Electoral District	Constituency	No. of Candidates	Deputy Elected	Party Membership
131	Buzlukskii – Orenburg oblast'	6	Aleksei Chernyshev	Agrarian Party
132	Orenburgskii – Orenburg oblast'	5	Tamara Zlotnikova	YABLoko
133	Orskii – Orenburg oblast'	7	Vladimir Volkov	Communist Party of the Russian Federation
134	Orlovskii – Orlov oblast'	9	Aleksandr Voropaev	Party of Russian Unity and Accord
135	Zheleznodorozhnyi – Penza oblast'	10	Valerii Goryachev	Republican Party of the Russian Federation
136	Pervomaiskii – Penza oblast'	10	Viktor Ilyukhin	Communist Party of the Russian Federation
137	Bereznikovskii – Perm oblast'	4	Vladimir Kraptsov	None
138	Kungurskii – Perm oblast'	5	Mikhail Putilov	Civic Union for Stability, Justice and Progress
139	Leninskii – Perm oblast'	7	Vladimir Zelenin	Communist Party of the Russian Federation
140	Sverdlovskii – Perm oblast'	5	Viktor Pokhmelkin	Russia's Choice
141	Pskovskii – Pskov oblast'	7	Evgenii Mikhailov	Liberal Democratic Party of Russia
142	Volgodonskii – Rostov oblast'	5	Sergei Ponomarev	Socialist Party of Workers
143	Kamenskii – Rostov oblast'	5	Boris Danchenko	None
144	Rostovskii-Pervomaiskii – Rostov oblast'	10	Alla Amelina	None
145	Rostovskii-Sovetskii – Rostov oblast'	9	Igor' Bratishchev	Communist Party of the Russian Federation
146	Taganrogskii – Rostov oblast'	6	Yurii Rodionov	None
147	Shakhtinskii – Rostov oblast'	4	Ivan Bespalov	Communist Party of the Russian Federation

Electoral District	Constituency	No. of Candidates	Deputy Elected	Party Membership
148	Ryazanskii – Ryazan oblast'	8	Konstantin Laikam	Civic Union for Stability, Justice and Progress
149	Shilovskii – Ryazan oblast'	6	Sergei En'kov	Agrarian Party
150	Novokuibyshevskii – Samara oblast'	7	Galina Gusarova	Women of Russia
151	Promyshlennyi – Samara oblast'	12	Nikolai Chukanov	None
152	Samarskii – Samara oblast'	10	Lyubov' Rozhkova	Communist Party of the Russian Federation
153	Syzranskii – Samara oblast'	6	Evgenii Gusarov	None
154	Tol'yattinskii – Samara oblast'	5	Vyacheslav Smirnov	Russian Movement for Democratic Reforms
155	Balakovskii – Saratov oblast'	5	Aleksandr Sergeenkov	Democratic Russia
156	Balashovskii – Saratov oblast'	3	Andrei Dorovskikh	Liberal Democratic Party of Russia
157	Saratovskii – Saratov oblast'	9	Aratolii Gordeev	Communist Party of the Russian Federation
158	Engel'sskii – Saratov oblast'	8	Nikolai Lysenko	National Republican Party of Russia
159	Sakhalinskii – Sakhalin oblast'	4	Boris Tretyak	None
160	Artemovskii – Sverdlovsk oblast'	5	Tamara Tokareva	Peasants Party of Russia
161	Verkh-Isetskii – Sverdlovsk oblast'	7	Larisa Mishustina	Russia's Choice
162	Kamensk-Ural'skii – Sverdlovsk oblast'	3	Sergei Mikheev	None
163	Nizhne-Tagil'skii – Sverdlovsk oblast'	4	Artur Veer	None
164	Ordzhonikidzevskii – Sverdlovsk oblast'	5	Yurii Brusnitsyn	None
165	Pervoural'skii – Sverdlovsk oblast'	5	Leonid Nekrasov	Party of Economic Freedom
166	Serovskii – Sverdlovsk oblast'	2	Andrei Selivanov	None
167	Vyazemskii – Smolensk oblast'	5	Vyacheslav Balalaev	Agrarian Party
168	Smolenskii – Smolensk oblast'	7	Aratolii Luk'yanov	Communist Party of the Russian Federation

Electoral District	Constituency	No. of Candidates	Deputy Elected	Party Membership
169	Michurinskii – Tambov oblast'	8	Aleksei Ponomarev	Communist Party of the Russian Federation
170	Tambovskii – Tambov oblast'	16	Tamara Pletneva	Communist Party of the Russian Federation
171	Bezhetskii – Tver oblast'	5	Vladimir Bayunov	Communist Party of the Russian Federation
172	Tverskoi – Tver oblast'	9	Tat'yana Astrakhankina	Communist Party of the Russian Federation
173	Tomskii Gorodskii – Tomsk oblast'	6	Vladimir Bauer	Russia's Choice
174	Tomskii Sel'skii – Tomsk oblast'	6	Stepan Sulakshin	Republican Party of the Russian Federation
175	Novomoskovskii – Tula oblast'	13	Vladimir Vasilev	None
176	Tul'skii – Tula oblast'	5	Eduard Pashchenko	Russia's Choice
177	Shchekinskii – Tula oblast'	10	Elena Bogdanova	Agrarian Party
178	Ishimskii – Tyumen oblast'	3	Stanislav Shkuro	None
179	Tyumenskii – Tyumen oblast'	10	Aleksandr Trushnikov	None
180	Leninskii – Ul'yanovsk oblast'	4	Valerii Sychev	None
181	Zasviyazhskii – Ul'yanovsk oblast'	6	Lyudmila Zhadanova	None
182	Zlatoustovskii – Chelyabinsk oblast'	6	Vladimir Grigoriadi	None
183	Kalininskii – Chelyabinsk oblast'	11	Vladimir Golovlev	Russia's Choice
184	Kyshtymskii – Chelyabinsk oblast'	6	Aleksandr Kushnar'	Russia's Choice
185	Magnitogorskii – Chelyabinsk oblast'	4	Aleksandr Pochinok	Russia's Choice
186	Sovetskii – Chelyabinsk oblast'	5	Vladimir Utkin	None
187	Borzinskii – Chita oblast'	5	Vladimir Surenkov	None
188	Chitinskii – Chita oblast'	6	Sergei Markedonov	None
189	Kirovskii – Yaroslavl oblast'	7	Evgeniya Tmikovskaya	None
190	Rybinskii – Yaroslavl oblast'	9	Anatolii Greshnevikov	None

Electoral District	Constituency	No. of Candidates	Deputy Elected	Party Membership
191	Babushkinskii – City of Moscow	10	Yulii Nisnevich	Democratic Russia
192	Varshavskii – City of Moscow	11	Sergei Kovalev	Russia's Choice
193	Zapadnyi – City of Moscow	11	Georgii Zadonskii	Democratic Russia
194	Kashirskii – City of Moscow	10	Irina Khakamada	Party of Economic Freedom
195	Medvedkovskii – City of Moscow	9	Viktor Mironov	None
196	Nagatinskii – City of Moscow	11	Andrei Volkov	None
197	Perovskii – City of Moscow	13	Aleksandr Osovtsov	Russia's Choice
198	Preobrazhenskii – City of Moscow	8	Aleksandr Zhukov	Dignity and Charity Movement
199	Severnyi – City of Moscow	13	Alla Gerber	Russia's Choice
200	Severo-Zapadnyi – City of Moscow	9	Yurii Vlasov	None
201	Universitetskii – City of Moscow	13	Aleksandr Braginskii	Russian Movement for Democratic Reforms
202	Tsentral'nyi – City of Moscow	16	Artem Tarasov	None
203	Sheremet'evskii – City of Moscow	11	Andrei Makarov	Russia's Choice
204	Yugo-Zapadnyi – City of Moscow	9	Pavel Medvedev	None
205	Yugo-Vostochnyi – City of Moscow	9	Boris Fedorov	Russia's Choice
206	Zapadnyi – City of St Petersburg	10	Vitalii Savitskii	Russian Christian Democratic Union – New Democracy
207	Severnyi – City of St Petersburg	20	Mikhail Kiselev	None
208	Severo-Vostochnyi – City of St Petersburg	11	Yulii Rybakov	Free Democratic Party of Russia
209	Severo-Zapadnyi – City of St Petersburg	12	Aleksei Aleksandrov	Russia's Choice
210	Tsentral'nyi – City of St Petersburg	7	Aleksandr Nevzorov	Russian National Council
211	Yuzhnyi – City of St Petersburg	9	Aleksandr Egorov	None
212	Yugo-Vostochnyi – City of St Petersburg	9	Sergei Popov	Russia's Choice
213	Yugo-Zapadnyi – City of St Petersburg	10	Mark Goryachev	Civic Union for Stability, Justice and Progress
214	Birobidzhanskii – Jewish autonomous oblast'	3	Anatolii Biryukov	Agrarian Party

Electoral District	Constituency	No. of Candidates	Deputy Elected	Party Membership
215	Aginskii Buryatskii – Aga Buryat auto. okrug	4	Bair Zhamsuev	None
216	Komi-Permyatskii – Komi-Permyak auto. okrug	6	Anna Vlasova	Women of Russia
217	Koryakskii – Koryak autonomous okrug	6	Mikhail Popov	None
218	Nenetskii – Nenets autonomous okrug	7	Artur Chilingarov	All-Russian Union 'Renewal'
219	Taimyrskii – Taimyr autonomous okrug	3	Aleksandr Vasil'ev	None
220	Ust'-Ordynskii – Ust'-Orda Buryat auto. okrug	2	Sergei Boskholov	None
221	Nizhnevartovskii – Khanty-Mansii auto. okrug	4	Vladimir Medvedev	None
222	Khanty-Mansiiskii – Khanty-Mansii auto. okrug	5	Eremei Aipin	Russia's Choice
223	Chukotskii – Chukchi autonomous okrug	5	Tat'yana Nesterenko	None
224	Evenkiiskii – Evenk autonomous okrug	9	Viktor Gayul'skii	None
225	Yamalo-Nenetskii – Yamal-Nenets auto. okrug	7	Vladimir Goman	None

Source: Rossiiskaya gazeta, 30 November 1993, pp. 4–12; 28 December 1993, pp. 2–6

Appendix 3

Regional Distribution of the Proportional (Party List) Votes in the December 1993 Elections to the State Duma

Key to Electoral Blocs and Parties

APR	Agrarian Party of Russia
New Names	Future of Russia–New Names
RC	Russia's Choice
CU	Civic Union
DPR	Democratic Party of Russia
D&C	Dignity & Charity
WR	Women of Russia
Cedar	Constructive Ecology Movement
CPRF	Communist Party of the RF
LDPR	Liberal Democratic Party of Russia
PRUA	Party of Russian Unity & Accord
RMDR	Russian Movement for Democratic Reform
YBL	Yavlinskii, Boldyrev, Lukin Bloc (YABLoko)

No.	Federal Territory	Turnout (%)	Votes for Electoral Blocs and Parties (%)													Votes Against (%)	Null & Void
			APR	New Names	RC	CU	DPR	D&C	WR	Cedar	CPRF	LDPR	PRUA	RMDR	YBL		
1	Rep. of Adygeya	61.73	5.49	1.48	8.15	1.43	5.24	0.54	7.13	0.55	28.87	18.11	9.96	2.18	10.88	2.20	5.06
2	Rep. of Bashkortostan	63.73	24.76	1.46	8.51	2.62	4.45	0.87	9.23	0.97	15.08	12.56	13.06	2.54	3.88	4.77	9.77
3	Rep. of Buryatiya	57.50	5.47	1.63	13.24	2.23	4.79	1.07	11.96	0.85	15.58	17.32	17.39	2.71	5.76	4.83	0.00
4	Altai Republic	65.59	8.74	1.62	9.31	1.26	4.83	0.66	12.47	1.00	11.02	17.04	26.55	2.34	1.62	4.84	6.17
5	Rep. of Dagestan	52.18	18.36	0.41	2.03	3.24	4.32	0.61	2.34	0.37	54.00	3.38	6.82	0.83	3.27	2.15	6.65
6	Rep. of Ingushetiya	45.42	0.69	0.39	1.65	4.17	71.07	0.56	2.76	0.49	6.44	3.20	4.90	1.57	2.11	8.60	3.22
7	Kabardino-Balkariya	61.14	12.87	0.65	6.62	1.77	5.32	0.59	4.62	0.62	20.08	8.79	31.53	2.40	4.24	1.88	1.45
8	Rep. of Kalmykiya	58.03	11.63	1.03	10.24	6.27	8.13	0.80	10.51	0.89	14.18	20.30	8.91	2.32	4.78	5.91	9.36
9	Karachai-Cherkess.	71.91	10.80	1.97	4.30	1.08	4.61	0.81	4.41	0.38	38.58	20.19	7.54	1.93	3.40	1.86	4.81
10	Rep. of Kareliya	55.11	2.60	1.42	21.80	1.95	5.43	0.72	12.69	0.60	7.32	21.09	9.05	4.12	11.21	4.61	13.88
11	Komi Republic	47.32	5.57	1.72	21.83	2.25	5.26	0.93	12.18	0.61	7.05	24.31	7.22	3.97	7.09	4.69	7.64
12	Rep. of Marii-El	57.05	14.17	1.65	11.42	1.76	6.62	1.34	10.32	1.64	12.55	24.47	6.49	3.07	4.51	5.96	6.19
13	Rep. of Mordoviya	62.13	12.46	0.93	7.65	1.59	4.89	0.54	6.14	0.62	18.74	35.34	4.03	1.68	5.39	2.46	2.47
14	Sakha (Yakutiya)	55.81	10.51	3.45	13.36	4.48	5.23	0.94	11.44	1.05	10.19	15.45	13.01	3.88	7.04	7.57	10.78
15	Rep. of North Osetiya	59.79	3.94	2.86	7.81	1.75	7.03	1.23	5.94	0.70	36.06	17.47	5.99	4.18	5.04	3.61	5.07
16	Rep. of Tatarstan	12.68	2.12	1.20	22.40	3.33	5.42	0.93	7.66	0.87	9.38	22.00	8.54	4.59	11.55	2.77	9.96
17	Rep. of Tyva	53.87	5.56	1.09	6.15	2.78	2.92	1.51	9.00	0.63	8.40	9.73	48.38	1.72	2.11	15.73	5.01
18	Rep. of Udmurtiya	44.25	11.07	1.92	16.19	1.88	5.34	1.11	14.70	1.01	11.14	17.59	7.00	2.87	8.18	4.48	9.95
19	Rep. of Khakasiya	45.63	6.70	2.23	15.35	5.10	5.56	0.65	10.42	0.74	10.89	27.45	6.55	4.51	3.85	5.19	8.59
20	Rep. of Chechnya	0.00	0.00	0.00	0.00	0.00	0.00	0.00	0.00	0.00	0.00	0.00	0.00	0.00	0.00	0.00	0.00
21	Rep. of Chuvashiya	62.55	12.75	2.08	8.90	1.86	9.11	0.94	8.50	0.77	19.73	22.53	4.83	4.57	3.43	6.46	4.49
22	Altai Krai	54.54	23.40	1.12	10.81	1.13	4.71	0.47	8.58	0.61	9.86	27.75	5.47	2.90	3.19	4.43	8.01
23	Krasnodar Krai	49.44	7.59	1.11	11.90	1.28	5.65	0.71	8.57	0.62	16.82	25.48	7.51	3.25	9.51	2.65	0.00

No.	Federal Territory	Turnout (%)	APR	New Names	RC	CU	DPR	D&C	WR	Cedar	CPRF	LDPR	PRUA	RMDR	YBL	Votes Against (%)	Null & Void
24	Krasnoyarsk Krai	51.75	7.84	1.31	13.56	1.76	4.98	1.09	9.28	0.64	9.06	31.17	6.56	5.04	7.29	4.18	0.00
25	Primorskii Krai	50.46	2.52	1.83	14.09	2.21	7.32	0.99	15.27	1.30	8.74	23.34	8.18	5.63	8.58	7.07	0.93
26	Stavropol' Krai	63.83	11.48	0.91	9.32	1.17	3.64	0.51	6.93	0.53	12.35	38.53	6.19	3.23	5.13	2.76	6.75
27	Khabarovsk Krai	24.09	1.83	2.18	19.09	2.22	6.07	1.20	12.91	1.92	12.07	19.90	7.53	5.82	7.27	7.45	8.56
28	Amur Oblast'	56.78	9.78	2.13	12.51	2.94	5.01	0.85	10.31	1.02	16.23	24.90	7.08	2.55	4.68	4.53	1.03
29	Arkhangelsk Oblast'	26.57	6.39	1.21	21.83	3.11	5.74	0.55	12.85	0.61	6.44	22.22	6.63	4.21	8.20	4.64	0.00
30	Astrakhan Oblast'	51.42	11.90	2.40	13.73	1.65	5.36	0.90	9.99	0.84	16.61	17.25	8.16	3.27	7.92	4.15	7.73
31	Belgorod Oblast'	64.11	10.23	0.84	10.02	1.41	4.64	0.71	7.12	0.59	15.90	37.07	4.70	2.20	4.57	5.75	5.30
32	Bryansk Oblast'	65.89	10.80	1.38	12.57	1.24	5.70	0.72	7.66	0.75	20.18	27.23	4.86	2.46	4.46	2.53	0.00
33	Vladimir Oblast'	60.47	7.36	1.25	16.92	1.66	5.47	0.67	9.65	0.58	9.55	29.49	6.42	3.27	7.73	4.03	7.52
34	Volgograd Oblast'	55.74	10.90	0.89	11.86	1.54	5.19	0.63	7.59	0.55	14.42	27.67	5.84	3.38	9.53	2.85	7.17
35	Vologda Oblast'	58.23	15.21	1.21	16.51	1.53	4.36	0.61	9.59	0.58	5.19	29.66	5.18	4.53	5.84	3.85	6.05
36	Voronezh Oblast'	59.53	11.99	0.77	11.91	1.39	7.23	0.50	5.96	0.74	14.54	30.63	4.02	2.47	7.84	3.01	5.96
37	Ivanovo Oblast'	57.77	6.82	1.36	16.60	5.64	5.07	0.94	8.85	0.64	8.67	28.24	7.16	3.18	6.82	4.65	7.87
38	Irkutsk Oblast'	41.97	4.95	1.75	16.85	2.35	6.13	0.86	13.24	0.94	9.50	21.48	8.88	6.37	6.71	5.18	0.00
39	Kaliningrad Oblast'	59.91	3.03	1.09	19.96	1.75	7.58	0.53	7.98	0.64	10.40	29.96	5.21	3.94	7.94	4.38	1.90
40	Kaluga Oblast'	63.63	10.13	1.14	16.58	1.95	5.36	0.56	6.80	0.65	14.31	28.06	4.62	2.87	6.97	3.34	9.45
41	Kamchatka Oblast'	42.16	1.13	1.99	15.51	1.74	6.40	0.83	8.21	1.57	5.05	27.16	8.46	4.33	17.61	6.17	2.98
42	Kemerovo Oblast'	44.27	5.61	1.22	13.74	1.64	7.45	0.70	10.65	0.98	9.57	29.42	5.71	6.47	6.83	4.68	9.84
43	Kirov Oblast'	57.93	15.27	1.22	12.48	1.93	5.27	0.96	9.96	0.70	8.74	27.53	5.34	3.06	7.54	4.30	7.97
44	Kostroma Oblast'	55.80	11.89	1.58	14.59	1.66	5.70	1.34	10.21	0.59	10.01	26.12	6.65	2.80	6.87	0.00	0.00
45	Kurgan Oblast'	61.23	11.39	1.57	11.60	1.73	7.35	0.75	15.53	0.98	12.62	23.72	5.58	3.18	4.00	14.83	8.37
46	Kursk Oblast'	64.67	11.46	1.26	10.64	1.10	4.41	0.48	5.02	0.60	20.03	33.48	4.11	2.61	4.79	3.12	5.84

Votes for Electoral Blocs and Parties (%)

No.	Federal Territory	Turnout (%)	Votes for Electoral Blocs and Parties (%)														Votes Against (%)	Null & Void
			APR	New Names	RC	CU	DPR	D&C	WR	Cedar	CPRF	LDPR	PRUA	RMDR	YBL		
47	Leningrad Oblast'	52.40	3.97	1.24	16.10	1.85	4.46	0.77	9.39	0.61	8.55	30.04	5.29	4.36	3.38	4.29	7.39
48	Lipetsk Oblast'	59.94	12.24	0.95	12.93	1.87	5.09	0.49	6.84	0.71	14.27	31.70	4.69	2.32	5.89	3.13	7.82
49	Magadan Oblast'	44.00	1.11	1.64	14.39	2.19	7.31	0.61	9.54	0.63	5.99	29.21	5.81	5.11	16.45	5.83	0.00
50	Moscow Oblast'	55.38	3.99	1.05	19.82	1.99	5.92	0.64	6.69	0.80	10.82	26.64	7.20	4.70	9.75	4.53	8.51
51	Murmansk Oblast'	62.88	1.30	1.50	23.47	2.37	6.97	0.66	7.82	0.85	5.67	24.26	6.44	4.43	14.25	4.88	3.98
52	Nizhny Novgorod Ob.	48.13	9.11	1.69	13.96	3.20	7.08	0.80	9.73	0.70	11.58	19.91	5.65	4.36	12.23	4.60	11.55
53	Novgorod Oblast'	57.91	6.91	1.13	13.21	2.41	6.14	0.78	9.52	0.62	9.25	29.60	10.08	2.74	7.61	3.68	6.04
54	Novosibirsk Oblast'	50.91	8.69	1.31	12.06	1.86	7.25	0.76	7.78	0.67	11.44	25.64	5.61	4.70	12.23	7.05	7.99
55	Omsk Oblast'	54.73	8.53	2.17	16.95	2.32	6.30	0.90	10.72	0.95	13.93	21.19	5.42	5.77	4.85	7.86	5.87
56	Orenburg Oblast'	55.96	17.79	1.21	13.16	2.13	5.82	0.61	7.82	0.64	13.20	22.55	5.59	3.54	5.94	4.26	8.20
57	Orlov Oblast'	65.77	7.03	0.87	9.58	1.23	5.48	0.51	6.04	0.63	25.69	31.80	4.69	2.31	4.13	3.58	4.63
58	Penza Oblast'	62.23	10.40	1.01	8.56	1.39	4.71	0.55	7.16	0.52	19.49	32.56	4.69	1.99	6.95	9.74	7.52
59	Perm Oblast'	45.27	4.86	1.91	27.12	2.47	5.00	0.84	12.24	0.83	6.91	14.81	9.85	4.92	8.24	3.73	6.38
60	Pskov Oblast'	68.26	8.94	1.21	10.13	1.04	4.06	0.67	8.23	0.56	9.50	43.01	4.88	2.15	5.62	3.04	3.73
61	Rostov Oblast'	55.70	7.52	1.03	12.30	1.30	6.24	0.69	8.26	0.65	17.31	22.28	12.11	2.86	7.44	2.83	6.49
62	Ryazan Oblast'	66.19	10.33	1.09	12.01	2.04	7.35	1.04	7.43	0.74	14.25	30.84	4.98	2.23	5.68	3.57	4.33
63	Samara Oblast'	48.64	6.33	1.77	16.26	1.77	6.74	0.82	10.09	0.85	16.44	19.67	5.74	4.77	8.75	4.13	0.00
64	Saratov Oblast'	63.01	7.64	1.01	12.30	2.72	6.45	0.57	9.90	0.69	15.28	26.63	5.68	2.53	8.59	3.48	13.48
65	Sakhalin Oblast'	49.05	1.43	1.69	9.60	2.71	6.55	0.73	10.43	0.88	8.91	36.86	8.35	4.24	7.62	5.34	7.12
66	Sverdlovsk Oblast'	49.42	3.97	1.84	25.20	2.17	5.51	0.84	8.38	1.20	5.79	17.72	9.81	9.40	8.17	5.56	7.27
67	Smolensk Oblast'	34.49	13.05	1.34	11.39	1.67	5.74	0.48	6.43	0.49	16.15	32.63	4.09	1.84	4.69	2.77	0.00
68	Tambov Oblast'	63.99	9.83	1.20	9.27	1.24	5.86	0.82	6.34	0.61	16.86	35.32	5.19	2.14	5.32	3.40	5.04
69	Tver Oblast'	63.95	13.87	1.06	14.13	1.66	7.71	0.59	7.72	0.55	12.46	25.48	5.65	3.09	6.04	1.29	2.04

No.	Federal Territory	Turnout (%)	Votes for Electoral Blocs and Parties (%)														Votes Against (%)	Null & Void
			APR	New Names	RC	CU	DFR	D&C	WR	Cedar	CPRF	LDPR	PRUA	RMDR	YBL		
70	Tomsk Oblast'	46.00	4.49	1.53	22.06	1.75	5.58	0.95	8.86	0.85	10.05	21.90	5.01	5.42	11.81	4.75	8.24
71	Tula Oblast'	60.89	6.56	1.55	14.69	1.66	5.56	0.77	8.24	0.72	12.00	30.35	6.32	2.93	8.66	3.87	6.45
72	Tyumen Oblast'	48.23	10.57	1.68	13.44	2.14	6.34	0.95	14.77	0.77	11.03	21.03	6.72	4.63	5.90	5.71	0.00
73	Ul'yanovsk Oblast'	55.11	13.98	1.17	12.23	1.65	5.52	0.69	8.04	0.69	17.50	24.57	6.17	3.00	4.78	5.41	7.78
74	Chelyabinsk Oblast'	51.67	4.06	1.47	23.58	2.61	4.69	0.76	8.52	2.46	7.49	20.38	6.77	5.84	11.34	4.19	8.93
75	Chita Oblast'	45.54	8.40	2.01	10.92	2.64	7.61	1.37	9.96	0.88	11.54	30.49	6.72	2.97	4.50	5.23	0.00
76	Yaroslavl' Oblast'	59.62	7.51	2.00	22.31	2.46	5.72	0.81	11.01	0.75	8.14	21.66	6.29	4.01	7.34	4.81	6.73
77	City of Moscow	51.57	1.43	0.77	34.73	2.23	5.56	0.56	4.35	0.75	11.03	12.82	6.48	7.20	12.08	3.58	5.81
78	City of St Petersburg	53.03	0.89	0.61	26.99	1.82	3.98	0.46	5.04	0.54	7.69	18.02	3.74	9.03	21.20	3.69	0.00
79	Jewish Auto. Oblast'	48.89	5.01	2.03	15.38	2.05	5.92	1.27	14.92	1.33	12.26	24.96	6.41	3.60	4.86	9.08	7.65
80	Aga Buryat A Okrug	63.30	21.49	1.69	9.50	2.09	5.65	1.08	9.02	0.46	9.75	14.38	19.22	1.66	4.00	7.83	0.00
81	Komi-Permyak AO	56.36	12.22	2.46	17.68	2.91	5.24	1.43	13.52	0.94	6.76	19.38	11.33	2.96	3.16	8.24	7.78
82	Koryak Auto. Okrug	56.12	1.50	1.93	14.88	2.54	7.81	0.90	12.51	1.09	7.30	24.07	9.58	3.98	11.92	8.57	0.00
83	Nenets Auto. Okrug	60.64	3.19	1.84	19.84	8.24	7.36	1.18	10.88	0.88	6.48	19.15	9.62	4.70	6.65	8.48	5.10
84	Taimyr Auto. Okrug	58.67	1.04	2.09	27.99	1.54	6.58	0.82	9.64	0.84	4.67	17.37	13.46	6.09	7.85	7.43	6.30
85	Ust-Orda Buryat AO	69.31	25.28	1.55	10.02	1.17	3.58	0.51	12.34	0.77	11.86	14.35	13.25	3.17	2.14	4.20	7.39
86	Khanty-Mansii AO	39.13	1.04	1.44	23.66	1.83	6.37	0.65	12.20	0.82	4.63	21.25	9.52	8.37	8.24	5.49	0.00
87	Chukchi Auto. Okrug	53.54	0.97	2.18	14.40	2.25	8.73	0.80	11.42	0.89	6.60	23.32	9.49	6.72	12.25	6.87	5.25
88	Evenk Auto. Okrug	60.53	3.58	1.55	15.36	1.72	7.32	0.90	17.39	1.07	7.45	20.94	10.48	4.29	7.94	5.59	4.41
89	Yamalo-Nenets AO	47.21	1.14	2.01	19.37	2.25	6.69	0.69	19.12	0.88	3.99	19.57	7.83	7.34	9.11	5.16	4.39

Sources: Byulleten' Tsentral'noi izbiratel'noi kommissii Rossiiskoi Federatsii, no. 12, 1994, pp.52–66; Organisational Department of the Office of the Presidential Administration and the Regional Affairs Department of the Government of the Russian Federation. The author would like to acknowledge the assistance of Hugh Jenkins, Stephen White and Richard Sakwa for their help in acquiring this material.

Map A3   Winning Parties (on the Party List) in the December 1993 elections to the State Duma in the Republics and Regions of the Russian Federation

Key to numbered regions

1 Leningrad Oblast'	11 Komi-Permyak AOkrug	21 Chelyabinsk
2 Tula	12 Krasnodar Krai	22 Ust-Orda Buryat AOkrug
3 Moscow	13 Adygeya	23 Aga Buryat AOkrug
4 Vladimir	14 Kalmykiya	24 Jewish Auto. Oblast'
5 Ivanovo	15 Karachai-Cherkessiya	
6 Lipetsk	16 Kabardino-Balkariya	
7 Mordoviya	17 North Osetiya	
8 Chuvashiya	18 Ingushetiya	
9 Marii-El	19 Chechnya	
10 Udmurtiya	20 Dagestan	

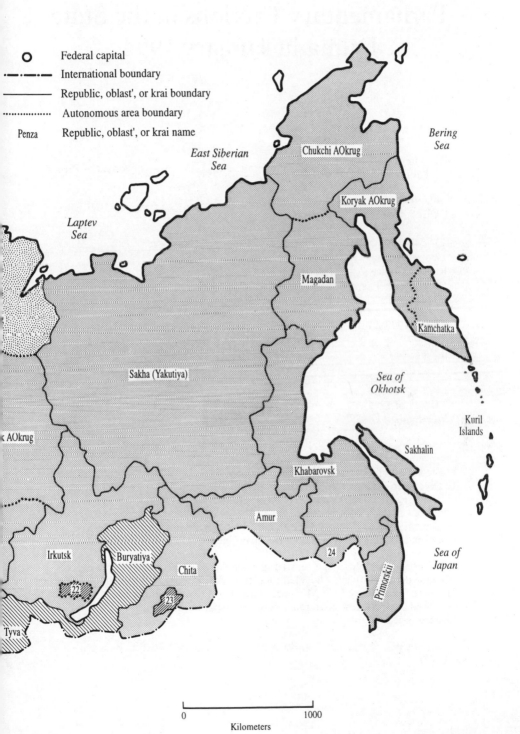

Federal capital

International boundary

Republic, oblast', or krai boundary

Autonomous area boundary

Penza Republic, oblast', or krai name

Appendix 4a

Parliamentary Factions in the State Duma in January 1994

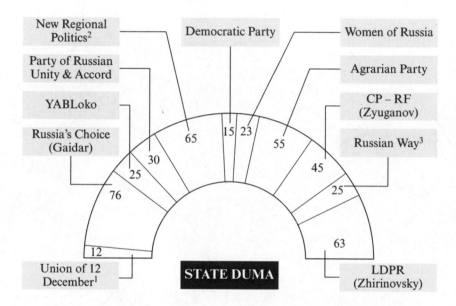

New Regional Politics[2]

Party of Russian Unity & Accord

YABLoko

Russia's Choice (Gaidar)

Democratic Party

Women of Russia

Agrarian Party

CP – RF (Zyuganov)

Russian Way[3]

65 15 23 55

30 45

25 25

76

63

12

Union of 12 December[1]

STATE DUMA

LDPR (Zhirinovsky)

1. The Union of 12 December – later renamed the Liberal Democratic Union of 12 December – is a faction of radical liberal-Westerners. When the faction was officially registered in the spring of 1994 it had a membership of 37. The Chairman of the Union is former Finance Minister Boris Fedorov. The parliamentary leaders of the faction are Aleksandr Braginskii and Irina Khakamada of the Party of Economic Freedom.

2. New Regional Politics is a centrist grouping largely composed of non-party-affiliated deputies. It is led by Vladimir Medvedev, President of the Union of Oil Producers. In January 1995 Medvedev and other members of the faction organized a constituent conference of a new social-political movement called Regions of Russia.

3. Russian Way is a nationalist, Russophile grouping led by Sergei Baburin.

Appendix 4b

Parliamentary Factions in the State Duma in January 1995

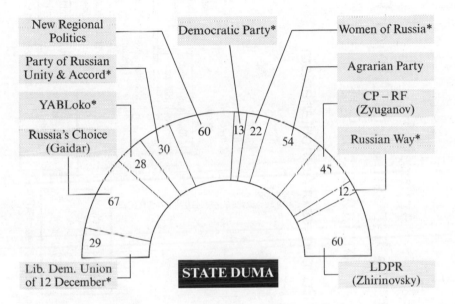

New Regional Politics — Democratic Party* — Women of Russia*

Party of Russian Unity & Accord* — Agrarian Party

YABLoko* — CP – RF (Zyuganov)

Russia's Choice (Gaidar) — 60 13 22 54 — Russian Way*

30 28 45

67 12

29 60

Lib. Dem. Union of 12 December* — STATE DUMA — LDPR (Zhirinovsky)

* According to house rules introduced in 1994, formal registration of parliamentary factions would be restricted to those groups with a minimum of 35 members. What this essentially amounted to was the loss of office space, staff and communication facilities for unregistered groups.

A number of other, very small parliamentary groupings also came into existence during 1994. These included the Russian Christian Democratic Union led by Valerii Borshchev (a breakaway group of a handful of deputies from Russia's Choice and YABLoko) and *Derzhava*, led by Viktor Kobelev (a former member of the LDPR).

At the time of going to press, a number of other parliamentary factions were in the process of being constructed. These included 'Duma 96' (made up of former Russia's Choice deputies and deputies from New Regional Politics) and 'Solidarity' (a pro-Yeltsin grouping).

Appendix 5
Axes of Conflict and Disposition of Major Political Forces in January 1995

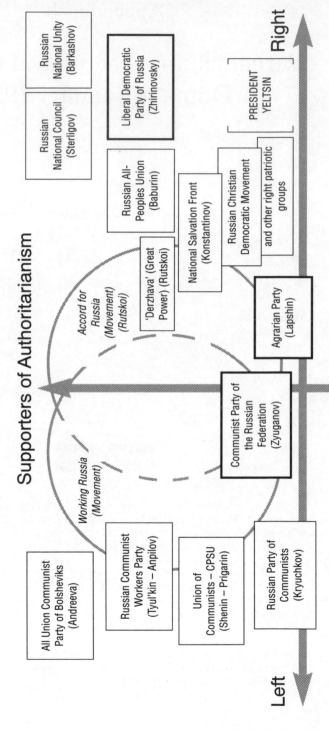

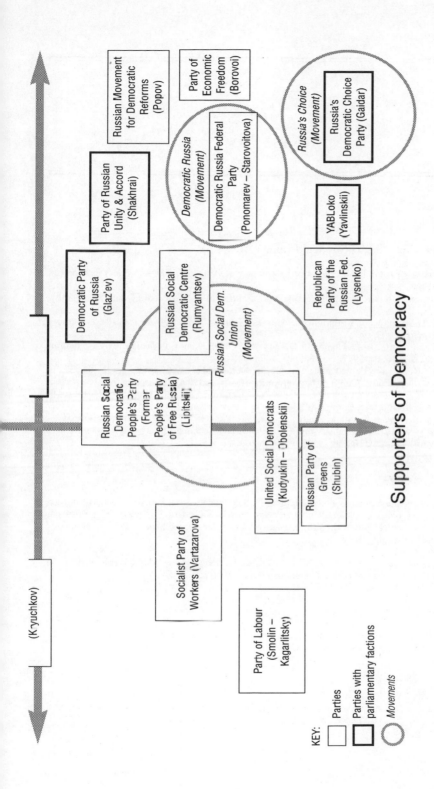

Supporters of Democracy

(Kryuchkov)

Russian Movement for Democratic Reforms (Popov)

Party of Economic Freedom (Borovoi)

Russia's Choice (Movement)

Russia's Democratic Choice Party (Gaidar)

Party of Russian Unity & Accord (Shakhrai)

Democratic Russia (Movement)

Democratic Russia Federal Party (Ponomarev – Starovoitova)

YABLoko (Yavlinskii)

Democratic Party of Russia (Glaz'ev)

Russian Social Democratic Centre (Rumyantsev)

Russian Social Dem. Union (Movement)

Republican Party of the Russian Fed. (Lysenko)

Russian Social Democratic People's Party (Former People's Party of Free Russia) (Lipitskii)

United Social Democrats (Kudyukin – Obolenskii)

Russian Party of Greens (Shubin)

Socialist Party of Workers (Vartazarova)

Party of Labour (Smolin – Kagarlitsky)

KEY:
▢ Parties
▣ Parties with parliamentary factions
◯ *Movements*

Source: Professor Aleksandr Buzgalin. Reprinted and updated with the kind permission of the author.

Notes

Introduction: The Theoretical Framework

1 Interview with Giuliano Gramsci (the younger of Antonio Gramsci's sons) in Moscow, 4 June 1994.
2 As cited in M.N. Gretskii, *Antonio Gramshi – Politik i Filosof* (Moscow: Izdatel'stvo Nauka, 1991), p. 97.
3 Perry Anderson, 'The Antinomies of Antonio Gramsci', *New Left Review*, 100, November 1976–January 1977, pp. 5–78.
4 See Lenin's letter to Plekhanov in January 1901 in V.I. Lenin, *Collected Works* (London: Lawrence & Wishart, 1977), vol. 34, pp. 55–7.
5 Lenin, 'Reformism in the Russian Social-Democratic Movement', ibid., vol. 17, p. 232.
6 Quintin Hoare and Geoffrey Nowell-Smith (trans and eds), *Selections from the Prison Notebooks of Antonio Gramsci* [hereafter *SPN*], (London: Lawrence & Wishart, 1986), p. 79.
7 Chantal Mouffe, 'Hegemony and Ideology in Gramsci', in Chantal Mouffe (ed.), *Gramsci and Marxist Theory* (London: Routledge & Kegan Paul, 1979), p. 181 (emphasis added).
8 Ernesto Laclau and Chantal Mouffe, *Hegemony and Socialist Strategy: Towards a Radical Democratic Politics* (London: Verso, 1985), p. 67.
9 *SPN*, p. 349.
10 Ibid., pp. 15–16.
11 Ibid., pp. 181–2.
12 Ibid., p. 195.
13 One of the most impassioned encounters on this issue was that between Norberto Bobbio and Jacques Texier in 1968; a landmark debate that has perpetually divided all Gramscian scholars ever since. For an English translation of this debate, see Mouffe (ed.), *Gramsci and Marxist Theory*, pp. 21–79.
14 *SPN*, p. 244.
15 Joseph Femia, *Gramsci's Political Thought: Hegemony, Consciousness and the Revolutionary Process* (Oxford: Clarendon Press, 1981), p. 37.
16 *SPN*, p. 324.
17 Ibid., p. 323.
18 Ibid., p. 235.
19 Mouffe, 'Hegemony and Ideology', p. 198.
20 As Boggs has pointed out, Gramsci's writings on bureaucracy share some affinity with those of Max Weber. See Carl Boggs, *Gramsci's Marxism* (London: Pluto Press, 1976), pp. 45–6.
21 *SPN*, pp. 275–6.
22 Ibid., pp. 237–8.
23 Ibid., p. 238.
24 Christine Buci-Glucksmann, 'State, Transition and Passive Revolution', in Mouffe (ed.), *Gramsci and Marxist Theory*, pp. 219, 220.
25 *SPN*, p. 268.

26 Ibid., p. 268 (emphasis added).
27 Ibid., p. 149.
28 Ibid., p. 150.
29 See D. Forgacs and G. Nowell-Smith (eds), *Antonio Gramsci: Selections from Cultural Writings* (London: Lawrence & Wishart, 1985), p. 108.
30 *SPN*, p. 360.
31 Ibid., p. 181.
32 Ibid., p. 53.
33 Stuart Hall, 'Postscript: Gramsci and Us', in Roger Simon, *Gramsci's Political Thought: An Introduction* (London: Lawrence & Wishart, 1991), pp. 114, 116.
34 See Eric J. Hobsbawm, 'Gramsci and Marxist Political Theory', in Anne Showstack Sassoon (ed.), *Approaches to Gramsci* (London: Writers & Readers Publishing Co-operative Society, 1982), pp. 20–36.
35 See ibid., p. 30.
36 Walter L. Adamson, *Hegemony and Revolution: A Study of Antonio Gramsci's Political and Cultural Theory* (Berkeley: University of California Press, 1980), p. 221.

Part I

Chapter 1 The Frailty of Russia's New Civil Society

1 Joseph Femia, *Gramsci's Political Thought: Hegemony, Consciousness and the Revolutionary Process* (Oxford: Clarendon Press, 1981), p. 46.
2 Ibid., p. 47.
3 Ibid., p. 47.
4 Mikhail Gorbachev, *Perestroika: New Thinking for Our Country and the World* (London: Collins, 1987), pp. 21–2.
5 This, for example, was an impression often given in Zdenek Mlynar's account of the Gorbachev reforms. See *Can Gorbachev Change the Soviet Union? The International Dimensions of Political Reform*, trans. Marian Sling and Ruth Tosek (Oxford: Westview Press, 1990).
6 See, for example, Thomas Remington, 'A Socialist Pluralism of Opinions: *Glasnost* and Policy-Making Under Gorbachev', in Alexander Dallin and Gail W. Lapidus (eds), *The Soviet System in Crisis* (Oxford: Westview Press, 1991), pp. 97–115.
7 Françoise Thom, *The Gorbachev Phenomenon: A History of Perestroika*, trans. Jenny Marshall (London: Pinter, 1989), p. 47.
8 This issue is well treated in Mary Buckley, *Redefining Russian Society and Polity* (Oxford: Westview Press, 1993).
9 The essence of this 'engagement', even by conservative forces, has been well documented by Vitalii Tret'yakov. Writing in the spring of 1991, Tret'yakov commented: 'Gorbachev has forced the nomenklatura publicly to fight for the retention of its power, and thus practically included it in the reformist activity. That is so because a public struggle, even if it is only over power and privileges, is a civilised, and not a conspiratorial mode of political action, and as such it contributes in the last analysis to the consolidation of reformist activity.' V. Tret'yakov, 'Apologya Gorbacheva ili epitafya perestroike', *Nezavisimaya gazeta*, 7 March 1991, p. 3.
10 For detailed studies on the emergence of informal associations, see, in particular, Judith B. Sedaitis and Jim Butterfield (eds), *Perestroika from Below: Social Movements in the Soviet Union* (Oxford: Westview Press, 1991); Victoria E. Bonnell, 'Voluntary Associations in Gorbachev's Reform Program', in Dallin and Lapidus (eds), *The Soviet System in Crisis*, pp. 151–60; Vladimir Brovkin, 'Revolution from Below: Informal Political Associations in Russia 1988–1989', *Soviet Studies*, vol. 42, no. 2, 1990, pp. 233–57; and Mike Urban, 'Politics in an Unsettled Climate: Popular Fronts and Informals', *Detente*, no. 14, 1989, pp. 3–8. For a useful Soviet interpretation of the *neformaly*, see A.V. Gromov and O.S. Kuzin, *Neformaly: Kto est' kto?* (Moscow: Mysl', 1990).
11 Leading the way in this sphere of sociological research was Tatyana Zaslavskaya. See, for

example, T.I. Zaslavskaya and R.V. Ryvkina, *Izvestiya sibirskogo otdeleniya akademii nauk SSSR: Seria ekonomiki i prikladnoi sotsiologii*, no. 1, January 1984.

For useful translations of some of Zaslavskaya's work, see *A Voice of Reform: Essays by Tat'iana I. Zaslavskaia*, ed. and intro. Murray Yanowitch (London: M.E. Sharpe, 1989); Tatyana Zaslavskaya, *The Second Socialist Revolution: An Alternative Soviet Strategy* (London: I.B. Tauris, 1990).

12 T. Yu. Znamenskaya, 'Sotsialisticheskii pliuralizm: obsuzhdenie za "kruglym stolom" APN i redaktsii "Sotsiologicheskikh issledovanii"', *Sotsiologicheskie issledovaniya*, no. 5, 1988, pp. 6–24.

13 Ibid., p. 10.

14 Interview with Malyutin in Moscow, 27 March 1991.

15 Andranik Migranyan, 'Vzaimootnosheniya individa, obshchestva i gosudarstva v politicheskoi teorii marksizma i problemy demokratizatsii sotsialisticheskogo obshchestva', *Voprosy filosofii*, no. 8, 1987, pp. 75–91.

16 Ibid., p. 79 (original emphasis).

17 Ibid., p. 80.

18 Ibid., p. 78.

19 Ibid., p. 91.

20 *Sovetskaya Kultura*, 24 June 1989.

21 *Literaturnaya gazeta*, 16 August 1989, p. 10.

22 Ibid. (emphasis added). See also Migranyan's article 'Dolgii put' k evropeiskomu domu', *Novyi mir*, no. 7, 1989, pp. 166–84.

23 *Pravda*, 26 November 1989.

24 Janina Frentzel-Zagorska, 'Civil Society in Poland and Hungary', *Soviet Studies*, vol. 42, no. 4, 1990, p. 769.

25 This is well demonstrated in an internal party document of the Moscow city party committee in 1990 (Information Bulletin no. 29, *izd*. Moscow Pravda, October 1990), where the assumption is still being made, even at this late stage, that the Party can still act 'as a transcendental instrument for the conciliation of interests' within society, without affecting any aspect of the traditional conception of power in the Soviet system.

For an instructive analysis of this document, see Rachel Walker, 'In Place of an Epitaph for the Party', *Russia and the World*, no. 20, 1991.

26 For the full text of the Law, see *Pravda*, 16 October 1990.

27 This phrase was originally used by Dimitrina Petrova in relation to the emergence of a civil society and political pluralism in Bulgaria. See Dimitrina Petrova, 'Political Pluralism in Bulgaria', *East European Reporter*, vol. 4, no. 4, 1991, p. 35.

28 Interview with Malyutin in Moscow, 27 March 1991.

29 See Yuri Krasin and Aleksandr Galkin, 'Grazhdanskoe obshchestvo: put' k stabil'nosti', *Dialog*, no. 3, 1992, p. 74.

30 See Steven Fish, 'The Emergence of Independent Associations and the Transformation of Russian Political Society', *The Journal of Communist Studies*, vol. 7, no. 3, 1991, pp. 324–8.

31 For a detailed review of the case and the state's defence, see Mikhail Fedotov, Andrei Makarov and Sergei Shakhrai, '"Delo KPSS" ili Kakuyu organizatsiyu myi poteryali', *Izvestiya*, 2 July 1992, p. 3.

32 For more detailed information on the 1932 Law, see B.I. Sergeev, 'Zakonodatel'stvo o dobrovol'nykh obshchestvakh: vchera, segodnya, zavtra', in D.A. Kerimov (ed.), *Novoe Politicheskoe Myshlenie i Protsess Demokratizatsii* (Moscow: Nauka, 1990), pp. 40–46.

The Russian parliament finally revoked the Law – somewhat conveniently, it has to be said – on 18 December 1991.

33 *BBC Summary of World Broadcasts*, 16 January 1993, SU/1588 B/2.

34 Based on comments made in an interview with Professor Aleksandr Buzgalin of the Party of Labour in Moscow, 8 January 1993.

35 For the full text of this presidential decree (No. 45), see *Rossiiskaya gazeta*, 16 January 1993.

36 Fish, 'The Emergence of Independent Associations', p. 326.

37 For the text of the Law, see *Rossiiskaya gazeta*, 8 February 1992.

38 See Julia Wishnevsky, 'Manipulation, Mayhem and Murder', *Transition*, vol. 1, no. 2, 1995, p. 38.

39 For the text of the statute which created the Federal Information Centre and for details of its structure, see *Rossiiskie vesti*, 26 January 1993.

40 Because of state demands that it purchase a year's supply of newsprint in advance, the much-respected *Nezavisimaya gazeta* has been able to appear only as a four-page, rather than an eight-page, newspaper since the end of 1994. The overall situation as regards excessive state interference with all the various channels of information and communication has been well summed up by Vladimir Tikhonov, a member of President Yeltsin's Consultative Council. What we have today, he has argued, 'is a curious state of affairs. . . . We have *glasnost'*, but it is [still highly] regulated. Evidently, what it boils down to is that we are not yet mature enough for what we seek. A democratic society is a society that enjoys freedom of speech. But the curious thing is the ban on that speech. From certain political groups, the president can expect anything, and read anything – any accusations, including the most criminal – and he will let it all pass by with a smile, whereas others tell the truth and receive an administrative punishment for their pains.' See *BBC Summary of World Broadcasts*, 30 November 1992. SU/1551 C2/6.

41 Fish, 'The Emergence of Independent Associations', p. 326.

42 Ibid., p. 327.

43 For a detailed discussion of many of the possible variants of de-statization and marketization, see Kazimierz Z. Poznanski (ed.), *Constructing Capitalism: The Re-emergence of Civil Society and Liberal Economy in the Post-Communist World* (Oxford: Westview Press, 1992), especially Chs 4–6, with contributions by Poznanski, Janos Kornai and Jozef M. van Brabant.

44 Fish, 'The Emergence of Independent Associations', pp. 327–8.

45 That the gender issue in contemporary Russian life does not feature as prominently as it undoubtedly deserves to do in the present study is partly due to reasons of space; but much more significantly due to the fact that an excellent, specialist analysis of this issue has recently appeared in print. See Anastasia Posadskaya *et al.* (eds), *Women in Russia* (London: Verso, 1994).

46 Neal Ascherson, 'From Moscow, on the Brink of Greater Nowheria', *The Independent on Sunday*, 15 December 1991, p. 25.

47 For some interesting comments on this, see Yevgeny Yevtushenko, *Fatal Half Measures: The Culture of Democracy in the Soviet Union*, ed. and trans. Antonina W. Bouis (London: Little, Brown, 1991).

48 *Rossiiskaya gazeta*, 12 December 1992, p. 3

49 Ernest Gellner, *Conditions of Liberty: Civil Society and Its Rivals* (London: Hamish Hamilton, 1994).

50 Interview with Professor Aleksandr Galkin at the Gorbachev Foundation in Moscow, 11 January 1993.

51 Vladimir Bibler, 'Demokratom byit' trudno: iz zametok o grazhdanskom obshchestve', in Yurii Afanas'ev *et al.*, *God posle Avgusta: gorech' i vybor* (Moscow: Literatura i politika, 1992), pp. 169–86.

For a thought-provoking philosophical account of civil society written by Bibler and published towards the end of the Gorbachev era, see 'O grazhdanskom obshchestve i obshchestvennom dogovore', in A.A. Protashchik (ed.), *Perestroika, Demokratiya, Sotsializm: Cherez Ternin* (Moscow: Progress, 1990), pp. 335–61.

52 In contrast to GDP, NMP did not include depreciation, nor did it include the output of 'services' such as banking, insurance, health, education, etc. The estimated difference between GDP and NMP was usually about 40 per cent.

53 *Rossiiskaya gazeta*, 21 January 1995, p. 4.

54 Mary Brennan, 'Free Fall: Social and Economic Collapse in Russia', Background Report for the Committee for Democracy and Civil Liberties in Russia, August/September 1994, p. 2.

55 See, for example, 'Russia's Crisis of Capitalism', *The Economist*, 15 October 1994, p. 44. For a report on Chernomyrdin's speech, see *BBC Summary of World Broadcasts*, 28 October 1994, SU/2138 B/1.

56 Two days after the crash the rouble managed to recover 25 per cent of its value. The political effects of 'Black Tuesday', however, were quite far-reaching, leading to a number of important ministerial changes and the resignation of the head of the Central Bank, Viktor Gerashchenko.

57 *Izvestiya*, 29 January 1994.
58 In a logging company in Yarenskii near Arkhangelsk, workers were apparently paid their August 1994 wages in kind in tampons (*The Economist*, 8 October 1994, p. 27).
59 *The Economist Intelligence Unit Country Profile, Russia 1993–94*, p. 31.
60 E. Fedorova, 'Inostrannyi kapital ne spshit v Rossiyu', *Finansovye izvestiya*, 9 June 1994, p. 2.
61 *The Economist* suggested that this was possible because the cost to the consumer of basic services such as rent, water and heating was still only a fraction of the actual production costs. It was also insinuated that a great many Russian citizens were able to avoid paying their taxes, thus leaving them with a higher disposable income (8 October 1994, p. 23).
62 'O situatsii v rossiiskoi ekonomike', *Nezavisimaya gazeta*, 13 September 1994, p. 3.
63 *Ekonomika i organizatsiya promyshlennogo proizvodstva (EKO)*, no. 8, 1994, p. 111.
64 Ibid.
65 *Izvestiya*, 15 October 1994, p. 1. The poll was carried out by the *Mneniye* Sociological Service. Of the 3,500 respondents from 30 regions of the Federation, 43.5 per cent said it was 'impossible to predict' when their living standards would improve; 20.1 per cent said it was 'too hard to say'; and 18.1 per cent replied 'never'. The remaining answers gave a range of periods from one to ten years.
66 Adam Smith, *The Wealth of Nations* (Harmondsworth: Penguin, 1970), p. 8.
67 See, for example, Richard Sakwa, *Russian Politics and Society* (London: Routledge, 1993), p. 243.
68 As cited in ibid., p. 212.
69 *Reuters*, 19 January and 12 February 1993.
70 Stephen Handelman, *Comrade Criminal: The Theft of the Second Russian Revolution* (London: Michael Joseph, 1994).
71 Ibid. Similar statistics were also cited in a BBC television documentary, 'Dirty Money: The Wild East', September 1994.
72 Ibid. See also *Rossiiskaya gazeta*, 12 February 1993, p. 13.
73 One of the most socially pernicious effects of the criminalization of the Russian economy is the impact it has had on the ordinary domestic housing market. Countless stories are told, for example, of pensioners being forced to bequeath their apartment to 'brokers' in return for a small cash supplement to their meagre pensions. If they then happen to survive for anything longer than a few months, they are invariably found murdered.
74 As cited in Handelman, *Comrade Criminal*, p. 77.
75 The claim by Georgii Shakhnazarov, a close aide and adviser of Mikhail Gorbachev, back in February 1992, that a two-party system could soon evolve in Russia continues to look somewhat unrealistic. See Georgii Shakhnazarov, 'U nas est' shans sozdat' dvukhpartiinuyu sistemu', *Izvestiya*, 17 February 1992, p. 3.
76 This is based on an earlier study I conducted, 'The Emergence of a Party Political System in Russia', *Reading Papers in Politics*, no. 10, May 1992.
77 The whole question of financing political parties was always slated to be one of the main prerogatives of a new Law on Political Parties. As yet, however, no such law has been enacted, despite frequent calls for its urgent necessity.
78 Viktor Kuvaldin, 'How to Make Way for a Multiparty System', *Moscow News*, no. 24, 1990, p. 8. See also L. Gordon and E. Klopov (eds), *Novye sotsial'nye dvizheniya v Rossii* (Moscow: Progress-Kompleks, 1993).
79 Interview with Professor Buzgalin in Moscow, 10 December 1993.
80 In the elections to the State Duma (the lower chamber of the new Federal Assembly), 225 seats were contested on the basis of single-member constituencies on a first-past-the-post outcome, while the remaining 225 seats were proportionally distributed according to party lists.
81 Andrzej Walicki, 'Russia, before the Coup and After', *Critical Review*, vol. 5, no. 1, 1991, p. 9.
82 Boris Kagarlitsky, *The Disintegration of the Monolith*, trans. Renfrey Clarke (London: Verso, 1992), p. 49.
83 Boris Kurashvili, *Strana na rasput'e* (Moscow, 1990), p. 21. As cited in Kagarlitsky, *The Disintegration*, p. 45.
84 Ibid., p. 48.

85 For an early illustration of this, see Viktor Sheinis, 'Kakaya platforma nam nuzhna', *Rabochii klass i sovremennyi mir*, no. 3, 1990, p. 8. See also 'Mnogopartiinost' u nas i u "nikh": izmeneniya sotsial'noi struktury sovetskogo obshchestva i ikh politicheskie posledstviya', *Dialog*, no. 6, 1991, pp. 46–53; 'The Soviet Multi-Party System: A Moscow Roundtable' (conducted by Michael E. Urban), *Russia and the World*, no. 18, 1990, pp. 1–6.
86 See, for example, Aleksandr Meerovich, 'The Emergence of Russian Multiparty Politics' in Dallin and Lapidus (eds), *The Soviet System in Crisis*, pp. 162–3.
87 Kagarlitsky, *The Disintegration*, p. 25.
88 Ibid., pp. 13–14.
89 Ibid., p. 14.
90 Ibid., p. 26 (emphasis added).
91 Interview with Andrei Kolganov in Moscow, 8 January 1993.
92 'The Left and Worker's Movements in the Former USSR', *Economy and Democracy*, no. 3, 1992, p. 4.
93 Claus Offe, 'Capitalism by Democratic Design? Democratic Theory Facing the Triple Transition in East Central Europe', *Social Research*, vol. 58, no. 4, p. 869.
94 According to Offe this can best be labelled ' "capitalism by design" or capitalism without capitalists as active promoters of their class interests'. Unlike Western capitalism, he argues, which relied on 'blind evolutionary emergences', the 'new class of entrepreneurs (and, correspondingly, the new class of employees, into which the previous "working people" see themselves reconstituted), [must be] created according to a blueprint designed by political elites' (ibid., p. 879).
95 Interview with Professor Aleksandr Buzgalin in Moscow, 5 January 1993.
96 See, for example, 'Rabochee dvizhenie Rossii segodnya', *Levaya gazeta*, no. 4, November 1992, pp. 3, 6.
97 *Moscow News*, no. 12, 19 March 1993, p. 3.

Chapter 2 How Many States; How Many Caesars?

1 As cited in Curt Gasteyger, 'Eastern Europe: between Reform and Resignation', *The World Today*, May 1992, p. 82.
2 As cited in Philip Hanson, 'Russia: Economic Reform and Local Politics', ibid., April 1993, p. 64.
3 See, for example, Peter Andras Heltai and Zbigniew Rau, 'From Nationalism to Civil Society and Tolerance', in Zbigniew Rau (ed.), *The Reemergence of Civil Society in Eastern Europe and the Soviet Union* (Oxford: Westview Press, 1991), pp. 129–44.
4 Paul Piccone, 'Paradoxes of Perestroika', *Telos*, no. 84, 1990, p. 15.
5 Ibid., p. 24.
6 An opinion poll in March 1992, for example, carried out by the Russian Academy of Sciences Institute of Socio-Political Research, indicated that 70.5 per cent of those polled were in favour of restoring the USSR. See *Sovetskaya Rossiya*, 19 March 1992. The poll was conducted almost a year to the day after the referendum on the future of the Union carried out across the USSR. In this earlier vote, 71.34 per cent of Russians had come out in favour of maintaining the territorial integrity of the USSR.
   This whole question of which State most Russian citizens had a greater sense of allegiance to was made even more complicated by the fact that for most of the first year after the disintegration of the Soviet Union, the Russian Constitution retained a number of clauses which contained a continuing reference to the USSR.
7 *Rossiiskaya gazeta*, 2 December 1992.
8 See the interview with Abdulatipov in *Pravda*, 19 February 1992.
9 The largest organized expression of hostility to the federal authorities' actions in Chechnya came at a meeting in Cheboksary in early January 1995. Organized by the President of the Chuvash Republic, Nikolai Fedorov, the meeting was attended by senior representatives from the republics of Bashkortostan, Karelia, Tatarstan, Mordovia, Udmurtia and Marii-El. Many commentators subsequently referred to the meeting as the 'Cheboksary Fronde' – using the analogy of the rebellious activities of those forces at the time of the reign of the

French autocrat Louis XIV. Other republics very hostile to the war included Sakha (Yakutia), Tyva and Buryatia.

10 For details of the Confederation's activities and the response of Chechnya's neighbours to the war, see Vadim Shorokhov, 'Groznyi na politicheskoi stsene', *Nezavisimaya gazeta*, 20 January 1995, p. 3.

11 This figure was cited by Ramazan Abdulatipov in an interview with Russian television in August 1992. See *BBC Summary of World Broadcasts*, 6 August 1992, SU/1452 B/2.

12 See, for example, the interview with President Shaimiyev in *Moscow News*, no. 18, 1992, p. 14. In February 1994 a formal Interstate Treaty was signed between Russia and Tatarstan. For details, see *Rossiiskaya gazeta*, 18 February 1994, p. 5.

13 A seventh republic, Kalmykia-Khalmg Tangch, had also proclaimed legal sovereignty back in October 1990. In March 1994, however, this claim was voluntarily rescinded by the Republic's President, Kirsan Ilyumzhinov, although not without considerable internal protest.

14 See Vladimir Yemelyanenko, 'The Country Will Collapse, if Vassals and Suzerains Survive', *Moscow News*, no. 6, 1993, p. 3.

15 See Leonid Wardomski, 'Wirtschaftsbeziehungen zwischen Zentrum und Regionen in Russland: Schwierige Suche nach einem Interessenausgleich', *Berichte des Bundesinstituts für ostwissenschaftliche und internationale Studien*, no. 18, 1994.

16 In the case of the self-proclaimed Urals Republic, in November 1993 President Yeltsin formally dissolved all such proclamations made by the Sverdlovsk authorities. Such presidential edicts, however, have largely been ignored.

17 For details of the Accord, see *Izvestiya*, 26 March 1992; *Mezhdunarodnaya zhizn'*, no. 4, 1993. The Accord was registered as a legal entity by the Russian Ministry of Justice at the end of January 1993. A useful survey of the whole Siberian situation can also be found in James Hughes, 'Regionalism in Russia: The Rise and Fall of Siberian Agreement', *Europe-Asia Studies*, vol. 46, no. 7, 1994, pp. 1133–61.

18 Valery Lavsky, 'Russian Regions Use the Threat of Self-isolation', *Moscow News*, no. 41, 1993, p. 8.

19 Two regions (Kemerovo and Altai), also pulled out of the Accord in disagreement with the excessive politicization of the movement. *Nezavisimaya gazeta*, 14 January 1994.

20 By autumn 1993, as many as 36 regions of the Federation were wholly or partly refusing to pay taxes into the central budget. This meant, in effect, that the central authorities were receiving less than half of their total tax revenue.

21 Some of the most prominent of these movements are the Kabard Adyge-Khase Party, the Avar People's Front, the Kumyk Tenglik Movement, the Ingush Niiskho Party, the Karachai National Movement, the Ittifak Party of Tatar Radicals and the Bashkir Urals Movement. *Megapolis-Express*, 3 March 1993, p. 13.

22 Ferenc Miszlivetz, 'The Unfinished Revolutions of 1989: The Decline of the Nation-State?', *Social Research*, vol. 58, no. 4, 1991, pp. 799–800.

23 See Richard Sakwa, *Russian Politics and Society* (London: Routledge, 1993), p. 410.

24 See, for example, Gennadii Burbulis's article, 'Will There be a New Authoritarianism?', *Chas pik*, no. 8, 1992, p. 5; and the reports on Burbulis's support for the authoritarian option in *Kommersant*, no. 12, 1992 and *Nezavisimaya gazeta*, 30 October 1992. Gavriil Popov has similarly not hidden his support for this option, as indicated in *Kommersant*, 27 October 1992. Mikhail Gorbachev also made an analysis of the extent to which Yeltsin was being encouraged to instigate a new authoritarianism in Russia, *Komsomolskaya pravda*, 4 July 1992; and this issue also repeatedly cropped up in the collection of articles in Yurii Afanas'ev *et al.*, *God Posle Avgusta: Gorech' i Vybor* (Moscow: Literaturi i Politika, 1992), though it should be emphasized that the likes of Afanas'ev, Elena Bonner, Lev Timofeev, Vladimir Lopatin and Yegor Gaidar have consistently and vociferously spoken out *against* the use of authoritarian or dictatorial measures. For other significant contributions on the debate concerning the desirability of the authoritarian/caesarist option, see Sergei Yakovlev's report in *Nezavisimaya gazeta*, 25 March 1993.

25 Tatyana Tolstaya, 'Boris the First', trans. Jamey Gambrell, *New York Review of Books*, 23 June 1994, pp. 3–7.

26 Ernesto Laclau, in his study of the related phenomenon of populism, appears to reach a

similar kind of conclusion when he argues that although populism is intrinsically a classless ideology, it can only ever emerge and sustain itself in relation to the ideology of a given class. Ernesto Laclau, *Politics and Ideology in Marxist Theory: Capitalism-Fascism-Populism* (London: Verso, 1989), pp. 172 3.

27 See Kagarlitsky, *The Disintegration*, p. 157.

28 *Nezavisimaya gazeta*, 3 September 1991. See also the interview with Vitalii Tret'yakov, the editor of *Nezavisimaya gazeta*, in *il Manifesto*, 20 September 1991, p. 2.

29 *Rossiiskaya gazeta*, 11 March 1993.

30 For the text of the decree 'On Stage-by-stage Constitutional Reform in the Russian Federation' and Yeltsin's television address, see *Izvestiya*, 22 September 1993. The *illegality* of the decree was never hidden, either by Yeltsin himself or by his key supporters. According to comments made by Foreign Minister Andrei Kozyrev, for example: 'The president's actions were contrary to Article 121 (b), of the constitution (which stipulates that the president cannot use his powers to suspend the activities of any lawfully elected bodies of state power). . . . If the president had not acted as he did, fundamental constitutional principles (the principles of people's power and checks and balances), would have been trampled on. The economic reform would have been buried and the unity and integrity of the Russian Federation would have been jeopardised', *BBC Summary of World Broadcasts*, 9 October 1993, SU/1815 C/3.

31 Many of these issues were officially taken up with the Russian authorities by such groups as Amnesty International.

32 Andrei Sinyavskii, 'Vse eto uzhe bylo', *Nezavisimaya gazeta*, 13 October 1993, p. 5.

33 For the text of the Constitution, see *Rossiiskaya gazeta*, 10 November 1993, pp. 3–6.

34 See the interview with Yeltsin in *Izvestiya*, 16 November 1993, p. 4.

35 It should be noted that most of these elements of the new Constitution came into force only after its first year in operation; and as will be made clear in Chapter 5, the actual outcome of the election did – ironically, perhaps – see a diminution in the stature of the President at the hands of the much more centrist-orientated Prime Minister, Viktor Chernomyrdin.

36 *BBC Summary of World Broadcasts*, 14 December 1993, SU/1871 B/1.

37 For details of allegations of falsification of the figures and claims of fraud, see *Izvestiya*, 4 May 1994, p. 4; *Nezavisimaya gazeta*, 28 June 1994, pp. 1, 5.

38 *The Guardian*, 11 December 1993, p. 26.

39 As cited in Renfrey Clarke, 'Stormy Criticism of Yeltsin's Constitution', *Green Left Weekly*, 1 December 1993, p. 23. See also Rumyantsev's analysis of the new Constitution in *Nezavisimaya gazeta*, 24 November 1993, p. 2.

40 'Svobodnykh vyborov ne budet', *Nezavisimaya gazeta*, 1 December 1993, pp. 1, 3.

41 Interview with *Izvestiya*, 16 November 1993, p. 1.

42 See, for example, his comments in the interview with *Literaturnaya gazeta*, 16 August 1989.

43 Ibid.; and *Latinskaya Amerika*, vol. 1, no. 3, 1990. In an interesting commentary on the actions taken by President Yeltsin in September and October 1993, however, Migranyan did raise serious doubts as to whether those actions would ultimately have a progressive impact or not. See Andranik Migranyan, 'Autoritarnyi rezhim v Rossii: kakovy perspektivy?', *Nezavisimaya gazeta*, 4 November 1993, pp. 1–2.

44 The analogy that is sometimes drawn between Yeltsin and Louis Bonaparte in the more critical sections of the Russian press should also be seen as an implicit recognition of the reactionary nature of Yeltsin's Caesarist tendencies. See, for example, Aleksandr Meshkov, 'Lui Bonapart ili General Peron? Posle 21 sentyabrya Rossiya vybrala pervogo', *Nezavisimaya gazeta*, 8 October 1993, p. 5.

45 *The Guardian*, 5 October 1993, p. 21.

46 Daniel Yergin and Thane Gustafson, *Russia 2010 and What It Means for the World* (London: Nicholas Brealey, 1994), pp. 169–76.

47 Samuel Huntington, *The Soldier and the State* (Cambridge: Harvard University Press, 1957); *Political Order in Changing Societies* (New Haven: Yale University Press, 1968).

48 For a useful discussion of this problem, see Yurii Deryugin, 'Rossiiskaya armiya: narodnaya ili "gosudareva"?', *Nezavisimaya gazeta*, 4 October 1994, p. 5.

49 The one possible Soviet-era exception was the Zhukov case in 1957. Openly accused of 'Bonapartism', Marshal Georgii Zhukov was later sacked as Defence Minister after he had played a prominent role in the defeat of the 'Anti-Party Group' in June of that year. For most

scholars, the charges were extremely far-fetched, and no one seriously believed that the army at that time had any real designs on political power.
50 Archie Brown, 'Political Leadership in Post-Communist Russia', in Amin Saikal and William Maley (eds), *Russia in Search of Its Future* (Cambridge: Cambridge University Press, 1995), p. 42.
51 Mikhail Gorbachev, 'Politika snova delaetsya "pod kovrom"', *Nezavisimaya gazeta*, 28 October 1994, p. 2.
52 The main army divisions that immediately 'defected' to the Yeltsin camp at this time were the Taman Motorized Rifle Division, the 106th Airborne Division and the Kantemirov Tank Division.
53 *Krasnaya zvezda*, 8 October 1993.
54 In a report in *Kuranty*, 9 October 1993, it was indicated that the staff of the Leningrad, Volga, Ural and Siberian military districts, as well as the Pacific Fleet, were sympathetic to the parliamentary forces.
55 Interview with the German ARD television network, 12 November 1993. For a fuller version of Yeltsin's account of the October 1993 events and the response of the military, see Boris Yeltsin, *The View from the Kremlin* (London: HarperCollins, 1994), pp. 241–94.
56 In January 1995 open opposition to the Chechen campaign led to the summary dismissal of four very senior generals, among them the Deputy Defence Minister, Colonel-General Boris Gromov (who had previously commanded the withdrawal of Soviet forces from Afghanistan).
57 Yurii Deryugin, 'Trevozhnye tendentsii v rossiiskoi armii', *Nezavisimaya gazeta*, 24 August 1994, pp. 1–2.
58 Ibid.
59 The dismissal of Burlakov came shortly after the murder of the investigative journalist for *Moskovskii Komsomolets*, Dmitrii Kholodov, who had done more than most to uncover instances of corruption in the higest echelons. Another prominent newspaper investigator into military corruption is Aleksandr Zhilin. See, for example, his report 'Generals in Business', *Moscow News*, no. 24, 1994.
60 Deryugin, 'Trevozhnye tendentsii', p. 1.
61 Interview with Lebed' on Channel 4 News, 10 November 1994. For his admiration of Pinochet and other political views, see his interview with *Nezavisimaya gazeta*, 15 September 1994, pp. 1, 3. According to one autumn 1994 poll, more than 70 per cent of the officers of the Moscow garrison thought that Lebed' should be made Defence Minister. It should also be remembered that some sections of Lebed's 'Dniester Republic' army travelled from Tiraspol to Moscow to defend the Russian parliament in October 1993.
62 According to *Nezavisimaya gazeta*'s monthly list of the country's 100 leading political figures, Lebed' had appeared from nowhere to lie in 13th position in August 1994 (1 September 1994, p. 5). The same newspaper also reported that plans were afoot in Tula (where Lebed' was stationed between 1985 and 1991), to set up a political movement to organize and co-ordinate his presidential bid. The movement apparently had the support of local intellectuals and the Afghan war veterans' association (16 September 1994, p. 1).

Part II The Hegemonic Combatants

Chapter 3 Westerners

1 Andrzej Walicki, *A History of Russian Thought from the Enlightenment to Marxism* (Oxford: Clarendon Press, 1988), Ch. 8, *passim*.
2 See, for example, the interview with the literary critic Vladimir Lakshchin in *Rossiya*, 4–10 December 1991; and Anatolii Golovatenko, 'Bol'shevizm kak otrazhenie russkoi kul'tury i zakonomernyi rezul'tat vzaimovnichtozheniya etiki i estetiki', *Nezavisimaya gazeta*, 27 November 1991.
3 Arnold van Gennep, *The Rites of Passage*, trans. Monika B. Vizedom and Gabrielle L. Caffee (London: Routledge & Kegan Paul, 1960).
4 See Vladimir Shlapentokh, *Soviet Intellectuals and Political Power: The Post-Stalin Era*

(London: I.B. Tauris, 1990); Boris Kagarlitsky, *The Thinking Reed: Intellectuals and the Soviet State from 1917 to the Present*, trans. Brian Pearce (London: Verso, 1988); and *The Disintegration of the Monolith*, trans. Renfrey Clarke (London: Verso, 1992). Both Shlapentokh and Kagarlitsky are explicit in categorizing two distinct phases of pro-Western intellectual development during the years of the Gorbachev era. I am assuming that both would accept that the post-Gorbachev, post-communist era did indeed usher in a distinctive *third* period of development.

5 See, for example, Shlapentokh, *Soviet Intellectuals*, Ch. 6, *passim*.

6 Yurii Afanas'ev *et al.*, *Inogo ne dano* (Moscow: Progress, 1988). Representing what many commentators at the time regarded as a 'manifesto' of liberal reformers, all the contributions, with virtually no exception, deliberately went out of their way to support the Gorbachev political leadership in its own reform ambitions and in its own methodology of seeking to implement a reform programme.

7 Larisa Popkova, 'Gde pyshnee pirogi?', *Novyi mir*, no. 5, 1987, pp. 239–41. It was later revealed that Popkova was a pseudonym for Larisa Piyasheva.

8 N Amosov, 'Real'nosti, idealy i modeli', *Literaturnaya gazeta*, 5 October 1988.

9 Vasilii Selyunin, 'Istoki', *Novyi mir*, no. 5, 1988, pp. 162–89.

10 Shlapentokh, *Soviet Intellectuals*, p. 157.

11 I am grateful for the review article by Paul Bellis, 'The Price of Prosperity', *Russia and the World*, no. 17, 1990, pp. 30–32, for drawing my attention to this collection.

12 L.I. Piyasheva, 'Kontury radikal'noi sotsial'noi reformy', in F.M. Borodkin, L. Ya. Kosals and R.V. Ryvkina (eds), *Postizhenie* (Moscow: Progress, 1989), pp. 264–78.

13 V.L. Sheinis, 'Perestroika na novom etape: opasnosti i problemy', in ibid. pp. 357–85; T.I. Zaslavskaya, 'Perestroika i sotsializm', in ibid., pp. 217–40. Zaslavskaya, however, to her credit [*sic*], did at least draw the line at advocating the positive inducements that could be attained if a sector of society was forced to sleep out in the streets and under bridges, something that had been suggested as a way of stimulating a more productive labour force by one economist, who eventually went on to become a key ideologue for the Russian Social Democratic Party! See *Sotsialisticheskaya industriya*, 11 November 1988.

14 Perhaps the foremost contributor at this time to this process of ideological de-legitimization and demythologization was Aleksandr Tsipko. See 'Istoki stalinizma', *Nauka i zhizn'*, nos 11 & 12, 1988 and nos 1 & 2, 1989; and 'Khuroshi li nashi printsipy?', *Novyi mir*, no. 4, 1990, pp. 173–204.

15 Oleg Bogomolov, *Ogonyek*, no. 35, 1990.

16 Shlapentokh, *Soviet Intellectuals*, p. 265.

17 See Alexander Rahr, 'Russia's "Young Turks" in Power', *RFE/RL Report on the USSR*, 22 November 1991, pp. 20–23.

18 Members of the council, for example, included Georgii Arbatov, Yegor Yakovlev, Svyatoslav Fedorov, Gavriil Popov, Vladimir Tikhonov, Daniil Granin and Oleg Bogomolov, among many others.

19 In some quarters as well, the main task of such older intellectuals was perceived now as akin to being 'guarantors' of the new process of transformation. See, for example, the comments made by *Ostankino*'s Igor' Malashenko in a television debate with several members of the Consultative Council in November 1992. *BBC Summary of World Broadcasts*, 30 November 1992, SU/1551 C2/8.

20 Ibid., C2/4.

21 See, for example, Vladimir Pankov, 'Propoved' o nashikh grekhakh. Russkaya dusha po prezhnemu bol'na kollektivizmom', *Nezavisimaya gazeta*, 25 December 1991.

22 See Patrick Flaherty, 'Perestroika and the Neo-Liberal Project', in Ralph Miliband and Leo Panitch (eds), *Communist Regimes: The Aftermath. Socialist Register 1991* (London: Merlin Press, 1991), pp. 145, 150.

23 Ibid., p. 144. See also Yeltsin's opening address to the Russian Constitutional Conference in June 1993 in *BBC Summary of World Broadcasts*, 7 June 1993, SU/1708 C1/3. For an earlier attack on the perversity of egalitarianism, see Gavriil Popov, 'O pol'ze neravenstva', *Literaturnaya gazeta*, 4 October 1989.

24 See Sue Curry Jansen's review of Marsha Seifert (ed.), *Mass Culture and Perestroika in the Soviet Union* in *The International Journal of Public Opinion Research*, vol. 4, no. 4, 1992,

p. 393. As the director of one Western advertising agency quickly discovered, what are often positive images in the Western consumerist mind may often be perceived differently in a Russian consumer's mind. By far the best forms of 'capitalist realism', he went on, were the simple, uncomplicated adverts that portrayed happy, smiling individuals. As cited in Madeleine Bunting, 'Dreams for Sale', *The Guardian Europe*, 6 September 1993, p. 19.

25 This desire for a greater degree of moral *glasnost'*, however, has caused a considerable degree of debate in the Russian media, even among those who would count themselves as firmly within the Westerners' camp. In one article, for example, paralleling the age-old debate in Western societies themselves over the desired limits of bourgeois moral values, Sergei Tikhomirov sought to analyse the ever-increasing numbers of homosexuals in post-communist Russsia as an intrinsically 'democratic problem'. Sergei Tikhomirov, 'Russkaya kul'tura v predchuvstvii "Sodomizatsii" ili Gomoseksualizm kak demokraticheskaya problema', *Nezavisimaya gazeta*, 16 June 1993, p. 5.

26 For details of the conference see 'Razgosudarstvlenie i privatizatsiya', *Ekonomika i zhizn'*, nos. 26 & 27, 1991, pp. 6–9.

27 *BBC Summary of World Broadcasts*, 30 November 1992, SU/1551 C2/3.

28 *Rossiiskie vesti*, 21 April 1993.

29 Erich Solov'ev, 'Iskushenie pravom', *Rossiya*, 27 May–2 June, 1992.

30 B. Vasil'ev, *Nedelya*, no. 12, March 1992.

31 *Polis*, no. 3, 1992, p. 73.

32 See, for example, Andrei Chereshnya, *Rossiya*, no. 41, 7–13 October 1992. Certainly, this kind of line has not always been easy to follow. Nevertheless, one very good example of this kind of restraint on the part of the Westerners has been their oft-repeated refusal to interfere in the problem of the status of the Crimea which, they have consistently argued, is an *internal* Ukrainian matter.

33 Arkadii Popov, 'Filosofiya raspada. Ob ideologii postsovetskogo natsional-patriotizm', *Nezavisimaya gazeta*, 10 April 1992.

34 Marina Pavlova-Sil'vanskaya, 'U Rossii est' shans ostat'sya velikoi derzhavoi', in Yurii Afanas'ev *et al.*, *God Posle Avgusta: Gorech' i Vybor* (Moscow: Literatura i Politika, 1992), p. 154.

35 *Sobesednik*, no. 31, August 1992, p. 3.

36 Oleg Bogomolov's article in *Ogonyek* was a good indication of the powerful images that can be conjured up by repeated references to universal values and universal human experience. For an even earlier espousal of this, see Chingiz Aitmatov, *Plakha Roman* (Moscow: Molodaya Gvardiya, 1987).

37 See, for example, Yeltsin's references to a condition of normalcy in *Rossiiskie vesti*, 21 April 1993.

38 As of early 1995, approximately 20 per cent of prices were still subject to some form of state regulation, primarily in the energy and telecommunications sector. A slightly higher proportion of price controls on basic consumer items were also in force at a local government level.

39 Ben Slay and John Tedstrom, 'Privatisation in the Postcommunist Economies: An Overview', *RFE/RL Research Report*, vol. 1, no. 17, 24 April 1992, p. 1.

40 For more details, see 'Privatizatsiya: Voprosy i otvety', *Izvestiya*, 28 September 1992, p. 4.

41 Essentially, the vouchers were securities issued by the state. Valid for one year, they could be used as a means of payment for shares in privatising companies throughout the Russian Federation (either directly or indirectly through investment funds); alternatively, the vouchers could simply be sold for cash.

42 *BBC Summary of World Broadcasts*, 9 April 1992, SU/1351 C1/4.

43 See, for example, *Izvestiya*, 23 August 1991; *Rynok*, no. 17, 1991, pp. 1, 2.

44 See *Izvestiya*, 20 May 1992, p. 4.

45 'Sotsial'no-ekonomicheskoe polozhenie Rossiikoi Federatsii v 1991 godu', *Ekonomika i zhizn'*, no. 4, 1992, pp. 4–5.

46 The main aspect of the 'post-voucher' phase of privatization was the emphasis on direct cash sales, which would have the aim of attracting 'strategic investors' with the necessary capital and entrepreneurial skills. For full details, see *Rossiiskaya gazeta*, 4 January 1994, pp. 2–8.

47 Sergei Rybak, 'Negosudarstvennyi sektor proizvel bol'shuyu chast' VVP', *Nezavisimaya gazeta*, 18 January 1995, p. 2.

48 *The Economist*, 12 November 1994, p. 41.
49 One journal regularly promoting a positive profile of newly emerging individual businessmen is *Delovye lyudi*.
50 Anthony Jones and William Moskoff, *Ko-ops: The Rebirth of Entrepreneurship in the Soviet Union* (Indianapolis: Indiana University Press, 1991), pp. 27–8.
51 Ibid., p. 28.
52 In 1994 Bunin published a book on his findings entitled *Businessmen of Russia: 40 Stories of Success* (Moscow: OKO, 1994).
53 Michael Burawoy, 'The End of Sovietology and the Renaissance of Modernisation Theory', *Contemporary Sociology*, vol. 21, no. 6, 1992, p. 783.
54 As cited in Stephen Handelman, *Comrade Criminal: The Theft of the Second Russian Revolution* (London: Michael Joseph, 1994), p. 89. According to Handelman, a classified Politburo resolution dated 11 June 1991 approved the transfer of 600 million roubles to commercial organizations and banks previously established by the Party. The resolution was signed by Mikhail Gorbachev (ibid., p. 90). According to the estimates of the Russian Economics Ministry, meanwhile, the CPSU's accounts between 1981 and 1991 indicated that the Party had at its disposal more than 450 billion 'hard currency' roubles (i.e. freely convertible to dollars), and up to 1 billion dollars in cash (as cited in ibid., p. 97).
55 See, for example, Rita di Leo, 'The Former USSR in Search of New Rules', *The Journal of Communist Studies*, vol. 9, no. 1, March 1993, pp. 10–11.
56 The first such commodity exchanges that appeared in 1990 were the Moscow Commodity Exchange and the Russian Commodity and Raw Materials Exchange. The latter was initially led by the high-profile figure of Konstantin Borovoi until his forced resignation in April 1994.
57 Jones and Moskoff, *Ko-ops*, pp. 110–18. In the aftermath of the demise of the USSR this body became known as the League of Russian Co-operators and Entrepreneurs, and under Tikhonov's continued leadership has regularly regarded itself as a mainstay of the Westerners' orientation.
58 S. Peregudov, I. Semenenko and A. Zudin, 'Business Associations in the USSR – and After: Their Growth and Political Role', Working Paper no. 110, April 1992, Department of Politics and International Studies, University of Warwick, p. 9.
59 For details of the constituent congress, see *Kommersant*, 3 April 1993; *Moscow News*, no. 15, 1993, p. 3. Gaidar, of course, had been forced to resign as acting PM in December 1992.
60 As cited in Sheila Marnie, 'Economic Reform and Poverty in Russia', *RFE/RL Research Report*, vol. 2, no. 6, 5 February 1993, p. 34. According to Elena Mezentseva, the wage differential between a secondary school teacher and a miner can often be anything up to 40 times. Elena Mezentseva, 'Women in Russia', *Labour Focus on Eastern Europe*, no. 42, 1992, p. 45.
61 Marnie, 'Economic Reform and Poverty', p. 34.
62 Georgii Ivanov-Smolenskii, 'Gornyaki i Metallurgi poryvayut s profsoyuzami Klochkova', *Izvestiya*, 28 October 1992, pp. 1, 2; *Trud*, 31 October 1992.
63 For more details on the miners' position, see Michael Burawoy and Pavel Krotov, 'The Economic Basis of Russia's Political Crisis', *New Left Review*, no. 198, March/April 1993, pp. 49–69.
64 *Pravda*, 19 November 1992.
65 See the comments made by Andrei Isaev, 'A New Role for the Russian Trade Unions', *Labour Focus on Eastern Europe*, no. 42, 1992, p. 11.
66 Daniel Singer, 'Priviligentsia, Property and Power', in Miliband and Panitch (eds), *Communist Regimes*, p. 214. See also the analysis of the motivations of the liberal intellectuals given by Michael E. Urban, *More Power to the Soviets: The Democratic Revolution in the USSR* (Aldershot: E. Elgar, 1990), p. 153.
67 Turnout at the referendum was 64.5 per cent. On question 1 (support for President Yeltsin), 58.7 per cent *of those who voted* expressed their support; on question 2 (the socio-economic programme), 53.0 per cent of those who voted expressed their endorsement; on question 3 (early presidential elections), 49.5 per cent said that there should be elections; and on question 4 (early parliamentary elections), 67.2 per cent voted in favour. *Rossiiskaya gazeta*, 6 May 1993.
68 Comments made by Nikolai Travkin in *Demokraticheskaya gazeta*, no. 1, 1990.

69 *Izvestiya*, 23 October 1992; *Moscow News*, no. 7, 1993, p. 2.
70 Television interview with Shostakovskii in *BBC Summary of World Broadcasts*, 15 May 1992, SU/1381 B/4–6.
71 Indira Dunaeva *et al.*, 'Formiruyutsya predvybornye bloki', *Nezavisimaya gazeta*, 16 October 1993, p. 1.
72 For details, see *Put' progress i sotsial'noi demokratii (programmnye tezisy SDPR)*, Moscow, October 1990.
73 Interview with Oleg Rumyantsev, *Nezavisimaya gazeta*, 13 May 1992. See also L. Byzov, 'Sotsial-Demokraty Rossiiskoi Federatsii: Kto oni?', *Narodnyi deputat*, no. 6, 1991, pp. 90–93.
74 See Georgii Ivanov-Smolenskii, 'Nishchayushchim massam mozhet ponravit'sya', *Izvestiya*, 12 May 1992, p. 2; *Rossiiskaya gazeta*, 13 January 1993.
75 Following the Party's fourth congress in May 1992, Boris Orlov was elected the Party's sole chairman, thus replacing the old system of having three co-chairmen, who were initially Aleksandr Obolenskii, Oleg Rumyantsev and Pavel Kudyukin. At the Party's fifth congress in May 1993, Orlov was himself replaced by Anatolii Golov. See Vladimir Ionov, 'Social Democrats Argue about Happiness', *Moscow News*, no. 20, 1993, p. 2.
76 *Izvestiya*, 13 May 1992, p. 1; *Moscow News*, no. 21, 1992, p. 2.
77 Georgii Ivanov-Smolenskii, 'Partiya Ekonomicheskoi Svobody vykhodit na stsenu', *Izvestiya*, 15 June 1992, p. 2; 'Partiya Ekonomicheskoi Svobody schitaet, chto resheniya VIII syezda nekonstitutsionny', *Izvestiya*, 19 March 1993, p. 2.
78 Ibid. See also *BBC Summary of World Broadcasts*, 7 December 1992, SU/1557 B/1.
79 Ibid. See also *Moskovskii Komsomolets*, 14 January 1993; *Nezavisimaya gazeta*, 11 February 1993; and the interview with Borovoi in *Nezavisimaya gazeta*, 10 March 1993, p. 4.
80 Carla Thorson, 'A Loss of Direction for Russia's Movement for Democratic Reforms', *RFE/RL Research Report*, vol. 2, no. 10, 5 March 1993, p. 13. On the nature of the RMDR, see also Popov's interview with *Moscow News*, no. 49, 1992, p. 4; and the reports on the founding congress in *Nezavisimaya gazeta*, 18 February 1992 and *Izvestiya*, 20 February 1992.
81 See *Nezavisimaya gazeta*, 18 February 1992; *Moscow News*, no. 27, 1992, p. 7.
82 For details and documents relating to the inaugural congress, see Rossisko-Amerikanskii Universitet, Institut Massovykh Politicheskikh Dvizhenii, *Partii, Assotsiatsii, Soyuzy, Kluby: Sbornik Materialov i Dokumentov*, Book 2 (Moscow: RAU-Press, 1992), pp. 33–44.
83 For details, see Vladimir Pribylovskii, *Slovar' Novykh Politicheskikh Partii i Organizatsii Rossii* (Moscow, November 1991), pp. 15–18. For specific details on Democratic Russia's involvement in Yeltsin's presidential campaign, see Michael E. Urban, 'Boris El'tsin, Democratic Russia and the Campaign for the Russian Presidency', *Soviet Studies*, vol. 44, no. 2, 1992, pp. 187–208.
84 Alexander Tsipko, 'No One Wanted to Win', *Moscow News*, no. 8, 1991, p. 7.
85 Georgii Ivanov-Smolenskii, 'Raskol v "DemRossii"', *Izvestiya*, 11 November 1991, p. 2.
86 *Kuranty*, 9 February 1991.
87 Ivanov-Smolenskii, 'Raskol', p. 2.
88 For details, see Julia Wishnevsky, 'The Rise and Fall of "Democratic Russia"', *RFE/RL Research Report*, vol. 1, no. 22, 29 May 1992, p. 26.
89 As cited in *Nedelya*, no. 45, 1991, p. 3.
90 E. Gellner, 'From the Ruins of the Great Contest. Civil Society, Nationalism, and Islam', *The Times Literary Supplement*, 13 March 1992, p. 10.
91 See his speech to a forum of 'democratic organizations' in *BBC Summary of World Broadcasts*, 19 April 1993, SU/1666 B/1.
92 Svetlana Babayeva, 'Businessmen-politicians', *Moscow News*, no. 15, 1993, p. 3.
93 In a report in *Nezavisimaya gazeta*, for example, it was announced that Konstantin Borovoi had been awarded the Medal of St Daniil, Prince of Moscow, 'for outstanding service in the restoration of the Russian Orthodox Church'. In the previous eighteen months, Borovoi had donated more than 2.5 million roubles to the Patriarchate of Moscow, to be used for the restoration of churches in the Russian capital. *Nezavisimaya gazeta*, 9 September 1992.
94 Keith Bush, 'Light at the End of the Tunnel', *RFE/RL Research Report*, vol. 2, no. 20, 14 May 1993, p. 66.
95 'Russia Reborn', *The Economist*, 5 December 1992, p. 4.
96 For the actual details of this particular survey, see Robert J. Shiller, Maxim Boycko and

Vladimir Korobov, 'Popular Attitudes towards Free Markets: The Soviet Union and the United States Compared', *The American Economic Review*, vol. 81, no. 3, 1991, pp. 385–400.
97 Albert E. Gollin, 'Public Opinion Research as Monitor and Agency in Revolutionary Times: Editor's Introduction', *International Journal of Public Opinion Research*, vol. 4, no. 4, 1992, p. 300 (emphasis added). The quotation refers to *Soviet* polling practices at the very end of 1989. Everything would suggest, however, that this continues to be the approach of Russian pollsters today. Many would perhaps suggest that the explicit relationship between polls and the actual *formation* of public opinion is the norm, not the exception, as Gollin would wish to imply from his American experience.
98 For details of the polls, see Mary Cline, 'Attitudes toward Economic Reform in Russia', *RFE/RL Research Report*, vol. 2, no. 22, 28 May 1993, pp. 43–9.
99 It is also regularly pointed out by the supporters of the pro-Western orientation that the number of workdays lost to strike action in 1992 was only one-sixth that of 1991, despite the deteriorating situation in the overall standard of living.
100 *Moscow News*, no. 10, 1993, p. 14.
101 Richard Sakwa, 'The Revolution of 1991 in Russia: Interpretations of the Moscow Coup', *Coexistence*, vol. 29, no. 4, 1992, pp. 339–41. The *minimalist* view, meanwhile, tends to assert that the old order collapsed under the weight of its own inadequacies and contradictions.
102 The 'storming of the winter palace' analogy, of course, took on even more salience following the dissolution of the Supreme Soviet in September 1993 and the forcible destruction of the parliamentary building in early October.
103 Interview in *Moscow News*, no. 25, 1993, p. 2.
104 V. Nikol'skii (ed.), *Slovarya sovremennogo slenga* (Moscow: Panorama, 1993).
105 One can perhaps get no better indication of this than the sight of Russian businessmen striking deals while playing a round of *golf* in the Moscow suburbs!
106 See also Kagarlitsky, *The Disintegration*, p. 66.
107 *BBC Summary of World Broadcasts*, 30 November 1992, SU/1551 C1/1.
108 *Rossiiskie vesti*, 21 April 1993 (emphasis added).
109 Ibid.
110 Michael Burawoy and Pavel Krotov, 'The Economic Basis of Russia's Political Crisis', *New Left Review*, no. 198, 1993, pp. 49–69.
111 Ibid., p. 64.
112 Ibid., p. 54 (emphasis added).
113 Burawoy, 'The End of Sovietology', p. 783.
114 Burawoy and Krotov, 'The Economic Basis', p. 69.
115 Simon Clarke, 'Privatisation and the Development of Capitalism in Russia', *New Left Review*, no. 196, 1992, p. 5.
116 Interview with Russian television, 18 February 1992. *BBC Summary of World Broadcasts*, 21 February 1992, SU/1310 B/8.
117 Larisa Piyasheva, 'Gde pyshnee pirogi?', *Nezavisimaya gazeta*, 25 November 1993, p. 4.
118 Interview with *Moscow News*, no. 12, 1993, p. 4.
119 See, for example, his speech to the 6th Congress of People's Deputies in April 1992, *BBC Summary of World Broadcasts*, 9 April 1992, SU/1351 C1/5.
120 In the case of Neft-Almaz-Invest, the illegality of their actions was never in doubt following the embezzlement of nearly six million pounds' worth of privatization vouchers. As for MMM, this was a share-selling company that operated according to the so-called 'pyramid' structure which guaranteed immediate vast profits to investors, funded by no other means than the income received from new contributors.
121 Stephen K. Wegren, 'Rural Reform and Political Culture in Russia', *Europe-Asia Studies*, vol. 46, no. 2, 1994, pp. 215–41.
122 A. Tsipko, ' "Demokraticheskaya Rossiya" kak bol'shevistskaya i odnovremenno pochvennicheskaya partiya', *Nezavisimaya gazeta*, 9, 13 April 1993, p. 5.
123 Interview with Mayak radio in *BBC Summary of World Broadcasts*, 25 October 1993, SU/1828 B/4.
124 The Yavlinskii bloc, in particular, regularly cited this as a reason for its inability to unite with Russia's Choice. Throughout the election campaign, the leaders of the bloc likened the existing process of privatization to a 'collectivization of industry' which had failed to produce

sufficient degrees of individual control within the newly privatized enterprises. It also attempted to differentiate itself from other pro-Western forces by laying greater stress on the need for economic de-monopolization rather than liberalization; on its desires to limit the outflow of foreign currency; and on its criticism that too much time had been wasted on the fight against inflation at the expense of other important goals. See, for example, the interview with Yavlinskii in *Nezavisimaya gazeta*, 8 December 1993, pp. 1–2.

125 *The Moscow Tribune*, 9 December 1993, p. 5.

126 For details of the founding of the movement, see *Izvestiya*, 15 June 1993. In the December 1993 elections the bloc was also formally given the support of the main part of the Party of Economic Freedom, the Constitutional Democratic Party and the Association of Independent Professionals (all of which had originally desired to take part in the elections as separate organizations from Russia's Choice), as well as by the minority faction of the Republican Party under the leadership of Stepan Sulakshin.

127 *Moskovskii Komsomolets*, 20 October 1993, p. 2.

128 As cited in *The Economist*, 29 January 1994, p. 29.

129 Interview with Russian Television in *BBC Summary of World Broadcasts*, 28 January 1994, SU/1907 B/4.

130 In the Democratic Choice Party, Gaidar was joined on the political council by, among others, Anatolii Chubais, Boris Zolotukhin and Sergei Yushenkov. His deputy, meanwhile, is Oleg Boiko. The inclusion of this thirtysomething businessman, head of the Olbi corporation and joint owner of the National Credit Bank of Russia, has undoubtedly secured the immediate financial future of the Party. As for the Democratic Russia Federal Party, the constituent conference in October 1994 elected Lev Ponomarev and Galina Starovoitova as its co-leaders. For details on the decision of other activists as to which party to join, see Evgenii Ikhlov, 'Kak ubivayut "Demrossiyu"', *Nezavisimaya gazeta*, 29 April 1994, p. 8.

131 For the text of the platform, see *Rossiiskie vesti*, 5 May 1994, p. 3. Other prominent 'Decembrists' in the State Duma include Irina Khakamada of the Party of Economic Freedom.

132 Vladimir Zharinov and Tai Pel'she, 'Nuzhno obyedinyat'sya zanovo', *Nezavisimaya gazeta*, 27 May 1994, p. 2.

133 Marina Sal'e, 'Vybros mnogopartiinosti', ibid., 9 June 1994, p. 2.

134 Marina Sal'e, 'Katastrofa liberal'nykh printsipov', ibid., 24 March 1994, p. 5.

135 See, for example, Aleksei Kiva, 'Tupiki i perspektivy rossiiskogo liberalizma', ibid., 11 May 1994, p. 5 and the earlier article by Viktor Volkonskii, 'Vozmozhen li v Rossii liberalizm?', ibid., 16 February 1993, p. 4.

136 *Segodnya*, 1 February 1994, p. 2. For a comprehensive outline of Gavriil Popov's change of direction following the December 1993 elections, see his article 'Tret'ya Model': Ob idee reformatorskoi tsentristskoi koalitsii', *Nezavisimaya gazeta*, 25 February 1994, p. 5. The change of direction in the RMDR's line, however, did not prevent its increasing political marginalization and in April 1995 there was no better indication of this than the departure of Anatolii Sobchak.

137 A. Migranyan, 'Ot VII syezda narodnykh deputatov k referendumu', *Nezavisimaya gazeta*, 16 February 1993, p. 5.

138 See *Mirovaya ekonomika i mezhdunarodnaya otnosheniya*, no. 9, 1993, pp. 20–32. According to the various authors who drew up this geographical map of anti-Westernization resistance, the most prominent areas of opposition (excluding Tatarstan and Chechnya), are the regions or republics of Bryansk, Kaluga, Orel, Ryazan, Tula, Nizhnii Novgorod (the region as a whole, not the city), Chuvashia, Marii-El, Mordovia, Belgorod, Kursk, Lipetsk, Tambov, Voronezh, Volgograd, Penza, Samara, Saratov, Ulyanovsk, Ingushetia, Dagestan, Karachaevo-Cherkessia, Kabardino-Balkaria, Adygeya, Kurgan, Orenburg, Chelyabinsk, Bashkortostan, Novosibirsk, Smolensk, Amur, Chita and Altai.

139 By far the most surprising defeat was that inflicted on the Westerners by the 'Communists of Leningrad' bloc in the St Petersburg city elections in October 1994.

140 *Rodina*, no. 4, 1993, p. 11.

141 See Allen Lynch, 'Postcommunist Political Dynamics: *Ex Uno Plura*', *RFE/RL Research Report*, vol. 3, no. 1, 7 January 1994, pp. 1–8.

142 Roman Solchanyk, 'The Politics of State Building: Center–Periphery Relations in Post-Soviet Ukraine', *Europe-Asia Studies*, no. 1, 1994, pp. 47–68. See also Jeremy Lester, 'Russian

Political Attitudes to Ukrainian Independence', *The Journal of Communist Studies and Transition Politics*, vol. 10, no. 2, June 1994, pp. 193–233.
143 Kagarlitsky, *The Disintegration*, pp. 42, 43.

Chapter 4 Russophiles

1 See, for example, Alexander Yanov, *The Russian New Right* (Berkeley: Institute of International Studies, University of California, 1978), and *The Russian Challenge and the Year 2000* (Oxford: Basil Blackwell, 1987); John B. Dunlop, *The Faces of Contemporary Russian Nationalism* (Princeton, NJ: Princeton University Press, 1983), and *The New Russian Nationalism* (New York: Praeger, 1985); Darrel P. Hammer, *Russian Nationalism and Soviet Politics* (Boulder, CO: Westview, 1988); Stephen K. Carter, *Russian Nationalism: Yesterday, Today and Tomorrow* (London: Pinter, 1990); and Walter Laqueur, *Black Hundred: The Rise of the Extreme Right in Russia* (London: HarperPerennial, 1994).
2 A good indication of this can be illustrated by the demotion and ultimate ambassadorial exile to Canada of Aleksandr Yakovlev following his orthodox Marxist critique of Russophilia in his November 1972 article in *Literaturnaya gazeta* (entitled 'Against Anti-historicism').
3 See, for example, Yanov's essay 'Russian Nationalism as the Ideology of Counterreform', in 'Russian Nationalism Today', *Radio Liberty Research Bulletin* (Special Edition), 19 December 1988.
4 Igor' Shafarevich, 'Rossiya naedine s soboi', *Nash sovremennik*, no. 1, 1992, p. 4.
5 Vladimir Krupin, 'Bor'ba s besami v Rossii', *Sovetskaya Rossiya*, 15 August 1992.
6 Igor' Ermolaev and Evgenii Mikhailov, *Nezavisimaya gazeta*, 5 March 1991.
7 Aleksandr Dugin, 'Organicheskaya demokratiya', *Nash sovremennik*, no. 10, 1992, p. 145.
8 See Yurii Sokhryakov, '"Russkaya ideya" i "amerikanskaya mechta"', *Perspektivy*, no. 11, 1991, p. 18; Valerii Sarychev, 'Rossiya v poiskakh "novoi" idelogii', *Rossiya*, 5–11 February 1992. For an interesting piece on the parallels between Russian and socialist exclusiveness, see Andranik Migranyan, *Demokratiya i Nravstvennost'* (Moscow: Znanie, 1989).
9 Aleksandr Dugin, *Politika*, no. 13, 1991.
10 For more details of the village prose school (encompassing such writers as Valentin Rasputin and Viktor Astaf'ev, among many others), see D.C. Gillespie, *Valentin Rasputin and Soviet Russian Village Prose* (London: Modern Humanities Research Association, 1986).
11 *Sovetskaya Rossiya*, 12 July 1992.
12 See, for example, Arsenii Gulyga, 'Formula Russkoi Kul'tury', *Nash sovremennik*, no. 4, 1992, pp. 145–6.
13 The idea of Russian patriotism as a unique phenomenon was primarily developed by F. Nesterov in *Svyaz' Vremen* (Moscow: Molodaya Gvardia, 1984).
14 Dugin, 'Organicheskaya demokratiya', pp. 142–3.
15 Ibid., p. 144.
16 Ibid., p. 147.
17 See, for example, Sergei Morozov, *Den'*, 21–7 June 1992.
18 For an early espousal of the Russian Idea in the latter period of the Brezhnev era, see Yurii Davydov, *Etika Liubvi i Metafizika Svoevolia* (Moscow: Molodaya Gvardia, 1982), pp. 263–71. See also Yurii Sokhryakov, '"Russkaya ideya" ...'; and Vladimir Krupin, 'Spasetsya Rossiya – spasetsya i mir', *Sovetskaya Rossiya*, 4 July 1992.
19 Shamil' Sultanov, 'Dukh Evraziitsa', *Nash sovremennik*, no. 7, 1992, p. 143. It is also interesting to note the comments of the French New Right ideologist Alain de Benoist: 'the metaphysical future of Russia and perhaps, owing to her example, the metaphysical future of Europe depends on the ideological, political, social and spiritual creative efforts of the Russian patriotic movement', *Den'*, no. 2, 1992.
20 Yurii Borodai, 'Tretii put'', *Nash sovremennik*, no. 9, 1991, p. 147.
21 *Literaturnaya gazeta*, no. 36, 2 September 1992.
22 Aleksandr Vodolagin, 'Vechnoe kocheve', *Den'*, 10–16 May 1992, p. 4.
23 See, for example, Ilya Glazunov, *Krasnaya zvezda*, 2 September 1992; Elgiz Pozdnyakov, 'The Soviet Union: The Problem of Coming Back to European Civilization', *Paradigms*, vol. 5, no. 1/2, 1991, pp. 55–6.

24 Aleksandr Dugin, 'Evraziiskoe soprotivlenie', *Den'*, no. 2, 1992.
25 *Den'*, 9–15 August 1992. See also Aleksandr Kazintsev, 'Rossiya: Uroki soprotivleniya', *Nash sovremennik*, no. 1, 1992, pp. 180–85.
26 See, for example, the comments made by Sergei Baburin in *Nezavisimaya gazeta*, 9 January 1992.
27 Shafarevich's book was published in *Nash sovremennik*, nos 6, 11, 1989.
28 Vladimir Shlapentokh, *Soviet Intellectuals and Political Power: The Post-Stalin Era* (London: I.B. Tauris, 1990), p. 221.
29 Richard Sakwa, 'The Revolution of 1991 in Russia: Interpretations of the Moscow Coup', *Coexistence*, vol. 29, no. 4, December 1992, p. 355.
30 This, for example, was the case with Aleksandr Prokhanov and Yurii Prokushev. See *Nezavisimaya gazeta*, 22 August 1991; *Literaturnaya Rossiya*, no. 35, 1991, p. 2.
31 According to some members of the *Soyuz* group, for example, the whole affair was nothing more than a 'paper coup'. See *The Guardian*, 18 September 1991. According to other reports, many patriotic groups opposed the coup because it up-staged and totally undermined their own preparations for a more thorough kind of *coup d'état*, provisionally planned to take place towards the end of the year. For details, see *Kuranty*, 24 August 1991. Yet another typical reaction was that voiced by Aleksandr Barkashov, leader of the Movement for Russian National Unity: 'Yes, we are always ready to give our support to serious measures of the kind [proposed during the August coup]. We have for several years been working out similar kinds of measures. From the beginning, however, we had serious doubts about co-operating with the putsch committee, since they were only Gorbachev people. For this reason, we did not rush to give them our support.' Interview with Barkashov, *Komsomolskaya pravda*, 29 November 1991.
32 *Izvestiya*, 1 July 1992.
33 'Slovo k narodu', *Sovetskaya Rossiya*, 23 July 1991, p. 1. Three days before the coup attempt another appeal, entitled 'From Words to Deeds', was published in *Sovetskaya Rossiya*, signed by the so-called 'Initiative Group of the People's Patriotic Movement'.
34 See the comparison made of the two documents by Natal'ya Ivanova, *Znamya*, no. 10, 1991, pp. 205–6.
35 'Obrashchenie k sovetskomu narodu', *Izvestiya*, 20 August 1991, p. 1.
36 Michael Hughes, 'The Never-Ending Story: Russian Nationalism, National Communism and Opposition to Reform in the USSR and Russia', *The Journal of Communist Studies*, vol. 9, no. 2, 1993, p. 53.
37 Sergei Kurginyan, 'Ya – ideolog chrezvychainogo polozheniya', in Sergei Kurginyan, *Sed'moi Stsenarii. Chast' vtoraya: Posle Putcha* (Moscow: Eksperimental'nyi tvorcheskii tsentr, 1992), p. 112. This article was originally published in *Putch: Khronika trevozhnikh dnei* (Moscow: Progress, 1991).
38 Kurginyan, 'Filosofiya Chrezvychaishchiny', in *Sed'moi Stsenarii. Chast' vtoraya*, p. 119.
39 Kurginyan, 'Vkhodim v revolyutsionnuyu situatsiyu', in ibid., p. 130.
40 Kurginyan, 'I nazvali ideologom putchistov', in ibid., pp. 148–9.
41 Carter, *Russian Nationalism*, p. 24.
42 For background details, see Darrel P. Hammer, 'Glasnost' and "The Russian Idea"', in Radio Liberty Research Bulletin (Special Edition), *Russian Nationalism Today*, 19 December 1988, pp. 20–21.
43 Ibid., p. 21.
44 See *Moskovskii literator*, no. 14, 24 March 1989; 'Nechustviushchie lyudi', *Nash sovremennik*, no. 2, 1989, pp. 125–51.
45 As quoted in Christian Schmidt-Hauer, *Die Zeit*, August 7 1991, p. 6.
46 See Kurginyan, *Sed'moi Stsenarii. Chast' pervaya*, pp. 5–8.
47 *Nezavisimaya gazeta*, 19 February 1991. The centre also received considerable financial support.
48 Its links with conservative elements were also confirmed during the days of the August 1991 coup, demonstrated very adequately by a decree upholding the privileged status of the centre. *Izvestiya*, 10 September 1991.
49 Sergei Kurginyan et al., *Postperestroika: Kontseptual'naya model' razvitiya nashego obshchestva, politicheskikh partii i obshchestvennykh organizatsii* (Moscow: Politicheskaya literatura, 1990).

50 Kurginyan, 'I nazvali ideologom', p. 146.
51 'Kommunizm nachinaet pobezhdat' v mirovom masshtabe', interview with *Komsomolskaya pravda*, 13 August 1991, p. 4.
52 Kurginyan, 'Politika v stile postmodern', in *Sed'moi Stsenarii. Chast' vtoraya*, p. 282.
53 Jeff Gleisner, 'Russia's Post-Industrial Patriots', *Russia and the World*, no. 17, 1990, p. 20.
54 Most notably in his three-volume series of collected writings, *Sed'moi Stsenarii*.
55 See the present author's interview with Buzgalin in *Labour Focus on Eastern Europe*, no. 44, 1993, p. 34.
56 See Gleisner, 'Russia's Post-Industrial Patriots', p. 20.
57 Karem Rash, 'Armiya i kul'tura', *Voenno-istorichesky zhurnal*, nos 2–5, 7–9, 1989.
58 *Nash sovremennik*, no. 5, 1990. For a review of Prokhanov's writings at this time, see Mark Galeotti, 'Life After the Party: Alexander Prokhanov's "Sufficient Defence"', *Russia and the World*, no. 18, 1990, pp. 7–9.
59 As cited in Galeotti, 'Life After the Party', p. 9.
60 *Moscow News*, no. 7, 1993, p. 1.
61 With an estimated 37 million believers identifying themselves with Russian Orthodoxy – even if many of these cannot be classified as practising believers – the political stakes in the struggle for Church backing are clearly very high.
62 For more specific details on this issue, see Wendy Slater and Kjell Engelbrekt, 'Eastern Orthodoxy Defends Its Position', *RFE/RL Research Report*, vol. 2, no. 35, 3 September 1993, pp. 48–55.
63 See, for example, 'Russkaya pravoslavnaya tserkov' budet otstaivat' traditsionnye tsennosti v otkrytoi zapadu rossii', *Nezavisimaya gazeta*, 5 June 1993, pp. 1–2.
64 Wendy Slater, 'The Russian Orthodox Church', *RFE/RL Research Report*, vol. 2, no. 20, 14 May 1993, pp. 92–5.
65 *Megapolis-Express*, no. 12, 31 March 1993.
66 This point was expressed very cogently by Metropolitan Kirill of Smolensk and Kaliningrad in an interview with *Nezavisimaya gazeta*, 5 June 1993, pp. 1–2.
67 For a useful commentary on the religious undertones of 'Post-perestroika', see Stephen D. Shenfield, 'Beware: God-builders at Work!', *Russia and the World*, no. 20, 1991. As the title of Shenfield's article points out, much of what the authors of 'Post-perestroika' had to say was not all that dissimilar in tone and style from the God-building movement of the Bogdanovists back at the time of the October 1917 Revolution.
68 Richard Kosolapov, 'Bednaya russkaya ideya', *Pravda*, 13 August 1992.
69 Ibid., 15 August 1992.
70 Ivan Vasil'ev, 'Dush i utroba', *Sovetskaya Rossiya*, 27 August 1992.
71 Interview with *Literaturnaya Rossiya*, 14 June 1991. In a later interview with *Nezavisimaya gazeta*, Zyuganov included in a list of the people he revered most: Jesus Christ, Mohammed, Confucius, Peter the Great, Lenin and Stalin! (4 November 1994, p. 5).
72 Ibid., 6 May 1991.
73 For a general overview of the effects of the increasing 'lumpenization' of society, see Yurii Igritskii, 'Mezhdu bezumiem lyumpena i alchnost'yu nuvorisha', *Nezavisimaya gazeta*, 2 November 1993 p. 5.
74 According to the calculations of Vladimir Pribylovskii, there were no fewer than 75 radical right-wing, Russophile groups in Russia at the beginning of 1994; and this figure did not include 'national-Bolshevik' organizations.
75 For details see *Sovetskaya Rossiya*, 30 December 1989, p. 3.
76 A brief analysis of the Social Patriots' performance in the 1990 elections can be found in John B. Dunlop, 'The Return of Russian Nationalism', *Journal of Democracy*, vol. 1, no. 3, 1990, pp. 120–21.
77 Vladimir Pribylovskii, *Slovar' novykh politicheskikh partii i organizatsii Rossii* (Moscow: Panorama, 1991), pp. 100–101.
78 For detailed studies on the Liberal Democratic Party, see Jeremy Lester, 'The Liberal Democratic Party of Russia – A Profile', *Labour Focus on Eastern Europe*, vol. 16, no. 1, 1994; and 'LDP: Eine Präsidentenpartei im Wartesaal', *Ost–West Gegeninformationen*, vol. 6, no. 3, 1994.
79 *Liberal'no-demokraticheskaya partiya Sovetskogo Soyuza. Dokumenty i materially*

(Moscow: Politizdat, 1991); see also the interview with Zhirinovsky in *Moscow News*, no. 17, 1990, p. 7.

80 Speaking in January 1994, the Mayor of St Petersburg, Anatolii Sobchak, confirmed that the LDP *was* a creation of the old CPSU and KGB. At a Politburo meeting shortly after the formal abolition of Article 6 of the old Soviet Constitution (granting the CPSU its leading role), Gorbachev is supposed to have said something along the lines of: 'A multiparty system is in the offing, so we must act before the event. We ourselves ought to set up the first alternative party, but one that would be malleable.' Sobchak also went on to say that the ultimate purpose of creating such a directed form of a multiparty system was to compromise any truly democratic or liberal parties that might emerge in the future. For details, see *Literaturnaya gazeta*, 12 January 1994; and *Chas pik*, no. 1, 1994. This account, perhaps not surprisingly, was vehemently denied by Gorbachev himself, although no evidence was offered substantially to refute the claims made.

81 Interview with Zhirinovsky in *Sovetskaya Rossiya*, 2 October 1991.

82 Right from the outset, the Zhirinovsky 'repertoire' has included such things as the forcible re-establishment of the Russian empire in its pre-1917 form; the dumping of nuclear waste on former Soviet republics which continue to resist proposals to re-establish a unified state; an economic blockade in similar circumstances; and the deliberate encouragement of inter-ethnic and religious wars, again on territories which refuse to succumb to Russia's will. A useful collection of his 'musings' has been conveniently put together in English translation in Graham Frazer and George Lancelle, *Zhirinovsky: The Little Black Book* (Harmondsworth: Penguin, 1994).

83 According to Zhirinovsky himself, five million of his supporters were young Russians. *Sovetskaya Rossiya*, 2 October 1991.

84 For details of the congress, see *Izvestiya*, 23 April 1991. For a broader appraisal of the organization, see Aleksei Kiva, ' "Soyuz" oderzhimykh: politicheskii portret deputatskoi gruppy, pretenduyushchei na ser'eznuyu obshchestvennuyu rol'', *Izvestiya*, 11 May 1991, p. 3. For a response to Kiva's article, see V. Alksnis, 'Za Soyuz v otvete', *Izvestiya*, 14 May 1991.

85 For an analysis of the organization see Otto Latsis, 'Ochen' staraya novaya vera', *Izvestiya*, 30 January 1992, pp. 1, 3.

86 For details of the congress, see *Nezavisimaya gazeta*, 9 January 1992; *Literaturnaya Rossiya*, 13 December 1991; and Marina Fuchs, 'Die russische Nationalidee als faktor im politischen Kampf fuer Reformen (II)', *Osteuropa*, vol. 43, no. 5, 1993, pp. 466–8.

87 It should be pointed out that in the case of both parties, their switch of allegiance away from Democratic Russia to a more Russophile stance caused a deep internal rift, and ultimately split the parties quite severely.

88 Nikolai Andreev, 'Zaimut li patrioty politicheskuyu stsenu siloi?', *Izvestiya*, 10 February 1992 pp. 1, 2; Otto Latsis, 'Neladno chto-to v nashem gosudarstve', ibid., p. 2.

89 Over the years, the literature on *Pamyat'* has become quite substantial. One of the best collection of documents on the organization is V. Pribylovskii, *Russkie Natsional'no-patrioticheskie organizatsii. "Pamyat'"*: *Dokumenty i teksty* (Moscow: Panorama, 1991).

90 For the text of Rutskoi's address to the congress, see *Patriot*, no. 6, February 1992.

91 *Obozrevatel'*, nos 2–3, February 1992; *Moscow News*, no. 29, 1992, p. 7.

92 Fuchs, 'Die russische Nationalidee', p. 465.

93 Ibid. See also Aleksei Kiva, 'Russkii Natsional'nyi sobor ugrozhaet navesti "poryadok" v strane', *Izvestiya*, 16 June 1992.

94 For an account of the emergence and the nature of the Soviet-era version of the Russian Communist Party, see Robert W. Orttung, 'The Russian Right and the Dilemmas of Party Organisation', *Soviet Studies*, vol. 44, no. 3, 1992, pp. 445–78. One indication of the way in which Russophile organizations had long debated the question of its orientation towards national-communists was the appearance in mid 1991 of an article which set out the *preconditions* which would have to be imposed on the communists if a fruitful partnership could ever emerge. Formulated by the leadership of the Republican People's Party of Russia, the preconditions were as follows. First, the communists should give up their atheistic convictions and accept the Orthodox religion as the primary ideological basis of Russian statehood.

Second, the main political goal of the communists should be the rebirth of a Russian national statehood, consistent with the form in which it existed before the October Revolution. Third, the party should be forced to change its name to something like the Party of Social Justice or the Party of Statehood and Order. And fourth, the material resources of the party should be equally redistributed among its new-found allies. Summing up, it was pointed out that the door to a new partnership with the Russophiles would remain open to the communists if they threw off their red jackets, which were soaked with the blood of the Russian people. *Nashe vremya*, no. 6, 1991, p. 4.

95 See *Obozrevatel'*, nos 2–3, February 1992; Viktor Aksyuchits, 'Ne razrushat', no sozidat", *Den'*, no. 10, 8–14 March 1992, p. 4.

As Nikolai Pavlov, one of the leaders of RAPU and the RPA, also pointed out in a later contribution to this debate: after years of being hounded by elements of the communist and KGB authorities, it was now possible to witness a former KGB General (Sterligov), and a former Central Committee Secretary (Zyuganov), jointly leading a Russophile movement (the Russian National Council). 'We are glad to see them in our ranks. But in order for them to win our full trust, they must travel together with us down the road that we have chosen.' *Literaturnaya Rossiya*, 11 September 1992.

96 Ibid., 13 March 1992.

97 'Spravedlivost', narodnost', gosudarstvennost', patriotizm', *Sovetskaya Rossiya*, 10 March 1992, p. 1.

98 For details of the bloc, see Vladimir Pribylovskii, 'Bloki i fraktsii rossiiskogo parlamenta', *Panorama*, no. 3, June 1992, pp. 17–18.

99 This was the period of long-standing demonstrations by the 'united opposition' outside the *Ostankino* television centre in Moscow. For details see, for example, *Nezavisimaya gazeta*, 20 June 1992, p. 8; *Izvestiya*, 13 July 1992.

100 *Sovetskaya Rossiya*, 22 September 1992.

101 Valerii Vyzhutovich, 'Front Natsional'nogo Spaseniya: Kommunisty i patrioty, shag vpered!', *Izvestiya*, 26 October 1992.

102 For details, see *Izvestiya*, 27, 29 October 1992; 16 February 1993.

103 Vyacheslav Bragin, 'Gde front – tam voina: kakie tseli stavit pered soboi Front Natsional'nogo Spaseniya', *Izvestiya*, 27 October 1992, p. 3. Other committed supporters of the NSF were the leaders of the August 1991 coup attempt, who were regularly in attendance at the Front's meetings. See, for example, 'Zavershilas' pervaya sessiya FNS', *Nezavisimaya gazeta*, 2 February 1993, p. 2.

104 For details of the non-affiliation of the RCDM, see *Moscow News*, no. 39, 1992, p. 8; for the non-affiliation of the RNC, see *Izvestiya*, 4 November 1992. Among the communist-orientated groups, neither the Russian Communist Workers Party nor the All-Union Communist Party of Bolsheviks (led by Nina Andreeva), ended up officially within the constituent ranks of the NSF.

105 A. Frolov, *Sovetskaya Rossiya*, 27 October 1992.

106 As cited in Jonathan Steele, 'Left and Right Gang up to Oust Yeltsin', *The Guardian*, 26 October 1992.

107 For details of the congress, see Valerii Vyzhutovich, 'Doigryvanie otlozhennoi partii', *Izvestiya*, 13 February 1993, p. 5; Otto Latsis, 'Programmnoe zayavlenie kompartii RF: nichego ne zabyli, nichemu ne nauchilis'", *Izvestiya*, 20 March 1993, p. 5.

108 Anna Ostapchuk, 'Kommunisty vnov' stanovyatsya samoi massovoi partiei strany', *Nezavisimaya gazeta*, 16 February 1993, p. 1.

109 The programme was published in *Sovetskaya Rossiya*, 2 March 1993.

110 *Sovetskaya Rossiya*, 22 September 1992. See also ibid., 2 March 1993; and the comments made by Zyuganov in *Literaturnaya Rossiya*, 12 February 1993.

111 For details of the congress, see *Sovetskaya Rossiya*, 24, 27 July 1993; *Nezavisimaya gazeta*, 27 July 1993; *Komsomolskaya pravda*, 7 September 1993.

112 See Pribylovsky's comments in *Russkaya mysl'*, 12–26 August 1993.

113 Interview with Professor Aleksandr Buzgalin in Moscow, 10 December 1993.

114 Indeed, the final opinion poll published on 1 December put the party's support at its lowest point in the electoral campaign, a mere 3.3 per cent.

115 In a clear act of defiance and provocation the front page of the newspaper featured a

photograph of Stalin and his top military staff, accompanied by the caption 'editorial colleagues of *Zavtra*'.

116 See, for example, Andrei Kolganov, 'The Chronicle of a Provocation', in *Bloody Coup in Russia*, special (third), issue of the informational bulletin The Left and Worker's Movements in the former USSR (Moscow: 1993), pp. 9–13; and Jonathan Steele, 'Chaos Theory', *The Guardian Weekend*, 13 November 1993, pp. 22–8.

117 *Rossiiskaya gazeta*, 17 June 1993.

118 *Pravda*, 24 September 1993, p. 1.

119 *BBC Summary of World Broadcasts*, 5 October 1993, SU/1811 C/15. In addition to Khasbulatov and Rutskoi, another convert to a more explicit pro-Russophile stance at this time was the head of the Constitutional Court, Valerii Zorkin. In interviews with *Den'* and *Sovetskaya Rossiya* in summer 1993 he spoke very warmly of the NSF and the Russophile ideas it had recently been expounding. See *Den'*, 1–7 August 1993; *Sovetskaya Rossiya*, 10 June 1993.

120 See, for example, the comments made by Dmitrii Rogozin in *Rossiya*, no. 46, 11–17 November 1992 .

121 *Den'*, 1–9 January 1993, pp. 2–3.

122 Liliya Shevtsova, 'Vlast' v Rossii: Problemy i tupiki konsolidatsii', in Afanas'ev *et al.*, *God posle avgusta*, p. 121.

123 See Mikhail Savin and Aleksandr Smagin, 'LDPR: slagaemye pobedy', *Nezavisimaya gazeta*, 18 December 1993, pp. 1–2.

124 For details of the survey, see *Izvestiya*, 30 December 1993; *The Guardian*, 31 December 1993. Later surveys also indicated strong support from the military, with some divisions and sectors giving him 80 per cent or more of the vote. The accuracy of these figures, however, should be treated with a little scepticism.

125 As quoted in *Izvestiya*, 4 January 1994, p. 7.

126 As cited in Enrico Franceschini, 'La strana squadra di Zhirinovskij', *La Repubblica*, 18 December 1993, p. 16. It is interesting to note that after the 1991 election campaign, Zavidia went on to buy the newspaper *Sovetskaya Rossiya* with a 4 million rouble loan from the Communist Party.

127 *Izvestiya*, 17 February 1994, p. 2. Kobelev did retain his overall membership of the LDP for a while, but finally broke with Zhirinovsky altogether in March.

128 *Kommersant Daily*, 23 February 1994, p. 3.

129 *Segodnya*, 7 April 1994, p. 2.

130 In an interview with *Forbes* magazine, Solzhenitsyn called the declarations of Zhirinovsky 'delirious, provocative and crazy'. He also described Zhirinovsky as 'an evil caricature of a Russian patriot'. 'It's as if someone wanted to use this figure', he went on, 'to show Russian patriotism to the world as a repulsive monster.' 9 May 1994, p. 122. Exactly the same charges were made in his first press conference on arrival in Vladivostok at the end of the month.

131 The most notable one being Aleksandr Sterligov of the Russian National Council, who allied himself with Zhirinovsky in a new pan-Slav parliament, set up in April 1994.

132 Norman R.C. Cohn, *Warrant for Genocide* (London: Eyre & Spottiswoode, 1967), p. 18.

Chapter 5 Centrists

1 Vladimir Mironov, 'Saga o tsentrizme', *Nezavisimaya gazeta*, 24 June 1993, p. 5.

2 V.B. Tikhomirov, 'Politika tsentrizma – put' k stabil'nosti?', *Sotsial'no-politicheskii zhurnal*, no. 8, 1992, p. 92.

3 *BBC Summary of World Broadcasts*, 4 March 1991, SU/1011 C1/2–5.

4 Leon Onikov, 'Illyuzii i prozreniya politicheskogo tsentrizma', *Izvestiya*, 1 November 1991.

5 The extent of the centrist orientation of the Gorbachev Foundation was made apparent on a number of visits to the Foundation throughout 1993 and 1994. A number of centrist parliamentary groups in the old Supreme Soviet also ran a theoretical-analytical centre geared towards elaborating a more concrete 'centrist ideology'.

6 Interview with Lipitskii, *Moscow News*, no. 39, 24 September 1993, p. 6.

7 V.I. Tolstykh *et al.*, *Tsentristskii proekt dlya Rossii* (Moscow: Institut Politiki, 1993), p. 7.

8 Interview with Professor Grigorii Vodolazov at the Gorbachev Foundation, Moscow, 12 January 1993.

9 As V.P. Lebedev succinctly expressed it in a round table organized by the centrist-orientated theoretical club 'The Free Word': 'When the Russian parliament proclaimed its sovereignty, the country effectively enacted a divorce from itself.' For details of the round table, see *Natsional'noe gosudarstvo: Chto eto takoe?* (Moscow, 1992), p. 50.

10 These fears were well expressed by Valentin Tolstykh in comments made in ibid., pp. 2–3. As Nikolai Travkin also once bluntly stated: 'The disintegration of the [USSR] today is the disintegration of Russia tomorrow.' See his speech to the third congress of the Democratic Party of Russia, *Materialy III Syezda DPR, 7–8 Dekabrya 1991g* (Moscow, 1992).

11 Interview with Evgenii Malkin at the Gorbachev Foundation, Moscow, 11 January 1993.

12 Tolstykh *et al.*, *Tsentristskii proekt*, p. 9.

13 Leon Aron, 'Boris Yeltsin and Russia's Four Crises', *Journal of Democracy*, vol. 4, no. 2, April 1993, p. 7.

14 Tolstykh *et al.*, *Tsentristskii proekt*, p. 9.

15 Viktor Volkonskii, 'Tretii put': A kuda zhe my idem?', *Nezavisimaya gazeta*, 16 November 1993, p. 4.

16 For a useful analysis of the different interpretations of corporatism in a Russian context, see Elizabeth Teague, 'Pluralism versus Corporatism: Government, Labor and Business in the Russian Federation', in Carol R. Saivetz and Anthony Jones (eds), *In Search of Pluralism: Soviet and Post-Soviet Politics* (Oxford: Westview Press, 1994), pp. 109–24.

17 For background information on the origin and significance of Eurasianism, see Nicholas V. Riasanovsky, 'The Emergence of Eurasianism', *California Slavic Studies*, no. 4, 1967, pp. 39–72; Leonid Lyuks, *Rossiya mezhdu zapadom i vostokom* (Moscow: Moskovskii filosofskii fond, 1993), pp. 76–91; and L.N. Gumilev, *Iz istorii Evrazii* (Moscow: Iskusstvo, 1993).

18 See Mark Bassin, 'Russia between Europe and Asia: The Ideological Construction of Geographical Space', *Slavic Review*, vol. 50, no. 1, 1991, pp. 13–17.

19 Sergei Agadzhanov, 'Novaya tsivilizatsiya v Rossii?', *Nezavisimaya gazeta*, 20 April 1993, p. 5.

20 For a translation of this article and a discussion of its significance, see *The National Interest*, Summer 1992, pp. 47–55.

21 Ibid., pp. 47–8.

22 Both V.P. Lebedev and A.A. Karamuza make these points very forcefully in *Natsional'noe gosudarstvo*, pp. 55, 75.

23 Tolstykh *et al.*, *Tsentristskii proekt*, p. 28. On the shared genetic heritage of the different peoples of the USSR, see the comments by Arkadii Vol'skii in *Pravda*, 9 September 1992.

24 For a useful survey of the Russophile interpretation of Eurasianism, see Aleksandr Yanov, 'Poslednii soldat imperii', *Novoe vremya*, no. 19, 1993, pp. 20–4. The main Russophile journal which acts as a mouthpiece for their understanding of Eurasianism is *Elementy*, which carries the subtitle 'Eurasian Review'.

25 *Nezavisimaya gazeta*, 17 November 1992. See also Aleksandr Vladislavlev, 'Lyuboi lider ne mozhet byt' odinochkoi', ibid., 3 August 1993, p. 5.

26 See, for example, comments made by Nataliya Narochnitskaya in *Literaturnaya Rossiya*, no. 34, 21 August 1992.

27 Aleksandr Tsipko, '"Demokraticheskaya Rossiya" kak bol'shevistskaya i odnovremenno pochvennicheskaya partiya', *Nezavisimaya gazeta*, 13 April 1993, p. 5.

28 Ibid.

29 S. Karaganov, *Russia – The New Foreign Policy and Security Agenda* (London: Centre for Defence Studies, 1992), p. 31.

30 Oleg Rumyantsev, 'Authoritarian Modernisation and the Social Democratic Alternative', *Social Research*, vol. 57, no. 2, 1990, p. 509.

31 Ernest Gellner's quip 'there is no guarantee that what was tragedy the first time will not also be a real tragedy the second time' might be even more suitable in Russia's present-day condition. See Ernest Gellner, 'Nationalism and Politics in Eastern Europe', *New Left Review*, no. 189, 1991, p. 132.

32 Tolstykh *et al.*, *Tsentristskii proekt*, pp. 37–8.

33 Nikolai Kulikov, 'Politicheskaya karta Rossii', *Oppozitsiya*, 12 December 1993, p. 1.

34 For details of these programmes, see Mikhail Leont'ev, 'Stabilizatsiya proizvodstva na trupe finansovoi sistemy', *Izvestiya*, 23 July 1992, p. 2; 'Trinadtsat' punktov programmy Vol'skogo', *Izvestiya*, 30 September 1992, p. 2; Andrei Lekant, 'Proekty', *Nezavisimaya gazeta*, 17 November 1992; and *Grazhdanskii Soyuz: K Rossii Edinoi, Sil'noi, Demokraticheskoi, Protsvetayushchei*, (Moscow, 1992). For a useful English summary, see also Michael Ellman, 'Russia: The Economic Program of the Civic Union', *RFE/RL Research Report*, vol. 2, no. 11, 12 March 1993, pp. 34–45.

35 Some of the main centrist economic theoreticians are Yurii Yaremenko, Director of the Institute for National Economic Forecasting; Evgenii Saburov, a former deputy Prime Minister and Economics Minister in the last RSFSR Silaev government and Director of the Centre for Research on Social Technology; Nikolai Petrakov, a former adviser to President Gorbachev and Director of the Institute for the Problems of the Market within the Russian Academy of Sciences; Professor Vilen Perlamutrov of the Academy of Sciences; and Viktor Ivanter from the Institute for National Economic Forecasting.

36 *BBC Summary of World Broadcasts*, 16 November 1992, SU/1539 C1/5.

37 Eric Lohr, 'Arkadii Volsky's Political Base', *Europe-Asia Studies*, vol. 45, no. 5, 1993, p. 823.

38 Iosif Diskin, 'Tsentrizm – glavnyi vrag?', *Nezavisimaya gazeta*, 23 October 1993, p. 4.

39 *BBC Summary of World Broadcasts*, 16 November 1992, SU/1539 C1/6.

40 See, for example, B. Kapustin, 'Nenaidennost' sebya – nepriznannost' drugogo', *Nezavisimaya gazeta*, 17 July 1992, p. 5.

41 *Rossiiskaya gazeta*, 31 October 1992, p. 5. See also his interview with *Nezavisimaya gazeta*, 4 November 1992. In a televised debate between Vol'skii and Boris Fedorov during the 1993 election campaign, it was the Chinese experiment that was at the heart of their disagreements.

42 Dzhon Ross, 'Pochemu ekonomicheskaya reforma poterpela krakh v vostochnoi evrope i Rossii, a v Kitae uvenchalas' uspekhom?', *Voprosy ekonomiki*, no. 11, 1992, p. 43.

43 Michael McFaul, 'Russian Centrism and Revolutionary Transitions', *Post-Soviet Affairs*, vol. 9, no. 3, 1993, p. 198.

44 Ellman, 'Russia: The Economic Program', p. 37.

45 As cited in Alexander Rahr, 'Upcoming Congress Will Test Yeltsin's Loyalty to Democrats', *RFE/RL Research Report*, vol. 1, no. 38, 25 September 1992, p. 8.

46 Simon Clarke, 'Privatisation and the Development of Capitalism in Russia', in Simon Clarke, Peter Fairbrother, Michael Burawoy and Pavel Krotov, *What About the Workers?: Workers and the Transition to Capitalism in Russia* (London: Verso, 1993), pp. 119–216.

47 See, for example, V.A. Naishul', *The Supreme and Last Stage of Socialism* (London: Centre for Research into Communist Economies, 1991); and 'Institutional Development in the USSR', *Cato Journal*, vol. 2, no. 3, 1992, pp. 489–96.

48 *Ekonomika i zhizn'*, no. 47, 1992, p. 3. See also Wyn Grant, 'Business Associations in Eastern Europe and Russia', *The Journal of Communist Studies*, vol. 9, no. 2, 1993, pp. 94–5; Peter Rutland, *Business Elites and Russian Economic Policy* (London: Royal Institute of Economic Affairs, 1992), pp. 11–12, 17–19.

49 Lohr, 'Arkadii Volsky's', pp. 821–2.

50 For further details, see ibid., p. 829; Rutland, *Business Elites*, p. 19.

51 By the summer of 1993 it was estimated that between 70 and 80 per cent of enterprises had been privatized according to the second variant. *Ekonomika i zhizn'*, no. 36, 1993.

52 For articles in favour of option 2, see Vol'skii's comments in *Izvestiya*, 30 September 1992; and Vladislavlev's comments in *Nezavisimaya gazeta*, 25 September 1992. For an overview of the general disapproval of the option by most Westerners, see Pekka Sutela, 'Insider Privatisation in Russia: Speculations on Systemic Change', *Europe-Asia Studies*, vol. 46, no. 3, 1994, pp. 417–35. Some radical Westerners such as Larisa Piyasheva, however, were very much in favour of at least the general idea that state property should be given away, if necessary, to the insiders themselves. A 'fourth variant' was also strongly supported by centrists which would have allowed labour collectives an automatic right to acquire no less than *90 per cent* of an enterprise's shares on even more favourable terms than those proposed in the second variant. This variant, however, was fundamentally rejected by the Westerners as a too explicit form of *nomenklatura* privatization.

53 As cited in Clarke, 'Privatisation', p. 227.

54 Simon Johnson and Heidi Kroll, 'Managerial Strategies for Spontaneous Privatisation', *Soviet Economy*, vol. 7, no. 4, 1991, pp. 308–9.

55 Ibid. See also Simon Clarke, Peter Fairbrother, Vadim Borisov and Petr Bizyukov, 'The Privatisation of Industrial Enterprises in Russia: Four Case Studies', *Europe-Asia Studies*, vol. 46, no. 2, 1994, pp. 179–214.

56 Clarke, 'Privatisation', p. 218.

57 The newspaper had originally been established in January 1990 as an organ of the Soviet Trade Union organization.

58 *Trud*, 22 April 1992.

59 *Rabochaya tribuna*, 10 July 1992. See also, D. Zanilov, 'V kotorom tretii', *Delovoi mir*, 11 July 1992, p. 1.

60 Simon Clarke, 'After the Coup: The Workers' Movement in the Transition to a Market Economy', in Clarke *et al.*, *What About the Workers?*, p. 192.

61 Aleksandr Rubstov, 'Mif o tsentre a takzhe o radikalakh i konservatorakh', *Nezavisimaya gazeta*, 22 October 1993, p. 5.

62 Nikolai Gulbinsky, 'Rutskoi, not Merely Russia's Dan Quayle . . .', *Moscow News*, no. 20, 1992, p. 6.

63 V. Kononenko, 'V Rossii nazrevaet ser'yoznyi pravitel'stvennyi krizis', *Izvestiya*, 5 December 1991, pp. 1–2. For more of Rutskoi's own views on his Siberian tour, see his interview with *Pravda*, 27 December 1991.

64 As cited in Vasilii Lipitskii, 'Razvilki nashei nedavnei istorii', *Nezavisimaya gazeta*, 12 August 1993, p. 2.

65 On this occasion it was in an interview with *Pravda*, 14 May 1993.

66 *Pravda*, 30 January 1992.

67 *Izvestiya*, 31 January 1992.

68 Given the content of this article, it was small wonder that the editors of *Izvestiya* carried a postscript making it clear that they had not commissioned Rutskoi to write such a piece. In a nice 'aside' they also went on to comment: 'Judging by its text, the Vice-President has not partaken of any holy communion at McDonalds – he has more than likely simply observed the queue while driving past in his car. Had he talked to people in the queue, he would have realized that they had gone there not for holy communion but for a bite to eat. Given the difficulties of finding something to eat in Moscow, McDonalds probably feeds more people than anywhere else.'

69 *Pravda*, 8 February 1992.

70 *Nezavisimaya gazeta*, 13 February 1992.

71 B.I. Koval' *et al.*, *Partii i Politicheskie Bloki v Rossii* (Moscow: Marko Media, 1993), p. 29.

72 For details, see the interview with Travkin and Mikhail Tolstoi in *Dialog*, no. 12, 1991, pp. 57–66; Rossiisko-Amerikanskii Universitet, Institut Massovykh Politicheskikh Dvizhenii, *Partii, Assotsiatsii, Soyuzy, Kluby: Sbornik Materialov i Dokumentov*, Book 2 (Moscow: RAU-Press, 1992), pp. 12–33.

73 As cited in Vera Tolz and Elizabeth Teague, 'Is Russia Likely to Turn to Authoritarian Rule?', *RFE/RL Research Report*, 24 January 1992, p. 7.

74 *Vserossiiskii Soyuz 'Obnovlenie' – Uchreditel'naya Konferentsiya: Materialy* (Moscow, 1992).

75 Koval' *et al.*, *Partii i Politicheskie Bloki*, p. 49; *Kommersant*, no. 23, 1–8 June 1992, p. 21.

76 Koval' *et al.*, *Partii i Politicheskie Bloki*, p. 159.

77 Two notable members of the faction, before its split with Democratic Russia, were Sergei Shakhrai and Sergei Baburin.

78 Lohr, 'Arkadii Volsky's', pp. 825–6.

79 Koval' *et al.*, *Partii i Politicheskie Bloki*, pp. 43–8; *Rossiiskaya gazeta*, 13 January 1993.

80 Analiticheskii tsentr zhurnala 'Dialog', 'Grazhdanskii Soyuz: Upushchennyi shans "demokraticheskogo" kapitalizma?', *Dialog*, nos 8–10, 1992, p. 14.

81 See, for example, *Grazhdanskii Soyuz: K Rossii Edinoi*.

82 McFaul, 'Russian Centrism', p. 211.

83 It is true, of course, that Civic Union's first choice for Prime Minister was Georgii Khiza, but it was certainly well satisfied with Chernomyrdin's appointment. This same period also witnessed the demotion of two of the most prominent Westerners, Mikhail Poltoranin and

Gennadii Burbulis; although their main candidate for demotion, Foreign Minister Andrei Kozyrev, survived the reshuffle. Evgenii Krasnikov, 'GS dumaet o posleel'tsinskoi Rossii', *Nezavisimaya gazeta*, 5 January 1993, p. 2.

84 Evgenii Krasnikov, 'Boris El'tsin vystupil na syezde "Grazhdanskogo Soyuza"', *Nezavisimaya gazeta*, 2 March 1993, p. 1.

85 Ibid., 17 April 1993, pp. 1–2. Further clarification of Yeltsin's positive re-evaluation of Civic Union was demonstrated in a rare interview he granted to *Pravda*, 2 March 1993.

86 Aleksandr Vladislavlev, 'Lyuboi lider'.

87 Evgenii Krasnikov, 'Forum Grazhdanskogo Soyuza otvergaet referendum', *Nezavisimaya gazeta*, 27 February 1993.

88 *BBC Summary of World Broadcasts*, 12 June 1993, SU/1713 i. Opinion polls throughout this period also indicated a significant lead for the centrist groups over their main rivals.

89 See, for example, Gordon M. Hahn, 'Opposition Politics in Russia', *Europe-Asia Studies*, vol. 46, no. 2, 1994, pp. 314–24. Andranik Migranyan also hinted at a similar interpretation in his article 'Yeltsin: Which Path to Choose?', *Moscow News*, no. 20, 1993, pp. 1–2.

90 A good example being *Grazhdanskii Soyuz: K Rossii Edinoi*, p. 19.

91 Evgenii Krasnikov, 'Mozhet byt', politicheskii tsentr nikuda ne provalilsya?', 3 July 1993, *Nezavisimaya gazeta*, p. 1.

92 Hahn, 'Opposition Politics', p. 324.

93 There were also significantly different approaches to the referendum *within* each component organization. See *Megapolis-Express*, 28 April 1993, p. 23.

94 See, for example, his reply to Migranyan and others in *Nezavisimaya gazeta*, 17 April 1993, p. 4.

95 The split between Gekht and Vol'skii recalled an earlier division in the Soviet industrial lobby between Vol'skii (as head of the Scientific and Industrial Union, the forerunner of RUIE), and Aleksandr Tizyakov. The latter, of course, went on to become a leading member of the State Emergency Committee during the August coup. It is also worth noting that Gekht himself supported the coup in principle, though an article he wrote in its defence at the time was luckily withdrawn from publication because the end of the coup just beat the typesetting deadline. *Vechernaya Moskva*, 14 November 1991.

96 The DPR's previous involvement with political alliances had been with Democratic Russia (prior to a split in November 1991 over the plans for the break-up of the USSR), and with the Popular Accord alliance, which had involved them in a brief association with Aksyuchits's Russian Christian Democratic Movement and Astaf'ev's Constitutional Democrats.

97 See, for example, Vyacheslav Shchepotkin, 'Mesyats trevozhnogo optimizma', *Izvestiya*, 30 January 1992, p. 2; and *Rossiya*, no. 28, 1992.

98 *BBC Summary of World Broadcasts*, 26 August 1993, SU/1777 B/3.

99 Ibid., 21 December 1992, SU/1569 B/5.

100 A major fear of Travkin's at this time, it seems, was an increasing division inside the ranks of the DPR. During the April referendum many local branches of the party had renewed their links with Democratic Russia. Within his own ruling council, meanwhile, his ideological secretary, Ilya Roitman, had even chaired a prominent public committee in support of Yeltsin. Severing the links with Civic Union, therefore, was a risk strategy designed to unify his party behind the exclusive DPR identity. For the most part it worked, although for a time the Moscow section was instrumental in setting up an interregional association of DPR branches that continued an affiliation with Civic Union. Krasnikov, 'Mozhet byt'', pp. 1–2.

101 Krasnikov, 'Mozhet byt'', p. 1. As Krasnikov went on to point out, to the extent that there was no fixed membership of Civic Union, this was formally correct, but otherwise Vol'skii was 'blowing in the wind' if he thought he could simply deny his very active role in the alliance.

102 Lev Ovrutsky, 'Rutskoism', *Moscow News*, no. 12, 1992, p. 7.

103 See, for example, Rutskoi's vehement attack on Ukrainian independence from Russia in *Rossiiskaya gazeta*, 20 May 1992.

104 For the text of this speech, see A.I. Podberezkin *et al.* (eds), *Neizvestnyi Rutskoi: Politicheskii Portret* (Moscow: Obozrevatel', 1994), pp. 275–81.

105 Of all the intellectuals Rutskoi was so fond of quoting, Ivan Il'in was the most regular and the most prominent. A professor of philosophy at Moscow University at the time of the

1917 Revolution, he was an ardent activist in the counter-revolutionary White movement, who was ultimately expelled from Russia in 1922. As a committed advocate of Russia's national and spiritual supremacy, Il'in's views were often compared with the emerging fascist doctrines elsewhere in Europe at this time.

106 *Pravda*, 14 May 1993.

107 *BBC Summary of World Broadcasts*, 12 July 1993, SU/1738 B/1–3.

108 Ibid., 7 August 1993, SU/1761 B/2–3.

109 Ibid., 25 August 1993, SU/1776 B/2.

110 See, for example, Grigorii Vodolazov, Boris Kapustin and Igor' Pantin, 'Peremeny v ideologii i praktike gosudarstva nazreli', *Nezavisimaya gazeta*, 27 August 1993, p. 2.

111 For claims made by Vol'skii on this basis, see *Obshchaya gazeta*, 19–25 November 1993.

112 A clear indication of the confusion inside Civic Union at this time was Rumyantsev's assertion that despite the fact that it was primarily supported by industrialists and enterprise directors, there was nevertheless scope for the Union to become a full-fledged Labour Party. For other instances of its lacklustre campaigning see, for example, *Segodnya*, 11 December 1993.

113 This, for example, was the viewpoint of Andrei Golovin in comments made on *Radio Moscow's World Service*, 14 May 1994.

114 See, for example, comments made by Vol'skii in an interview with *Nezavisimaya gazeta*, 18 June 1993, p. 5.

115 Mironov, 'Saga', p. 5.

116 See, for example, Umirserik Kasenov, ' "Doktrina Kozyreva" – Rossiiskii Variant "Doktriny Monro"?', *Nezavisimaya gazeta*, 12 March 1994, pp. 1, 3.

117 In an inaugural address to the Federation Council in January 1994, Yeltsin himself openly spoke of Russia's 'vocation to be the first among equals here'. In an address to the first joint sitting of the two chambers of the Federal Assembly in February 1994, meanwhile, he referred to the fact that all the republics of the former USSR were 'gradually being cured of the euphoria of being able to swim in the raging sea [of independence]'. *Rossiiskaya gazeta*, 12 January, 25 February 1994.

118 For the full text of Nazarbaev's plan, see *Nezavisimaya gazeta*, 8 June 1994, pp. 1, 3. For the likes of Sergei Kurginyan, the proposal was not so much 'premature' as *immature* in its specifics. Kurginyan was also very critical of the 'hidden motives' behind Nazarbaev's suggestion. See his article 'Soderzhanie novogo intergratsionizma', ibid., 7 July 1994, p. 5.

119 *Rossiiskie vesti*, 7 August 1993. He also cited his allegiance to centrism throughout the 1993 election campaign.

120 As cited in Wendy Slater, 'The Diminishing Center of Russian Parliamentary Politics', *RFE/RL Research Report*, vol. 3, no. 17, 29 April 1994, p. 18.

121 The probable consequences of this new sense of responsibility on Chernomyrdin was just one of the themes covered in a seminar held in the Gorbachev Foundation in early February 1994 devoted to the 'Chernomyrdin Phenomenon'.

122 *Rossiiskaya gazeta*, 29 April 1994.

123 Anatolii Dolgolaptev, ' "Filadel'fiiskoe sitechko" ', *Nezavisimaya gazeta*, 7 December 1993, p. 5.

124 Of the country's main political parties represented in parliament, the only non-signatories were Zyuganov's Communist Party, the Agrarian Party, a number of nationalist organizations and Grigorii Yavlinskii's *YABLoko* faction. Even Vladimir Zhirinovsky's LDP was persuaded to give its affirmation. Yavlinskii refused to sign the Accord, partly because he thought it was a meaningless repetition of provisions that for the most part could already be found in the Constitution, and partly because he did not want to sign a document that included Zhirinovsky's signature.

125 Stepan Sulakshin, 'Tsentrizm – politicheskaya kul'tura budushchego', *Nezavisimaya gazeta*, 17 May 1994, p. 5.

126 In particular, one can frequently find these days references to a form of Yeltsinist 'centrism'. See, for example, Oleg Senatov, 'I eshche o tsentrizme', *Nezavisimaya gazeta*, 26 August 1993, p. 8.

127 Vladislav Inozemtsev, 'Spor o rossiiskom tsentrizme prodolzhaetsya', *Nezavisimaya gazeta*, 9 October 1993, p. 4.

128 In January 1995 Travkin quit the DPR altogether, claiming that as he had recently become a minister without portfolio in Chernomyrdin's government, he could no longer accept the official opposition stance of the party.

129 There has been some debate as to whether Gorbachev promised Yeltsin, when he left office in December 1991, that he would not formally engage in politics any more. Yeltsin said he did; Gorbachev has said that he merely promised that he would not use his Foundation as an *explicit* base for a new political party. For an interesting insight, meanwhile, into the current ideas of the former Soviet leader, see his interview with *Nezavisimaya gazeta*, 6, 7 July 1994, pp. 1, 3.

130 Clarke, 'Privatisation', p. 240.

Chapter 6 Possibilities for a Future Socialist Hegemony

1 Göran Therborn, 'The End of the Future', *Marxism Today*, November 1991, p. 24.

2 *Za rabochee delo*, no. 13, November 1993.

3 Author's interview with Aleksandr Buzgalin in Moscow, 5 January 1993. Published in *Labour Focus on Eastern Europe*, no. 44, 1993, pp. 31–4.

4 The main articles in this period have been in *Sovetskaya Rossiya*, 3 July 1993 and 28 August 1993. Two booklets have also been written by Zyuganov: *Drama vlasti* and *Derzhava* (Moscow: Informpechat', 1994). For a useful analysis, meanwhile, of Zyuganov's political character, see Petr Aleev, 'Vot takoi, on Zyuganov . . . ', *Alternativy*, no. 4, 1994, pp. 71–84.

5 Nicolas Berdyaev, *Konstantin Leontiev*, trans. George Reavey (London: Geoffrey Bles, 1940), p. vii.

6 As quoted in Andrzej Walicki, *A History of Russian Thought: From the Enlightenment to Marxism* (Oxford: Clarendon Press, 1988), p. 308.

7 Ibid., p. 305.

8 See, for example, Andrei Sokolov, 'Mnogie kommunisty nedovol'ny svoim liderom', *Nezavisimaya gazeta*, 21 January 1995, p. 2.

9 Boris Slavin, 'Otkaz ot marksizma pogubit kompartiyu. (Otkrytoe pis'mo Zyuganovu G.A.)', *Mysl'*, no. 10, 1994, p. 2.

10 For the text of the letter, see 'Russia After the General Elections', *Informational Bulletin of the Left and Workers' Movements in the Former USSR*, no. 4, 1993/no. 1, 1994, pp. 50–51.

11 As cited in Tamara Deuscher (ed.), *Isaac Deutscher: Marxism in Our Time* (London: Jonathan Cape, 1972), pp. 110–11.

12 Boris Slavin, 'Etot trudnyi natsional'nyi vopros', *Alternativy*, no. 4, 1994, pp. 27–8.

13 'Natsional'naya problema: "Levyi vzglyad" ', ibid., pp. 85–113.

14 See the interview with Medvedev in *New Left Review*, no. 189, 1991, p. 98.

15 Author's interview with Ludmilla Vartazarova in Moscow, 10 January 1993.

16 Denisov's comments were reported to the author in an interview with Aleksandr Buzgalin in Moscow, 10 December 1993. The interview was subsequently published in *Labour Focus on Eastern Europe*, no. 47, 1994, pp. 2–16.

17 For Kalashnikov's speech and the full text of the SPW's new programme, see *Levaya gazeta*, no. 1, April 1994, pp. 3–7.

18 *Moskovskie novosti*, no. 8, 1992, p. 11.

19 For a detailed report on the programme, see Andrei Kolganov, 'Gumanisticheskaya ekonomika: antikrizisnaya programma demokraticheskikh levykh', *Solidarnost'*, no. 31, 1992, p. 7.

20 Konstantin Sumnitel'nyi, 'Toward a Portrait of the Workers' Movement in Russia', *Socialist Alternatives*, vol. 2, no. 2, 1993, p. 86.

21 It is also worth noting that most of the new unions strongly supported Yeltsin at the time of the October 1993 parliamentary rebellion.

22 For more details of AFL–CIO involvement in Russian trade-union affairs, see P. Bracegirdle and D. Seppo, 'The AFL–CIO Comes to the Community of Independent States', *Socialist Alternatives*, vol. 2, no. 2, 1993, pp. 173–98; Renfrey Clarke, 'US Labour Missionaries – No Blessing for Russian Workers', *Russian Labour Review*, no. 3, Summer 1994, pp. 3–5.

23 Boris Kagarlitsky, 'Levye v Rossii: nadezhdy, neudachi, bor'ba', *Svobodnaya mysl'*, no. 11, 1994, p. 38.

24 For details of the congress, see *Levaya gazeta*, nos 3, 4, 1992.

25 Kagarlitsky, 'Levye v Rossii', p. 39.

26 B.P. Kurashvili, *Kuda idet Rossiya?* (Moscow: Slovo, 1994).

27 The accusations referred to come from the pen of the Polish intellectual Adam Michnik.

28 Michael Burawoy, 'The End of Sovietology and the Renaissance of Modernization Theory', *Contemporary Sociology*, vol. 21, no. 6, 1992, p. 785.

29 Taking part in the round table (which was also covered by national television), were: Aleksandr Buzgalin (Co-ordinator of the Congress of Democratic Left Forces and a member of the Executive Committee of the Party of Labour); Boris Kagarlitsky (also a member of the Executive Committee of the Party of Labour and a consultant for the Russian Federation of Independent Trade Unions); Boris Slavin (member of the Central Executive Committee of the Communist Party of the Russian Federation and a deputy editor of *Pravda*); Vladimir Khazanov (member of the Political Council of the Russian Party of Communists); Galina Rakitskaya (founder of the Committee for the Support of Working Class Movements); Aleksei Prigarin (Secretary of the Union of Communists); Vladimir Kizima (member of the Presidium of the Socialist Party of Ukraine); Sergei Novikov (member of the Political Council of the Russian Party of Communists); and Igor' Gotlib (member of the Movement for Democracy, Social Progress and Justice).

30 Jacques Derrida, 'Spectres of Marx', *New Left Review*, no. 205, 1994, p. 33.

31 Author's interview with Ludmilla Bulavka in Moscow, 31 May and 4 October 1994.

32 In Bulavka's view, the Left has little choice but also to make an appeal using this emotional language through the propagation, for example, of what she calls a Russian democratic Soviet culture. It should be done, however, in a proper dialectical way; i.e. by means of irrational language, one can still teach the principles of rational concepts.

33 In the first quarter of 1994 alone there were 288 strikes, 30 more than in the whole of the previous year. The main sectors affected were coal mining and all the other natural resource industries, telecommunications, engineering, defence, education and health.

34 Comments made at the June 1994 Moscow round table.

35 Author's inteview with Andrei Kolganov, 4 October 1994.

36 It is interesting to note that according to a report in *Rossiiskie vesti*, 19 August 1994, p. 1, Gennadii Zyuganov has recently come up with a programme for infiltrating the trade unions, which he now sees as his 'paramount task'. This move followed complaints, expressed at a plenary meeting of the CPRF's Central Executive Committee in March 1994, that he was not doing enough to win the downtrodden workers over to the party's aspirations.

37 For specific details of their proposals, see A. Buzgalin and A. Kolganov, 'Self-Management as a Key to the Economy of XXI Century'; A. Kolganov, 'Collective Ownership and Self-Management', in A. Buzgalin (ed.), *Economy and Democracy* (Moscow: Economic Democracy, 1992), pp. 7–27, 151–68.

38 For details of the draft law, see Kurashvili, *Kuda idet Rossiya?*, pp. 256–64.

39 One such 'doubting Thomas' convert away from self-management schemes appears to be Boris Kagarlitsky. See, for example, his comments in an interview with *Labour Focus on Eastern Europe*, no. 46, 1993, p. 21; and his comments in *Russian Labour Review*, no. 3, Summer 1994, p. 45.

For a brief analysis of the failures of the STK movement, see Poul Funder Larsen and David Mandel, 'The Left in Russia', in Ralph Miliband and Leo Panitch (eds), *The Socialist Register 1994* (London: Merlin Press, 1994), pp. 271–4.

40 According to Vadim Dam'e, there are essentially three versions of self-management currently on offer. The first, and most radical, is an *integral* interpretation of this concept which acts as a model for the whole of society, not just its economic structures. The second version refers more specifically to the operational mechanisms of enterprises. Such enterprises would remain in the overall hands of the state or some other socialized form of ownership, but workers' collectives would be given managerial control of the day-to-day activities of the enterprise, and would determine the use to which profits could be put. Likewise, some form of overall market requirements would be preserved. The third version, meanwhile, equates the notion of self-management with a specific form of privatization in which the workers' collective assumes

full ownership rights over the property of the enterprise. As Dam'e goes on to make clear, the three versions would result in an absolutely different form of social model if ever they were realized in practice. See the interview with Dam'e, 'Sushchestvuet li budushchee u rossiiskikh levykh?', *Intervzglyad*, no. 3, 1992, pp. 20–21.
41 Comments made at a presentation at an international symposium of the association 'Scholars for Democracy and Socialism', Zelenograd, 1 June 1994.
42 Author's interview with Aleksandr Buzgalin, Moscow, 10, 13 December 1993. This, for example, is the basis of Buzgalin's prominent involvement in such organizations as the Movement in Defence of Democracy and Civil Rights.

Chapter 7 In Lieu of a Conclusion

1 As cited in Ryszard Kapuscinski, *Imperium*, trans. Klara Glowczewska (London: Granta, 1994), p. vi.
2 This was the main charge made by Aleksandr Solzhenitsyn in his address to the State Duma in October 1994.
3 Irina Khakamada, 'Uroki dekabrya, fevralya, marta', *Nezavisimaya gazeta*, 26 April 1994, p. 5.
4 The stated aim of the new electoral bloc, which was supported publicly by President Yeltsin, was to counter the threat posed by the political extremism of individuals such as Zyuganov and Zhirinovsky and the political forces around them. Of the mainstream parties, only Sergei Shakhrai's Party of Russian Unity and Accord gave Chernomyrdin his full backing. The initial reaction of other prominent party political leaders such as Yegor Gaidar and Grigorii Yavlinskii was largely very hostile. Given the close association of companies such as Gazprom, there were immediate widespread allegations of misappropriation of state funds by the new 'party of power'. Even if it survives these scandals, there must nevertheless be a serious doubt as to whether its 'preservation of the status quo' orientation will prove a potential vote-winner with the Russian public.
5 James Meek, 'Legions of the Gullible Clamour for Their Slice of the Good Life', *The Guardian*, 27 July 1994, p. 10.
6 Leszek Kolakowski, 'The Myth of Human Self-Identity: Unity of Civil and Political Society in Socialist Thought', reprinted in C. Kukathas, D.W. Lovell and W. Maley (eds), *The Transition from Socialism: State and Civil Society in Gorbachev's USSR* (Melbourne: Longman Cheshire, 1991), p. 49.
7 Certainly the murder of the popular television commentator Vladislav List'ev at the beginning of March 1995 sent such a shock wave through the population that the clamour for 'something to be done' appeared well-nigh universal.
8 See, for example, the interview with Yegor Gaidar in *Nezavisimaya gazeta*, 30 September 1994, p. 5.
9 Towards the end of 1994 a big debate was started on the prospects for a social democratic hegemony in Russia, and in particular whether Russian political culture was amenable to this kind of orientation or not. See, for example, Vadim Belotserkovskii, 'Sotsial-demokratiya v antisotsial-demokraticheskoi strane', *Nezavisimaya gazeta*, 10 November 1994, p. 5; and the interview with Oleg Rumyantsev in ibid., 29 October 1994, pp. 1, 3.
10 Aleksandr Solzhenitsyn, 'Kak nam obustroit' Rossiyu', *Komsomol'skaya pravda*, 18 October 1990, p. 10.
11 The Westerners, of course, have long known of Solzhenitsyn's plans to return to his homeland, and they have not been idle. Every now and then an article would appear on Solzhenitsyn, and hidden amid the compliments to the man and the writer one could clearly detect a subtle discrediting of virtually all the ideas he has ever propagated. Parallel references to the Ayatollah Khomeini's return to Iran were often drawn, with all the implications that this entailed for a new 'fundamentalist' onslaught; and there were frequent allusions to an exiled Buddha spitting upon all those who had supposedly lost their old faith.
12 The findings of the opinion poll were cited in Vladimir Lysenko, 'Avtoritarnyi rezhim neizbezhen', *Nezavisimaya gazeta*, 22 December 1994, p. 2.
13 In the parliamentary debate on the Chechen war at the beginning of 1995, Baburin's faction 'Russian Way' was split down the middle on the question of support.

14 Just to add to the broad picture of supporters and opponents of the war: in the ranks of the former stood such groups as Sergei Shakhrai's Party of Russian Unity and Accord and the Democratic Party of Russia, along with individuals such as Sergei Mavrodi. In the ranks of the opponents stood the Agrarian Party, the Women of Russia parliamentary faction and such individuals as Aleksandr Rutskoi, Aleksandr Lebed' (because of the manner in which the war was conducted), and Aleksandr Solzhenitsyn, who argued that Chechnya should be not only allowed but encouraged to secede from Russia, on condition that it give up traditional Russian parts of the Republic.

15 See, for example, the powerful open letter, a virtual declaration of political war against Yeltsin (signed by Leonid Batkin, Yurii Burtin, Irina Uvarova and Yelena Shumilova), in *Moskovskie novosti*, 25 December 1994, p. 1.

16 As cited in Vladimir Guliyev, *Rossiiskie vesti*, 1 February 1995.

17 As cited in Mikhail Petrachev, 'Prezident – 96: figury, litsa, obrazy', *Nezavisimaya gazeta*, 11 November 1994, p. 1.

18 Daniel Yergin and Thane Gustafson, *Russia 2010 and What It Means for the World* (London: Nicholas Brealey, 1994).

19 Vladimir Voinovich, *Moscow 2042* (London: Picador, 1989).

20 Kapuscinski, *Imperium*, p. vi.

Index

Note: Italicized page numbers refer to information in tables and maps.